Turn On, Tune In, Drift Off

Turn On, Tune In, Drift Off

Ambient Music's Psychedelic Past

VICTOR SZABO

OXFORD
UNIVERSITY PRESS

OXFORD
UNIVERSITY PRESS

Oxford University Press is a department of the University of Oxford. It furthers the University's objective of excellence in research, scholarship, and education by publishing worldwide. Oxford is a registered trade mark of Oxford University Press in the UK and certain other countries.

Published in the United States of America by Oxford University Press
198 Madison Avenue, New York, NY 10016, United States of America.

Library of Congress Control Number: 2022941436

ISBN 978–0–19–069931–4 (pbk.)
ISBN 978–0–19–069930–7 (hbk.)

DOI: 10.1093/oso/9780190699307.001.0001

Paperback printed by Marquis, Canada
Hardback printed by Bridgeport National Bindery, Inc., United States of America

For Zephyr, who loves drone

Contents

Acknowledgments

This book has many hearts. I thank those individuals who took the time to share their insights and memories with me through conversations and interviews, first and foremost Stephen and Leyla Rael Hill, whose hospitality, generosity, and deep knowledge made an entire chapter of this book possible. Many thanks also to Gavin Bryars, Kevin Foakes, Kevin Braheny Fortune, Christopher Hobbs, Laraaji, Charlemagne Palestine, Steve Roach, Jonah Sharp, Michael Stearns, and Jennifer Teibel-Ballow for providing depth and clarity to this book's narrative.

I thank the librarians and staff at the Special Collections of the New York Public Library for the Performing Arts, the Dolph Briscoe Center for American History at the University of Texas–Austin, the Library & Archives of the American Craft Council, and the Graduate Theological Union Archives at the University of California—Berkeley. Thanks again to Jennifer Teibel-Ballow, and to Jonathan Een Newton, for providing access to and guidance through the archived materials of Syntonic Research, Inc.

I consider myself lucky to have such friendly and supportive colleagues among the faculty and staff at Hampden-Sydney College. Thanks to them, with special thanks to the H-SC librarians and staff who made research easy, and to those faculty colleagues and friends in my cohort for joining me in much-needed off-time revelry. I'd also like to thank those H-SC students whose fresh perspectives on ambient and popular music fueled the writing of this book. Warmest thanks to my cherished colleagues and friends in the H-SC Fine Arts Department for their unwavering support, community spirit, and commitment to having good fun along the way. I also thank the College's Committee on Professional Development and Dean's Office, especially Dean of the Faculty Mike McDermott, for generously supporting this project financially through Summer Research Fellowships, the William W. Elliott Professorship, and conference travel funding.

Many thanks to my editor, Norm Hirschy, for his gracious encouragement and flexibility throughout the book-writing process. This book also benefited greatly from the reviews provided by the anonymous readers appointed by Oxford University Press, whom I thank for their time and thoroughness.

I deeply appreciate the feedback and encouragement of my many fellow scholars and music geeks throughout this process, including Christa Bentley, Joshua Busman, Mark Butler, Chris Campo-Bowen, Theo Cateforis, Laurel Chartow, Norma Coates, Erik DeLuca, Mike D'Errico, Jarek Ervin, Robert Fink, K. E. Goldschmitt, Sumanth Gopinath, Ted Gordon, Mack Hagood, Karl Hagstrom-Miller, Robin James, Brian Jones, Kevin Karnes, Anthony Kwame Harrison, Elizabeth Lindau, Andrew Mall, Sean Peterson, Alex Reed, Will Robin, Paul Roquet, Travis Thatcher, David Toop, Steve Waksman, Kristina Warren, Eric Weisbard, Rachel Devorah Wood, and Brian Wright. I am also grateful for the feedback of my interlocutors during the many stages of this project at the regular meetings of the American Musicological Society, the International Association of Popular Music–US chapter, the Society for American Music, and the Society for Minimalist Music, as well as at the Future of Pop, FuturePresentPop, Ambient@40, Over and Over, and Embracing the Margins meetings. My appreciation also goes out to the organizers of these events.

Thanks to my mentors during my graduate study at the University of Virginia, where this project began, especially those who offered feedback and guidance throughout the writing of my dissertation: my advisor, Fred Everett Maus, and Ted Coffey, Rita Felski, Bonnie Gordon, and Michael Puri. Thanks are also due to the excellent librarians and library staff at the UVA Libraries, especially those who worked at the Music Library during my time there. A special shout-out to Nadine Hubbs for modeling sparkling popular music scholarship for me when I was an undergraduate student at the University of Michigan, and for wisely directing me toward UVA to continue my studies.

Big, big thanks (and also *little tiny* thanks) to the dear friends who gave thoughtful commentary on earlier versions of this text, including Craig Comen, Kevin Davis, Stephanie Doktor, Stephanie Gunst, and Lee Wachocki. Extra special thanks to Amy Coddington, my writing and conference buddy extraordinaire, who throughout this process provided precious perspective, written feedback, daily motivation, and tasty (re)treats.

Thanks to my family, especially my sister Natalie and brother-in-law Jorge, as well as the Coyles, who continue to make Ohio feel like home. Thanks also to my extended family of hometown friends—Robin Lau Cooper, Carrie Cuy, Lauren Liu, Patti Longoria, Suzie McGinness, Jennifer Page, Erin Ward Stublarec—for keeping me grounded with laughter and love.

Having saved the best for last, I cannot possibly express enough gratitude to my partner and best friend, Ian Coyle, who has offered boundless emotional support, patience, consolation, sympathy, and intellectual (as well as literal) sustenance, all of which kept me going throughout this process. Ian—I am incredibly lucky to have you by my side. Thank you!!

Finally, thanks to Oxford University Press for permitting me to publish here several updated and recontextualized writings from formerly published works. Portions of the Introduction and chapter 2 were previously published in *Journal of the American Musicological Society* 74, no. 1 (Spring 2021): 43–90. Portions of the Introduction and chapter 3 were previously published in *Twentieth-Century Music* 14, no. 2 (June 2017): 305–33. Portions of chapters 3 and 4 were published in *The Routledge Companion to Popular Music Analysis: Expanding Approaches*, ed. Ciro Scotto, Kenneth M. Smith, and John Brackett (New York: Routledge, 2018), 144–58. Portions of chapter 4 were published in *The Oxford Handbook of Electronic Dance Music*, ed. Robin James and Luis Manuel Garcia-Mispireta (New York: Oxford University Press, 2021), doi: 10.1093/oxfordhb/9780190093723.013.33.

PART 1
TURN ON . . .

. . . to Ambient Audio

Preface: On Ambient Audio

A familiar scenario: You turn on an audio playback device, tune in to some music, and drift off. Your awareness dissolves into waves of vibration. You seem to float, glide, swim through patterned tones and textures. The sound soothes as it recedes into your periphery. Music for ambience.

Perhaps also familiarly, you have chosen, for this purpose, audio produced to create ambience. Discreet music: uniform, predictable, and understated, music without obtrusive changes in instrumentation or volume to draw the ear, music without harmonic or rhythmic surprises. Minimal music: sheer, simple, and uncluttered, rafts of sustained tones (ground made into figure) or scant wisps of melody (figures become ground). Hypnotic music: tones drone and motifs recur, irregularly, but certainly, like a breeze, or like rippling water, variably elaborated or truncated. Spacious music: in their steady state, the sounds elude focus, seeking environment, surrounding; but the sounds also simulate space in other ways as melodies echo across instruments, as tones bloom into full resonance, and as source sounds melt into reverberation, excitements of air singing, overlapping, dissipating. Music to foster atmosphere, yes; but also atmospheres made into audio, immersive sound worlds for getting lost in, for transforming moods and transporting minds, for sedation and succor. Ambience as music.

This is ambient music, and it has a history. In fact, it has many overlapping histories, most of which converge on recording artist Brian Eno's *Discreet Music* (1975) and four-part *Ambient* series (1978–82), albums often cited as origins of the genre.[1] *Discreet Music* was, by Eno's own account, the experimental pop artist's first solo album of ambient music, but *Ambient 1: Music for Airports* (1978), a four-track LP conceived as music for use in airports, introduced the term "ambient music" to the world in the

[1] Books identifying Eno's records as origins of the ambient music genre include Seth Kim-Cohen, *Against Ambience and Other Essays* (New York: Bloomsbury Academic, 2016); John T. Lysaker, *Brian Eno's Ambient 1: Music for Airports*, Oxford Keynotes (New York: Oxford University Press, 2018); Paul Roquet, *Ambient Media: Japanese Atmospheres of Self* (Minneapolis: University of Minnesota Press, 2016); and Eric Tamm, *Brian Eno: His Music and the Vertical Color of Sound* (London: Faber & Faber, 1988).

liner notes as "an atmosphere, or a surrounding influence: a tint."[2] Ambient music, Eno asserted, would be both functionally and aesthetically different from "conventional background music" like Muzak, Inc.'s symphonic pop arrangements.[3] Rather than merely "adding stimulus" to the environment, ambient music would "induce calm and a space to think." And ambient, apparently unlike Muzak's "lightweight and derivative" muzak, should "accommodate many levels of listening attention without enforcing one in particular; it must be as ignorable as it is interesting."[4] For his record, Eno created four tape-loop-based tracks that could, in an airport setting, produce a consistent field of sound for passersby to easily enter or leave. Hefty silences and an uncluttered midrange made room for PA announcements, while clean synthesized timbres and ample reverb stylized the airport as a welcoming, open-air modern marvel.

Most people, however, have come to know *Music for Airports* not via airports, but rather as a studio album. Released on major international pop/rock label Polydor, *Airports* initiated the *Ambient* LP series in which Eno and collaborators sketched out several forms ambient music might take.[5] Muzak's muzak, given this context, provided a less relevant point of contrast than did the albums of "mood music" (aka "mood albums") introduced by Paul Weston & His Orchestra on LPs like *Music for Dreaming* (1945) and *Music for Easy Listening* (1950), a concept replicated by various performers to great popularity throughout the 1950s and '60s (*Music for Washing and Ironing*!) and ironized in *Music for Airports*'s title.[6] Eno likely had these albums, now consigned to many a thrift store record bin, in mind when in 1977 stating his

[2] Brian Eno, "Ambient Music," liner notes to *Ambient 1: Music for Airports*, Editions EG, AMB001, 1978, LP.

[3] Starting in 1936, Muzak, Inc., wired streams of their arrangements to businesses for commercial use. On the history of Muzak, see Stephen H. Barnes, *Muzak: The Hidden Messages in Music*, vol. 9, Studies on the History and Interpretation of Music (Lewiston, NY: The Edwin Mellen Press, 1988); Jerri Ann Husch, "Music of the Workplace: A Study of Muzak Culture" (PhD diss., University of Massachusetts, 1984); Simon C. Jones and Thomas G. Schumacher, "Muzak: On Functional Music and Power," *Critical Studies in Mass Communication* 9, no. 2 (June 1992): 156–69; Joseph Lanza, *Elevator Music: A Surreal History of Muzak, Easy-Listening, and Other Moodsong* (New York: Picador, 1995), 22–54; Hervé Vanel, *Triple Entendre: Furniture Music, Muzak, Muzak-Plus* (Urbana: University of Illinois Press, 2013), 46–83.

[4] Eno, "Ambient Music." The Muzak service became so widespread by the mid-twentieth century that US Americans began referring colloquially to any publicly programmed background music as "muzak."

[5] Major collaborators included composer-performers Harold Budd (*Ambient 2: The Plateaux of Mirror*) and Laraaji (*Ambient 3: Day of Radiance*). Several other performers and engineers assisted with Eno's solo albums in the series.

[6] On the history of the mood album, see Keir Keightley, "Music for Middlebrows: Defining the Easy Listening Era, 1946–1966," *American Music* 26, no. 3 (Fall 2008): 314–21; Lanza, *Elevator Music*, 67–132; Jennifer Messelink, "Mood Albums," *Journal of Popular Music Studies* 33, no. 3 (2021): 45–49.

intention to make "disposable" records for home use, records that would be "like having nice curtains or nice lights in the room. I'd sell them very cheap in a plain package that says *Waking up Music, Breakfast Music*, that kind of thing. They'd be like ordinary records physically, they'd just not come with the aura of art, so one wouldn't be frightened of having the things for a couple of weeks and then getting rid of them."[7] And yet, in 2022, copies of *Music for Airports*, and of Eno's albums generally, are rare to come by at yard sales or second-hand shops. *Airports* has since been reissued several times, while in the United States original vinyl copies easily run for $50. The aura of art lingers.

By contrast, the aura of art was nowhere to be found, during the early 2010s, in the Charlottesville, Virginia, SPCA rummage store record bins where I first encountered Syntonic Research, Inc.'s *Environments: Disc 2* (1970). Immediately drawn in by the garishly colored "listening test responses" on the back ("I feel much more relaxed."—"A surrealistic experience . . . "—"Very heavy stuff."), I was intrigued to read below these testimonials what I recognized as a description of ambient music: *Tintinnabulation (Contemplative Sound)*, a "computer synthesized" recording of bells, provides a "long duration environmental sound source" that listeners should find "useful for both meditation and relaxation." My later playback revealed five remarkably realistic bells with uncannily long reverb being struck at random intervals and interspersed with silence, a recording that indeed, as the back states, "seems to float in the air" as a "physical presence." From there, I sought out its predecessor, *Environments: Disc 1* (1969), which also boasted multifont, multicolor listener testimony on the back ("better than a tranquilizer!"), as well as the claim that, "Unlike music, *Environments* affects the subconscious without deadening the mind's ability to think." Side A's *The Psychologically Ultimate Seashore*, a digitally randomized recording of ocean waves, indeed provided me, as the back promised, a "sensuous sound environment" and "source of constant amazement."

These discoveries spurred me to seek out more proto-ambient music not, as frequently found in academic studies of the genre, in Muzak or its avant-garde alternatives, but rather in what I now call *ambient audio*: slow, spare, spacious audio sold as an artful personal medium for creating atmosphere, fostering contemplation, transforming awareness, and stilling the body.

[7] Vivien Goldman, "Eno: Extra Natty Orations," *Sounds*, February 5, 1977, Rock's Back Pages, https://www.rocksbackpages.com/Library/Article/eno-extra-natty-orations.

This unity of audio production design and promotional concept, not yet conventionalized by genre labels like "ambient" in the international music market until the 1980s and '90s, found nascent form in an assorted range of popular audio productions now more commonly associated with new age music, psychedelic and progressive rock, nature sounds records, and jazz than with muzak or avant-garde composition: records like Steven Halpern's *Spectrum Suite* (1976), Tangerine Dream's *Phaedra* (1974), Wendy Carlos's *Sonic Seasonings* (1972), and Paul Horn's *Inside* (1968).

In the context of ambient audio, *Music for Airports* appears less an avant-garde take on Muzak than a secularized twist on Tony Scott Trio's *Music for Zen Meditation (and Other Joys)* (1965), a collection of delicate free improvisations featuring Tony Scott on clarinet, Shinichi Yuize on koto, and Hōzan Yamamoto on shakuhachi—and a record of discreet, minimal, spacious, hypnotic audio often absent from histories of ambient music. As Scott wrote in the notes, the trio came together "in the spirit of Zen" after Yamamoto asked to join Scott and Shinichi's ongoing improvisational practice.[8] And experiencing Zen music, as popular Buddhism writer Alan Watts elaborated in the notes, can be like meditating, a way of realizing your oneness with the universe by "letting go one's thoughts and feelings, whatever they may be, and allowing them to settle into quietness, to the point where the sensation of the separate 'I' gets rid of itself."[9] The dispassionate sensitivity, deep focus, and mutual generosity displayed through the trio's improvisations inspire such still-minded receptivity. The modal, loosely imitative duets comprising most of the tracks peaceably work as background, but their quiet intensity also rewards rapt listening. Indeed, the album seems as much "for" accompanying meditation (and/or other joys) as "for" providing a gateway, through close listening, to a meditative state—an inducement, by way of recorded sound, of *satori*.[10]

But *Music for Zen Meditation*, despite also providing a calming, ignorable-yet-interesting spin on the mood album, is frequently cited, to quote Scott's

[8] Tony Scott, liner notes to *Music for Zen Meditation (and Other Joys)* by Tony Scott, Shinichi Yuize, and Hōzan Yamamoto, Verve, V6-8634, 1965, LP.

[9] Watts, liner notes to *Music for Zen Meditation*. Watts was the most widely read Western ambassador to Zen Buddhist thought during the postwar years; see James William Coleman, *The New Buddhism: The Western Transformation of an Ancient Tradition* (New York: Oxford University Press, 2002), 63–64.

[10] Indeed, inducing a meditative state may well have been the intention of the Japanese musicians whose musical training was rooted in, and inseparable from, Zen tradition. On this inseparability, see Jay Keister, "The Shakuhachi as Spiritual Tool: A Japanese Buddhist Instrument in the West," *Asian Music* 35, no. 2 (2004): 99–131.

New York Times obituary, as an "early example of New Age music."[11] The term "new age," which in the late 1960s referred to the material culture around psychedelic experience, alternative spirituality, and holistic health that was rooted in the California counterculture, eventually also found use during the mid-to-late 1970s as a descriptor for any music associated with this milieu. *Music for Zen Meditation* and its 1965 follow-up, *Music for Yoga Meditation (and Other Joys)*, both early products of this material culture, also portended various stylistic conventions that coalesced around the "new age" term in the early to mid-1980s as major labels, retailers, and print media in the United States more widely adopted the genre tag: group improvisation, folklike melodies, cross-cultural fusion, and a therapeutic framing. Eno's ambient music did not. While ambient music was initially bundled with the emergent category of new age in popular media discourses, it solidified as a separate genre between the mid-'80s and mid-'90s as artists, critics, and listeners conventionalized it in contrast to new age's industry-based construction and aligned it instead with relatively highbrow avant-garde, electronic, and rock scenes and markets.[12] Ambient music's reification in subsequent histories and canons as separate from (and seemingly more progressive, conceptual, and artistic than) new age—and from the many popular styles adjacent to it, including modal jazz and psychedelic rock—has conditioned listeners to think these musics and histories separately, rather than as entwined lineages within the broader phenomenon of ambient audio.

Some deconditioning is in order. As *Turn On, Tune In, Drift Off* demonstrates, ambient music took shape relative to a host of late-twentieth-century audio productions conceived and commodified as personal atmospheres for intoxication and cerebration, for meditation and aesthetic contemplation, hypnosis and gnosis, concentration and cool. From the 1960s to the century's end, as sophisticated audio production technologies became increasingly available and affordable through consumer markets globally, independent artists and producers across avant-garde and popular idioms developed ambient audio via such varied productions as nature sounds records, experimental compositions and sound installations, "space music" radio, acid rock improvisations, cosmic rock albums, dub mixes, electronic

[11] Margalit Fox, "Tony Scott, Jazz Clarinetist Who Mastered Bebop, Dies at 85," *New York Times*, March 31, 2007, https://www.nytimes.com/2007/03/31/obituaries/31scott.html.

[12] "Industry-based" is a genre form discussed in Jennifer C. Lena, *Banding Together: How Communities Create Genres in Popular Music* (Princeton, NJ: Princeton University Press, 2012). According to Lena, industry-based genres commonly develop out of scene-based and/or avant-garde genre forms.

dance music compilations—and, of course, music explicitly identified as "ambient."[13] These artists took high-fidelity ideals of spatial immersion and mental transportation to dreamy, fantastical conclusions, exploring and exploiting the potential for electronically enhanced audio to deliver listeners into imaginary spaces and new states of awareness.[14] Their productions commonly involved the automated sustainment and/or cycling of sounds; displacement effects like delay and phasing; spatialization techniques like reverb, panning, and echo; as well as instrumental mixing, timbral modification, and microtuning, all of which could induce disorientation, dissociation, and deconcentration in listeners.[15] These composers and producers often stressed the contemplative side of these psychoacoustic intoxications, making room and time in their sonic environments for listeners to observe the effects of these sounds on the sensorium. Many also located the primary value of their work in such contemplation.

Turn On, Tune In, Drift Off charts the formation of the ambient music genre via the mind-altering, mood-bending, often stilling, and yet also unsettling worlds of ambient audio. The book takes a trip through various landmark productions and related discourses—including marketing rhetoric, artist manifestos and interviews, and music criticism—that between roughly the mid-1960s and mid-'90s plotted the conventions of what would become known and sold as ambient music (or simply "ambient"). The sounds and scenes on this trip include, but also extend before and beyond the music and influences of Brian Eno, illustrating how ambient's genre formation, far from the invention of one person, took place across myriad popular styles and their various overlapping sociocultural, technological, market, intellectual, and artistic domains. And while nonexhaustive—many different routes could be forged through the vast and still-underexplored universe of ambient audio—this journey, as its commencement at *Music for Zen Meditation* and *Environments* hints, traverses cultural territory routinely avoided in academic studies of ambient despite its strong connection to the genre's

[13] On the growing availability of audio production technology in the US consumer market during this time, see Paul Théberge, *Any Sound You Can Imagine: Making Music/Consuming Technology* (Middletown, CT: Wesleyan University Press, 1997).

[14] On the immersive and transportive ideals of high-fidelity audio, see Tim J. Anderson, *Making Easy Listening: Material Culture and Postwar American Recording* (Minneapolis: University of Minnesota Press, 2006), xliii–xliv; Peter Doyle, *Echo and Reverb: Fabricating Space in Popular Music Recording, 1900–1960* (Middletown, CT: Wesleyan University Press, 2005); Albin Zak, *The Poetics of Rock: Cutting Tracks, Making Records* (Berkeley: University of California Press, 2001), 76–77.

[15] Michael Hicks, *Sixties Rock: Garage, Psychedelic, and Other Satisfactions* (Urbana: University of Illinois Press, 1999), 58–74.

aesthetics: namely, the psychedelic counterculture of the 1960s, the overlapping New Age milieux of the '70s and '80s, the electronic dance music subcultures of the '80s and '90s, and the coincident coevolution of therapeutic audio and "head music" across North American and European alternative media and independent music markets.

In mapping ambient music's genesis relative to these countercultural formations, my approach in this book countervails the habit, especially within academic scholarship, of rooting the genre primarily in the conceptual lineage of avant-garde art while paying scant attention to parallel and overlapping processes of commodification in popular media and music markets.[16] Instead, I observe the continuity of Eno and others' self-consciously "ambient" experimentation with the prior and concurrent mass-market experiments in ambient audio against which ambient's genre boundaries ultimately took shape. These continuities have since been obscured by genre divisions and art canons—not least the division between popular and art music that the ambient genre itself blurred. Ambient music, while appearing in name to be an asocial and suprastylistic artform, was in truth a socially savvy stylization of the intoxicating affective and embodied pleasures of psychedelic drone- and loop-based atmospheric audio for a presumptively white hip and high-middlebrow consumer market.

Hence, unlike accounts that conceptualize ambient music outside the strictures of genre—David Toop's indispensable *Ocean of Sound* comes to mind, as does Mark Prendergast's *The Ambient Century*—this book focuses on ambient music's commodification, illuminating how "ambient" emerged in the late twentieth century as a singular genre among genres, and style among styles. In particular, it traces how the expressive openness, detachment, disorientation, moodiness, and cerebral aspirations now associated with ambient music largely found form in the psychedelic and new age countercultures, and how musicians, critics, and industry professionals came to conventionalize this audio as "ambient" according to idealizations of hip highbrow white masculinity as exemplified in the figure and music of Brian Eno, and in contradistinction to popular genres codified as relatively mainstream, middlebrow, nonwhite, and feminine.

[16] See, for instance, Joanna Demers, *Listening through the Noise: The Aesthetics of Experimental Electronic Music* (New York: Oxford University Press, 2010), 117–20 and 164; Thom Holmes, *Electronic and Experimental Music: Technology, Music, and Culture*, 3rd ed. (New York: Routledge, 2008); Kim-Cohen, *Against Ambience*; Alan Licht, *Sound Art: Beyond Music, Between Categories* (New York: Rizzoli, 2007); Lysaker, *Brian Eno's "Ambient 1"*; Vanel, *Triple Entendre*.

In tracing this process of commodification, I hope to make evident some of the blind spots in discourses wherein ambient music idealistically appears absent of convention or sociocultural meaning. I wager that an ongoing critical assessment of ambient music's socioaesthetics,[17] and the classed, gendered, and raced terms by which it has conventionally set its expressive parameters, might in fact serve as a starting point for rerouting the processes of commodification and conventionalization its proponents have long claimed to defy. Accordingly, this book also wagers that a meditation on ambient music's psychedelic past, beyond expanding received notions of ambient and psychedelic music alike, might also motivate ambient audio's makers to revisit and reconceive the sorts of awareness that its erstwhile creators have long struggled to adequately spread.

Overview

Lester Bangs, one of the most adventurous of late-twentieth-century rock critics, in 1980 delivered a remarkably prescient meditation on the emergent meaning of "ambient" as an environmental, seemingly anonymous audio resource for mood and motivation. His reflection might well be read as a *précis* of this very book:

> As rock has moved from being the rebellious sound of a counterculture to that of mainstream America, and as the mean age of its listenership has gone up, the predominant sound has gotten tamer. Housewives now leave the rock-'n'-roll station on while they do dishes. That's ambient, and so is disco. Meanwhile, "environment" records featuring the sounds of waves rolling in on the seashore or birds chirping in the trees are selling like crazy. Eno himself has remarked with some surprise that his ambient records are

[17] Although the term "socioaesthetics" is not entirely common in music studies, I use it in this book to capture the framework often assumed in much anglophone popular music studies scholarship, as well as in a good deal of scholarship elsewhere in cultural studies, (ethno)musicology, and music theory, wherein the social and aesthetic value of music are seen as essentially intertwined, and thus important to analyze in tandem. A good starting place for considering this framework can be found in Simon Frith, "Towards an Aesthetic of Popular Music," in *Music and Society: The Politics of Composition, Performance, and Reception*, ed. Richard Leppert and Susan McClary (New York: Cambridge University Press, 1987), 133–49. This framework is certainly compatible with the use of the term "socioaesthetics" in philosophy to imagine an expansion of the aesthetic into mediated and commodified "ambience"—see Anders Michelsen and Frederik Tygstrup, eds., *Socioaesthetics: Ambience-Imaginary* (Leiden, The Netherlands: Brill, 2015)—but my use of the term is more precisely rooted in the long-standing development of these ideas in music and cultural studies.

> actually outselling his song discs. In reality, we're rapidly reaching a point where, in the broadest sense, the two are interchangeable . . . As people feel more unnerved and threatened by the external world around them, the aural Valium of ambient recordings will eventually supplant Muzak altogether. In fact, disco DJs (in New York City, at least), with experience in bringing whole rooms full of people up and down again and again nightly, have been fantasizing about the political possibilities of sonic/rhythmic crowd control for at least three years now. We'll see how far they get.[18]

Along these lines, this book chronicles the mainstreaming and codification of countercultural ideals within the late-twentieth-century recorded music market in ambient audio genres, as well as the growth of audio cultures that treat nature sounds, ambient music, and electronic dance music (like disco) alike as drugless highs ("aural Valium") and sources of ambience and affect. We will, indeed, see how far they get, at least by the end of the twentieth century. And in fact, we will also venture a bit further by asking what and how these practices of audio production and codification also *mean* socially, culturally, and aesthetically.

To elaborate: The forthcoming book contains an introductory chapter, four body chapters, and a brief coda. The introductory chapter offers an exposition of the book's overarching narrative while highlighting some of the core themes, scenes, and concerns that run through the four body chapters. The first chapter focuses on Syntonic Research, Inc.'s *Tintinnabulation (Contemplative Sound)*, from the second *Environments* disc, as a chief example of the emergent high-middlebrow commodification of minimalist audio as psychedelic sound. The second chapter offers a peek into the first decade of *Music from the Hearts of Space*, a Bay Area–based program on Pacifica Radio that from 1973 to 1982 crystallized the ideals of the local grassroots spirituality network through the delivery of the DJs' ethereal "space music." A coda to this second chapter describes the industry-based mainstreaming of new age music in the 1980s, and the sounds and associations that clustered around the new age genre in light of this popularization. On the whole, these first two body chapters illustrate not only the commodification and popularization of countercultural ideals through ambient audio, but also how the heady, high-minded experimentation now commonly associated with ambient music has deep roots in psychedelic and new age art and culture.

[18] Lester Bangs, "Pop Music in the Eighties," *Stereo Review*, January 1980, 76.

The third and fourth chapters of this book document how ambient emerged as a self-standing genre of music, an emergence that largely occurred through rhetorical and stylistic distinctions from psychedelic, new age, and other popular genres. The third chapter focuses on the formative ambient albums of Brian Eno and his collaborators, mainly *Discreet Music* and the albums of the *Ambient* series, describing how these records and their framing mapped the coordinates by which later artists would establish a distinctive lineage for the ambient genre. The fourth chapter documents the popularization of ambient music as a self-standing genre between the late 1980s and the mid-1990s by way of its emergence as a subgenre of electronic dance music. It traces the sounds and tropes by which ambient attained distinction from other electronic dance music styles, as well as the rhetorical means by which ambient became raced, gendered, and classed relative to these other styles as a highbrow white male domain. Finally, a coda to the book offers some insights into the many promising directions ambient artists have explored since the turn of the twenty-first century, and it proposes these developments as trajectories from which to imagine a more expansive place and meaningful social role for the ambient music genre today.

Introduction

Highs for Highbrows? How We Got from Head Music to Ambient Music

Head Music and the Psychedelic Counterculture

"Rock's the first head music we've had since the end of the baroque."[1] So announces poet and journalist Chester Anderson in the opening to his widely reprinted paean to the art of the audile high, "Notes for the New Geology." The essay first appeared in the February 1967 issue of *The Oracle*, a San Francisco underground newspaper with ornate visual designs and visionary prose that assumed a readership of heads—namely the "pot heads" and "acid heads" of the Bay Area counterculture. Head music, Anderson writes, is at once mind and body music, to be apprehended holistically with the sensate consciousness of vibrating flesh. Rock does not simply communicate messages; it is a pulsating sensational matrix that listeners can plug into, a vehicle for entrancing the mind, loosening the body, and heightening feeling: "Repeated patterns (ostinati) & drones induce an almost instant light hypnosis (just like grass), locking the mind on the music at hand & intensifying all the other reactions. Long, open chords lower the blood pressure: crisp, repeated chords raise it." Noting the sense of "musical space" intuitively arising from these visceral responses, Anderson concludes by musing, prophetically, that "an arranger/composer who knew all this, especially if he had electronic instruments to work with, could play a listener's body like a soft guitar."[2]

Did Anderson hear rock as ambient audio?[3] Certainly central to Anderson's rendering lies the notion of rock as an ambient *medium* that

[1] Chester Anderson, "Notes for the New Geology," *San Francisco Oracle*, February 1967, 2. Anderson later clarifies that rock's similarity to "baroque music" lies in what he calls its "mosaic structure of tonal & textural contrast: tactility, collage" (2).

[2] Ibid., 23.

[3] As I define it in the Preface, ambient audio is "slow, spare, spacious audio sold as an artful personal medium for creating atmosphere, fostering contemplation, transforming awareness, and stilling the body."

Turn On, Tune In, Drift Off. Victor Szabo, Oxford University Press. © Oxford University Press 2023.
DOI: 10.1093/oso/9780190699307.003.0001

affects and augments personal embodiment and perception. His formulation taps into the historical meaning of "ambience" as a medium or milieu, i.e., an "aggregate of influences or conditions which shape or determine the being, development, life, or behavior of a person or thing."[4] Accordingly, Anderson gestures fervently to the philosophy of Marshall McLuhan, the Canadian media theorist whose vision of an electronically interconnected "global village," informed by an understanding of media as "human environments," resonated with the '60s counterculture.[5] Rock, writes Anderson, echoing McLuhan's formulations, is an "electronic extension of the central nervous system" that invites listener "participation" and "extended awareness."[6] "The medium is indeed the message," Anderson avers with reference to McLuhan's best-known slogan, "and rock knows what that means."[7]

Anderson's conception of rock as an ambient medium of altered awareness likewise conjures the conceptual framework of the *psychedelic* through which ambient audio, and ultimately ambient music, found form. The word "psychedelic," first coined in 1957 by British psychiatrist Humphry Osmond to characterize LSD as "mind manifesting," by this time commonly linked certain types of art to hallucinogens' perceptual effects.[8] Psychedelic light shows, for instance, recreated the visual deformations and recolorations caused by acid or psilocybin, while psychedelic rock audibly evoked, through various formal and studio techniques, the temporal and kinesthetic distortions of the LSD trip. The point of most such art was not merely to represent the hallucinogenic trip but also to create or induce one, with or without drugs.[9] Immersing audiences in variegated spaces of light and sound, entrancing listeners with hypnotic repetitive patterns, and overloading the senses with intense stimuli became common tactics of instigating psychedelic art's highs. So did the experiments in electronic audio production, especially the echoing, amplification, and timbral manipulation of droning and repetitive guitar patterns, that brought such varied rock acts as The Beatles, Jimi

[4] Leo Spitzer, "Milieu and Ambiance: An Essay in Historical Semantics," *Philosophy and Phenomenological Research* 3, no. 1 (September 1942): 2.

[5] Marshall McLuhan, *Understanding Media: The Extensions of Man*, 2nd ed. (New York: Mentor, 1964), viii, 19.

[6] Anderson, "New Geology," 23.

[7] Ibid., 2.

[8] On the coinage of the word "psychedelic," see Martin A. Lee and Bruce Shlain, *Acid Dreams: The Complete Social History of LSD: The CIA, the Sixties, and Beyond*, rev. ed. (New York: Grove Press, 1992), 54–55.

[9] Michael Hicks, *Sixties Rock: Garage, Psychedelic, and Other Satisfactions* (Urbana: University of Illinois Press, 1999), 59.

Hendrix, Jefferson Airplane, the Grateful Dead, and Pink Floyd under the umbrella of the psychedelic around this time.

Limitations plague both popular and scholarly conceptions of psychedelic music, a term that continues to be chiefly associated with the woozy, ornate style of rock that became internationally lucrative from the mid-'60s into the '70s.[10] As Anderson himself points out, rock's mind-altering effects extend far beyond "psychedelic" styles; the head music "high" is an "avant garde art form" and an "intensely synthesizing art" upon which "no limitations . . . are valid."[11] The limitless potential of electrified sound to alter perception and embodiment, beautifully represented in Anderson's "head music" vision, extends far out beyond psych rock, narrowly conceived, to all sorts of music and audio. In '60s San Francisco alone, artists and amateurs alike intentionally blurred avant-garde and pop sensibilities in exploring the potential of electronic sound to overwhelm the senses and entrance audiences. From the performances of the 1964 Trips Festival, where attendees were encouraged to play their own electronic "gadgets" alongside improvisations by The Grateful Dead and synth-maker Don Buchla;[12] to the theatrical surrounds of USCO (The US Company), in which music blaring and sounds screeching alongside kinetic light and film projections would dissolve into a stream of tape-looped "Om's";[13] to the everyday improvisations of Ken Kesey's Merry Pranksters, who quite literally brought their extemporaneous tape-delay experiments on the road (and later to their famous Acid Tests);[14] to the

[10] See Hicks, *Sixties Rock*; Ann Johnson and Mike Stax, "From Psychotic to Psychedelic: The Garage Contribution to Psychedelia," *Popular Music and Society* 29, no. 4 (October 2006): 411–25; Edward L. Macan, *Rocking the Classics: English Progressive Rock and the Counterculture* (New York: Oxford University Press, 1997); Russell Reising, "Melting Clocks and the Hallways of Always: Time in Psychedelic Music," *Popular Music and Society* 32, no. 4 (October 2009): 523–47; Sheila Whiteley, *The Space between the Notes: Rock and the Counter-Culture* (London: Routledge, 1992). Joseph Lanza overrides some of these limitations in his history of psychedelic aesthetics in 1960s easy-listening pop, a history that dovetails well with this book's; see Joseph Lanza, *Easy Listening Acid Trip: An Elevator Ride through Sixties Psychedelic Pop* (Port Townsend, WA: Feral House, 2020). Some authors have considered certain styles of electronic dance music in terms of psychedelia; see Matthew Collin, *Altered State: The Story of Ecstasy Culture and Acid House*, rev. ed. (London: Serpent's Tail, 2009); Simon Reynolds, *Energy Flash: A Journey through Rave Music and Dance Culture* (Berkeley: Soft Skull, 2012). Accounts bridging psychedelic rock, soul, and electronic dance music include Jim DeRogatis, *Turn On Your Mind: Four Decades of Great Psychedelic Rock* (Milwaukee: Hal Leonard, 2003); William Echard, *Psychedelic Popular Music: A History through Musical Topic Theory* (Bloomington: Indiana University Press, 2017).

[11] Anderson, "New Geology," 2, 23.

[12] Charles Perry, *The Haight-Ashbury: A History* (New York: Wenner, 2005), 42–47; Trevor Pinch and Frank Trocco, *Analog Days: The Invention and Impact of the Moog Synthesizer* (Cambridge, MA: Harvard University Press, 2002), 94–97.

[13] Fred Turner, *From Counterculture to Cyberculture: Stewart Brand, the Whole Earth Network, and the Rise of Digital Utopianism* (Chicago: University of Chicago Press, 2006), 51.

[14] Tom Wolfe, *The Electric Kool-Aid Test* (New York: Picador, 1968), 58–59, 67–72, and 138.

meditative, long-duration explorations of microtuning, drone, and echo in the hyperfocused and hyperextended music of the "hypnotic" (later "minimalist") school of experimental composition;[15] audio artisans inspired by psychedelic experience conspired to vibrate listeners' bodies, and melt listeners' minds, into altered states. Practitioners valued the immediacy of embodied experience as the stuff of art, and they embraced electronic audio production technologies as a common means of shocking, puzzling, and soothing the senses into new configurations. Psychedelic music, under this broader conception of the term, synthesized earlier developments in avant-garde experimentalism, Western popular music, and Asian art to create occasions for mental transportation and awareness expansion. With this history in mind, ambient music's genre formation may be understood as a taming and reframing of the mind- and mood-altering potentials of psychedelic music, a chief area of ambient audio exploration in the 1960s and '70s.

Many more ingredients make up the sociocultural, technological, and intellectual brew in which ambient music fermented, but the psychedelic counterculture of the 1960s and '70s, and the concurrent commodification of electronic audio as an agent of altered consciousness, is perhaps the most commonly overlooked context for its growth. A mass culture phenomenon from the beginning, fused together by the popular art that facilitated its spread, the psychedelic counterculture embraced electronic sound as both experimental art and mind-altering medium. Inspired by the antiauthoritarianism of the New Left civil rights and student movements, these mostly white and middle-class boomer youth across North America and Europe "turned on" to drugs like marijuana and LSD, and to the body-shaking and head-spinning sounds of the electric guitar and synthesizer, as totems and affirmations of their dissidence.[16] Many, in the process, "tuned in" to different modes of apprehending the world, finding themselves confronting

[15] The full extent of scholarship on minimalist music is too broad to list here; some comprehensive resources include Robert Fink, *Repeating Ourselves: American Minimal Music as Cultural Practice* (Berkeley: University of California Press, 2005); Christophe Levaux, *We Have Always Been Minimalist: The Construction and Triumph of a Musical Style*, trans. Rose Vekony (Oakland: University of California Press, 2020); Keith Potter, Kyle Gann, and Pwyll Ap Siôn, eds., *The Ashgate Research Companion to Minimalist and Postminimalist Music* (Burlington, VT: Ashgate, 2013); Edward Strickland, *Minimalism: Origins* (Bloomington: Indiana University Press, 1993); Richard Taruskin, "A Harmonious Avant-Garde?," in *The Oxford History of Western Music*, vol. 6: *Music in the Late Twentieth-Century* (New York: Oxford University Press, 2005), 351–410.

[16] With loci in the San Francisco Bay Area and New York City, the mass psychedelic counterculture overlapped with, but also remained distinct from, the New Left civil rights and student movements across the United States and Europe. For a clear description of the differences between the New Left and psychedelic countercultures, see Van Gosse, *Rethinking the New Left: An Interpretative History* (Gordonsville, VA: Palgrave Macmillan, 2005), 204.

existential truths and transcendental experiences scarcely acknowledged in nationalist and corporatist narratives of material prosperity and social progress. And while some went so far as to "drop out" of corporate labor or the consumer market, for instance by participating in grassroots labor or housing cooperatives, most opted for the symbolic withdrawal of the psychedelic trip. A consumption-based ethic of sensory de-familiarization and perceptual self-examination arose alongside the widespread idea that new social relations could arise out of individual therapeutic interventions. Psychedelic drugs and electrified music alike instrumentalized this lifestyle ethic.

It is no coincidence that the catchcry of countercultural disaffiliation "turn on, tune in, and drop out" so overtly collapsed human drug user and electronic audio device. The motto, popularized by acid guru Timothy Leary (on Marshall McLuhan's recommendation to coin a catchphrase), sloganized what Leary called a "politics of the nervous system" that regarded humans, synthetic chemicals, and electronics as co-extensive, and that prescribed the transformation of individual consciousness as a practice of social liberation.[17] Envisioning society as a cybernated nervous system uniting the electronic and organic, Leary argued that LSD and electronic music alike could "reprogram" humans to undo the military-industrial complex's "sensory conditioning."[18] Relatedly, McLuhan famously regarded electronic media, especially audio, as "extending" the human nervous system beyond its inborn capacities into a global sea of freeform informational and sensational exchanges.[19] Promoting ideals of fluidity, communalism, and material transcendence, both Leary and McLuhan understood audio as a gateway through which, to borrow an image from counterculture historian Theodore Roszak, the human individual could enter "wholly into the grand symbiotic system of nature, letting its currents and nuances flow through him."[20]

As Roszak's technonatural image suggests, the psychedelic counterculture took a far more optimistic, if still ambivalent view of electronic technology than suggested by the shallow media portrayal of the antimodern and technophobic "hippie." While the media "establishment" of the mid–late '60s

[17] Timothy Leary et al., "The Politics of the Nervous System," *Bulletin of the Atomic Scientists* 18, no. 5 (May 1, 1962): 26–27.

[18] Timothy Leary, *The Politics of Ecstasy* (Berkeley: Ronin, 1998), 33, 45.

[19] McLuhan, *Understanding Media*, 19.

[20] Theodore Roszak, *The Making of a Counter Culture: Reflections on the Technocratic Society and Its Youthful Opposition* (Berkeley: University of California Press, 1995), 247.

and early '70s were representing the new countercultural eco-consciousness with images of barefoot flower children, socially engaged hip "dropouts"—the "turned-on underground" of "the electronic generation," as Leary called them—were busy reimagining the look, sound, and role of technology within their everyday environments.[21] Although skepticism abounded around large-scale and automated technologies, which symbolized the technocratic ideals of instrumental rationality, efficiency, order, and control that countercultural youth rejected,[22] electricity also held promise as a universalizing "second nature" that could route around social, individual, and even physical boundaries to create a new cybernetic (or posthuman, as it would later be theorized) collectivity.[23] If, as countercultural luminary Buckminster Fuller gushed in 1970, "we are technology, the universe is technology," then it stood to reason, however paradoxically, that technologies could be deliberately designed and used to bring the body and mind closer to a state of nature.[24] This pragmatic reasoning owes a great deal to cybernetics, a research field that in the mid-twentieth-century studied the interactivity of entities nonorganic and organic, or technological and natural, together as entwined components of behavioral and informational feedback systems.[25] Amplified audio, understood as one such entity, had the potential to alleviate (if not

[21] Leary, *The Politics of Ecstasy*, 165.

[22] Leo Marx, "The Idea of 'Technology' and Postmodern Pessimism," in *Technology, Pessimism, and Postmodernism*, ed. Yaron Ezrahi, Everett Mendelsohn, and Howard P. Segal (Amherst: University of Massachusetts Press, 1995), 20. As Marx explains, a small but significant stream of US intellectuals and artists since the nineteenth century criticized technocratic idealism that treated instrumental rationality, functionalism, and efficiency as ends in themselves. This line of criticism found great popularity in the United States following the Second World War, especially with the counterculture (19–23). See also Leo Marx, *The Machine in the Garden: Technology and the Pastoral Ideal in America* (New York: Oxford University Press, 1967).

[23] On the relationship between cybernetics and posthumanism, see N. Katherine Hayles, *How We Became Posthuman: Virtual Bodies in Cybernetics, Literature, and Informatics* (Chicago: University of Chicago Press, 1999).

[24] Buckminster Fuller, "Pirated Transcription of Interview Videotaped by Raindance Corporation," *Radical Software* no. 1, Summer 1970, 5. Ironically, the notion of technoholistic therapy traces back to late-nineteenth-century neurological discourses that anxiously represented the nervous system as susceptible both to actual electric energy and to the figurative "shocks" of urban modernity; see Shelley Trower, "'Nerve-Vibration': Therapeutic Technologies in the 1880s and 1890s," in *Neurology and Modernity: A Cultural History of Nervous Systems, 1800–1950*, ed. Laura Salisbury and Andrew Shail (New York: Palgrave Macmillan, 2010), 148–49 and 156.

[25] Some early overviews of cybernetics from this time period include W. Ross Ashby, *An Introduction to Cybernetics*, 2nd ed. (London: Chapman & Hall, 1957); Norbert Wiener, *Cybernetics: Or Control and Communication in the Animal and the Machine*, 2nd ed. (New York: MIT Press and John Wiley & Sons, 1961). On the influence of cybernetics and systems theory on the counterculture, see Daniel Belgrad, *The Culture of Feedback: Ecological Thinking in Seventies America* (Chicago: University of Chicago Press, 2019); Andrew G. Kirk, *Counterculture Green: The Whole Earth Catalog and American Environmentalism* (Lawrence: University of Kansas Press, 2007); Turner, *From Counterculture to Cyberculture*.

ameliorate) the anxieties of the modern world by affording users opportunities to alter their disposition and outlook.

This notion, of course, was not new. In the 1930s, the Muzak Corporation started piping light classical and dance music, made and streamlined for mood regulation, into public spaces of leisure and commerce in the United States; while light music on the radio became a favored source of relaxing background entertainment in the home.[26] A decade later, North American radio programs featuring light music and sweet jazz began marketing themselves as undemanding "easy listening," and record labels started selling "mood music" albums of orchestral arrangements of familiar tunes to adult audiences as accompaniment to physical relaxation and mental drift.[27] For '60s countercultural youth, however, no music better encapsulated the technocratic docility and bourgeois snobbery of the adult middlebrow square than the bland "light" fare offered up by easy-listening radio, mood music, and Muzak.[28] High-minded heads often shared with highbrow critics and intellectuals disdain for these sonic symbols of corporate conformity and aspired refinement. Unlike cultural elites, however, heads also held out hope for the transformative and transportive possibilities of immersive, amplified, and mass-reproduced sounds to dissolve barriers between mind and body, to ease inner space into harmony with its outer environments, and to contribute to a spiritually nourishing cultural ecosystem.[29]

It just needed to sound different.

Inside Ambient Audio

Malachi's *Holy Music* (1967), according to poet and counterculture luminary Allan Ginsberg, "approaches music in spirit of consciousness—meditation: altar, flowers, herbs, incense, silence, communion with selves,

[26] On the history of Muzak, see note 3 of the Preface. On radio listening practices in the 1930s, see David Goodman, "Distracted Listening: On Not Making Sound Choices in the 1930s," in *Sound in the Age of Mechanical Reproduction*, ed. David Suisman and Susan Strasser (Philadelphia: University of Pennsylvania Press, 2010), 15–46.

[27] On "easy listening," see Keir Keightley, "Music for Middlebrows: Defining the Easy Listening Era, 1946–1966," *American Music* 26, no. 3 (Fall 2008): 309–35. On the history of the mood music album, see note 6 of the Preface.

[28] On the relationship between easy-listening mood music and middlebrow taste, see John Howland, *Hearing Luxe Pop: Glorification, Glamour, and the Middlebrow in American Popular Music* (Oakland: University of California Press, 2021), esp. 114–47; Keightley, "Music for Middlebrows."

[29] On the history of the concept of "ecosystem" in environmental sciences, see A. J. Willis, "The Ecosystem: An Evolving Concept Viewed Historically," *Functional Ecology* 11, no. 2 (April 1997): 268–71.

hush and darkness and improvisation."[30] Verve Records released the album of understated head music after a label rep discovered Malachi, born John Morgan Newbern, improvising on his twelve-string guitar in a Berkeley church, and invited him to record at a San Francisco studio. Newbern, initially inspired by the rhythm'n'blues, jazz, and rock'n'roll he was raised with in Memphis, attributes his "strongest" influences on the album to Arabic maqam-based music, Japanese kabuki, Chinese opera, and Indian classical music, as well as his study of Buddhism, all of which he attempted to synthesize on the record's 37-minute modal improvisation.[31] Titled "Evening Vibrations," the unrehearsed performance slowly waxes and wanes in intensity as Newbern explores the prepared open-tuned guitar's register and timbre alongside an ever-present undulating Jew's harp drone, as well as occasional hand percussion, Native American chant, and ponderous pools of silence. Although impactful within the Bay Area scene, and selling over 100K copies nationwide,[32] Verve could not figure out how to market the LP, and critics had difficulty finding substance in the record that they, nonetheless, recognized as "an adequate background" and a "medium" for achieving a "meditative mood"—should the buyer find the ability to "listen from the inside."[33]

Paul Horn's *Inside* (1968), too, provided audiences a medium for achieving a meditative mood—in this case, from inside the reverberant marble dome of the Taj Mahal. Horn, an established jazz clarinetist and flautist, was in April 1968 filming a documentary about transcendental meditation, which he had studied (alongside The Beatles) earlier that year. Having heard, during his first visit, the vocal incantations of the Taj Mahal dome's mausoleum guard echoing endlessly in the dome air, Horn returned late one evening with his flute—and recording engineer—to capture the sound of the instrument in the space. Horn's modal, largely pentatonic improvisations, at times in dialogue with a friend of the guard's vocal calls, create billowy plumes of reverberation within which Horn's playing sweeps, dances, and dives. Released on the Epic label, the record found critical acclaim (a "beautiful, deeply spiritual experience" produced with "incredible ambience" and "otherworldly

[30] Allan Ginsberg, liner notes to *Holy Music* by Malachi, Verve, V6-5024, 1967, LP.

[31] John Wisniewski, interview with John Morgan Newbern, *Alternative Culture Magazine*, 2006, http://alternativeculture.com/music/malachi.htm.

[32] Sales estimate comes from review of *NOT FOR SALE . . .* by Malachi, *Cash Box*, January 30, 1988, 22.

[33] Bertram Stanleigh, review of *Holy Music* by Malachi, *Audio*, June 1968, 49; N.H., review of *Holy Music* by Malachi, *Hi-Fi/Stereo Review*, February 1968, 126.

beauty," according to Gene Lees of *High Fidelity*), and was ultimately canonized as a new age classic, with sales upward of 750,000 copies.[34] Though later reissued as *Inside the Taj Mahal* with the majestic structure on front, the original pressing of *Inside* placed Horn's face on the cover, staring at the viewer, implying that the title refers as much to the interior of the listening self as that of its environing space.

That same year, La Monte Young and Marian Zazeela's *Dream House*, now an intermittently ongoing sound and light installation in Manhattan, then presented Young's most ambitious effort yet to "get inside of sounds" and "experience another world."[35] The experimental avant-garde composer with roots in jazz performance, a strong interest in psychedelics, and a growing fascination with Hindustani raga had for a decade been combining heavy amplification with drones in his compositions and collaborative improvisations. *Dream House* offered (and continues to offer) a spatialized extension of this practice.[36] Attendees enter a room suffused with magenta lights and calligraphic shadows designed by Marian Zazeela (Young's spouse), as well as a thick cluster of microtuned oscillator-generated sine waves constantly streaming from loudspeakers in the four corners. As participants move their bodies, whether in place, or through the space of the room, Young's seemingly static drones attain a dynamic quality as different drones successively come to the fore of audition. Time contracts in the windowless room as the drones beckon states of entrancement and disorientation. Like various other '60s avant-garde works linked to the countercultural milieu, *Dream House* occasioned psychoacoustic perceptual shifts, discoveries of complexity within seeming simplicity, and heightened awareness of a continuously surrounding sonic "now."

Although typically categorized apart today—*Holy Music* as psychedelic folk or rock, *Inside* as jazz fusion or new age, *Dream House* as minimalism or sound art—these audio productions from the late 1960s commonly illustrate characteristics of both art and artist that would become conventionalized in the following decades as "ambient." Compositionally, all involve reverberation, drones, and sustained tones as means of producing ambience and modulating listener awareness. Conceptually, all gesture to spiritual,

[34] Gene Lees, review of *Inside* by Paul Horn, *High Fidelity*, November 1969, 140; Paul Horn, *Inside Paul Horn: The Spiritual Odyssey of a Universal Traveler* (New York: HarperCollins, 1990), 78.

[35] La Monte Young, "Lecture 1960," *Tulane Drama Review* 10, no. 2 (1965): 81–82.

[36] For more on *Dream House*, see Jeremy Grimshaw, *Draw a Straight Line and Follow It: The Music and Mysticism of La Monte Young* (New York: Oxford University Press, 2011), 114–41.

introspective, and transportive auditory experiences. As artists, Newbern, Horn, and Young, all white men with significant training and investment in Black American popular styles and interest in Asian musics,[37] downplay their own expressive presence and identity in the creation of cool, depersonalized moods. And all produce sonic spaces in which audiences, from the inside, might achieve contemplative and altered states of mind. For these reasons, while genre labels other than "ambient music" might best describe their sound, I consider all of these productions examples of ambient audio.

Audio design, a term uncommon in music studies outside technical discourse in sound engineering, provides a useful framework for the fusion of production and composition, and of functional and aesthetic concerns, undertaken by the creators of ambient audio.[38] It also highlights the relevance of visual design to ambient audio's early formations, for throughout the 1960s and '70s, countercultural designers of all sorts aspired to liberate minds by altering space. Assemblages, happenings, multimedia installations, lightshows, magic theaters, kinetic environments, mirror rooms, interactive labyrinths, sensoria, domes, bubbles, inflatables—the psychedelic concept of audio as an ambient medium developed in parallel, and sometimes combination, with these environmental experimentations.[39] Principles of openness, formlessness, and flow guided psychedelic artists and designers who, in the words of design critic C. Ray Smith, "aim[ed] at expanded consciousness through expanded spaciousness."[40] And while ambient sound was frequently a component of these environmental designs, contemporaneous producers and musicians also found that audio alone could simulate—nay, *create* spaces inside which minds could expand, inside which bodies could relax, and inside which listeners could disappear.

For many artists of the psychedelic counterculture, space had symbolic value as both container and passage for the expanded mind. Vast spaces were found to catalyze experiences of self-transcendence—disembodiment,

[37] Throughout this book, I capitalize "Black" where associated with a specific ethnic identity and/or community; I maintain the common "black" and "white" elsewhere to refer to the racial classifications.

[38] On framing audio production in terms of design, see Adam Krims, "The Changing Functions of Music Recordings and Listening Practices," in *Recorded Music: Performance, Culture and Technology*, ed. Amanda Bayley (Cambridge, UK: Cambridge University Press, 2010), 68–85.

[39] Alastair Gordon, *Spaced Out: Radical Environments of the Psychedelic Sixties* (New York: Rizzoli, 2008).

[40] C. Ray Smith, *Supermannerism: New Attitudes in Post-Modern Architecture* (New York: Dutton, 1977), 140.

disindividuation, ego loss—that psychedelic explorers often valued as noetic evidence of a transindividual, communal, or cosmic consciousness. Spaces of worship, nature, and outer space held special fascination as gateways to temporal and spatial infinitude. And in the 1960s and '70s, advancements in high-fidelity audio reproduction, digital audio processing, and consumer-grade production technology permitted not only the replication of extraordinary spaces (as in Horn's *Inside*), but also the design of entirely new ones.

Thanks to the technological advancements of decades prior, recording artists and producers during this time increasingly moved away from the working idea of documenting or recreating sonic events as they occurred in real space, and toward the fabrication of wholly unique audio images or environments. As with psychedelic ambient audio's reinvention of easy listening, this was not a new discovery so much as a development of possibilities hinted at throughout recorded sound's history. Even from the early days of acoustic recording, record makers ensconced music and its listeners in an aura of ambient sounds.[41] The development of electric recording in the early–mid 1920s soon entailed microphonic techniques for rendering what media scholar Peter Doyle calls "pictorial spatialities" and three-dimensional *mises en scènes* in popular song recording.[42] During the postwar high-fidelity era, the advancement of techniques in audio signal processing like echo and reverb, stereophonic sound, and multitrack recording and mixing increasingly permitted audio producers to generate immersive and transportive ambiences.[43] And in the 1960s and '70s, an array of consumer-grade electronic audio equipment became freshly available and affordable to artists without major-label, university, or government funding. For those working in a pop idiom, the amplified sound of electric guitars, charged with the subversive energy of Black American music, continued to emblematize rock's potential to bypass the linear, square, conformist conditioning of the

[41] Hear, for instance, the noisy crowds and steam whistles preceding "God Save the Queen" on Russell Hunting's "The Departure of the Troopship" (ca. 1899–1902) or the trilling birds pervading the Mayfair Orchestra's 1917 recording of Albert W. Ketèlby's *In a Monastery Garden*.

[42] Peter Doyle, "From 'My Blue Heaven' to 'Race with the Devil': Echo, Reverb and (Dis)Ordered Space in Early Popular Music Recording," *Popular Music* 23, no. 1 (2004): 33.

[43] On the rise of high-fidelity popular music production, see Tim J. Anderson, *Making Easy Listening: Material Culture and Postwar American Recording* (Minneapolis: University of Minnesota Press, 2006); Peter Doyle, *Echo and Reverb: Fabricating Space in Popular Music Recording, 1900–1960* (Middletown, CT: Wesleyan University Press, 2005); Virgil Moorefield, *The Producer as Composer: Shaping the Sounds of Popular Music* (Cambridge, MA: MIT Press, 2005); Albin Zak, *The Poetics of Rock: Cutting Tracks, Making Records* (Berkeley: University of California Press, 2001).

technocratic establishment;[44] but these sounds could now also be dynamized with filter and modulation effects, layered with 4- or 8-track recording, spatialized with tape delay and spring reverb units, and supplemented with electric pianos and synthesizers. Experimental artists meanwhile took to tape and synthesizers for their accessibility to those without formal musical training, for their automatability, and for their capacity to generate pitches and noises outside standard intonation. These developments in timbre, texture, spatialization, instrumentation, and automation not only empowered recording artists and producers to refine audio for use as ambience but also allowed them, in so doing, to treat ambience as an expressive sonic form in its own right.

This ambiguity at the heart of ambient audio design—music for ambience, but also ambience as music—underpinned ambient audio's aesthetic development in the last decades of the twentieth century. In his genre-coining manifesto, Brian Eno famously condensed this ambiguity in his decree that ambient music should be "as ignorable as it is interesting," leading many to construe "ambient" as chiefly marking the quality or pedigree of what would otherwise be background music (as in the opening line of the 1979 *New York Times* review of *Music for Airports*: "Avant-garde Muzak?").[45] More precisely, however, the "ambient" in ambient music (and audio) at base describes audio *production* in terms of ambience, attributing an atmospheric quality to its design regardless of listeners' ignorance or interest.

To design audio as ambience, ambient audio's producers, then as now, used spatialization techniques (e.g., amplification, panning, reverb, delay), techniques of durational extension (e.g., drone, looping, modular repetition, harmonic cycles), sampled or simulated nonhuman sounds (e.g., insects chirping, motors whirring, church bells), and/or uncoordinated textures (e.g., independent loops; free-rhythm parts). Some scholars and producers describe these elements of recorded audio as aspects of the "staging" of musical performances or events;[46] but in ambient audio, these techniques do not commonly support attention-grabbing human expressions like lyrics, emotive vocals, melodic hooks, or performed gestures, which are typically staged

[44] Farley Miller, "Popular Music and Instrument Technology in an Electronic Age, 1960–1969" (PhD diss., Montreal, McGill University, 2018), esp. 81–92.

[45] Ken Emerson, "Brian Eno Slips into 'Trance Music,'" *New York Times*, August 12, 1979, D22.

[46] On staging, see Serge Lacasse, "'Listen to My Voice': The Evocative Power of Vocal Staging in Recorded Rock Music and Other Forms of Vocal Expression" (PhD diss., University of Liverpool, 2000); William Moylan, *Recording Analysis: How the Record Shapes the Song* (New York: Routledge, 2020), 322–32; Simon Zagorski-Thomas, *The Musicology of Record Production* (Cambridge, UK: Cambridge University Press, 2014), 70–91.

foreground and center in recorded music. With these indices and icons of human subjectivity minimized or omitted, ambient audio assumes the appearance of an unoccupied environmental space or mood, and invites the listener to inhabit the audio as one's own atmosphere (or stage, as it were). Features like titles, visual accompaniments, and audio samples or textures associated with certain environments may additionally "set the stage" for audiences to recognize and treat ambient audio as ambience.[47]

While the producers and promoters of easy-listening muzak in the postwar years often stipulated that their sounds should specifically sit in the background, the producers of ambient audio more often left it open-ended, and up to listeners, how to interact with the ambiences therein. To use the terminology of perception theorist James J. Gibson, ambient audio's designs invited audiences to perceive a multiplicity of *affordances*, or opportunities for (inter)action that may be subconsciously or consciously located "in" environmental features, "in" the sound.[48] Take, for instance, Moog synthmaster Wendy Carlos's 1972 album, *Sonic Seasonings*, which producer Rachel Elkind describes as "a sonic ambience" that both "enhances the listener's total environment" and, at the same time, "takes the listener *out* of his environment and into the countryside of his fantasy."[49] As Elkind observes, ambient audio might either augment audiences' actual physical surroundings or replace these surroundings entirely. These place-enhancing and transportive affordances can likewise apply to listeners' consciousness in and of the body, as ambient audio might heighten awareness of sound and its embodiments, and yet might also encourage states of disengagement—detached mood, physical relaxation, mental drift. It might even, depending on set and setting,[50] elicit contemplation of its efficacy as a personal medium, occasion attentive absorption in the process of relaxation, afford concentration on other

[47] Musicologist Simon Zagorski-Thomas calls this "functional staging," noting how recorded music's virtual spaces may afford uses like focused listening, dance, or background playback; see Zagorski-Thomas, *Musicology of Record Production*, 84–86.

[48] On Gibson's theory of affordances, see James J. Gibson, *The Ecological Approach to Visual Perception*, Classic Edition, Psychology Press Classic Editions (1986; repr. New York and London: Psychology Press, 2015), 119–35. Applications of Gibson's theory to the analysis of recorded music and its uses may be found, for example, in Eric F. Clarke, *Ways of Listening: An Ecological Approach to the Perception of Musical Meaning* (New York: Oxford University Press, 2005); and Tia DeNora, *Music in Everyday Life* (New York: Cambridge University Press, 2000).

[49] Rachel Elkind, liner notes to *Sonic Seasonings* by W. Carlos, Columbia, KG 31234, 1972, LP.

[50] "Set and setting," a core concept in psychedelic research coined by Timothy Leary and his Harvard group of researchers, describes the set of expectations and environmental settings that condition psychedelic experience; see Ido Hartogsohn, *American Trip: Set, Setting, and the Psychedelic Experience in the Twentieth Century* (Cambridge, MA: MIT Press, 2020), 8–15.

activities, or spur withdrawal into dreamy reminiscence. And while all sorts of audio, as various media scholars have noted, make available these atmospheric, transportive, contemplative, and tranquilizing affordances, ambient audio's designers often reflexively prepare and thematize these affordances in sound, as well as through visuals, titles, and genre categorization.[51]

Both before and after Eno's ambient music coinage, ambient audio's designers also frequently blended and blurred symbols of technology and nature through mixtures of the synthetic and organic, controlled and spontaneous, in effect metaphorizing audio technology's own environmental embedding. Overtly synthesized sounds shade samples of wilderness; acoustic instruments boast unnatural enhancements and modifications; unsynchronized loops of sound and silence interact unpredictably with one another; layers of free-rhythm sound simulate the uncoordinated textures of natural surrounds. So sounds Beaver & Krause's *In a Wild Sanctuary* (1970) in which Moog synth and Hammond organ create "environmental impressions" of the natural outdoors; or Carlos's *Sonic Seasonings*, which "electronically orchestrated" the sounds of nature "into an amalgam of the natural and the synthetic."[52] Even where electronic modification is scant, as on Henry Wolff and Nancy Hennings's *Tibetan Bells* (1972), familiar sounds appear unfamiliarly electrified; in this case, the sustained tones of Tibetan bells and singing bowls contain peculiarly alien resonances that, as the musicians write in the liner notes, are "reminiscent of impulses of electronic origin."[53] Such insinuations of acoustic nature's electric provenance hint at an ecology in which electronic technologies are "naturalized" or merged into the personal sphere, and in which the self arrives at a more "natural" state within a cybernetic ecology—a technologized ecology itself made manifest by ambient audio.

At the same time as ambient audio's early producers thematized technology's integration into timeless nature, they also used techniques of continuous durational extension like drones, sustained tones, loops, and

[51] On these various functions of recorded audio, see Jody Berland, "Locating Listening," in *The Place of Music*, ed. Andrew Leyshon, David Matless, and George Revill (New York: Guilford, 1998), 129–50; Michael Bull, *Sound Moves: IPod Culture and Urban Experience* (New York: Routledge, 2007); DeNora, *Music in Everyday Life*.

[52] Liner notes to *In a Wild Sanctuary* by Beaver & Krause, Warner Bros. Records, WS 1850, 1970, LP; Elkind, liner notes to *Sonic Seasonings*.

[53] Liner notes to *Tibetan Bells* by Henry Wolff and Nancy Hennings, with Drew Gladstone, Island Records, SMAS 9319, 1972, LP. Not all of the album's electronic-sounding effects occur for acoustic reasons; some of the taped instruments are indeed reversed and/or layered in post-production to create otherworldly reverberations.

echoes as a means of approaching timelessness itself. Without a foreground to throw them in relief, these layers of sonic consistency can dissolve into a spatialized environmental presence, cocooning listeners in continuous sound and affording focus on other activities. Yet, seemingly paradoxically, extreme reduction of consistent sounds to a sparse pitch collection and texture can also induce altered states of sonic- and self-awareness (especially at high volumes) by drawing attention to timbral, textural, and temporal details often missed in listening to non-steady-state music. These techniques became markedly associated with the "minimalist" avant-garde of the 1960s, especially La Monte Young and his colleagues Terry Riley and Steve Reich, whose practices of extreme reduction and durational extension were informed as much by psychedelics as by jazz, rock'n'roll, Moroccan devotional music, and Hindustani raga improvisation. Such techniques of extension and reduction, however, were also features of the ambient audio of Malachi, Paul Horn, and Irv Teibel (founder of the *Environments* series)—all of whom abstracted these techniques from similar influences. As the next section elaborates, the sublimely sparse sonic "nows" of ambient audio's minimalist designs, packaged and promoted through rhetoric of the "drugless trip," ultimately posed an alternative to the "lowbrow," everything-all-of-the-time hedonic excesses of the psychedelic counterculture—essentially courting, at once, hip youth, highbrow listeners, and hip- and highbrow-aspirant adult consumers seeking less invasive routes to trance and transcendence.

Ambient Audio's Holistic Highs and the New Age Movement

Q: What do fasting, meditation, tantric sex, tai chi, and minimalist sound have in common?

A: They are among the "250 Ways for Altering Your Consciousness without Drugs" as cataloged in countercultural writer and editor Ed Rosenfeld's 1973 volume *The Book of Highs*. Who needs psychedelic rock to feed your head when you can try metronome watching (#196: "A most effective hypnotic induction device"), repetition tapes (#247: "A loop tape that repeats, exactly, the same sound, word, or phrase over and over again"), bells (#210: "Ringing bells can get you high. The bigger the bell the better"), or continuous light and sound environments (#230: "Young and Zazeela call this kind of sound environment 'House Hums'")?[54] These minimalist techniques of extreme sonic reduction and extension, according to the book's introduction by alternative-medicine researcher Dr. Andrew Weil, should be understood as "techniques of focusing awareness" that shape "expectations and environment" to facilitate, if not create, meditative states of mind. "Meditation and other self-reliant methods of getting high tend to make us better able to function in ordinary reality," Weil concludes. "The better we get at getting high and staying there, the more we integrate the conscious and unconscious spheres of our mental life. This integration is the key to wholeness (health) of body and mind."[55]

Rosenfeld and Weil's framing of minimalist, meditative ambiences as drugless "highs" for healthy being illustrates ambient audio's drift from the '60s counterculture's heady politics of the nervous system into the instrumented, pragmatic holism of 1970s New Age.[56] From the psychedelic counterculture's reorientation of values around personal freedom, humanity, nature, and eternity sprung discourses and tools seeking to remedy the relationship between individuals and these various wholes (the whole self, the whole of humanity, the whole earth, the cosmos). *The Book of Highs* accordingly stood as one of a proliferation of 1970s "alternative" media dedicated to holistic awareness development. Alternative consumer markets for techniques like psychotherapy, yoga, meditation, and biofeedback developed in response to, and as nonpsychiatric solutions for, the ills of Western individualism and mass-consumerist excess—alienation, anxiety, experiential fragmentation.[57] East and South Asian religious philosophies and practices meanwhile populated what sociologist Wade Clark Roof calls the "spiritual marketplace" of the 1960s and '70s United States, out of which countercultural boomers developed pluralistic, process-oriented, and individualistic

[54] Edward Rosenfeld, *The Book of Highs: 250 Methods for Altering Your Consciousness without Drugs* (New York: Quadrangle/The New York Times Book Co., 1973), n. pag.

[55] Ibid., n. pag.

[56] I capitalize New Age when referring to the alternative spirituality counterculture that developed in the 1970s United States, while using the common "new age" with reference to the music genre.

[57] The spread of holistic personal media coincided with the rise of antipsychiatric sentiment as countercultural values took hold in the US mainstream; as Healy notes, "psychiatry's legitimacy was sharply challenged between 1965 and 1975." David Healy, *The Creation of Psychopharmacology* (Cambridge, MA: Harvard University Press, 2009), 174; see also 129–77; Nicolas Henckes, "Magic Bullet in the Head? Psychiatric Revolutions and Their Aftermath," in *Therapeutic Revolutions: Pharmaceuticals and Social Change in the Twentieth Century*, ed. Jeremy A. Greene, Flurin Condrau, and Elizabeth Siegel Watkins (Chicago: University of Chicago Press, 2016), 65–96.

practices of "personal growth" to counter these ills.[58] Several developed ambient audio to facilitate such growth.

The holistic framing of ambient audio, and its promotion as a gateway to cosmic consciousness, developed with the rise of the Human Potential, New Consciousness, New Age, and Awareness movements of the 1970s United States.[59] Now best known under the broad banner of the New Age, these interlocking grassroots movements put ambient audio in service of what Roszak called the "new ecological awareness" of the 1970s: an awareness of one's oneness with one's environments.[60] New Agers encouraged ventures beyond objective reason into subjective states of selflessness and environmental connection, states that individuals might carry into their everyday lives should they learn how to "get high and stay there." Roszak describes these states as involving a "relaxed attention" that brings awareness "out of the head and its verbal abstractions into the here-and-now immediacies of the body, the senses, the visionary imagination."[61] Ambient audio became produced, packaged, and promoted as environments through which selves might achieve these states of "flow and plasticity."[62] The goal, as humanistic psychologist and Human Potential beacon Abraham Maslow put it, was to bring all individual selves "beyond individuality . . . into something which is more inclusive than the individual person"[63]—a something that many New Agers understood in terms of a supraindividual "planetary," "cosmic," or "unitive" consciousness.[64] The discourses that arose around ambient audio

[58] Wade Clark Roof, *Spiritual Marketplace: Baby Boomers and the Remaking of American Religion* (Princeton: Princeton University Press, 1999), esp. 77–110.

[59] The Awareness movement and its discourses of holism are most methodically covered, if also roundly criticized, in Edwin Schur, *The Awareness Trap: Self-Absorption Instead of Social Change* (New York: Quadrangle/The New York Times Book Co., 1976). Other comprehensive accounts include Nicholas Campion, *The New Age in the Modern West: Counterculture, Utopia and Prophecy from the Late Eighteenth Century to the Present Day* (New York: Bloomsbury Academic, 2016); Nevill Drury, *The Elements of Human Potential* (Longmead: Element Books, 1989); Wouter J. Hanegraaff, *New Age Religion and Western Culture: Esotericism in the Mirror of Secular Thought* (Leiden, The Netherlands: E.J. Brill, 1996); Paul Heelas, *The New Age Movement: The Celebration of the Self and the Sacralization of Modernity* (Cambridge, MA: Blackwell, 1996); Sarah M. Pike, *New Age and Neopagan Religions in America* (New York: Columbia University Press, 2004); Theodore Roszak, *Unfinished Animal: The Aquarian Frontier and the Evolution of Consciousness* (New York: Harper & Row, 1975); Paul Williams and Brian Edgar, "The Primal Is the Political: Psychotherapy, Engagement, and Narcissism in the 1970s," *American Quarterly* 70, no. 1 (March 2018): 79–100.

[60] Roszak, *Unfinished Animal*, 4.

[61] Ibid., 245.

[62] Ibid., 245.

[63] Anthony J. Sutich, "The Founding of Humanistic and Transpersonal Psychology: A Personal Account" (PhD diss., The Humanistic Psychology Institute, 1976), 172.

[64] Dane Rudhyar, *The Planetarization of Consciousness: From the Individual to the Whole* (New York: Harper & Row, 1970); Peter Russell, *The Global Brain: Speculations on the Evolutionary

in turn recalled, sometimes directly, theories of vibration and temperament running back through the Classical era to Greek antiquity in which musical sounds were understood to sympathetically attune the self to the "harmony" of nature and the universe.[65]

But not everyone who bought ambient audio bought into this vision of a new transpersonal consciousness. Indeed, New Age techniques and technologies were quite easily—and popularly—commodified for individualistic consumption. Sociologist Sam Binkley has described these commodities as facilitating a counterculture-inspired lifestyle ethic of "getting loose," a "practiced release" or controlled relinquishment of self-control into spontaneity and a more natural, relaxed state.[66] This reflexive praxis of self-management used "mediators of lived immediacy" like self-help books, electronic meditation timers, incense, and home audio to foster states of somatic relaxation and heightened presence to the present.[67] These lifestyle media, Binkley explains, spread alongside a widespread desire among white middle-class US Americans for stability, safety, and control in the wake of a politically and socially tumultuous decade—yet a stability that did not sacrifice the reflective values and sense of youthfulness inherited from the psychedelic counterculture. And as the 1970s pressed on into the '80s, these media and their retailers became enormously popular in association with the New Age appellation—including a wide variety of ambient audio that began appearing in "new age" record slots in the early–mid 1980s.

Of course, New Age media caught on so well in the 1970s and '80s because neither the mantra of holistic living, nor the quest for relaxed awareness, ever fundamentally challenged the tenets of exploitative capitalism and neocolonial globalism that enabled the mass dissemination of these media in the first place. During this time, various cultural critics decried the therapeutic material culture of the consciousness movement for its "privatism" and "narcissism" diverting attention away from social and interpersonal problems.[68]

Leap to Planetary Consciousness (Los Angeles: J.P. Tarcher, 1983). On unitive consciousness, see also chapter 2, section 3.

[65] For instance, see Alain Daniélou, "The Influence of Sound Phenomena on Human Consciousness," trans. Paul Huebner and Ralph Metzner, *Psychedelic Review* 7 (1966): 20–26. Trower historicizes this phenomenon by way of conceptions of the Aeolian harp at the turn of the nineteenth century; see Shelley Trower, "Nerves, Vibration and the Aeolian Harp," *Romanticism and Victorianism on the Net*, no. 54 (2009), doi:10.7202/038761ar.

[66] Sam Binkley, *Getting Loose: Lifestyle Consumption in the 1970s* (Durham, NC: Duke University Press, 2007), 16.

[67] Ibid., 10.

[68] Christopher Lasch, *The Culture of Narcissism: American Life in an Age of Diminishing Expectations* (New York: W.W. Norton, 1978); Michael Rossman, *New Age Blues: On the Politics of*

Scholars have since also noted how New Age commodities counteract cultural disenchantment and anxiety on an individual level but, far from redressing the social and economic inequalities of Western welfare states, actually exacerbate them by becoming status symbols for mostly white middle-class consumers.[69] New Age's interiorized "spirituality" discourses have meanwhile uncritically accommodated individuals to economic and social conditions that cause suffering, rather than attuning individuals to that suffering, an aim of Buddhism that westernized yoga practices often conveniently set aside.[70] Along these lines, mediators of immediacy like ambient audio continue to sell buyers the confidence to determine their own destinies in lieu of institutional and community support, ultimately producing ever more socially isolated subjects.[71] In effect, New Age media's social praxis amounts to little more than trickle-down tranquility, helping only the best-positioned to relax into their most authentic selves.

At the same time, critics' reduction of New Age media to their commodification—and accordingly, to their complicity in the rise of neoliberalism—ultimately deflates and flattens what was originally a transpersonal and humanistic world-building affair.[72] Participants in the New Age movement assiduously built alternative media networks and markets not just to promote individual healing, but also to populate a universally transformative planetary environment. Drawing on cybernetics and systems theory, builders of the New Age saw these networks as part of a global media ecology to which anyone on earth could conceivably "tune in"; and so, as historian Fred Turner writes, "the choices that individuals made in the cultural realm became freighted with truly cosmic, evolutionary significance."[73] Spreading audible ambiences for contemplative "here-and-now" attunement meant creating spaces for people to realize a potential for transpersonal connection rooted in our species's "deep" ancient past. For musician Michael Stearns, the

Consciousness (New York: E.P. Dutton & Co., 1979); Schur, *The Awareness Trap*; Tom Wolfe, "The 'Me' Decade and the Third Great Awakening," *New York Magazine*, August 23, 1976, 27–48.

[69] Kimberly J. Lau, *New Age Capitalism: Making Money East of Eden* (Philadelphia: University of Pennsylvania Press, 2000), 136.

[70] Jeremy Carrette and Richard King, *Selling Spirituality: The Silent Takeover of Religion* (New York: Routledge, 2005), 101.

[71] Paul Roquet, *Ambient Media: Japanese Atmospheres of Self* (Minneapolis: University of Minnesota Press, 2016), 14.

[72] Neoliberalism, broadly speaking, defines the economic and ideological project of shifting power and resources from the public sector to the private, and of shifting the responsibility for maintaining personal autonomy from the social collective to individuals.

[73] Turner, *From Counterculture to Cyberculture*, 45.

ambient audio he calls "space music" permits "discovery of what it means to be human beyond the habitual ways we continually recreate our lives."[74] Self-described ambient musician Steve Roach similarly speaks of accessing "ancestral memories" through atmospheric "sound worlds" that provide listeners the "feeling of being connected to something infinite."[75] Such glimpses of infinity were not understood as merely therapeutic, but rather as starting places for rethinking and remaking humanity relative to a far vaster temporal and spatial scale. Although New Agers were naïve for thinking the consumer market could accommodate such lofty communal and universalist goals, consumer capitalism's inability to do so was not the failure of New Age's practitioners alone.

Moreover, the neoliberalism critique of New Age media became, itself, a popular means of authenticating commodities and art that drew on the same values and forms as those cultivated within the New Age movement. "Not New Age," as cultural studies scholar Ryan Hibbett observes, became a recurring claim since the 1980s among music creators, critics, and fans wishing to distance their favored ambient audio from the "hokey, easily marketed set of values" represented by New Age's therapeutic commodification.[76] In anglophone music discourses, such claims were of a piece with rock culture and criticism's broad rejection of "pop" between the late '60s and century's end, an authenticating binary that Kelefa Sanneh in 2004 influentially dubbed "rockism."[77] Whereas "pop," from the "rockist" perspective, sacrificed ethical and artistic ideals of authenticity to mainstream conformism and trivial functionalism, rock retained a sense of seriousness, integrity, and opposition to "mass culture" while yet participating in it.[78] Ironically, rock's high-middlebrow distancing from new age music became another form of commodified "awareness," even while the indie and alternative rock cultures of the 1980s and '90s, much like the New Age counterculture of the '70s, valued scaled-down and decentralized markets as more authentic avenues for distribution and community-building.[79]

[74] Michael Stearns, email message to author, February 1, 2019.

[75] Steve Roach, interview with author, December 6, 2018.

[76] Ryan Hibbett, "The New Age Taboo," *Journal of Popular Music Studies* 22, no. 3 (2010): 283.

[77] Kelefa Sanney, "The Rap against Rockism," *New York Times*, October 31, 2004, https://www.nytimes.com/2004/10/31/arts/music/the-rap-against-rockism.html.

[78] On rock's oppositional stance toward "mass culture," see Keir Keightley, "Reconsidering Rock," in *The Cambridge Companion to Pop and Rock*, ed. John Street, Simon Frith, and Will Straw, Cambridge Companions to Music (Cambridge: Cambridge University Press, 2001), 109–42.

[79] On this resistance to corporate control, see Simon Frith, "Art versus Technology: The Strange Case of Popular Music," *Media, Culture & Society* 8, no. 3 (1986): 163–79.

It was through these authenticating discourses that Brian Eno's concept of "ambient music" came to represent, for hip and highbrow musicians and consumers, a more artful form of ambient audio than new age. This had not always been the case—Eno's early ambient work, until around the mid-1980s, found little love among rock and art music critics; while ambient music, as a category, was widely recognized by music catalogers, writers, and scholars as one of many emergent styles or subgenres of ambient audio *alongside* and/or *as part of* new age.[80] After all, by the time Brian Eno released *Ambient 1: Music for Airports* in 1978, precedents had been set for the promotion of gentle atmospheric music to "induce calm" and create "a space to think" by Bay Area–based New Agers like Steven Halpern, Iasos, and Stephen Hill and Anna Turner of the radio program *Music from the Hearts of Space*. Eno, however, framed his easy-listening sounds not in terms of loose living, cosmic connection, or drugless highs, but rather as an avant-garde reinvention of background music.

Highs for Highbrows?

From Eno's own perspective, the expansion of awareness wagered by his ambient music was not holistic, but artistic—an experiment in expanding tastes. The concept directly challenged the trenchant perception among Western cultural elites, including high-middlebrow rockists, that background music was *déclassé*: at best, an unseemly indulgence of base sensation and, more profoundly, a failure of moral education and social respectability. The reverent display of attentive musical listening, popularized through the rise of bourgeois individualism in the late eighteenth- and early nineteenth-century Western Europe and subsequently cemented through the romantic "sacralization" of European art music, had become a sign of spiritual refinement and, in turn, a sign of superior social status.[81] As Pierre Bourdieu most

[80] Leslie Berman, "New Age Music?," in *Not Necessarily the New Age: Critical Essays*, ed. Robert Basil (Buffalo, NY: Prometheus, 1988), 250–68; Patti Jean Birosik, *The New Age Music Guide* (New York: Collier Books, 1989); J. Gordon Melton, Jerome Clark, and Aidan A. Kelly, *New Age Encyclopedia* (Detroit: Gale Research Inc., 1990); David H. Cope, *New Directions in Music*, 5th ed. (Dubuque, IA: WM. C. Brown Publishers, 1989), 395; John Schaefer, *New Sounds: A Listener's Guide to New Music* (New York: Harper & Row, 1987), 12.

[81] The term "sacralization" to describe this phenomenon comes from Lawrence W. Levine, *Highbrow/Lowbrow: The Emergence of Cultural Hierarchy in America* (Cambridge, MA: Harvard University Press, 1988). See also James H. Johnson, *Listening in Paris: A Cultural History* (Berkeley: University of California Press, 1995). The musicologist Andrew Dell'Antonio traces similar ideals of listening back further to discourses about music among nobility in

fully theorized in *Distinction*, his landmark 1979 sociology of taste in 1960s France, the display of calm attentiveness in the presence of art was the hallmark of "legitimate" tastes, whereas "popular" tastes demanded subordination of artistic form to technical function.[82] According to this binary logic, background music could never attain the symbolic and status-conferring "cultural capital" enjoyed by "legitimate" art; the very notion of music "as ignorable as it is interesting," according to this logic, would have seemed deeply ironic, even oxymoronic. Yet by the time Bourdieu published *Distinction*, the dismantling of the legitimate/popular art binary was well underway. Western cultural critics, philosophers, and producers in the 1960s and '70s had announced a new era of "postmodernism" in which divisions between art and popular culture, high and low, were imagined dissolved. This cultural shift, in actuality, did not entail an elimination of taste-based hierarchies so much as nuance popular culture's role in determining them, with high-status cultural producers stratifying popular music and empowering certain pop forms.[83] Concomitantly, this period saw a shift among high-status consumers from snobbish exclusion of popular culture to a "discriminating omnivorousness" through which highbrows and high-middlebrows strategically demonstrated their aesthetic disposition and venerated disinterested modes of cultural production.[84] Eno's creation of a calming-yet-artistic muzak, from this perspective, was a demonstration of his own considerable symbolic capital as a well-known rock star—and a bold attempt to receive a return on investment.

It paid off. Ambient music, which gained popularity in tandem with the growth of the new age genre during the 1980s, fully developed into its own

seventeenth-century Italy; see Andrew Dell'Antonio, *Listening as Spiritual Practice in Early Modern Italy* (Berkeley: University of California Press, 2011).

[82] Pierre Bourdieu, *Distinction: A Social Critique of the Judgement of Taste*, trans. Richard Nice (1979; repr. Cambridge, MA: Harvard University Press, 1984), 28–62.

[83] Bernard Gendron, *Between Montmartre and the Mudd Club: Popular Music and the Avant-Garde* (Chicago: University of Chicago Press, 2002), 7; David Brackett, "'Where's It At?': Postmodern Theory and the Contemporary Musical Field," in *Postmodern Music/Postmodern Thought*, ed. Judy Lochhead and Joseph Auner (New York and London: Routledge, 2002), 207–31.

[84] Richard A. Peterson and Roger M. Kern, "Changing Highbrow Taste: From Snob to Omnivore," *American Sociological Review* 61, no. 5 (October 1996): 904. On the modes and parameters of omnivorous discrimination by highbrows, see Bethany Bryson, "Anything but Heavy Metal: Symbolic Exclusion and Musical Dislikes," *American Sociological Review* 61, no. 5 (October 1996): 884–99; Josée Johnston and Shyon Baumann, "Democracy versus Distinction: A Study of Omnivorousness in Gourmet Food Writing," *American Journal of Sociology* 113, no. 1 (July 2007): 165–204. Musicologist John Howland posits that these changes stem from emergent cross-brow consumer attitudes in the 1950s and '60s; see Howland, *Hearing Luxe Pop*, 180–81.

translocal music scene and marketing category of recorded music in the early–mid 1990s when electronic music DJs and producers turned to Eno's musical legacy for inspiration, and when independent record labels subsequently touted certain styles of recorded electronic music with the tag. This fragmentation of the market for ambient audio occurred via negotiations of value in musician, media, and fan discourses distinguishing ambient from contemporaneous hip middlebrow styles like jazz fusion, soft rock, house, and perhaps most importantly, new age. Eno's coinage, within these discourses, specified ambient audio that was relatively experimental, restrained, and textural compared to the more overtly sentimental, sweet, melodic fare that had become associated with "new age." "Unlike New Age music's flawless emulsions," *Melody Maker* critic Paul Oldfield characteristically reasoned in 1990, "Eno's ambient is fabulously complex."[85]

The commodification of drone- and loop-based head music in the 1990s as "ambient" echoed earlier patterns in ambient audio's validation relative to other popular styles. New age in the 1980s, for instance, was marketed as more youthful than symphonic-pop easy-listening, and yet also more mature than psychedelic rock or pop—a means not just of a hedonic "high," that is, but of providing holistic "awareness." Formerly, psychedelic and progressive rock's champions in 1960s into the 1970s themselves positioned rock as authentic art in comparison to youth-oriented rock'n'roll and pop.[86] Avant-garde minimalism had meanwhile attained distinction as cutting-edge concert music for hip highbrows—despite its own roots in ambient audio, blues-based popular music, and psychedelic culture. In short, proponents of ambient audio throughout its history located the audio's potential to attract hip and high-middlebrow markets, and they touted the audio's tasteful design to attract these consumers. I hence define ambient audio, in part, by its production and promotion as an "artful" medium—an artfulness, as much in the framing of the sounds as in the sounds themselves, that provided contrasts from popular genres racialized as nonwhite, gendered as feminine, and classed as low-middlebrow or middlebrow.

The genre codification of recorded music as "ambient" cemented a high-middlebrow market for culturally omnivorous audiophiles of a new generation

[85] Paul Oldfield, "Eno: Patter of Life and Death," *Melody Maker*, October 13, 1990, 53.

[86] The racing of rock as a mostly white genre during the 1960s, in comparison to the more overtly racially mixed categories of rock'n'roll and pop, bolstered rock's elevated status; see Jack Hamilton, *Just around Midnight: Rock and Roll and the Racial Imagination* (Cambridge, MA: Harvard University Press, 2016); Maureen Mahon, *Black Diamond Queens: African American Women and Rock and Roll* (Durham: Duke University Press, 2020).

to engage in the psychedelic practice of using audio to reorient consciousness. Ambient's commodification as such was predicated on a symbolic rejection of the "easy" high—the shortcut to immediacy and transcendence—implied by styles like house, new age, and psychedelic rock. Ambient music's critics and historians have often sidelined or disavowed the relevance of these styles to ambient's development, even as they regard ambient records as contemplative agents that can heighten attention to the present moment, expand awareness of the conditions of one's perception, and send listeners on virtual "trips."[87] Much like the naming of contemporaneous avant-garde music as "minimalist," "ambient" downplayed the sedating, intoxicating, and transportive properties of the music, which threatened the category's legitimacy as art, through rhetorics of experimentation, contemplation, concentration, control, and cool. In essence, "ambient music" sold ambient audio, in soberer terms, as highs for highbrows.

Lest this claim seem far-reaching, consider that Eno himself, in a 1982 essay, identified psychedelic music as a distinct forerunner of his own experiments in ambience: "I always thought that psychedelia was about discovering space in music," wrote Eno as he reflected on the recorded audio assemblages of Jimi Hendrix, The Beach Boys, Jefferson Airplane, and The Byrds as precedents in creating "associations of place" through recorded sound.[88] That same year, in another interview, Eno lamented that rock no longer carried, for him, the "spiritual quality" to which psychedelic musicians once aspired. "Despite all the criticism that's been made of psychedelic music," he continued, "it certainly was committed to the production of an expanded awareness."[89] That ambient music captured the mystical wonder of the psychedelic high was neither lost on pop critic Simon Reynolds, who, at the crest of ambient's rise to the pop mainstream in 1993, described ambient as "the ultimate destination of the psychedelic impulse. Technically, in that psychedelia pioneered stereo and the illusion of spatial dimension; spiritually, in that ambience is the heavenly end of the psychedelic trip."[90]

[87] See, for example, Belgrad, *The Culture of Feedback*, 109–37; Kyle Chayka, *The Longing for Less: Living with Minimalism* (New York: Bloomsbury Publishing USA, 2020), 98–101; Seth Kim-Cohen, *Against Ambience and Other Essays* (New York: Bloomsbury Academic, 2016); John T. Lysaker, *Brian Eno's "Ambient 1: Music for Airports,"* Oxford Keynotes (New York: Oxford University Press, 2018).

[88] Mick Brown, "On Record: Brian Eno," *Sunday Times Magazine*, October 31, 1982, 94.

[89] George Rush, "Brian Eno: Rock's Svengali Pursues Silence," *Esquire*, December 1982, 132.

[90] Simon Reynolds, "Easy Lizzzzning," *Melody Maker*, October 2, 1993, 50.

And yet, to regard ambient as a psychedelic intoxicant might seem unintuitive to anyone who has long considered the category, as philosopher John T. Lysaker describes it, primarily a conceptual demonstration that "music also operates ambiently."[91] Most of popular music's audiences, however, have long intuited music's ambient activity without explicit artistic demonstration, despite depictions of this operation in media discourses as intoxicating, dangerous, even addictive. At least since the popularization of radio in the 1920s, North American intellectual elites and public health experts cautioned against "background" or "distracted listening" as an injurious mode of consumption that, like illicit drugs, impinged on listeners' objectivity and mental soundness.[92] What might be more accurately termed *deconcentrated listening* was understood to endanger individual productivity and autonomy, both of which, as art scholar Jonathan Crary explains, had since the late nineteenth century been measured by the subjective capacity to focus on certain stimuli among many—that is, by the ability to pay attention. By this cultural logic, any practice of ceding concentrational control to autonomic technologies and techniques, be it hypnosis, television, or recorded music, threatened to dull the mental acuity of the ideally self-sufficient and cognitively disciplined subject.[93] The use of audio as an ambient medium, which could be more generously understood as a voluntary and selective technique of managing awareness and behavior, was hence perceived by cultural authorities as an unhealthy habit. Composer Aaron Copland, for instance, advised against "abusing" the "sensuous" plane of listening, a "brainless but attractive" escape akin to dreaming in which one "bathes in the sound" without thinking about it.[94] Philosopher and sociologist Theodor W. Adorno compared "unconcentrated" radio listeners to habitual smokers, describing the typical "distracted" listener as an "addict" who copes with social atomization and loneliness by manufacturing, through musical technology, "an illusionary private realm, where he thinks he can be himself."[95] Composer and acoustic ecologist R. Murray Schafer railed against the deconcentrated consumption of automated sounds, not just in

[91] Lysaker, *Brian Eno's "Ambient 1,"* 110. A similar thesis is entertained in Mark Edward Achtermann, "Yes, but Is It Music? Brian Eno and the Definition of Ambient Music," in *Brian Eno: Oblique Music*, ed. Sean Albiez and David Pattie (New York: Bloomsbury Academic, 2016), 85–104.

[92] Goodman, "Distracted Listening."

[93] Jonathan Crary, *Suspensions of Perception: Attention, Spectacle, and Modern Culture* (Cambridge, MA: MIT Press, 1999), esp. 17–46 and 65–79.

[94] Aaron Copland, *What to Listen for in Music* (1939; repr. New York: McGraw-Hill, 1957), 10–11.

[95] Theodor Adorno, *Introduction to the Sociology of Music*, trans. E. B. Ashton (1962; repr. New York: Continuum, 1976), 15–16.

his denunciation of Muzak as mind-numbing "audioanalgesia," but also in calling drones in music an "anti-intellectual narcotic."[96] No wonder ambient audio's promoters so often headed off at the pass these excoriations of deconcentrated listening by supplying rhetoric that stressed record listeners' playback control and attentional flexibility, and that emphasized the music's ability to confer focus rather than dissolve it. Eno's "ambient music" coinage in many ways codified these accrediting discourses, selling to skeptics a different relationship with deconcentrated listening and remaking what was once considered an intoxicant into, as Lysaker describes *Airports*, the "seminal sounds" of an avant-garde artist.[97]

As this description suggests, cultural elites' anxiety around deconcentrated listening stemmed not only from ambient media's supposed threat to listeners' rationality but also, relatedly, from an idealized masculinity. Focused music listening has, at least among elite men in Western Europe and the United States, held long-standing association with intellectually penetrative manly "activity" in contradistinction to the feminized "passivity" of the deconcentrated listener (and of listeners in general).[98] Feminist thinkers have accordingly deconstructed this gendered binary by identifying ways in which deconcentration does not preclude listener activity or awareness, as in Pauline Oliveros's reframing of the binary as a spectrum between a detail-oriented, linear "focal attention" and an environmentally oriented, inclusive "global attention,"[99] or in musicologist Elisabeth Le Guin's description of the "consensual blurring or refraction of attention" that can occur while listening to ambient audio.[100] Yet since this time, ambient music has attained status as virile, "seminal" atmospheric art in comparison to the "soft-focus" sounds of "hopelessly effeminate" middlebrow genres like easy-listening (as music theorist Rebecca Leydon has described its gendering by midcentury

[96] R. Murray Schafer, *The Soundscape: Our Sonic Environment and the Tuning of the World* (1977; repr. Rochester, VT: Destiny Books, 1994), 96, 79.

[97] Lysaker, *Brian Eno's "Ambient 1,"* 1.

[98] Dell'Antonio, *Listening as Spiritual Practice*; Fred Everett Maus, "Masculine Discourse in Music Theory," *Perspectives of New Music* 31, no. 2 (Summer 1993): 264–93. Rhetorical emphasis on music listeners' activity, as Maus suggests, may thus "serve as a masculine denial of the listener's feminized role" (282). Maus, it should be said, argues here that this feminization applies to music listening in general, not just deconcentrated listening, in distinction to the activity of music analysis and theorization.

One sociological study observed the effects of this binary in gender role socialization, as young women more commonly than men acknowledged using music as a background activity; see Peter G. Christenson and Jon Brian Peterson, "Genre and Gender in the Structure of Music Preferences," *Communication Research* 15, no. 3 (June 1988): 299.

[99] Pauline Oliveros, *Software for People* (Baltimore: Smith, 1984), 216.

[100] Elisabeth Le Guin, "Uneasy Listening," *Repercussions* 3, no. 1 (Spring 1994): 9.

audiophiles) and new age, offering masculinist and highbrow consumers an invitation to deconcentration that does not threaten their masculinity or intellect.[101]

As in rock or experimental genre discourses in the late twentieth century, ambient's claim to highbrow status benefited not only from its association with masculinity relative to other popular genres, but also from its racialization as a relatively white genre. Throughout the late twentieth century, various anglophone genres have tacitly found coherence as white traditions—most often by banding together, through stylistic labels, the sounds of primarily white artists reinterpreting Black American, African, and Asian traditions through techniques of subtraction, depersonalization, and disembodiment like electronic manipulation, conceptualism, and abstraction. In ambient's immediate history, nowhere was this more evident than in the codification of white experimentalist composers' long-duration riffing, droning, cyclical polyrhythm, and looping—all common techniques in US popular, African, and Asian musics—as "minimalist music."[102] Often through the automation of tape and synthesizer, as well as through conceptual and technical abstraction (e.g., Reich's "process" music) and reduction to steady-state elements, these compositions became described as blank and empty—merely a function of their own automaticity rather than of the composers' authorship or performers' physicality—and hence also transcendent, pure, or universal (as Reich wrote of electronic tape manipulation, "All music turns out to be ethnic music").[103] The racial identity of their composers was not incidental, but rather intrinsic, to the framing of their music as "minimalist"; as musicologist Lloyd Whitesell has sharply argued, the rhetorical construction of this music as wholly abstract negations maps onto the social construction of racially white subjects as unmarked or "without properties."[104] This is all not merely to say that minimalism (and later ambient) involved cultural

[101] Rebecca Leydon, "The Soft-Focus Sound: Reverb as a Gendered Attribute in Mid-Century Mood Music," *Perspectives of New Music* 39, no. 2 (Summer 2001): 98. See also Keightley, "Music for Middlebrows," 326–27.

[102] On the relevance of US popular, African, and Asian musics to minimalism, see Sumanth S. Gopinath, "Contraband Children: The Politics of Race and Liberation in the Music of Steve Reich, 1965–66" (PhD diss., Yale University, 2005); Martin Scherzinger, "Curious Intersections, Uncommon Magic: Steve Reich's 'It's Gonna Rain,'" *Current Musicology* 79 (2005): 207–44; and Allison Welch, "Meetings along the Edge: Svara and Tāla in American Minimal Music," *American Music* 17, no. 2 (1999): 179–99.

[103] Steve Reich, "Music as a Gradual Process," in *Writings on Music, 1965–2000*, ed. Paul Hillier (New York: Oxford University Press, 2002), 35.

[104] Lloyd Whitesell, "White Noise: Race and Erasure in the Cultural Avant-Garde," *American Music* 19, no. 2 (2001): 184. Whitesell borrows this characterization of white subjectivity from Richard Dyer, *White: Essays on Race and Culture* (New York: Routledge, 1997), 80.

appropriation, but rather, more specifically, that the conventionalization of this music as "minimalist" (or "ambient") tacitly constructed the genre as a chiefly white tradition, and framed its sounds as expressions of whiteness, thereby bolstering its cultural status.

Ambient's headiness likewise found highbrow acceptance in the 1990s, by way of a racialized mind-body binary, through the canonization of white artists in its historical lineage, and through the concomitant abjection of black-coded popular styles from its discourses. As ambient became reinterpreted in the early 1990s as a subgenre of electronic dance music, its rhetorical boundaries became explicitly configured around its physically stilling affordances ("dance music that isn't dance music!," to quote a 1993 DJ Mag headline on ambient).[105] Ambient's emergent genre discourses and culture meanwhile found association with mostly white producers and DJs who audibly renounced the body-shaking function of electronic dance music (EDM) styles while yet retaining their grooves and flows, creating music that became commonly described as "beatless."[106] Implicitly, these negations of EDM's dancing function became delineated according to idealizations of hip white masculinity—disembodied, detached, cerebral—as media discourses largely disregarded the relevance of equally heady jazz/fusion, soul, R&B, dub, hip hop, and deep house by Black artists to the nascent genre. As artists and popular media represented ambient music as the emanation of disembodied mind(s), rather than of socialized and embodied individuals, factors of race (and class and gender) continued to remain marginal to media discourses about the music, even as these factors shaped the genre's boundaries and canons.

In summary, like the elevated cultural status of minimalism and progressive rock before it, ambient music's highbrowing was predicated, in part, on its rhetorical remove from a multiracial popular field, and from the feminized commercialism and functionalism this popular field represented. Indeed, to some extent, the framing of this very book as a reckoning with ambient's psychedelic past inadequately captures the genre's broad indebtedness to nonwhite artists given this frame's focus on the predominantly white psychedelic, New Age, and EDM countercultures of the Bay Area and London, and given the general association of psychedelic culture with racial whiteness.[107] A revision

[105] *DJ Mag*, August 26–September 3, 1993, front cover. See Fig. 4.1 in chapter 4.

[106] Marc Weidenbaum, *Selected Ambient Works Volume II*, 33⅓ Series (New York: Bloomsbury Academic, 2014), 11–32.

[107] On race and music in the Bay Area psychedelic counterculture, see Nadya Zimmerman, *Counterculture Kaleidoscope: Musical and Cultural Perspectives on Late Sixties San Francisco* (Ann

of ambient's history might indeed look very different with Miles Davis's 1959 *Kind of Blue*, rather than Scott's *Music for Zen Meditation* or Syntonic Research's *Environments*, taken as a chief point of origin; Davis's album, after all, like most ambient audio after it, used modal harmonic frameworks, explored introspective moods, communicated a sense of cool and calm, and embodied for consumers worldwide a high-middlebrow sign of refinement.[108] Ambient (and psychedelic) music's roots in improvised traditions like jazz or Hindustani raga are only hinted at throughout here, and a more methodical accounting of ambient music's relationship with these forms has yet to be written.[109]

Nevertheless, as this book should make clear, ambient music's formative discourses centered the creations of hip and/or highbrow white men, and they negotiated the genre's boundaries and pleasures by way of appeals to highbrow masculinity and white hipness. Ambient music's popular and scholarly discourses have largely lacked such sociocultural analyses, perhaps in part because the music's atmospheric appearance so neatly aligns with the cultural logic wherein upwardly mobile whiteness is socially unmarked and universalizable. In undertaking this discourse analysis, particularly in this book's second half, I hope to particularize this logic as a function of the category's presumptive high-middlebrow whiteness; or in the words of race theorist Hazel V. Carby, to "make visible what is rendered invisible when viewed as the normative state of existence: specifically the white point in space from which we tend to identify difference."[110] From this perspective, ambient's seemingly blank atmospheres might instead be seen as socioaesthetic expressions—including of racial whiteness, of upwardly mobile middle-classness, and of masculinity—through which artists

Arbor: University of Michigan Press, 2008). On race and the Bay Area New Age counterculture, see Hans A. Baer et al., "The Holistic Health Movement in the San Francisco Bay Area: Some Preliminary Observations," *Social Science & Medicine* 47, no. 10 (1998): 1499; Ron Eglash, "Cybernetics and American Youth Subculture," *Cultural Studies* 12, no. 3 (1998), 401; and Williams Brian Edgar, "The Primal Is the Political," 88–89. On the whiteness of psychedelic countercultures more broadly, see Arun Saldanha, *Psychedelic White: Goa Trance and the Viscosity of Race* (Minneapolis: University of Minnesota Press, 2007).

[108] Richard Williams attests to the primacy of Davis's *Kind of Blue* in relation to minimalism and ambient audio; see Richard Williams, *The Blue Moment: Miles Davis's* Kind of Blue *and the Remaking of Modern Music* (London: Faber & Faber, 2009).

[109] David Toop does substantially engage with jazz and the art of raga in his study of ambience in twentieth-century music; see Toop, *Ocean of Sound: Aether Talk, Ambient Sound and Imaginary Worlds* (London: Serpent's Tail, 1995).

[110] Hazel V. Carby, "The Multicultural Wars," *Radical History Review* 54 (1992): 12.

and listeners have attained "higher" states of mind and "chiller" modes of embodiment.

Ambient Music's Socioaesthetic Meanings

This book's exploration of ambient music's psychedelic past, given the genre's reframing and redesigning of psychedelic and new age head music as experimental audio, necessarily contends with matters of taste and artistic validation. Much scholarship that likewise contends with ambient's status relative to other popular and programmed music largely focuses on the genre's discursive positioning as "high environmental art," as literary critic and philosopher Timothy Morton describes Eno's "Ambient Music" screed, and the rhetorical means by which this art "polices the boundaries between itself and kitsch."[111] Accordingly, several scholars argue or insinuate that allegations of aesthetic superiority, avant-garde credentials, or "subcultural capital" alone distinguish ambient music from other programmed and popular musics.[112]

Yet while the "cultural empowerment" of ambient audio as ambient music, to use philosopher Bernard Gendron's terminology, is a large part of this history, it is not the whole story.[113] Genres, after all, can scarcely be reduced to advertisements of cultural validity, although they do get used in this manner; for even highbrow genres mediate aesthetic pleasures and social affinities by promising subjective experiences of recognition, identification, familiarity, attachment, detachment, and interpretation.[114] Marketing inventions, moreover, have musical consequences; for recorded music's creators must navigate the systems of genre that at once organize sonic conventions, mark social affinities, and generate hierarchies of value.[115] Yet sociologies of genre that strictly focus on music's reception within social hierarchies often look past

[111] Timothy Morton, *Ecology without Nature: Rethinking Environmental Aesthetics* (Cambridge, MA: Harvard University Press, 2007), 152. See also Hibbett, "The New Age Taboo."

[112] Anahid Kassabian, *Ubiquitous Listening: Affect, Attention, and Distributed Subjectivity* (Berkeley: University of California Press, 2013), 5; Sarah Thornton, *Club Cultures: Music, Media and Subcultural Capital*, US Edition (Hanover, NH: University Press of New England, 1996), 71; Kembrew McLeod, "Genres, Subgenres, Sub-Subgenres and More: Musical and Social Differentiation within Electronic/Dance Music Communities," *Journal of Popular Music Studies* 13, no. 1 (2001): 59–75.

[113] Gendron, *Between Montmartre and the Mudd Club*, 4–6.

[114] These pleasures of attachment are theorized extensively in Rita Felski, *Hooked: Art and Attachment* (Chicago: University of Chicago Press, 2020), esp. 1–40 and 94–120.

[115] On systems of genre, see John Frow, *Genre* (New York: Routledge, 2005), 124–28.

how artists participate in genre through particular sonic, intertextual, and affective techniques that afford certain social and aesthetic pleasures.

Each of this book's chapters hence investigates the techniques, themes, styles, affects, and expressive meanings by which Irv Teibel, Stephen Hill, and Anna Turner designed head music as ambient audio, and by which now-canonic ambient artists such as Brian Eno, Harold Budd, Laraaji, The Orb, and the KLF popularly reframed and redesigned ambient audio as ambient music. These analyses, in sum, answer a number of lingering questions: How do the aesthetic tropes and expressive conventions established by canonic ambient records substantiate ambient music as a coherent genre? What does ambient music *mean* as a socioaesthetic expression, and how has it acquired these meanings?[116] What stylistic and affective devices create value for its repeat listeners? And, given ambient's history of genrification via elitist discourses of value, is it possible for ambient music to develop into something more socially and culturally inclusive while yet retaining its artistic identity and value—and if so, how?[117]

To begin summarizing these findings, it bears mentioning that ambient music is neither unique nor prophetic in being "as ignorable as it is interesting"—a maxim of Eno's often taken as a core principle of the genre. Indeed, I posit that *no* ambient audio, holistically understood, can be wholly reduced to its function as a personal enhancement medium. However "ignorable" a piece of ambient audio seems—however much it appears "designed to negate itself as content, creating a perceptual absence rather than attention-grabbing presence," as media scholar Mack Hagood writes of "orphic media" like white noise machines—ambient audio's sensuous textures, affective charges, and aesthetic presentations matter, whether or not anyone pays attention to them while the audio plays.[118] This is *especially* true at a time when most recorded musics are treated, by most people, as both ignorable and interesting. Ambient music's continued appearance as a singular genre among (interesting) popular genres thus raises questions about what might be specifically "interesting" about it.

In comparing these ambient audio productions, it becomes evident that ambient music's best-known producers found value in improvising with and

[116] On my use of the term "socioaesthetic(s)," see note 17 of the Preface.

[117] Agents of distribution (i.e., record labels, promotional media) market—idealize, conventionalize, and canonize—these sounds, to varying degrees of popular success, in terms of genre, a process Rick Altman calls "genrification"; see Altman, *Film/Genre* (London: BFI, 1999).

[118] Mack Hagood, *Hush: Media and Sonic Self-Control* (Durham: Duke University Press, 2019), 22.

abstracting from an array of preexisting sounds and styles, a value already observable in psychedelic and new age music throughout the 1960s and '70s. Ambient audio's producers commonly regarded themselves as filters or conduits through which they translated surrounding sounds and styles into audio atmospheres, although what made their music "ambient" had less to do with any specific sonic sources than with the atmospheric appearance and calming affordances of their audio.

Critic and composer David Toop, as with other ambient adherents, has hence made a strong case for conceptualizing ambient as an uncategorizable "way of listening" to music as part of one's environments, a way of listening that takes the "erosion of categories" like genre for granted.[119] And yet, this very anticategorical approach to sonic and stylistic sourcing became a conventional feature of ambient music's genre culture and discourses as ambient's sonic conventions ossified along other lines. While "ambient" continued to imply the presence of slow sustained tones and reverberant sonic spaces, genre discourses ever more repeated, as announced in a byline of a 1993 *DJ Mag* article, the notion that "with ambient music there are no rules."[120] The sense of limitless possibility involved in ambient audio's abstractive playfulness and stylistic resourcefulness may accordingly be seen as part of the parcel of pleasures promised by the ambient genre tag. Ironically, this convention of ambient music preserved the experimentalist ethos and universalist aspirations of earlier head music as psychedelic rock and new age came to represent, despite their experimental and eclectic roots, highly conventionalized styles.

This investigation also finds that ambient music's sonic, visual, poetic, and conceptual designs, as with much ambient audio informing the genre, commonly aestheticize their own environing and escapist functions. In conveying value beyond "mere" functionality, ambient audio records frequently metaphorize through sound, image, title, and concept their own observable features as immersive audio media: namely their technological foundation, atmospheric appearance, and transportive effects. This finding contradicts the frequent assertion that ambient records lack aesthetic and thematic qualities, and thus "obviate questions of interpretation," as musicologist Cecilia Sun puts it, or "express only their own occurrence and do nothing but relay potential," as composer and aesthetic theorist Eldrich Priest writes.[121]

[119] Toop, *Ocean of Sound*, 62, iii.

[120] Andy Crysell, "Ambi-grooves," *DJ Mag*, August 26–September 8, 1993, 20.

[121] Cecilia Sun, "Resisting the Airport: Bang on a Can Performs Brian Eno," *Musicology Australia* 29, no. 1 (2007): 136; Eldritch Priest, "Felt as Thought (or, Music Abstraction and the Semblance of

While such assertions are understandable, since the name "ambient" appears generically descriptive of the music's atmospheric function and appearance, the tendency to read ambient music as semiotically vacuous and expressively neutral may be more inspired by the notion of pure functionalism than reflective of ambient music's conventional sonic techniques, thematic representations, and expressive tendencies.

In typically presenting little more than sustained tones, looped melodies, harmonic cycles, fleeting sounds, and overt production effects like echo and timbral filtering, ambient records and their head-music antecedents not only elude sustained attention, but also aestheticize their own technological mediations. These features, in other words, not only ease the withdrawal of sound into the background of listeners' awareness, but also double, through musical technique, the automatism of the playback technology that enables this withdrawal. Form here doesn't just follow function; it re-presents the concealed form of its functioning. Endless drones and invariant loops with overt timbral modifications and syntheses expose the audio's "hidden nature" as an electronically automated feature of the listening environment. Yet ambient audio can also belie its technological inscription, often appearing "natural" in its free-rhythmic, improvisational spontaneity. The combination of automated production techniques with naturalistic effects thematizes, or serves as a "metacommunication," about its ambient purposing as a "natural simulation" or "simulated nature."[122] In line with this thematization of the mediation of space and self, ambient productions commonly collapse various symbolic binaries mapping onto the technological and the natural: impersonal and personal, synthesized and organic, nonhuman and human, isolative and connective, and stable and transient. Again, these mixtures find precedent in the ambient audio of the psychedelic and New Age countercultures, and yet have since become conventionalized as a distinctive feature of ambient music.

Along with these technonatural mixtures, affective ambivalence between comfort and unease has become a conventional means of distinguishing ambient music from other genres of ambient audio. To this point, one

Affect)," in *Sound, Music, Affect: Theorizing Sonic Experience*, ed. Marie Thompson and Ian Biddle (New York: Bloomsbury Academic, 2013), 53.

[122] On genre metacommunications, see Frow, *Genre*, 17; on the interpenetration of nature and simulation, see N. Katherine Hayles, "Simulated Nature and Natural Simulations: Rethinking the Relation between the Beholder and World," in *Uncommon Ground: Toward Reinventing Nature*, ed. William Cronon (New York & London: W. W. Norton & Company, 1995), 409–25.

oft-passed-over line of Eno's "Ambient Music" manifesto specifies just what kind of "interest" Eno had in mind for his ignorable music: "Whereas conventional background music is produced by stripping away all sense of doubt and uncertainty (and thus all genuine interest) from the music," Eno writes, "Ambient Music retains these qualities." On *Music for Airports*, for example, Eno retained a sense of uncertainty within his largely predictable, sustained musical textures by building in temporal variability, modal ambiguity, and harmonic mercuriality. What resulted, as in most of his and others' ambient works, were mixed moods somewhere between the certain and uncertain.

In describing how ambient music's recorded designs produce ambivalent or mixed moods, my analyses partly elaborate upon the work of media scholars Tia DeNora and Anahid Kassabian, who have theorized how recorded music provoke physiological responses in both attentive and inattentive listeners.[123] As these authors explain, audio's "haptic images" or concrescences of sound, like touch, initiate bodily responses, which are usually followed by thoughts, feelings, and changes in composure.[124] Yet as these images are sustained temporally, as I analyze them, they may also be talked about in terms of their *moods* or global affects. While ambient music's slow-moving, space-making haptic images typically suggest calm and repose, their global affects tend toward the moody side of mood—the anxious, depressed, estranged, or forlorn—in contrast to the often uplifting, effusive, sentimental, or gently intimate calm now largely associated with new age. Mood music chronicler Joseph Lanza has accordingly described ambient music as "elevator noir," a darker shade of mood music in which, as Lanza writes hyperbolically, "misanthropes . . . play havoc with the canons of harmony and melody in the service of bad vibes."[125] By offering up moods involving dread, melancholy, alienation, or uncertainty in a depersonalized, spacey, and calm manner, ambient recordings provide their listeners the unconventional pleasure of electing to feel ambivalent. The appeal of impersonal ambivalence, perhaps ironically, can be understood as very much socially conditioned (though not determined): subjects disposed to such appeal might include individuals conditioned to self-identify independently of their bodies and emotions (a mode historically, but not exclusively, readily available to educated and/or elite white men) and individuals given to seeking

[123] Kassabian, *Ubiquitous Listening*, xxvi–xxix and 33–50; DeNora, *Music in Everyday Life*, 75–108.
[124] Kassabian, *Ubiquitous Listening*, xvi–xvii.
[125] Lanza, *Elevator Music*, 196.

detachment from the crowd (introverts, intellectuals, hipsters, artists).[126] As media scholar Paul Roquet insightfully remarks in his study of Japanese ambient media, ambient art's affective and aesthetic forms commonly register an "ambivalent calm" that both preserves a sense of artistic integrity while permitting the emotional autonomy of its audiences.[127] To this day, ambient music more often than not delivers technologized sounds to unpredictable mixtures of serenity and loneliness and wakefulness and wistfulness, often sponsoring detachment while triggering melancholy, or vacillating unpredictably between plateaus of energy or shades of feeling, or rendering those shades of feeling opaque or mysterious.

This stylistic tendency toward affective ambivalence, given ambient music's thematization of the technological mediation of space, may offer further grounds for interpreting ambient records as registering skepticism of their own personally enhancing social disengagements. Ambient music, in other words, may itself expressively and aesthetically reflect the "technologically mediated solitude" that ethnomusicologist Michael Bull observes of all mobile music media, along with the mixtures of connective "warmth" and isolative "chill" that these media provide.[128] The music's ever-shifting, bittersweet moods, in other words, can reflect unease surrounding the management of space and mood that audio playback equipment makes possible. This ambivalence, along these lines, may be interpreted sociologically and culturally as a passage for identification among listeners who share ambivalence about ambient audio's easy enhancements. Ambient music's auras of doubt and detachment affirm listeners' awareness of their own personal boundaries and subjective agency, even as these listeners seek comfort in ambient audio's sonic embrace. The application of the "ambient" genre term, in this light, may be understood as registering uncertainty about the social escapism that ambient audio affords. Ambient recordings not only flirt with, but also expressively hint at the danger of "audioanalgesia" and the "illusionary" and "brainless" states of sensuous deconcentration about which background

[126] Literary critic Rita Felski, for instance, describes modern intellectualism as rooted in a "suspicious sensibility"; see Rita Felski, *The Limits of Critique* (Chicago: University of Chicago Press, 2015), 14–51. See also Sara Ahmed, "A Phenomenology of Whiteness," *Feminist Theory* 8, no. 2 (2007): 149–68; Phil Ford, "Somewhere/Nowhere: Hipness as an Aesthetic," *Musical Quarterly* 86, no. 1 (Spring 2002): 49–81; Robin James, "In but Not of, of but Not in: On Taste, Hipness, and White Embodiment," *Contemporary Aesthetics* 2 (2009); Eve Kosofsky Sedgwick, "Paranoid Reading and Reparative Reading; or, You're So Paranoid, You Probably Think This Introduction Is About You," in *Touching Feeling: Affect, Pedagogy, Performativity* (Durham: Duke University Press, 2003), 123–51.

[127] Roquet, *Ambient Media*, 18.

[128] Bull, *Sound Moves*, 5, 8–9.

music's early critics warned. Yet characteristically, ambient music's more desirable worlds also involve the inadequacies of our own, ideally allowing listeners to achieve distance from these inadequacies while retaining awareness of them. Also ideally, ambient's textures may help re-enchant the world that its listeners hold in doubt, deepening and sharpening their capacity to slow down, open up, and take it all in.

But what if they don't? Whether ambient music's ambivalence actually promotes awareness of the isolating and socially atomizing effects of recorded audio, or whether it indulges and capitulates to this isolation, remains a gnawing question. Writers like Paul Roquet and Seth Kim-Cohen have tended toward the latter interpretation of ambient music and media, echoing the neoliberal critique of New Age's techniques and technologies of self-development. As Roquet explains, ambient music's ambivalence promotes a semblance of personal control over one's environment without actually changing the conditions of anyone's mood, focus, and comportment to begin with. As the cliché goes, ambient music treats the symptoms, not the cause.[129] And although ambient musicians have rarely aspired to the lofty revolutionary and evolutionary ideals of the psychedelic and New Age countercultures, sound artist Kim-Cohen has nonetheless taken ambient's seemingly apolitical functionalism to task for failing to address the sociopolitical crises and economic injustices that make its escapism possible, in essence accommodating audiences to conditions hostile to collectivization.[130] For these authors, the individualistic freedom and control afforded by ambient audio's uneasy detachments are neither collectively nor individually sustaining, both reinforcing workaday personal isolation while also silencing or precluding the possibility of sociocultural difference.

That ambient music makes neoliberal atomization bearable through intoxicating isolationism, rather than through any gesture toward communal or collective experience, remains an even thornier issue than its therapeutic instrumentalization. As some critics explain, the problem with ambient-music therapy has less to do with its melancholic withdrawal from the world than with the sociopolitical defeatism that its chosen melancholy encourages. As philosopher Robert Hullot-Kentor writes, overtly echoing Adorno, ambient music's spatialized chill reinforces the "technical subjectivity" of the addict who, more than anything, wants to be left alone,

[129] Roquet, *Ambient Media*, 14.

[130] Kim-Cohen, *Against Ambience*, 3–81. Mack Hagood undertakes a similar critique of "orphic media" like noise-canceling headphones; see Hagood, *Hush*, esp. 9–17.

rather than to return to the world renewed or curious.[131] In an even more trenchant critique, Timothy Morton calls ambient art a symptom of "beautiful soul syndrome," a reflexive mode of "ecological consumerism" that fetishizes transformative experiences of self-dissolution-into-alien-atmosphere. These habitual intoxications, Morton explains, paradoxically romanticize the alienation of the "beautiful soul" from an imagined "natural" state of being, disempowering that person from recognizing their extant imbrication within a worldly sociopolitical ecology, and thus confirming their day-to-day feelings of isolation from a transformable world.[132] All such critics take issue with ambient music's affectively mixed flirtations with the isolative "void," the trippy "dream," and distant "nature" as attractive capitulations to the impossibility of finding ambivalent calm in the world "out there."

These critiques, I submit, are valid insofar as they take at face value one of the most pervasive and pernicious illusions perpetuated in discourses around ambient music—namely that it is something *other* than popular music, be it abstract highbrow conceptualism or personal sound-bath therapy. Indeed, ambient music's producers and purveyors, as I describe in this book, have long bracketed out how social, cultural, market, stylistic, and expressive factors inform their art's production and reception. Ambient music's designs often calmly sustain this illusion of social purity in taking on the appearance of timeless "technological" and "natural" presence disconnected from the commodified sociality of popular culture, as if it had been hovering there all along. Its enshrinement of the individual/private over the collective/public is also exactly what engenders the notion that it is above the common considerations of commodified sociality.

It is not. With this in mind, I do not seek to repudiate ambient's isolationist illusionism so much as reorient it within the social world of popular audio production and consumption from which it originally drew. In identifying ambient music's roots in popular audio, I locate a starting place for the insights of popular-music criticism and cultural musicology to inform ambient music's discourses, and for disentangling its socioaesthetic pleasures

[131] Robert Hullot-Kentor, "From Uplift to Gadgetry: Barbiero, Eno, and New Age Music," *Telos* 82 (Winter 1989–90): 155. (Thanks to Sumanth Gopinath for this reference.) Similarly, David Toop has criticized the ossification of ambient music as "any droning, slow, dreamy, drifting" electronic music that seems uniquely configured for optimizing individual productivity over cultivating community-minded intimacy and vulnerability; see David Toop, "How Much World Do You Want? Ambient Listening and Its Questions," in *Music beyond Airports: Appraising Ambient Music*, ed. Monty Adkins and Simon Cummings (Huddersfield: University of Huddersfield Press, 2019), 1–20.

[132] Morton, *Ecology without Nature*, 109–23.

from its elitist media and scholarly construction. For instance, as feminist and queer musicologists and 21st-century music critics regularly affirm, popular music does not need to save the world, or sustain a revolutionary politics, to have redeemable social value. Fostering personal comfort and autonomy within an uncomfortable and unjust world has its own virtues; if nothing else, the pleasures of escapist and "easy" art can be hard-won and productive for socially embattled subjects. Elizabeth Le Guin acknowledges as much in her reading of ambient music as a feminist pleasure, as does popular-music scholar Jason King in his praise of smooth soul's "ambient" testaments to collective intimacy.[133] And while ambient's pleasures of affective ambivalence, disaffiliation, and personal introspection have become genrified, through the ambient name, as hip and highbrow pleasures for the upwardly mobile, these pleasures are neither exclusive to this market, nor do they preclude collectivization across cultural divisions.

This book, in reframing ambient music as a popular genre, hence modestly aims to reorient perceptions and discussions of this practice in social and cultural terms—i.e., not as pure isolationism or a passage into psychological interiority, but rather as a socioaesthetically informed and commodified lifestyle technique around the mediation of consciousness and mood. To view ambient music as a popular genre is to look at it less as a personal practice, and more as a collective (if also commercial) enterprise; less as a "withdrawal" from or "solution" to social ills, and more as a means of summoning strength with and through the social everyday; less as a "technology of the self" or "high environmental art," and more as an agent of self-dispossession into more desirable worlds.[134] This might provide a starting point from which ambient's discussants collectively understand and engage with the alterations of awareness ambient music permits, and in the ways in which we might integrate these modes of awareness—these highs, as it were—more holistically into our hypercommericalized social lives.

Ambient music's psychedelic past reveals the promises and perils of romanticizing the personal highs of ambient audio in terms of expanded ecological awareness. The individualistic cultivation of holistic mind-body awareness is not enough to "get high and stay there," since the "there" must also

[133] Le Guin, "Uneasy Listening"; Jason King, "The Sound of Velvet Melting: The Power of 'Vibe' in the Music of Roberta Flack," in *Listen Again: A Momentary History of Pop Music*, ed. Eric Weisbard (Durham, NC: Duke University Press, 2007), 172–99.

[134] The sociologist Antoine Hennion rethinks taste similarly as a "collective, instrumented, and reflexive activity"; see Antoine Hennion, "Loving Music: From a Sociology of Mediation to a Pragmatics of Taste," *Scientific Journal of Media Education* 34, no. 17 (2010): 27.

be actively maintained through historically and materially informed social activity. And throughout head music's history, as I document, participants have found ways to collectivize around ambient audio, be it the multimedia mayhem of the psychedelic counterculture, the building of New Age alternative media networks, the collaborations of the experimentalist music world, or the DJ-led gatherings of the ambient EDM underground. In hindsight, these collective groundswells around head music collapsed as participants took for granted the reified marketing constructions that scaled up, narrowcasted, segmented, and translated into (sub)cultural capital the foundational (trans)humanist and utopian ambitions of the psychedelic counterculture.

I submit, then, that recognizing the universalist aspirations embedded in ambient music's psychedelic past as part of an ongoing historical socioaesthetic practice may equip genre participants to understand ambient art in terms of the making of a peaceable, livable reality for everyone, rather than (just) as an emblem of underground cool, a cerebral conceptual exercise, or an escape pod for middle-class heads from an unkind world. In acknowledging how ambient music's cultural history and sonic conventions developed in tandem with its commodification, the possibility arises that shared ground might be found outside this conventionalized history in overlapping musical traditions and social communities. And in revisiting the psychedelic counterculture's transpersonal and cosmic visions, the possibility also arises that ambient artmaking might address the catastrophic conditions (unevenly) threatening all global life in the twenty-first century, not just through the quiet creation of interiorized trips, but also through loudly engaging with the spread, out there, of a new ecological sympathy.

PART 2

TUNE IN . . .

. . . to Ambient Music's Psychedelic Past

1

Inside *Environments*'s Psychedelic "Psychological Sound"

Introduction

> There was an Atlantic album about five years ago of a computer-generated piece to be played very quietly. The hall-like tones were supposed to calm people and make them relax. It made visiting children stop crying.
>
> Eno is only five years late with this one.
>
> —Miles, *New Musical Express* review for Brian Eno's *Discreet Music* (1975)

Irving "Irv" Teibel (1938–2010) (Fig 1.1) liked to reminisce that his idea to sell nature sound records as "psychological sound" had such obvious untapped potential in 1968, it was as if he had awoken on top of an elephant.[1] The photo engineer and electronic music enthusiast had, in reality, divined the plan after recording ocean sounds for a film by drone musician and experimental filmmaker Tony Conrad and his then-wife, actress and codirector Beverly Grant, to be titled *Coming Attractions* (1970). The Conrads had found inspiration in a minimalist tape by the drummer (and soon-to-be earth artist) Walter De Maria, *Ocean Music* (1968), which featured the crashing of ocean waves giving way—extremely slowly—to the thrashing of cymbals over a ten-minute splice in its latter half. Teibel, too, created an entrancing, long-playing ocean waves recording, but to different ends. At the suggestion of his friend Louis Gerstman, a Bell Labs engineer who had experience working with white noise's various product applications, Teibel decided to repurpose the sounds recorded for the film as a

[1] Jennifer Teibel-Ballow, email message to author, May 3, 2013.

Turn On, Tune In, Drift Off. Victor Szabo, Oxford University Press. © Oxford University Press 2023.
DOI: 10.1093/oso/9780190699307.003.0002

Figure 1.1. Irving "Irv" Teibel, creator of the *Environments* series. Courtesy of Syntonic Research, Inc. Used by permission.

concentration aid.[2] To optimize the audio's consistency, he and Gerstman fed forty seconds of the ocean waves tape into an IBM 360, looped the segment, and used a random number generator to continually modify the resonant filters for roughly thirty minutes. The next day, Teibel pitched to Tony Conrad his idea to sell the looping ocean sounds as a "tranquilizer" and

[2] Irv Teibel, "Mother Nature Goes Digital," in *Digital Deli*, ed. Steve Ditlea (New York: Workman, 1984), 224–25; see also Mack Hagood, *Hush: Media and Sonic Self-Control* (Durham: Duke University Press, 2019), 134–39. Gerstman is best known for having pioneered a computer-based program to synthesize speech using filtered white noise, completed in 1961 in collaboration with John Larry Kelly Jr. at Bell Labs.

"psychedelic experience."[3] The filmmakers, however, had no interest in the proposed venture, so they and Teibel parted ways.

As the Conrads went on to commission a soundtrack from minimal music luminaries La Monte Young, Terry Riley, John Cale, and Charlemagne Palestine for their (still) obscure feature, Teibel brought minimalist collages of recorded sound to middle-class consumers all around the country under the pretense of "psychological" efficacy. Teibel released *Environments: Disc 1* in September 1969 in the guise of a company called Syntonic Research, Inc. The enterprising engineer promoted its ocean sounds (side A) and chirping birds (side B) as "psychological sound" designed to subliminally enhance user focus and alertness. The record sold so well that in June 1970 Teibel landed a distribution deal with Atlantic Records. Over the decade, he would go on to release eleven total *Environments* records under the Syntonic name, selling over a million records nationwide, and garnering features in such publications as the *New York Times*, *Newsweek*, *Rolling Stone*, and *High Fidelity Magazine*.

This chapter historicizes *Environments* and avant-garde minimalism together as concurrent and overlapping explorations of the psychological—and psychedelic—affordances of recorded cyclical and droning sounds. Whether avant-garde aesthetics directly shaped *Environments* is debatable; Teibel never claimed experimental electronic music or sound art as an influence on *Environments*, although he had, leading up to the series, visited composer Karlheinz Stockhausen's lab, dabbled in composing *musique concrète*, and taken a Moog synthesizer course at the New School for Social Research. De Maria has also plausibly insinuated that Teibel was well aware of *Ocean Music* and possibly in possession of the recording when he created *Seashore*.[4] But irrespective of these possibilities, both Teibel and experimental composers simultaneously found fascination in the immersive potential of recorded steady-state sounds. While experimentalists like Young and Palestine improvised with drones and amplification to flood and flummox the senses, Teibel exploited the droning and cyclical nature of "nature"—the lapping of the ocean, sheets of rain, buzzing cicadas, breeze-blown bells—to similarly intoxicating effect. His marketing rhetoric moreover echoed the terms by which Columbia Masterworks sold the trance-inducing music of composers

3 Hagood, *Hush*, 129.

4 Oral History Interview with Walter De Maria, interview by Paul Cummings, October 4, 1972, Archives of American Art, Smithsonian Institution.

Steve Reich and Terry Riley as inducing drug-like experiences of altered consciousness—that is, in Teibel's words, as "psychological sound."

Tintinnabulation (Contemplative Sound), Side A of *Environments: Disc 2* (1970) [Fig. 1.2], most clearly crystallizes the form in which Teibel fashioned recorded minimalism as both environmental feature and psychological salve. The recording, in which a set of unusually tuned bells clang softly for thirty minutes, delivered the hypnotic techniques of source-sound reduction and temporal extension associated with avant-garde minimalism to middle-class consumers seeking solitude and sedation. This aesthetic connection has been largely passed over by *Environments*'s lay and scholarly historians. Audio enthusiasts popularly remember *Environments* as the first of many "nature sounds" records made for relaxation, while diehards also recognize them as some of the earliest commercial records produced using digital

Figure 1.2. Album cover to Syntonic Research, Inc.'s *Environments: Disc 2* (Atlantic, 1970).

signal processing.[5] Media scholar Mack Hagood, noting the records' similarity to Eno's ambient music, also analyzes *Environments* as innovative "orphic media," or sonic facilitators of spatial and social control.[6] Few existing sources, however, take full stock of the records' pioneering designs, which were at once attractively polyvalent in their rhetorical and visual packaging while also mesmerizingly, even profoundly, simple in sound.

This chapter's investigation of psychedelic art and the early marketing of recorded minimal music during the latter half of the 1960s sheds light on the formative contexts for Teibel's germinal realization of ambient audio. With sustained focus given to the promotional rhetoric and designs of the records themselves, using *Tintinnabulation* as its chief example, it demonstrates how *Environments* embodied the ideals and lifestyle practices of the psychedelic counterculture as it packaged and popularized the hypnotic sonic minimalism of its avant-garde participants for a mass middle-class market.[7] In so doing, this chapter provides a piece of the larger (and still incomplete) puzzle of the interactions between avant-garde experimentalism and popular culture, between minimalist and psychedelic music, and between fine art and consumer technology around the turn of the 1970s.

Designing the Drugless High

Naturalizing Audio as "Psychological Sound"

Q: What are Environments, exactly?

A: Environments are not like any other phonograph discs ever released before. In essence, they are psychological sound designed to help people do things, rather than provide them with aural entertainment.

—liner notes to *Environments: Disc 2* (1970)

[5] See, for example, Mike Powell, "How a New Age Hustler Sold the Sound of the World," *Pitchfork*, November 2, 2016, https://pitchfork.com/features/cover-story/reader/natural-selection/.

[6] On "orphic media," see Hagood, *Hush*, 3–4 and 21–28.

[7] Minimalist composers' interactions with the psychedelic counterculture are thoroughly detailed in David W. Bernstein, ed., *The San Francisco Tape Music Center: 1960s Counterculture and the Avant-Garde* (Berkeley: University of California Press, 2008). On La Monte Young's countercultural and psychedelic connections, see Jeremy Grimshaw, *Draw a Straight Line and Follow It: The Music and Mysticism of La Monte Young* (New York: Oxford University Press, 2011), 93–96; Legs McNeil and Gillian McCain, *Please Kill Me: The Uncensored Oral History of Punk* (New York: Penguin, 1997), 4. On Steve Reich's countercultural connections, see Ross Cole, "'Fun, Yes, but Music?' Steve Reich and the San Francisco Bay Area's Cultural Nexus, 1962–65," *Journal of the Society for American Music* 6, no. 3 (August 2012): 315–48; Sumanth Gopinath, "Reich in Blackface: Oh Dem Watermelons and Radical Minstrelsy in the 1960s," *Journal of the Society for American Music* 5, no. 2 (May 2011): 139–93.

The sleeve notes accompanying *Environments: Disc 2*, as is typical of the rhetoric throughout the series, propose that users apply the enclosed "psychological sound" toward personal well-being and domestic well-doing. They at times identify alterations of mood or focus as goals in themselves, as when recommending the records for relaxation, concentration, and/or stimulation. At other times, Syntonic describes these subjective shifts as equipping users for activities like reading, meditating, studying, socializing, sex, or sleeping. But Syntonic insists, whatever the sounds' recommended applications, that *Environments*'s "psychological" efficacy stems from their peripherality to user focus; as the liner notes state, *Environments*'s recordings are "designed to be heard, rather than listened to."[8]

Syntonic's ostensible design for "hearing" rather than "listening" served as a crucial part of *Environments*'s promotional design as "functional" audio rather than as entertainment or art. The binary frame of "hearing" as passive auditory sensing, and "listening" as active attention to sounds and their meanings, dovetailed with contemporaneous rhetorics of "functional music," a formulation that arose in the United States after World War II as a way of marking music's usefulness as a technology of human behavior management.[9] Postwar anglophone producers and propagators of "functional music" avowed that expressions of feeling, or aesthetic concerns like beauty and style, were beside the point of functional music's educative, therapeutic, and/or psychological applications, and they accordingly claimed to jettison expressive and aesthetic concerns in pursuit of "functional" effectiveness.[10] Most prominently, the Muzak Corporation, whose instrumental arrangements of pop standards wafted through US businesses from the mid-1930s through midcentury to boost production efficiency and stimulate

[8] Liner notes to *Environments: Disc 2* by Syntonic Research, Inc., SD 66002, 1970, LP.

[9] Simon C. Jones and Thomas G. Schumacher most concisely define functional music as a "social technology in the control and regulation of work, consumption, and public space." Simon C. Jones and Thomas G. Schumacher, "Muzak: On Functional Music and Power," *Critical Studies in Mass Communication* 9, no. 2 (June 1992): 156. This book's discussion of functional music excludes the less-relevant history of *Gebrauchsmusik* ("functional music" or "utility music"), a polemical term from Weimar Germany that both described and prescribed an alternative to the dominant concert hall paradigm of autonomous or absolute music. See Stephen Hinton, *The Idea of Gebrauchsmusik: Musical Aesthetics in the Weimar Republic with Reference to the Works of Paul Hindemith* (New York: Garland, 1989).

[10] Everett Thayer Gaston, a notable developer of music therapy, maintained that functional music should not abandon aesthetics, even though appreciation is not its aim; see E. Thayer Gaston, "Psychological Foundations for Functional Music," *American Journal of Occupational Therapy* 2, no. 1 (February 1948): 1–8.

consumer spending, advertised its product as "functional" to communicate that the music *intentionally* precluded emotional and intellectual involvement. "We always have to be careful that the arrangements aren't too intrusive," commented Donald O'Neill, Muzak's VP of Research, in 1957. "After all, this is basically music to hear, not to listen to."[11]

Teibel's promotion of *Environments* as "psychological sound," published under the anonymous authority of Syntonic Research Inc., echoed Muzak's strategies of marketing music as fine-tuned for psychological "function" through institutionalized experimentation. Muzak, which sold its programs to companies rather than consumers directly, touted a "stimulus progression" technique of modulating musical "stimulus" (tempo, rhythm, instrumentation, and orchestra size) over long spans of time to maximize auditors' productivity.[12] The technique, Muzak asserted, had been developed through military-funded experimentation and approved by a "Board of Scientific Advisors," a group of "specialists in the physiological and psychological applications of music."[13] Teibel's dubious corporate posture similarly supported *Environments*'s claims of having resulted from "extensive research on auditory stimulation" and exhaustive product testing ("Over *3000* playbacks were obtained before noticeable wear occurred"). Targeting individual record buyers directly, colorful testimonials (usually labeled "Listening Test Responses") took up the back of each record with claims like "Speeds up my reading!" and "I feel more relaxed" speaking to the records' ease of use (see Fig. 1.3). Although Syntonic Research did, in fact, solicit listener feedback during the latter half of the 1970s, the veracity of the responses on the early records remains questionable.[14]

[11] Stanley Green, "Music to Hear but Not to Listen to," *Saturday Review*, September 28, 1957, 56. By the late 1960s, "muzak" colloquially referred to most any music, by Muzak or otherwise, publicly programmed to create "psychological" or behavioral effects other than aesthetic enjoyment. O'Neill's claims were later echoed by Bing Muscio, president of the Muzak corporation from 1966 to 1980, who insisted on branding Muzak as "nonentertainment" music, or music that does not require emotional and intellectual involvement. "With Muzak," Muscio announced proudly, "you can hear without listening." Derryn Hinch, "Hearing without Listening," *Sydney Morning Herald*, September 17, 1972, 127. For more sources on Muzak, see Note 3 in Preface.

[12] Stephen H. Barnes, *Muzak: The Hidden Messages in Music*, vol. 9, Studies on the History and Interpretation of Music (Lewiston, NY: Edwin Mellen Press, 1988), 91; Jones and Schumacher, "Muzak," 159–60.

[13] Muzak, *Stimulus Progression Number Three (Christmas)*, Muzak S-2563, n.d., LP.

[14] Steve Gerstman attests that Teibel made up most of the "Listening Test Responses"; see Hagood, *Hush*, 141.

the most sensuous recordings ever made!

"BETTER THAN THE REAL THING" "A Gentle, Subtle Trip"
"APARTMENT NEVER SEEMED SO PLEASANT BEFORE.." "AMAZING!"
"Great for reading..." "...HAVEN'T FELT THIS GOOD SINCE MY VACATION"
"Can't get over how clear my thinking is" "infinitely flexible..."
"THE HIPPEST RECORD EVER!" "PLAY IT CONTINUALLY..."
"...cured my insomnia!" "...MY FAVORITE RECORD"
"READING SPEED DOUBLED..." "Never heard anything like it!"
"...fantastic for making love!" "NEVER GET TIRED OF IT"
"BETTER THAN A TRANQUILIZER!" "room seemed brighter"

If you've ever had trouble reading, relaxing, sleeping, or just plain concentrating, ENVIRONMENTS will be a source of constant amazement to you. You've never heard a recording before quite like this one.

Above are a few of the many enthusiastic comments received during extensive listening tests conducted prior to the release of this record.

The first of an extensive series, ENVIRONMENTS represents a totally new type of recorded sound -- psychologically perfect aural environments which can be left on indefinitely without fatigue or boredom.

The outcome of extensive research on auditory stimulation, ENVIRONMENTS Disc One is not only pleasurable to listen to, but also represents the only effective means of easily coping with the ever-increasing problem of disturbing noise. At normal playback levels (or less), this disc effectively masks most irritating noises to an amazing degree, in much the same way a deodorizer neutralizes disagreeable odors.

You don't listen to this record -- you hear it. If played stereophonically, the sound seems to be all around you, creating an unusually sensuous sonic environment. Unlike music, ENVIRONMENTS affects the subconscious without deadening the mind's ability to think.

There are several other unusual features which make these recordings even more unique. For one thing, either side of this disc can be played at any phonograph speed, from 45rpm down to 16 2/3rpm, in full stereo. All that's required is a slight adjustment of your phonograph's tone controls to compensate for the speed change. This amazing capability of variable speed playback is no mere novelty -- the sounds produced at different speeds dramatically affect your respiration, heartbeat, and metabolism. In addition, the unusual characteristics of the disc groove, as well as the use of highest grade pressing materials guarantee extreme durability, thus assuring you of extensive distortion-free playback with minimum wear.

At the slowest speed, each side of this disc will play uninterrupted for an entire hour, more than twice the playing time of any other stereo LP! If you make the slight modification detailed within, this single record is capable of providing a continuous stereo environment which can be left on indefinitely.

Unlike sound effects recordings or other similar sound sources, the superb stereo sound on this disc has been achieved through the collateral use of a specially programmed computer interface. This accounts, in part, for the record's amazing ability to be played at any speed, as well as its ultra-dimensional presence and dynamic range.

Produced by Syntonic Research, Inc.
ATLANTIC RECORDING CORPORATION, 1841 BROADWAY, NEW YORK, NEW YORK 10023

Figure 1.3. Back cover to Syntonic Research, Inc.'s *Environments: Disc 1* (Atlantic, 1969).

Because Teibel packaged and promoted *Environments* for personal uses in domestic rather than public settings, a more apt comparison may be the easy-listening "mood music" album (aka "mood album"), which, like Muzak, sold orchestral arrangements of familiar tunes through "functional" framings.[15] Paul Weston and His Orchestra most influentially introduced the concept in the latter half of the 1940s with titles that explicitly sold music as accompaniment to mental activities like dreaming and reminiscing. The emergence of the long-playing record in 1948 helped the concept take off; although Weston's

[15] For sources on mood albums, see Note 6 in Preface.

earliest theme albums first appeared in 1945 as albums of 78-rpm discs, the idea caught on like wildfire once these "easy" environments could be fostered with little user intervention, with the craze peaking between the mid-1950s and early '60s.[16] Indeed, mood music was not so much musically innovative as it was promotionally inventive, since the music's style had been sold for well over a decade as "semiclassical" or "light" music.[17] Mood music LPs simply retooled, packaged, and marketed this existing music as a programmable consumer technology.[18]

Teibel's repurposing of the nature sounds LP as "psychological sound" innovated along similar lines as the mood album. *Environments*'s recordings (Table 1.1) mostly involved nature sounds, which Syntonic marketed as a "new concept in stereo sound," even though records of birdsong and thunderstorms had been commercially available for almost as long as phonograph discs themselves.[19] By 1970 labels like Audio Fidelity and Folkways had for decades sold album-length nature "field guides" for archival and educational purposes.[20] Teibel, however, refashioned the nature sounds LP by creating sound collages taking up the entirety of each side, and by packaging them with a "functional" concept.

In media theory terms, Teibel innovated in promoting the *Environments* discs as "technologies of the self," tools for extending user agency and feeling

[16] Jennifer Messelink, "Mood Albums," *Journal of Popular Music Studies* 33, no. 3 (2021): 45–49.

[17] On the origins of light music (*leichte Musik*), see Derek B. Scott, "Other Mainstreams: Light Music and Easy Listening, 1920–70," in *The Cambridge History of Twentieth-Century Music*, ed. Anthony Pople and Nicholas Cook, The Cambridge History of Music (Cambridge: Cambridge University Press, 2004), 307–35; Derek B. Scott, *Sounds of the Metropolis: The 19th-Century Popular Music Revolution in London, New York, Paris, and Vienna* (New York: Oxford University Press, 2008).

[18] Keir Keightley, "Music for Middlebrows: Defining the Easy Listening Era, 1946–1966," *American Music* 26, no. 3 (Fall 2008): 333, fn. 33. As Keightley further explains, mood music emerged around the same time that radio programs of "light music" marketed themselves as offering familiar, intellectually undemanding background music. As one station manager put it in 1949, "You don't have to stop what you're doing in order to listen to our program." Ibid., 317.

[19] Commercial wildlife sounds recordings date back to 1910, when the German branch of the Gramophone company released Carl Reich's recording, "Actual Bird Record Made by a Captive Nightengale." See Cheryl Tipp, "An Overview of Early Commercial Wildlife Recordings at the British Library," *IASA Journal*, no. 37 (2011): 47–54.

[20] Whereas most field guides identified different animal or nature sounds track by track, *Evening in Sapsucker Woods* (Cornell, 1958) was likely the first to include a montage of nature sounds on a full LP side, challenging listeners to "identify the species announced . . . on the first side of the record." For an extensive (though nonexhaustive) list of early commercial field guide recordings and sound effects records, see Eugene Endres, "There's a Tweeter in My Tweeter," *High Fidelity Magazine*, June 1971, 61–65.

Table 1.1. Recordings of the *Environments* LP series.

Track Title	Disc	Copyright Date	Sounds[a]
"The Psychologically Ultimate Seashore"	1	1969	ocean waves
"Optimum Aviary"	1	1969	birds
"Tintinnabulation (Contemplative Sound)"	2	1970	bells
"Dawn at New Hope, Pennsylvania"	2	1970	birds, insects, dogs
"Be-In (A Psychoacoustic Experience)"	3	1971	chatter, shouting, singing, drums (1969 gathering in Central Park)
"Dusk at New Hope, Pennsylvania"	3	1971	insects, birds, dogs
"The Psychologically Ultimate Thunderstorm"	4	1974	rain, thunder
"Gentle Rain in a Pine Forest (Synthetic Silence)"	4	1974	rain, birds, insects
"Ultimate Heartbeat"	5	1974	amplified human heartbeat
"Wind in the Trees"	5	1974	wind, leaves rustling, birds, dogs, cows
"Dawn in the Okefenokee Swamp"	6	1974	insects, frogs, toads, birds, water
"Dusk in the Okefenokee Swamp"	6	1974	insects, frogs, toads, birds
"Intonation"	7	1976	"om" mantra (multiple voices)
"Summer Cornfield"	7	1976	insects
"Country Stream"	8	1974	rippling water, insects, birds
"A Wood-Masted Sailboat"	8	1974	rippling water, creaking boards, wind on sails
"Pacific Ocean"	9	1979	ocean waves, gulls
"Caribbean Lagoon"	9	1979	rippling water, insects, birds
"English Meadow"	10	1978	birds, rippling water
"Night in the Country"	10	1978	insects, wind
"Alpine Blizzard"	11	1978	wind, banging shutters
"Country Thunderstorm"	11	1978	farm animals, thunder, rain

[a] Sounds include both actually recorded sounds and synthesized/simulated sounds.

in everyday life.[21] Since the 1920s, recorded and broadcast music consumers had become accustomed to programming music as a "background" for their own personal activities, much thanks to the automated sustainment of sound allowed by radio, and later by the record changer and long-playing record.[22] While cultural elites decried this sort of listening as "distracted" or "deconcentrated," middle-class consumers became adept at using music, as Tia DeNora puts it, as "an opportunity to structure the parameters of action."[23]

At the same time as Teibel riffed on existing practices of packaging recorded music as "functional" technologies of self-management, he also boasted that *Environments*'s natural sounds were more psychologically effective than functional music.[24] Teibel largely attributed this effectiveness to the timelessness of "nature" itself; as the liner notes to *Environments: Disc 1* stated, nature sounds "have subtle structures which are difficult to subconsciously memorize. Unlike playing a song over and over again, an *Environments* disc becomes more effective the more it is repeated." *Environments*'s variably occurring natural sounds, in contrast to the predictable tune that predictably wears over repeat listens, seem to unfold outside human time. In claiming that *Environments*'s sounds can be heard "over and over again" without tiring the listener, Teibel depicted his records as personal technologies as timeless and durable as nature itself. This framing spilled over into the records' other promotional and visual rhetoric as well (see Fig. 1.4).

Relatedly, Teibel asserted *Environments*'s superiority over functional music on the basis of its universal appeal. "The problem with music as a

[21] The term "technologies of the self" originates in Michel Foucault's late lectures on the topic; see Michel Foucault, *Technologies of the Self: A Seminar with Michel Foucault*, ed. Luther H. Martin, Huck Gutman, and Patrick H. Hutton (Amherst: University of Massachusetts Press, 1988).

[22] Susan J. Douglas, *Listening In: Radio and the American Imagination* (New York: Random House, 1999), 27; David Goodman, "Distracted Listening: On Not Making Sound Choices in the 1930s," in *Sound in the Age of Mechanical Reproduction*, ed. David Suisman and Susan Strasser (Philadelphia: University of Pennsylvania Press, 2010), 15–46.

[23] Tia DeNora, *Music in Everyday Life* (New York: Cambridge University Press, 2000), 20. DeNora's sociology of music in everyday life directly responds to the prescriptivism of Theodor Adorno, who most succinctly articulated a music sociology against "deconcentrated" listening in his *Introduction to the Sociology of Music*, see esp. 15–16. See also Tia DeNora, *After Adorno: Rethinking Music Sociology* (New York: Cambridge University Press, 2003).

[24] On the mood- and energy-based affordances of recorded music, see DeNora, *Music in Everyday Life*, 46–74.

Figure 1.4. Irv Teibel and *Environments: Disc 7* in nature (ca. 1976). Courtesy of Syntonic Research, Inc. Used by permission.

background sound is *taste*," as Teibel stated in one interview. "Each listener responds differently."[25] Even functional music cannot help but encroach on listeners' aesthetic sensibilities, Teibel liked to argue, whereas nature has nothing to do with taste because it is universally enjoyed. These claims to

[25] Julie M. Kerns, "Profile: Music in the Key of Life," *Austin Magazine*, April 1984, 34.

Environments's superior effectiveness, however, typically invoked subjective discernment and preference through an inapt comparison with publicly programmed "muzak" (bold type reflects my emphasis, italics reflects Teibel's):

> **I've known people who hate muzak so much that they will actually stick pencils through the grille of the speaker and ruin the muzak speaker just because they hate to listen to it!** Now, that's not muzak's fault so much as it's *music*'s fault. The aspect of trying to tell a person what is good and bad about music turns out to be a big task. Music is man-made, and music started out as an emulation of nature. . . . Now, suddenly, for the first time in the history of man, you can actually take these environmental sounds, and do things with them. It was an idea whose time had come. Once I came up with the idea, and started working on it, and seeing how effective it was with people, and how **they really enjoyed it a thousand times more than listening to music that they didn't want to listen to**, that they could listen to the same sound over and over and over again and not get tired of it—that was something that really, truly amazed me.[26]

Environments's home listeners, of course, would not need to jab pencils into their own speakers to stop the audio they themselves put on. Teibel's comparisons to muzak hence slyly masked the fact that *Environments*'s sounds were *not* as inevitable as nature—nor even as perennial as elevator music—since they would be bought, programmed, and played by their own discerning users. Both Teibel's rhetorics of nature and his comparisons to muzak served to "naturalize" products as timeless and universal, despite the fact that *Environments* had to appeal to consumer discernment as much as any other audio recording. "There are magical sounds in this world, and you don't really have to choose them," as Teibel would say in his appeal to prospective buyers. "It is something built into your psyche, and it has nothing to do with taste."[27]

The naturalization of *Environments* as universally suitable "psychological sound" not only circumvented questions of taste by conveying a lack of

[26] Irv Teibel, "Forum: Irv Teibel," interview by Eileen Remen, Longhorn Radio Network, February 5, 1983, UT KUT Longhorn Radio Network Records, Dolph Briscoe Center for American History, University of Texas at Austin, Box 2/25-83.

[27] Leah Rae, "Environmental-Sound Maestro Listens for 'Magic' Everywhere," *Buffalo News*, October 15, 1989, G7.

expressive intention, it also framed the sounds as suitable for placement in the periphery of the user's focus. This rhetoric obscured the active role of its carefully designed audio production, titles, liner notes, and visuals in guiding users toward the ambient use of audio. The carefully consistent designs of the extended audio collages on each side, for instance, afforded background use by paving the record grooves smoothly and continuously, their spans uninterrupted by potentially obtrusive discontinuities like loud animal sounds, track changes, textural shifts, or musical phrases. Their engineered consistency drastically reduced the probability that any subsequent event would be unique, and thus worthy of attention and/or response (as might, ironically, occur "in nature").

The titular "*Environments*" likewise suggested treating the recorded sounds as an atmosphere or surround. But, of course, it also identified the sounds' origins in "the environment," an idiomatic expression that arose in the United States around the end of World War II as a way of designating nonindustrial "nature." These double meanings can collapse in listening as electronically automated playback allows the audio to appear to users as experientially "natural," or second nature, in its ongoingness. *Environments*'s title hence not only reflexively anticipated that the sounds would blend into listeners' auditory environments, but it also thematized the naturalization of audio technology at the periphery of consumers' ongoing aural perceptions. In so positioning the recordings as outside the user's perceptual frame *and* outside culture, Teibel's promotional rhetoric dissolved the assumed boundaries between the technological and natural into the "psychological" promise of ambient audio.

Selling *Tintinnabulation*'s "Contemplative Sound" as Psychedelic

> The Environments concept is far broader than the mere simulation of natural sounds.
>
> —liner notes to *Environments: Disc 2* (1970)

Bells are not nature sounds per se, but their sounds, often played by wind as by people, do symbolize a proximity to "nature" not enjoyed by most urban or suburban dwellers. Though once a symbol of encroaching industrial modernity, bells, like the beach or the zoo, have come to represent a quasi-controlled zone between human industry and wilderness.[28] Since the late nineteenth century, bells have circulated as nostalgic emblems of the authentic village community;[29] as one author observed in 1870, the sounds of village bells suggest "rural peace and contented lives . . . where life is calm and equable, and less worry enters into the lives of those who there reside."[30] For Europe's descendants and immigrants on the American continents, the ringing of church bells would also represent a nostalgic link to the soundscapes of the old world.[31] Teibel's inclusion of a bell sounds recording on the second *Environments* release tapped into this symbolic history of distance from modern urbanity—as did its first public appearance.

Tintinnabulation (Contemplative Sound) debuted at a January–March 1970 exhibition called Contemplation Environments at New York's Museum of Contemporary Crafts (now the Museum of Arts and Design).[32] The American Craftsman's Council designed the exhibition "to provide city dwellers with places for solitude and inner communion."[33] In the catalog, Director Paul Smith imagined the gallery as a return to the "daily, direct access to nature" unavailable within the city's "overcrowded, noisy, dehumanized communities."[34] The museum displayed sixteen total physical environments that were arranged by their respective makers to produce calming, introspective moods. Exhibition visitors could follow a single path that wove through a steel booth decorated with moss and wood, a stroboscopic "crystal waterfall," giant plastic tubes with sound-controlled lighting, and a platform activating

[28] John Fiske, *Reading the Popular* (Boston: Unwin Hyman, 1989), 44–46.

[29] Aimée Boutin, "'Ring Out the Old, Ring In the New': The Symbolism of Bells in Nineteenth-Century French Poetry," *Nineteenth-Century French Studies* 30, nos. 3–4 (Spring–Summer 2002): 268; Alain Corbin, *Village Bells: Sound and Meaning in the 19th-Century French Countryside*, trans. Martin Thom (New York: Columbia University Press, 1998), 307–8.

[30] F. P. and H. G. S., "The Power of Sounds," *The Eclectic Magazine of Foreign Literature, Science, and Art*, vol. 12 (October1870), 488; reprinted in Gouverneur Morrison, ed., *Bells: Their History and Romance* (Santa Barbara: J.F. Rowny Press, 1932), 201.

[31] See Ilaria Serra, *The Imagined Immigrant: Images of Italian Emigration to the United States Between 1890 and 1924* (Teaneck, NJ: Fairleigh Dickinson University Press, 2009), 246; Mark Michael Smith, *Listening to Nineteenth-Century America* (Chapel Hill: University of North Carolina Press, 2001), 113.

[32] The American Craftsmen's Council (later, the American Craft Council, or ACC) founded the Museum in 1956 to foster public interest in contemporary US American craftsmanship. Paul J. Smith, director from 1963 to 1987, envisioned the Museum as a community center where visitors could interact with local art, design, and performance through exhibitions, concerts, educational seminars, and lectures. "Museum History," The Museum of Arts and Design, last modified July 1, 2014, accessed July 15, 2014, http://madmuseum.org/about/museum-history; American Craftsmen's Council, *Proceedings of The First World Congress of Craftsmen*, June 8–19, 1964 (New York City: Columbia University, 1964), 72.

[33] American Craftsmen's Council, "Contemplation Environments," *ACC Outlook*, January 1970, 2.

[34] Paul J. Smith, *Contemplation Environments* (New York: Museum of Contemporary Crafts, 1970), 3.

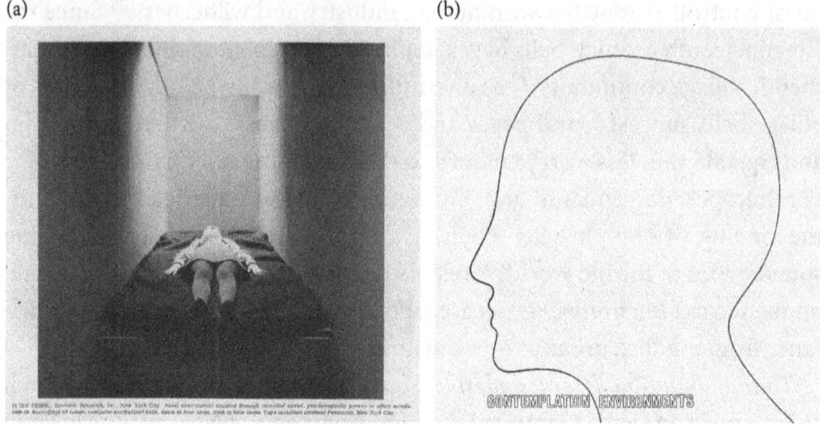

Figure 1.5. Front cover and exhibit image from the 1970 *Contemplation Environments* exhibition catalogue at the Museum of Contemporary Crafts. Courtesy of the American Craft Council.

lights and a warm "air shower." Several exhibited interiors permitted only single inhabitants, with each space exerting a "quieting, peaceful influence on the mind and emotions of the individual who enters it."[35] Teibel's exhibit was one of four spaces featuring sound, and the penultimate along the exhibition path. Visitors could enter one of three corridors playing *Tintinnabulation, Seashore, Dawn at New Hope, PA*, or *Dusk at New Hope, PA*, and listen (or zonk out) to the soothing sounds, abed, while staring up through a skylight (see Fig. 1.5).

In keeping with its original reception context, *Environments: Disc 2*'s packaging promoted retreat into the "meditation and relaxation" that its sonic design permitted. The subtitle marked the bell sounds as "contemplative sound," while the testimonials adorning the back cover announced the records' sedative power:

> I simply found it impossible to think of the things that disturb me, which, to me, is a high form of inner peace.
>
> These Environments bring peace and serenity—not easy to come by and much appreciated.

[35] Ibid.

> Very calming . . . helps me to sleep easier and speeds up my reading. . . . I feel much more relaxed.

Such descriptions equated "contemplative" with calm, an equation mediated by an aural design made to afford relaxation into present-moment awareness. As with the ocean and bird sounds recordings, Teibel devoted the full side of the LP disc to a single type of sound repeated, at various lengths, at random intervals; played at 33 1/3 rpm, each of *Tintinnabulation*'s bells strikes between roughly ½ to 5 seconds after the last, averaging at a placid 1½ seconds between strikes. The collection of bells establishes a narrow dynamic range and constrained repertory of five pitches, with their individual speeds of attack, decay lengths, and tone color also generally consistent throughout the track's considerable length. Users, expecting further sonic consistency, might readily relax focus and perceive the track's overall homogeneous texture as a composite drone with individual elements fading in and out of audibility. Alternatively, users might attend to local auditory phenomena such as rhythmic displacement or beating frequencies; or they might notice how their own perception of these phenomena changes over time as their focus shifts, expands, and contracts. Or, perhaps, they read, or snooze, or do the dishes—whatever the case, *Tintinnabulation*'s sonic invariants establish a controlled temporal shelter, not unlike the spatial seclusions of the museum exhibition, wherein inhabitants may forego future-focus and relax into an expanded present.

Teibel accordingly advertised *Environments*'s capacity to act as a psychological relaxant through comparisons with anxiety-quelling drugs. Early on, he called *Environments* a "decongestant for the mind" that speeds metabolism, lowers blood pressure, and cures insomnia.[36] "Better than a tranquilizer!" announced one "user" on the back of *Environments: Disc 1*. Syntonic's claims rode high on the unparalleled sales of prescription tranquilizers like Librium (in the 1960s) and Valium (the best-selling brand pharmaceutical in the Western world throughout the 1970s).[37]

Yet Syntonic's comparisons of *Environments* to chemical relaxants and analgesics coincided with the claim that its sounds might recalibrate,

[36] Linda Wolfe, "The Urban Strategist: Perchance to Sleep," *New York Magazine*, November 2, 1970, 70.

[37] Andrea Tone, "Tranquilizers on Trial: Psychopharmacology in the Age of Anxiety," in *Medicating Modern America: Prescription Drugs in History*, ed. Andrea Tone and Elizabeth S. Watkins (New York: New York University Press, 2007), 169.

rather than dull, users' perceptual faculties. Testimonials on the back of *Environments: Disc 2* express wonder at *Tintinnabulation*'s perception-warping, hallucinogenic agency:

> A surrealistic experience . . . the strange harmonics and "super-reality" of the sounds generate their own sense of reality . . . my friends came over and we just sat and listened for hours . . .
>
> I imagined shapes and colors I had never thought of before . . .
>
> The closest thing to real "head music" I've ever heard.
>
> The whole room seemed to change as the needle tracked the first groove. Very heavy stuff.

Like the "very heavy" rock dubbed "psychedelic" by '60s "heads," Syntonic did not merely propose to mirror psychedelic effects with *Environments*; they promised to supplant the very substances that produced them.[38] Several *Environments* releases were touted as drug replacements; see, for instance, the cheeky quote from High Times Magazine on the front cover of *Environments: Disc 9* calling the record "highly addictive." The liner notes to *Tintinnabulation*'s 1990 CD reissue made this proposition most plain, stating, "Many people have compared Tintinnabulation . . . to a very pleasant 'recreational drug' experience."[39]

Yet Syntonic took care to represent *Environments* as a relatively mindful alternative, rather than accompaniment, to psychedelics; as they further state in the rerelease,

> Environments are psychologically-based sound, and this would put the series in the category of "head music," but unfortunately, "head music" today is synonymous with "trip music" and "drug music," which infers that a person can best appreciate the sound when he is "high" or "tripping," which usually isn't the case. Many of the reply cards packed with the first album were returned to us with the notation that the ocean sound was the

[38] Michael Hicks, *Sixties Rock: Garage, Psychedelic, and Other Satisfactions* (Urbana: University of Illinois Press, 1999), 58–59; Jim DeRogatis, *Turn on Your Mind: Four Decades of Great Psychedelic Rock* (Milwaukee: Hal Leonard, 2003), 12.

[39] Syntonic Research, Inc., liner notes to *Environments 2*, Atlantic 81765-2, 1987, CD.

> best "natural high" the person had heard. Sound can be a powerful tool, if a person can learn to use it, instead of subjecting himself to it in a passive manner.[40]

Syntonic sold *Tintinnabulation*'s "natural high" on the promise of subjective control ("learn to use it") that would purportedly be absent under the influence of drugs. This included the user's ability to control the parameters of their "high" with playback technology; liner notes often emphasized that audiences may freely alter or stop the sound at any time. "The problem with substances taken internally for relaxation purposes is that one often has no control over their effects once they are in the body," plainly states the *Environments 2* CD notes. Yet, with *Tintinnabulation*, "there are no unpleasant side effects and you are always in complete control. If the effect is too powerful, all you need do is reach for a knob or switch." The back of the original LP explained that users can simply adjust the playback settings according to their needs: "Tintinnabulation can be played at any speed, from 78 to 16rpm, in full stereo. At different speeds, the sounds change in tone and apparent size. . . . The effect, unlike real bells, is fully controllable by the use of your volume, bass, and treble controls." What made *Tintinnabulation* such a "powerful" substitute for drugs, according to such assertions, was the ability it gave users to actively modulate their head trip. Syntonic's rhetoric concomitantly implied flexible attention on the part of users who might focus on sound while optimizing their "surrealistic" psychoacoustic effects, or while appreciating the quality of Syntonic's cutting-edge audio simulation.

To this end, *Environments: Disc 2*'s packaging does not directly explain how Syntonic created their "super-real" bells, but rather raises the nature of *Tintinnabulation*'s "reality" as a tantalizingly obscure prospect for the user to investigate through playback. Next to the title on the back, Syntonic vaguely notes that *Tintinnabulation*'s bells are "computer synthesized" without explicating the recording's digital origins.[41] This cursory mention draws attention

[40] Ibid.

[41] Given the general inaccessibility of digital synthesis tools to mass-market consumers at the time, Teibel most likely created the recording, with the assistance of Lou Gerstman, on the same IBM-360 he used to create *The Psychologically Ultimate Seashore*. Due to the limited capabilities of this early digital technology, Teibel probably recorded actual bells, then digitally resynthesized them based on a spectral analysis of the bell sounds' constituent frequencies.

to the bell sounds' *almost*-realness: While bearing remarkably rich inharmonic overtone structures compared to most digital simulations of the time, the long, flat sustains of the bell sounds also seem an unnatural result of their slow, dull attacks. Their uncanniness does not require close attention to notice, but it may inspire closer contemplation of the sounds' artificial provenance. The notes also attribute *Tintinnabulation*'s strange aural appearance to an "oriental theory of harmonics" used in production, a blanket orientalism that marks the bells' deviation from common Western tuning while also drawing attention to the ambiguity of the bells' fundamental pitches in relation to their inharmonic spectra.[42] As the upper partials of each bell sound loudly, leaving each fundamental tone either indistinguishable from the partials or inaudible entirely, closely attentive listeners may discover a complex multiplicity fracturing the bells' once-seeming unity.

Syntonic further spurred active auditory engagement with *Tintinnabulation*'s psychedelic effects by encouraging investigation of the bell sounds' ambiguating effects on perception. "Imagine five different bells," the packaging implored prospective users, "each as big as an average room, which are sounded very, very softly and reverberate for minutes afterwards. The sound seems to float in the air, slowly moving around the room as a physical presence." Attentive listening reveals the description to be hyperbolic—the bells do not seem much larger than a small closet, no one bell reverberates for longer than ten seconds, and none changes position in the stereo field once struck. Yet strangely, Syntonic's fantastical depiction does capture something of *Tintinnabulation*'s diffuse spatial presence in playback as one's listening focus on the bells softens. As the bell sounds flicker between object of focus and medium of perception, the line between the "actual" qualities of the sounds "themselves," and the impressions the textured recording bestows on a room or a listener, can become blurry. Trails of vibrating metal dissipate like perfume into air; one easily loses track of the bells' veridical "reality" relative to the resonance of one's own room. *Tintinnabulation*'s descriptions encourage such alternation between listening and not-listening, or between hard and soft focus, as a means of discerning—or enjoyably conflating—sonic causes and perceptual effects.

[42] On the relationship of orientalism in '60s psychedelic music to US neocolonialist policy, see Nadya Zimmerman, *Counterculture Kaleidoscope: Musical and Cultural Perspectives on Late Sixties San Francisco* (Ann Arbor: University of Michigan Press, 2008), 52–90.

By calling attention to the bells' ontological ambiguity ("real" or "super-real"?), *Tintinnabulation*'s listening responses and liner notes promote users' active participation in alternately seeking and relinquishing certainty of their own perception through shifts in aural attentiveness. Although Syntonic recommends, at points, that users ignore *Tintinnabulation* and treat it as part of their environment, they also depict users noticing the bells' sounds and actively observing their ambiguating effects on perception. These descriptions, in short, frame *Tintinnabulation* as both cause *and* gauge of altered consciousness. By advertising *Tintinnabulation* as a technology for defamiliarizing perception, and by representing this defamiliarization as an end in itself rather than as a means to some secondary mood or activity, Syntonic expanded the catalogue of *Environments*'s uses to include such "nonfunctional" activities as sensory exploration and aural contemplation. "Psychological," meet psychedelic.

The "Drugless Trip" in Psychedelic Art and Media Design

From today's perspective, the comically heady rhetoric of *Environments: Disc 2* reads nakedly as what Thomas Frank dubs "hip consumerism," a marketing strategy of rationalizing commodity consumption as rebellion.[43] From the series' beginning, Teibel packaged *Environments* for affluent adults who fashioned themselves as adventurous as Height-Ashbury or East Village "hippies." Emphasizing its youthfulness, Syntonic boasted hilariously on the LP's Atlantic release, "Teenagers are the record's biggest fans; they call it everything from 'the ultimate trip' to 'sensual rock.'" The way Syntonic speaks *about* teenagers, rather than addressing them directly, is telling; the idea, of course, was not to sell *to* youth so much as to sell a youth*ful* product to a mass market of upwardly mobile adult LP buyers.[44] With this in mind, Teibel's

[43] Hip advertisers, Thomas Frank argues, essentially rebranded '50s US liberalism's commitments to individualism and mass-culture skepticism as youthful; see Frank, *The Conquest of Cool: Business Culture, Counterculture, and the Rise of Hip Consumerism* (Chicago: University of Chicago Press, 1997), 9–17. Fred Turner traces this emphasis on individualism in the United States further back to antifascist mass media producers in the late 1930s; see Turner, *The Democratic Surround: Multimedia and American Liberalism from World War II to the Psychedelic Sixties* (Chicago: University of Chicago Press, 2013), 15–38.

[44] On the market orientation of LPs toward adult buyers in the postwar years, see Keir Keightley, "Long Play: Adult-Oriented Popular Music and the Temporal Logics of the Post-War Sound Recording Industry in the USA," *Media, Culture, and Society* 26, no. 3 (2004): 375–91.

discs might appear as glowing confirmation of some historians' thesis that the '60s counterculture's most lasting legacy has been the establishment of a reliably hip-hunting adult consumer base; San Francisco art historian Thomas Albright, for instance, proposes that "the real revolution of the 1960s was the transformation of practically everything—including the notion of 'revolution' itself—into a merchandisable commodity, in the service of an omnivorous consumerism."[45]

Environments and the hip consumerism it represents, however, may just as well be seen as a natural extension of the psychedelic counterculture's utopian political, social, and aesthetic investments, which largely derived from and thrived within the consumer culture the counterculture symbolically rejected. Although the counterculture's intrepid inner explorers regarded industrial-scale technologies with suspicion as "technocratic" agents of social management, many also found self-administered small-scale electronics potentially useful agents of social detachment, sensory contemplation, and communal attunement.[46] By 1970 consumer electronics like records and speakers had long been embraced by counterculture communalists antipathetic to large corporations and bureaucratic labor structures. Media consumption took symbolic and expressive forms that afforded imaginary retreats from "the Establishment," albeit in consort with commodities and their advertisements, not against them. Countercultural figureheads like Timothy Leary, Stewart Brand, and Marshall McLuhan spoke of "tuning in" to a new communal consciousness prepared by consumer technologies and home electronics. Teibel's "Syntonic Research" coinage captured this very idea of harmonization with the environment via electronic audio, for "syntonic" not only means "in tune" with or "tuned into" one's environment in a psychological sense, but it also once described, during the early years of wireless telegraphy, the mutual attunement of radio receivers and transmitters at particular frequencies.[47] Syntonic's

[45] Thomas Albright, *Art in the San Francisco Bay Area: 1945–1980* (Berkeley: University of California Press, 1985), 182. See also Joseph Heath and Andrew Potter, *Nation of Rebels: Why Counterculture Became Consumer Culture* (New York: HarperCollins, 2004).

[46] Fred Turner, *From Counterculture to Cyberculture: Stewart Brand, The Whole Earth Network, and the Rise of Digital Utopianism* (Chicago: University of Chicago Press, 2006), 11–102. Theodore Roszak coined the term "technocracy" to describe the organizational control of the military-industrial complex against which the countercultural individual rebels; see Theodore Roszak, *The Making of a Counter Culture: Reflections on the Technocratic Society and Its Youthful Opposition* (Berkeley: University of California Press, 1995), 5–6.

[47] Hugh G. J. Aitken, *Syntony and Spark: The Origins of Radio* (New York: John Wiley & Sons, 1976), 39–43.

psychedelic promotional concept and institutional posturing, far from a watered-down co-optation of "authentic" countercultural dissent from the outside, elaborated on existing countercultural practices of media design and commodification.[48]

Earlier in the '60s, McLuhan conceptualized this media-oriented countercultural praxis in recommending the creation and deployment of electronic "anti-environments" to retrain human perceptions of everyday reality.[49] Within the artistically designed anti-environment, McLuhan reasoned, electronics could appear in unfamiliar forms and contexts, drawing attention to the "psychic and social consequences of technology" by "provid[ing] us with the means of perceiving the environment itself."[50] Anti-environments, in other words, could undergird a countercultural praxis of dehabituating consumer perceptions of mass media by hijacking these media's own electronic means of involvement.

One may well regard *Environments* as a mass-reproduced, scaled-down variation of the psychedelic anti-environments that cropped up throughout the San Francisco Bay Area and New York City in the 1960s. Sometimes inspired by McLuhan's writings, and more often motivated by drug experience, psychedelic artists concocted mixed-media extravaganzas of amplified music and sound, abstract projections, and spinning lights with the intention of bringing inhabitants to contemplate the shared conditions of their altered perception. In the Bay Area alone, one could find ample opportunities for sensory revelation and wide-eared wonder through electronic sound, from spectacular surround-sound performance spaces such as Vortex and Audium, to lit-up events like the Trips Festival, rock concerts at the Fillmore West, happenings and performances put on by collectives like the San Francisco Tape Music Center and USCO, and Ken Kesey's and The Warlocks' freak-out experiments with tape delay and guitar feedback during Kesey's Acid Tests.[51] As historian Michael Kramer has written of the Acid Tests, such

[48] For further critiques of, and alternatives to, the co-optation narrative, see Richard Dyer, "In Defense of Disco," in *On Record: Rock, Pop, and the Written Word*, ed. Simon Frith and Andrew Goodwin (New York: Pantheon Books, 1990), 351–58; Phil Ford, *Dig: Sound and Music in Hip Culture* (New York: Oxford University Press, 2013); Frank, *The Conquest of Cool*; and Turner, *From Counterculture to Cyberculture*.

[49] Marshall McLuhan, *Understanding Media: The Extensions of Man*, 2nd ed. (New York: Mentor, 1964), viii–xi.

[50] McLuhan, *Understanding Media*, ix.

[51] On Vortex, see Cindy Keefer, "'Raumlichtmusik': Early 20th Century Abstract Cinema Immersive Environments," *Leonardo Electronic Almanac* 16, nos. 6–7 (2009). On the San Francisco

events provided opportunities for young US Americans "to experiment with new kinds of democratic assembly within an enigmatic swirl of extreme sonic and visual stimulation."[52] And while these events often courted psychedelic drug-taking, chemical experimentation was but one of many means of retooling the collective psyche. As historian Fred Turner describes, psychedelic "surrounds" were made to work, with or without the aid of drugs, to "shut down the analytical mind, awaken the unconscious, and allow individuals to come together in communities organized around a shared state of awareness."[53]

Much as Teibel would later, '60s anti-environmental practitioners across the Bay Area and New York City commonly proposed that their surrounds would deliver safe, legal, and participatory psychedelic experiences. For instance, although San Francisco writers Ken Kesey and Stewart Brand with SF Tape Center composer Ramon Sender first conceptualized their upcoming 1966 Trips Festival along the same lines as Kesey's Acid Tests, they eventually opted to advertise it less controversially as a "non-drug re-creation of a psychedelic experience." The handbill announced, with McLuhanite flair, that "the TRIP—or electronic performance—is a new medium of communication & entertainment."[54] The Festival itself stormed inhabitants' perceptions with torrents of amplified sounds that included thunder machines, psych rock jams by The Grateful Dead, and experimental free improvisations by composer-performers Pauline Oliveros and Don Buchla. Audience members also participated in the noisemaking, whether by unwittingly producing sounds for Kesey to record, amplify, and play back, or by bringing their own electronic "gadgets" for amplification.[55] Light projections, satirical theater productions, beat poetry readings, film screenings, and dance troupes rounded out the spectacle. No doubt aided by the innocuous allure of the "drugless trip," the event was massively popular, attracting over six-thousand

Tape Music Center, see Bernstein, *The San Francisco Tape Music Center*. On USCO, see Turner, *From Counterculture to Cyberculture*, 48–58; and Turner, *The Democratic Surround*, 284–89. On the Trips Festival, see Charles Perry, *The Haight-Ashbury: A History* (New York: Wenner, 2005), 39–48; Trevor Pinch and Frank Trocco, *Analog Days: The Invention and Impact of the Moog Synthesizer* (Cambridge, MA: Harvard University Press, 2002), 94–97. On Kesey, see Tom Wolfe, *The Electric Kool-Aid Test* (New York: Picador, 1968).

[52] Michael J. Kramer, *The Republic of Rock: Music and Citizenship in the Sixties Counterculture* (New York: Oxford University Press, 2013), 47.

[53] Turner, *The Democratic Surround*, 260.

[54] Pinch and Trocco, *Analog Days*, 95.

[55] Ibid.

admissions over the course of the weekend, and gaining coverage in magazines such as *Newsweek*, *Time*, and *Life*.

The Trips Festival anticipated waves of art-pop-crossing anti-environmental experimentation among psychedelic artists and scene-makers in Teibel's home of downtown Manhattan. Blending theater, sound, kinetic art, light art, and intermedia, these spectacles garnered large crowds and media attention as they fed hip audiences' appetites for audio amplification and the "enlarged" artistic experience.[56] A number of nightclubs and parties took on the aura of a mixed-means art happening: Andy Warhol's Exploding Plastic Inevitable from 1966–67 blended multiple film projections, strobe lighting, pop records, dancing, and intensely loud performances by The Velvet Underground and Nico into confrontationally disorienting mélanges.[57] The East Village's Electric Circus shortly thereafter combined rock and experimental electronic music with carnivalesque theater, lights, and projections, creating according to one *Life* reviewer "an experience total but temporary—a safe psychedelic."[58] In 1968, Ruffin Cooper Jr. and Richard Currie, in collaboration with various lighting designers, set designers, theater actors, music soundtracks, projections, and a fog machine, devised a Soho-based "loft party" called Cerebrum, in which visitors could pass through variously designed "platforms" or environments.[59]

One could also find similar experiments in the "total environment" taking place at small art galleries in California and New York: The Bay Area–based art collective USCO, short for "The Company of Us," toured the United States with wild surrounds of stroboscopic lights, electronic noise, and projections, bringing to audiences what *Life* magazine called a "drugless trip."[60] California artist James Turrell had meanwhile begun producing environmental light shows in gallery spaces by mirroring external light sources like neon signs, traffic lights, and the shadows of passing cars onto gallery space

[56] On the importance of the "enlarged" media experience to the New York counterculture, see John Gruen, *The New Bohemia* (New York: Grosset & Dunlap, 1966), 123–24.

[57] Branden W. Joseph, "'My Mind Split Open': Andy Warhol's Plastic Inevitable," in *Summer of Love: Psychedelic Art, Social Crisis and Counterculture in the 1960s*, ed. Christoph Grunenberg and Jonathan Harris, vol. 8, Tate Liverpool Critical Forum (Liverpool: Liverpool University Press, 2005), 239–59; Jean Wainwright, "Mediated Pain: Andy Warhol's Exploding Plastic Inevitable," in *Across the Great Divide: Modernism's Intermedialities, from Futurism to Fluxus*, ed. Christopher Townsend, Alex Trott, and Rhys Davies (Newcastle upon Tyne, UK: Cambridge Scholars Publishing, 2014), 158–86.

[58] John Stickney, "Non-Toxic Psychedelia for Squares," *Life*, August 11, 1967, 12.

[59] David Kaufman, *Ridiculous! The Theatrical Life and Times of Charles Ludlam* (New York: Applause Theatre & Cinema Books, 2002), 167–68.

[60] "Psychedelic Art," *Life*, September 9, 1966, 61.

walls, then mixing these images with light projections.[61] And in New York, Rudi Stern and Jackie Cassen had begun crafting "kinetic light" environments involving stroboscopic fountains of water, painted projections, and sound tunnels.[62] (Stern and Cassen, like USCO, would later be invited by the Museum of Contemporary Crafts to participate in the same Contemplation Environments exhibition as Teibel.)

It might seem a stretch to compare *Environments*'s relatively tame sonic atmospheres to such audiovisual spectaculars. Whereas '60s anti-environments summoned collectives to revel in gaga multimedia simultaneity, exploded formal deconstructions, raucous rock, and alien geometries, Syntonic's *Environments* helped consumers amplify their domestic solitude with quiet, steady-state sonic images of nature, creating comfort just as would the "wallpaper, sofa, or air conditioner."[63] Perhaps the anti-environmental energies of psychedelic youth were more directly transmitted by the drugless trips of Jimi Hendrix's *Electric Ladyland* or Pink Floyd's *Atom Heart Mother*. Teibel's records, however, scaled and domesticated the psychedelic counterculture's synesthetic, acid-fueled practices of disorientation into a cozily familiar, digestible, and "safe" experience of psychedelic immersion for both hip youth *and* the hip-hopeful high-middlebrow hi-fi audiophile. *Environments*'s discreet and tasteful design neatly and inclusively packaged the introspective ideals and disaffiliative ethics of the '60s psychedelic counterculture for the broader, not necessarily communalist US middle-class market.

Environments's sales pitch arrived at the forefront of a larger trend in the 1970s and '80s United States of selling personal media for relaxation and self-connection to an assumed white middle-class adult mainstream. Self-help books, guides to meditation and yoga, and other such therapeutic media promoted what cultural studies scholar Sam Binkley calls a "softer mode of self-discovery" than that provided by the mixed-media environments and loud rock of unruly '60s youths.[64] Teibel's strategy to position the records between hip countercultural and middlebrow adult orientations forecasted this consolidation of a growing submarket of environmentally friendly, mostly liberal

61 "View from Hill and Main," *Newsweek*, October 27, 1969, 111.

62 Allan Katzman, "As the Crow Flies," *The East Village Other*, January 1–15, 1968, 9.

63 S. K. Oberbeck, "Sonic Tonic," *Newsweek*, November 10, 1969, 127.

64 Sam Binkley, *Getting Loose: Lifestyle Consumption in the 1970s* (Durham, NC: Duke University Press, 2007), 34.

high-middlebrow consumers—who would later be dubbed, sometimes derisively, "new age" or "yuppie"—as a target demographic for such products.

Given the presumption of this market's whiteness among promoters, it bears mentioning that *Environments* emerged at the tail end of the "white flight" of white US American urbanites to the quietude of the suburbs. *Environments* can be understood, relative to this context at the turn of the '70s, as a technologized substitute for white flight, given its ability to produce depoliticized private spaces for urban dwellers amid ongoing demands for political recognition among racial and ethnic minorities.[65] *Environments*'s nature-based "white noise," from this perspective, may have presented white consumers a symbolic retreat from the "black noise" of cultural and political expressions rooted in Black American identity.[66]

Teibel's promotional rhetoric also took advantage of changing attitudes toward cannabis within the white US American middle class. Despite Syntonic's assertions to the contrary, *Environments*'s promotion as a "drugless trip" permitted the possibility of its usefulness as an accompaniment to "high times," profiting off what one *Life* journalist in 1967 called "[t]he greatest mass flouting of the law since Prohibition"—the popularization of cannabis as a recreational drug.[67] Prior to the mid-'60s, middle-class US adults generally associated pot with the Black working class and unruly "beatniks"; but over the latter half of the decade the flower gained respectability among middle-class liberals by way of acceptance among white college students, bohemians, and rock musicians. By the end of the '60s, cannabis would become familiar to many adults who would never trek to Woodstock, let alone the Trips Festival; a Summer 1970 article on the trend estimated that 25–30 million Americans would have had some experience with weed by the end of the year.[68] *Environments*'s promotional design played into this trend. Although Teibel advertised *Environments* as "safer than pot," various users got the message encoded in its splendid record jackets and psychedelic rhetoric that the records might be used in conjunction with the drug; as one

[65] On the relationship between audio technologies' production of personal space and race, see Hagood, *Hush*, 177–219.

[66] I borrow "black noise" from hip-hop scholar Tricia Rose, who uses it to describe how expressions of Black American youths are othered as "noise"; see Tricia Rose, *Black Noise: Rap Music and Black Culture in Contemporary America*, Music Culture (Hanover, NH: Wesleyan University Press, 1994).

[67] Albert Rosenfeld, "Marijuana: Millions of Turned-On Users," *Life*, July 7, 1967, 17. See also Lee, *Smoke Signals*.

[68] Sam Blum, "Marijuana Clouds the Generation Gap," *New York Times Magazine*, August 23, 1970, 29.

user told Syntonic on a feedback card, *Environments* should be played "inside with friends smoking a joint."[69] Such associations did not always find favor with *Environments*'s buyers, as evidenced by one self-described "prude" from Montana who wrote to Syntonic that the record jackets "gave [my friends] the idea I was into hypnotism or purchased this at a pot party."[70] Public opinion remained divided on cannabis long after the '60s, and this division cut through *Environments*'s consumer base. Nonetheless, by the early '70s, word had spread via mainstream media that marijuana was, by most scientific accounts, a technology of consciousness less addictive than alcohol and prescription pills. The trend worked in Teibel's favor.

In addition, Teibel's promotional strategy responded to a growing demand in the 1970s for more accessible and less invasive alternatives to pharmaceuticals. Distrust of psychiatry, and of tranquilizers in particular, had fomented from several corners of the United States and Europe throughout the '60s.[71] Scientific studies had exposed the addictive character of several popular prescription sedatives, and prominent articles attested to the staggering rates of tranquilizer consumption at the time.[72] For the hip (and hip-aspiring), meanwhile, the stereotypical pill-popping housewife represented the pinnacle of unthinking conformity; tranquilizer takers, more and more nonusers suspected, were "tuning out" the realities of the world.[73] Syntonic's subdued psychedelia rebutted the dutiful mindlessness assumed of the sedative-popping ice queen, presenting a more "natural" and nonaddictive ataractic for consumers who aspired to be more attuned to the world—and more rational—than these feminized "pillheads."

Evidently not wanting to be outdone, the record label Audio Fidelity, which had made a name for itself in the 1950s and '60s as a leader in stereophonic sound-effects records, chased the hip potential of *Environments* by releasing knockoffs *Ambience One* and *Ambience Two*, both subtitled *An Adventure in Environmental Sound*, in August 1970. The *Ambience* records, recorded "on location" by producer Eddie Newmark, almost exactly copied the *Environments*

[69] Questionnaire completed by K. Brown for Syntonic Research, Inc., date unknown. Archived by Syntonic Research, Inc.

[70] Correspondence from R. Fishburn to Syntonic Research, Inc., May 18, 1983. Archived by Syntonic Research, Inc.

[71] On antipsychiatry sentiments in the 1960s and '70s, see Martin Halliwell, *Therapeutic Revolutions: Medicine, Psychiatry, and American Culture, 1945–1970* (New Brunswick, NJ: Rutgers University Press, 2013), 267–70; Ido Hartogsohn, *American Trip: Set, Setting, and the Psychedelic Experience in the Twentieth Century* (Cambridge, MA: MIT Press, 2020), 231–41.

[72] Tone, "Tranquilizers on Trial," 170.

[73] Ibid., 171.

design concept, with full-side recordings of ocean waves, birdsong, a field, and a fireplace purposed, according to the packaging, for "relaxation and renewal" and to help users "talk, make love, eat, sleep, study, think . . . the uses are infinite."[74] Also like Syntonic, Audio Fidelity sought to "bridge the generation gap" with *Ambience*'s psychedelic hipness; press releases boasted the records' appeal to "college" and "other progressive areas" while hinting vaguely that the albums, played at different speeds, can produce "different, fascinating sounds."[75] *Environments*, however, far outlasted *Ambience*, in part thanks to Atlantic's broader distribution during the series' early years, but also thanks to *Environments*'s superior, and indeed hipper, visual and audio design.

Environments's coy visual design presciently established a market orientation across the "loose" hip counterculture and "safe" square middlebrow. Despite its psychedelic premise, its visual aesthetic contrasted sharply with the "ragged" unevenness of underground late-'60s graphic design, or the florid contours of the psychedelic rock poster (and, increasingly, of youth-targeted hip marketing), tempering these signifiers of unbounded spontaneity with contained corporate sheen.[76] Its streamlined, hard-edged layout more nearly abided by standards of modernist European graphic design that most professional or "aboveground" US American designers had adopted by the late 1960s.[77] The clean rows of text conveyed the calculating rationality of mass culture's stereotyped organization man, delivering a straight-laced sales pitch as the title winks at the customer in bright, bold colors. With sumptuously large nature photographs buttressing titles in all-lowercase Helvetica—a corporate typeface if there ever was one—and, of course, the seal of Syntonic Research, Inc.'s approval, the records literally wore on their sleeves their status as hip commodities.[78]

Environments's approach to product packaging, from the naïve perspective of 1960s hip advertising and underground design, might have been seen as confused.[79] Yet the records' utilitarian look added a sly, knowing, and modern edge to the soft romantic vision of nature and personal retreat they

[74] "Audio Fidelity Plans Series on Environment," *Billboard* 82, no. 85 (June 20, 1970), 66.

[75] "AF Sets Its Own 'Environments' LPs," *Cash Box*, June 20, 1970, 12.

[76] Lorraine Wild and David Karwan, "Agency and Urgency: The Medium and Its Message," in *Hippie Modernism: The Struggle for Utopia*, ed. Andrew Blauvelt (New York: Distributed Art Publishers, 2015), 46.

[77] Wild and Karwan, "Agency and Urgency," 46–47.

[78] Design historian Lars Müller calls Helvetica the "ultimate corporate typeface of the '60s and '70s"; see Lars Müller, *Helvetica: Homage to a Typeface* (Baden, Switzerland: Lars Müller, 2002), n. pag.

[79] Frank, *The Conquest of Cool*, 50, 93.

proposed, elevating the irony at the heart of the *Environments* project: After all, while the records proposed to reunite users with the natural world shut out of their homes, they would at the same time accommodate users to their isolation from nature, and even reinforce it by providing immersive sonic seclusion. The overtly manufactured professionalism of *Environments*'s visual design shrewdly incorporated this irony, symbolically resolving the apparent contradiction between romantic environmentalism and modern functionalism by illustrating the former's containment by the latter. While its sounds harken for the return of nature lost, restoring a romantic vision of wholeness that has become irreparably damaged by modernization, Syntonic's presentation at the same time acknowledges through cool abstraction the technologized world from which the records really come.[80] This abstraction, which made the records familiarly "functional" from a modern design perspective, extended an olive branch to hip consumers, symbolizing what musicologist Phil Ford calls the "ironic consciousness" of the Cold War hipster in bracketing and providing a vantage on "the system."[81]

Environments's studied ambivalence between the organic and manufactured, increasingly a feature of late-1960s and '70s underground countercultural design, had precedents in earlier atmospheric music and media sold to a hip-aspirant mass middle class.[82] Most notably, as Joseph Lanza has detailed, easy-listening psychedelic pop during the mid–late 1960s brought "trippy" production effects and arrangements to the orchestral easy-listening idiom. In keeping with the colorful times, producers and arrangers introduced unusual instruments, mysterious timbres, and surreal production effects to conventional pop song structures and arrangements of familiar tunes. In doing so, they struck a balance "between psychological mayhem and peace of mind" to match the ethos of the psychedelic era without alienating "middle-of-the-road" tastes.[83]

Meanwhile, when British engineer Edward Craven Walker invented and sold the lava lamp as a novelty decoration in 1964, his original inspiration was the swinger's cocktail glass; only later did the lava lamp became

[80] On romanticism and environmental holism, see Timothy Morton, *Ecology without Nature: Rethinking Environmental Aesthetics* (Cambridge, MA: Harvard University Press, 2007), esp. 14, 22.

[81] Ford, *Dig*, 63–67 and 121–26.

[82] On the appropriation of "professional" aesthetics in late 1960s and '70s underground design, see Wild and Karwan, "Agency and Urgency," 48–57.

[83] Joseph Lanza, *Easy Listening Acid Trip: An Elevator Ride through Sixties Psychedelic Pop* (Port Townsend, WA: Feral House, 2020), 24.

connected to the counterculture, with Walker himself pronouncing, "If you buy my lamp, you won't need drugs."[84] The novelty decorative item, as art historian Jennifer L. Roberts explains, provided a container for the counterculture's plasmic aesthetics, creating a simultaneously fluid and mechanistic design, internally boundless yet bottled from without.[85] A similarly contained fluidity could be found in the design concept for audio system psychedelic lighting units, which small manufacturers advertised in popular music and hobbyist electronic magazines later that decade. Users could attach to their hi-fis "color organs" that would move colored-light projections in response to the pitch content, bass, or drums, lighting a space as unpredictably as the music flowed while being yet limited by the few included colors. The devices' manufacturers imagined their consumers to be "timid adults" who wanted to "feel swingy, with never the risk of getting busted."[86] Such visual designs, like *Environments*'s, captured the "swingy" safety of the drugless trip by expressively integrating the natural and artificial, spontaneous and planned, organic and abstract, mysterious and rational, open and bounded.

The controlled looseness of *Environments*'s visual design matched the contained randomness of the recordings' spare audio designs. In the case of *Tintinnabulation*, the timbral spectrum, texture, pitch content, and dynamic range are all consistently constrained from the outset, permitting listeners to predict (and if desired, ignore) how the recording would continue to sound over its length. The pitch, loudness, timing, and duration of each subsequent bell strike, however, happens unpredictably; even the pitch content of each constituent bell strike sounds ambiguous due to the abundant inharmonic overtones in each. As with the visual design, global invariabilities in the audio contain localized spontaneity, producing an expressively ambivalent "loose control" for the presumed hip middlebrow listener. This combination of control and unpredictability in *Tintinnabulation*'s psychedelic design, as I discuss in this chapter's concluding sections, likewise characterized concurrent expressive practices and promotional rhetoric by avant-garde musicians whose trippy psychoactive sounds, not unlike Teibel's middlebrow-market

[84] Stephen van Dulken, *Inventing the 20th Century: 100 Inventions That Shaped the World* (London: The British Library, 2000), 156.

[85] Jennifer L. Roberts, "Lucubrations on a Lava Lamp: Technocracy, Counterculture, and Containment in the American Sixties," in *American Artifacts: Essays in Material Culture*, ed. Jules David Prown and Kenneth Haltman (East Lansing: Michigan State University Press, 2000), 167–89.

[86] Len Buckwalter, "The Eerie World of Psychedelic Lights," *Elementary Electronics*, November–December 1968, 105.

missives, formed bridges between the art world and a nascent market of hip high-middlebrow adult consumers.

Selling Recorded Minimalism as Ambient Audio

Inside the '60s NYC Experimental Underground's Meditative Drones

Although *Environments* shared a design concept of the immersive drugless trip with the dizzying anti-environments of the '60s psychedelic counterculture, its stripped-down audio designs promoted a more unimodal and probative form of sensory contemplation than did these Bay Area and NYC-based multimedia extravaganzas. The automated, homogeneous, and spare sound of *Tintinnabulation*, especially, came closer to the drone- and loop-based music cultivated by a loosely affiliated network of contemporaneous composers of these same cities' experimental avant-gardes. Artists such as La Monte Young, Terry Riley, Pauline Oliveros, Tony Conrad, Walter De Maria, Charlemagne Palestine, and Steve Reich in various ways used drone and automated repetition to make music out of extremely prolonged minimal units of sound. The technologized techniques of durational extension in this "hypnotic" school of composition promoted awareness of sound's vibrational presence within the body and afforded listeners psychoacoustic and sensory exploration.[87] The long drone and continuous loop, later understood as "minimalist" compositional techniques, likewise lent *Tintinnabulation* (as with much later ambient music) to such contemplative uses.[88]

La Monte Young, widely considered today one of minimalism's primary originators, found footing in his explorations of the psychedelic affordances of audio technology. Departing from the formalism of his serialist compositional training, Young in the late 1950s began experimenting with loud sustained sounds in order to get "inside" them and "experience another world."[89] Through such pieces as *2 Sounds* (1960), in which three (!) simple

[87] On early uses of the term "hypnotic" to describe minimalist music and its composers, see Edward Strickland, *Minimalism: Origins* (Bloomington: Indiana University Press, 1993), 242–43.

[88] Timothy Johnson most explicitly describes minimalist musics in terms of compositional technique; see Timothy Johnson, "Minimalism: Aesthetic, Style, or Technique?," *The Musical Quarterly* 78, no. 4 (1994): 742–73.

[89] La Monte Young, "Lecture 1960," *Tulane Drama Review* 10, no. 2 (1965): 81.

sustained sounds are played continuously on separate speakers, Young found that amplified drones could provide immersive aural environments in which listeners could observe their own embodied audition,[90] much in the same way psychedelic users, according to Timothy Leary, directly sense "the processes which physicists and biochemists and neurologists measure."[91] Starting around 1963, Young helped organize The Theater of Eternal Music, a group of musicians who probed these processes through constrained micro-tonal drone improvisations. Group members included calligrapher, vocalist, and lifelong partner Marian Zazeela; as well as composer/performers Terry Riley, John Cale, Angus MacLise, and future Teibel-commissioner Tony Conrad. The group's efforts to "get inside" the sounds were aided by amplification starting in 1964, Zazeela's magenta lights and calligraphic shadows in 1965, and cannabis before every show.[92] For the performers, marijuana seemed to ease access to the vibrational properties of sound; as Young put it, the drug "allows you to go within yourself and focus on certain frequency relationships and memory relationships in a very, very interesting way."[93] Young went on to obsessively explore microtonal frequency ratios as a means of accessing higher or transcendent realities. His work manifested ethnomusicologist Alain Daniélou's proposition in a 1966 issue of *Psychedelic Review* that certain frequency ratios in music may produce "cosmic" revelations of what lies beyond the threshold of perception, revelations that may have "considerable effects on our psycho-physiological condition."[94]

A nearer precedent for *Tintinnabulation* from the New York hypnotic underground may be found in the early work of Charlemagne Palestine, a drone enthusiast who got his start in sonic immersion by improvising on the twenty-six-bell carillon in Midtown's St. Thomas Episcopal Church between 1963 and 1970. Palestine now recalls how playing the gargantuan bells closely to his body introduced him to the "physical, visceral" side of sound; recordings from 1965 evince his interest in creating droning reverberation through repetition, and in the rhythmic and vibrational patterning emergent from their combination, both aspects of the Balinese and Javanese gamelan

[90] Grimshaw, *Draw a Straight Line and Follow It*, 75.

[91] Timothy Leary, "The Religious Experience: Its Production and Interpretation," *Psychedelic Review* 1, no. 3 (1964): 328–29; as quoted in Grimshaw, *Draw a Straight Line and Follow It*, 94.

[92] Keith Potter, *Four Musical Minimalists: La Monte Young, Terry Riley, Steve Reich, Philip Glass*, Music in the Twentieth Century (New York: Cambridge University Press, 2000), 67.

[93] Potter, *Four Musical Minimalists*, 67.

[94] Alain Daniélou, "The Influence of Sound Phenomena on Human Consciousness," trans. Paul Huebner and Ralph Metzner, *Psychedelic Review* 7 (1966): 21, 26.

music that at the time beguiled Palestine.[95] (Tony Conrad, upon hearing Palestine's carillon improvisations in 1969, asked him to play the bells for *Coming Attractions.*) Palestine also began diving into dense, dissonant pipe organ drones around this time, creating several-hour-long performances of what he called "meditative sound environments" that, as he has described with characteristic rhapsody, generated "sonorous continuums lush dense internal rhythms only tone against tone beatings overtones helmholtz would orgasm. . . ."[96]

At the NYU School of the Arts Intermedia Program, meanwhile, Palestine was creating drone environments with the Buchla synthesizer, experimentation that he likened to "real space travel."[97] These activities led Palestine to write a letter directly to Syntonic Research in January 1970 on behalf of the Intermedia program:

> Some of us are working with Sound Environments which a company like yours might find interesting. We are examining the physical effects of sound on listeners using various sound stimuli. For example, Mood Environments, created electronically, and Natural Environments. We also have many ideas dealing with the future of the Sound Environment which might be of interest to you.[98]

A collaboration with Teibel never came to fruition, though the two did become casual acquaintances, with Teibel visiting Palestine at the carillon, and with the two even touring the ARP synthesizer factory together.[99] While Palestine today does not recall speaking with Teibel about the significant overlap between their practices, his retrospection of his time at the NYU Intermedia program certainly resonates with Teibel's stated claims for *Tintinnabulation*: "I was makingggg droness also a meditative sound to transcend the racketttyyycrackkketttyyy of the big citiess,, we were imagininggg alternativessszzz!!"[100]

95 Charlemagne Palestine, sleeve notes to Charlemagne Palestine, *Bells Studies*, Alga Marghen alga049, 2015, LP; Charlemagne Palestine, interview with author, August 8, 2016.

96 Charlemagne Palestine, "Charlemagne Palestine" (unpublished manuscript, 1997). Palestine refers here to Hermann von Helmholtz (1821–94), whose book, *On the Sensations of Tone as a Physiological Basis for the Theory of Music* (1862), influentially demonstrated that musical tones are comprised composed of multiple constituent frequency waves.

97 Palestine, "Charlemagne Palestine."

98 Correspondence from Charlemagne Palestine to Syntonic Research, Inc., January 12, 1970. Archived by Syntonic Research, Inc.

99 Charlemagne Palestine, email message to author, July 4, 2016.

100 Charlemagne Palestine, email message to author, August 8, 2016.

Palestine and Young, despite the relative austerity of their drones, shared with the environmental trips of the psychedelic counterculture a fascination with the mind-altering effects of corporeal ensconcement in patterned sound. Yet while most "downtown" experimental composers like Young showed little interest in becoming part of the classical music establishment, they also commonly distanced their own pop-informed practices from jazz and rock, maintaining their music's art-world credibility while disavowing commercial motivation. "Even the minimalists . . . knew which side their music stood on," as critic and composer Kyle Gann recalls. "[T]he poverty of avant-garde musicians became a badge of integrity."[101] Listeners and promoters less invested in art-world orthodoxies, however, recognized the hypnotic effects of sonic drone and looping repetition in avant-garde minimalism as occupying the same sonic and psychological territory as mass-market head music.

The Man Can't Bust Our Minimalism

When John McClure, director of Columbia's flagship classical brand Columbia Masterworks, in 1967 first witnessed the music of La Monte Young and his experimental contemporaries, McClure was both struck by its resemblance to psychedelic rock and yet "shocked" to find rock artists and writers better informed on the topic than he.[102] He set out to establish a new series, titled "Music of Our Time," as a showcase for avant-garde contemporary music, and hired experimental composer David Behrman to produce the series. The two imagined that Music of Our Time could attract both classical buyers exploring beyond the canon as well as college students with a taste for underground rock.[103] "Musical tastes were changing fast," Behrman recalls. "It was clear to executives who ran record companies that new 'hits' appealing to young people were liable to break out from unknown sources."[104] It had also become clear to Behrman that the entrancing loop-based music

[101] Kyle Gann, *American Music in the Twentieth Century* (New York: Schirmer, 1997), 291, 293. See also Richard Taruskin, "A Harmonious Avant-Garde?," in *The Oxford History of Western Music*, vol. 6: *Music in the Late Twentieth-Century* (New York: Oxford University Press, 2005), 391–92.

[102] Michael Hicks, "Mass Marketing the American Avant-Garde, 1967–1971," *American Music* 35, no. 3 (2017): 283.

[103] "Trendsetters Examine New Trends in Classical Music," *Billboard*, October 8, 1966, 52.

[104] David Behrman, "Music of Our Time," liner notes to John Cage/Morton Feldman, *Music for Keyboard 1935–1948/The Early Years*, New World Records 80664-2, 2007, CD.

of composers Steve Reich and Terry Riley had hit (and hip) potential, and so Columbia packaged and marketed Reich's *Come Out* (composed 1966, released by Columbia in 1967) and Riley's *In C* (composed 1964, released 1968) as cutting-edge, psychedelic, and anti-establishmentarian sounds for young adult buyers.

Steve Reich's *Come Out*, now regarded as a milestone in the minimalist music canon, was first introduced to the record buying public in November 1967 through the *New Sounds in Electronic Music* LP, one of seven Music of Our Time records released that month on Columbia's classical budget line Odyssey. Two thousand copies went out to stores—a wide net relative to most experimentalists' limited pressings at that point. Reich's piece followed Richard Maxfield's *Night Music* (1960), an antiphony of furiously squawking sawteeth, on Side A; on the flip, Pauline Oliveros's *I of IV* (1966) featured square waves howling against the distant moaning of tape-delayed combination tones. All three pieces exploited looping tape to create spectacular, vertiginous, and often unpredictable stereo effects. Columbia's description on the back insinuated that young rock listeners were the targets for these electronic missives. "An entire generation has grown up with the sound of amplified guitars, reverb, tape delay and electronic synthesizers in its ears," it read. "Each work bears the mark of an original musical personality of the new 'electronic' generation."[105]

Columbia's *New Sounds* represented just one of many efforts by classical labels to peddle avant-garde electronic sounds to hip youth during the late '60s. By the middle of 1968, labels like Vanguard and Limelight were also cross-marketing recorded music by such avant-garde composers as Charles Ives, Edgard Varèse, John Cage, Pierre Henry, and Karlheinz Stockhausen through progressive rock radio and music magazines.[106] Columbia's print advertisements were perhaps the most overtly youth-baiting as they clumsily adopted the progressivism of the spreading counterculture to appeal to potential consumers' hipness. "ELECTRONIC AND OTHER SOUNDS OF THE FUTURE—TODAY!" cried out one Music of Our Time advertisement. "It takes cool to appreciate today's 'new' music," ventured another (see Fig. 1.6). The trend hit a peak in early 1969, when Columbia released its notoriously trying-too-hard "But The Man Can't Bust Our Music" ad in

[105] Liner notes to *New Sounds in Electronic Music* by Steve Reich, Richard Maxfield, and Pauline Oliveros, Odyssey, 32 16 0160, 1967, LP.
[106] Hicks, "Mass Marketing the American Avant-Garde," 291.

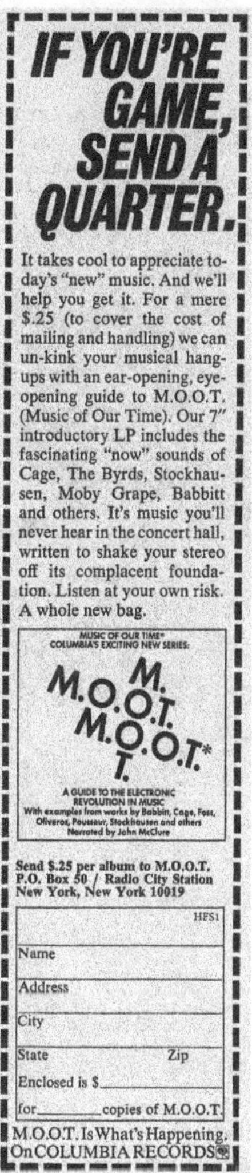

Figure 1.6. "It takes cool to appreciate today's 'new' music." Music of Our Time advertisement. (*Hi-Fi / Stereo Review*, March 1968, 118.)

Rolling Stone (Fig 1.7).[107] The full-page spread depicted six jailed college-age protesters jamming out, evidently, to the likes of Ives and Stockhausen. "The Establishment's against adventure," it read, which was why readers should "arm" themselves with Ives's "ear-shaking portraits of great dissenters" and Varèse's "musical anarchy." Also featured in the ad: Terry Riley's *In C*, with

[107] *Rolling Stone*, March 1, 1969, 27.

Figure 1.7. "But The Man can't bust our music." Music of Our Time advertisement. (*Rolling Stone*, March 1, 1969, 27.)

a caption calling the record "The only legal trip you can take. A hypnotic sound experience."

Despite the ridicule rock fans mounted on Columbia's campaign, Riley's record sold remarkably well, and is generally considered to be minimalism's first major market success. Although it wouldn't match the unprecedented sales of Wendy Carlos's *Switched-On Bach* LP, concurrently released on Columbia Masterworks, *In C* still sold in the tens of thousands, finding such broad crossover appeal that composer Robert Carl has referred to it as the "second premiere" of the piece.[108] The sales further demonstrated heads' special interest in the music of the "hypnotic" school, as already evidenced by Reich's largely bohemian crowds at the Soho Park Place Gallery and Riley's all-night improv shows at clubs like The Electric Circus.[109] Audiences in New York and San Francisco did not need Columbia's heavy-handed rhetoric to clarify these composers' relevance to the countercultural worldview, but Columbia's promotion did afford Riley and Reich purchase in a formative minimalist canon.[110]

The Music of Our Time series, as musicologist Michael Hicks points out, presciently identified in the art of recorded electronic music the possibility for crossover and synthesis across art/pop divisions, particularly thanks to the music's design-based resemblance to painting and sculpture.[111] But the old divisions proved strong. Music of Our Time ceased toward the end of 1970 as Columbia shifted their marketing budget toward the more lucrative fields of song-based pop and rock. Reich and Riley meanwhile edged away from association with rock as critics began calling the composers' music "minimalist," borrowing the tag, not coincidentally, from an existing movement in painting and sculpture. Over the 1970s, Reich and Riley's art-world associations gradually superseded those that they had forged in the prior decade with the psychedelic counterculture. Yet as Columbia's campaign shows—and as rock audiences recognized—much "minimalist" music first came into its own as psychedelic ambience.

Designing Minimalist Records as Ambient Audio

Columbia, like Reich and Riley themselves, located the value of their drone- and repetition-based records in the sounds' psychoactive effects. Like Teibel with *Tintinnabulation* later, Columbia pitched Reich and Riley's minimalist drones and loops as gateways to altered consciousness. Understood within the framework of recorded audio design, rather than the work-oriented

[108] Thom Holmes, *Electronic and Experimental Music: Technology, Music, and Culture*, 3rd ed. (New York: Routledge, 2008), 219; Robert Carl, *Terry Riley's* In C, Studies in Musical Genesis, Structure, and Interpretation (New York: Oxford University Press, 2009), 71–96.

[109] Ross Cole, "'Sound Effects (O.K., Music)': Steve Reich and the Visual Arts in New York City, 1966–1968," *Twentieth-Century Music* 11, no. 2 (2014): 217–44, especially 234; Potter, *Four Musical Minimalists*, 134.

[110] Hicks, "Mass Marketing the American Avant-Garde," 295; see also Carl, *Terry Riley's* In C.

[111] Hicks, "Mass Marketing the American Avant-Garde," 296.

interpretive frame standard to most art music scholarship, these pieces may be found commensurate with *Environments* on the basis of their shared minimalist designs and psychedelic affordances.[112] This concluding section explores the continuities in rhetoric and audio design alike between Reich and Riley's early minimalist records and *Tintinnabulation*, regrouping and reframing these records together through their shared realization of droning and repetitive sounds as ambient audio.

In the mid-'60s, Reich's own writings surrounding his tape-loop-based music—which Reich framed as "process music"—often referred to the music's psychoactive effects. The composer's notes for *Come Out* on the *New Sounds* LP, for instance, describe listening experiences of discovering acoustic, compositional, and performed minutiae that often go unnoticed when focusing on formal, semantic, or expressive features: "By restricting oneself to a small amount of material organized by a single uninterrupted process," Reich wrote, "one's attention can become focused on details that usually slip by." Reich's landmark 1966 essay "Music as a Gradual Process" described these details as the "psycho-acoustic byproducts" and "mysteries" of listening to music based on "gradual processes" like loops slowly phasing out of sync.[113] Although he never used the word "automation," Reich pointed out that the perception of such minutiae becomes possible thanks to the cognitive certainty instilled by a transparently automated piece of music. As a result, Reich wrote, listeners may simply ignore the composer's intentions, and instead turn toward details "occurring for their own acoustic reasons" like tonal density, textural grain, overtone structure, rhythmic patterning, and fleeting micro-melodies.[114] Reduction and automation, in short, afford listeners awareness of the sound's vibrational materiality and psychoacoustic effects.

This is hardly to say that Reich's music circumvented any sort of affect or meaning. On the contrary, the gradual processes carefully crafted by Reich

[112] The approach echoes Robert Fink's comparison of 1960s and '70s pulse-pattern minimalism with "barococo" and disco record listening; see Robert Fink, *Repeating Ourselves: American Minimal Music as Cultural Practice* (Berkeley: University of California Press, 2005), chapters 1 and 4. Other notable exceptions to work-oriented hermeneutic interpretation be found in Robert Carl's and Cecilia Sun's examinations of recordings of Riley's *In C*, in which both note these records' connections to the countercultural youth market; see Carl, *Terry Riley's* In C, 71–96 and Appendix; Cecilia Sun, "Experiments in Musical Performance: Historiography, Politics, and the Post-Cagian Avant-Garde" (PhD Dissertation, University of California, Los Angeles, 2004), 144–210.

[113] Steve Reich, "Music as a Gradual Process," in *Writings on Music, 1965–2000*, ed. Paul Hillier (New York: Oxford University Press, 2002), 35.

[114] Reich, "Music as a Gradual Process," 35.

and his "minimalist" contemporaries generate potentially rich hermeneutic possibilities.[115] Minimalism scholar Sumanth Gopinath, for instance, has detailed how *Come Out*'s multiplicative splitting of Harlem Six member Daniel Hamm's voice from one to two stereo-separated tracks, then again from two to four, then four to eight, has the potential to be heard as symbolizing a movement from Hamm's individual oppression to Black urban collectivization.[116] The unhappy entropy resulting from the interaction between Hamm's speech and the phasing process also generates a paranoid affect that, as one *Billboard* record reviewer described, can come across "relentlessly disturbing."[117] This paranoia, Gopinath explains, may be heard as capturing a political "structure of feeling" around the criminalization of African American men in the 1960s, a historically particular mood that continues to resonate forcefully with the United States' long history of anti-Black racism and violence.[118]

Despite these lasting resonances, however, discourses surrounding the piece from the mid-1960s into the '70s indicate that contemporaries more readily heard *Come Out* as a springboard to unusual personal experiences rather than to political understandings. Reich's own introduction on the *New Sounds* LP positions Hamm's trial as mere pretext to a peculiar auditory experience of the listener improvising with hearing: "At any given moment," Reich concludes, "it is open to the listener as to which pattern within the pattern he hears."[119] Some early reviewers of the piece also found its transformative perceptual effects a more pertinent takeaway than its political meanings. Fellow tape music composer Tod Dockstader in 1968, for instance, dismissed the piece's political content while praising how it brings the listener out of "clock" time "into a very non-European time experience."[120] Alan Rich, in a 1970 *New York Magazine* concert review, similarly wrote how *Come Out* brought him into an ecstatic state that allowed him to observe himself in the process of "examining, almost as an outsider, what was going on inside my head—the

115 See, for instance, Rebecca Leydon, "Towards a Typology of Minimalist Tropes," *Music Theory Online* 8, no. 4 (2002).

116 Sumanth Gopinath, "The Problem of the Political in Steve Reich's 'Come Out,'" in *Sound Commitments: Avant-Garde Music and the Sixties*, ed. Robert Adlington (New York & Oxford: Oxford University Press, 2009), 136–37.

117 "Album Reviews," *Billboard*, November 25, 1967, 47.

118 Gopinath, "The Problem of the Political," 138.

119 Liner notes to *New Sounds in Electronic Music* by Steve Reich, Richard Maxfield, and Pauline Oliveros, Odyssey 32 16 0160, 1967, LP.

120 Tod Dockstader, review of *New Sounds in Electronic Music* (LP), *Electronic Music Review*, July 1968, 33.

same sort of thing I found myself doing, almost like a census-taker, the first time I turned on."[121] Such descriptions emphasized the sounds' impact on the process of perception, depicting Reich's sounds as providing new angles on listening, space, time, and self, and as opening fields of focus beyond the habitual. The techniques that make *Come Out* hermeneutically rich, it turns out, also afford listeners a sort of sensory introspection normally passed over on the way to meaning.

Some musicologists have similarly noted how Reich's automated techniques of looping and phasing direct listeners beyond externalized sonic details toward their own bodily responsiveness to sound. Martin Scherzinger, with reference to *Come Out*'s predecessor *It's Gonna Rain*, has called this shift from formal and semiotic discernment to the visceral feeling of vibration in time a "phenomenological reversal" at the core of minimalist music listening.[122] Kerry O'Brien has likewise explained how Reich implicitly understood process-based listening as similar to yogic breathing in its ability to put participants in touch with their own bodies.[123] In Carolyn Abbate's broader terms, Reich's drone- and loop-based music can be understood to lead the listener astray from "gnostic" reflection upon musical meaning, and toward the "drastic" sensory epiphany of music's taking place through or upon oneself.[124] It calls attention to the embodied nature of perception and feeling-in-the-making.

Terry Riley thought about his loops similarly. For Riley, minimalist techniques like droning and looping were more interesting for their capacity to act as an "opening toward consciousness" than for their ability to generate unique compositional forms.[125] Columbia overtly promoted this dynamically introspective aspect of loop-based listening on the back cover of Riley's 1968 *In C* release (Fig. 1.8), which featured an extensive introduction to the piece by Paul Williams, editor-in-chief of germinal underground rock rag *Crawdaddy!* Here, Williams pays special attention to the listener's sense of embodiment and control while under the music's sway. He begins

[121] Alan Rich, "Over and Over and Over and . . .," *New York Magazine*, May 25, 1970, 54.

[122] Martin Scherzinger, "Curious Intersections, Uncommon Magic: Steve Reich's 'It's Gonna Rain,'" *Current Musicology* 79 (2005): 213.

[123] Kerry O'Brien, "'Machine Fantasies into Human Events': Steve Reich and Technology in the 1970s" (paper presented at the American Musicological Society Annual Meeting, Louisville, KY, November 14, 2015).

[124] Carolyn Abbate, "Music: Drastic or Gnostic?," *Critical Inquiry* 30, no. 3 (Spring 2004): 505–36.

[125] William Duckworth, *Talking Music* (New York: Schirmer Books, 1995), 169. Relatedly, Riley has also stated that smoking cannabis for the first time "was probably the most influential thing that happened in my life." Potter, *Four Musical Minimalists*, 104–5.

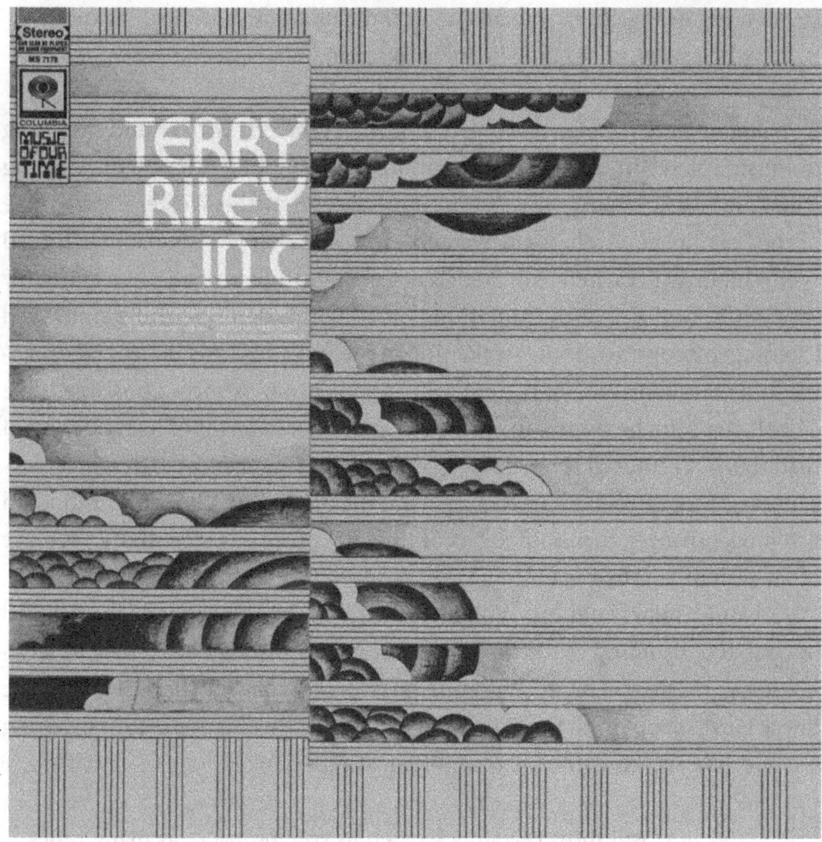

Figure 1.8. Album cover to Terry Riley's *In C* (Columbia, 1968).

by positioning himself not as an advertiser, but rather an "experiencer" of music's drastic force:

> The experience of music is not fully in the ears. If it were, we could concern ourselves with sound and its permutations to the exclusion of all else that musicians might be interested in. Since it is not, we must realize that we listen partly with our memories, allowing what we hear to clash and sing with the patterns already established in our minds; that we listen somewhat with our bodies, responding to music's rhythm as a form to impose on the nervous energy and emotional energy within us, waiting to be released; that we listen mostly with our souls, music serving primarily as some sort of magical matrix that, passing over the scattered pieces of our consciousness,

> can bring us together, can make us as individuals (and groups) inexpressibly whole. A piece of music happens to a man.[126]

Williams here differentiates two modes of concern with sound: listening to music solely "in the ears," and a more fully embodied mode of listening with "memory," "body," and "soul." In a reversal of the Western stereotype of the "ear" as passively inclusive and exposed relative to the active, lidded eye, Williams's detached "ear" here is discerning and rationalistic, exclusively probing "sound and its permutations."[127] Williams describes fully embodied listening, by contrast, as an awakening of mental, physical, and social capacities that, arguably, make the sound's apperception as music possible. Like Teibel after him, he frames the recorded audio not in terms of its reduction of material, but rather in terms of its "psychological" capacities to heighten perception, reorganize the senses, and foster introspection. This fully embodied listening, however, turns out to be contingent upon one's receptivity: "A piece of music happens to a man."

As would Teibel later on, Williams neutralizes the feminized threat posed by "passive" listening on the listener's rationality through an appeal to technological mastery. For as Williams goes on to remind the reader, music doesn't just "happen" to the listener of Columbia's *In C*, since record listening is a selective and controllable technological experience:

> Yes, and *In C* will most certainly happen to you, probably as many times as you choose to play it, certainly as a fresh experience each time. It will transfix, arouse and awaken you. This may be true of the music of subways and garbage cans outside your window in the morning; but the virtue of the recorded performance is that it is subject to the will of the listener. It is good to have things done to one's head; it is not always pleasant to lose all control over what is done to you, or when and how it is done.[128]

Williams here emphasizes the record's technological controllability, as would Teibel later; *In C*, he says, is "a voluntary, unpredictable, absorbing experience" lasting as long as the music sounds. In other words, as he later puts it,

[126] Paul Williams, liner notes to *In C*, Columbia Masterworks, MS 7178, LP, 1968.

[127] Jonathan Sterne conveniently outlines these clichéd contrasts between audition and vision, most famously made in the writings of Marshall McLuhan, in what he calls the "audiovisual litany"; see Sterne, "Sonic Imaginations," in *The Sound Studies Reader*, ed. Jonathan Sterne (New York: Routledge, 2012), 9.

[128] Williams, liner notes to *In C*.

"The nature of your trip is determined by you." Through an emphasis on this controllability, Williams, ahead of Teibel, anticipated, validated, and compensated for the feminized passivity assumed of listeners who, softly focused, let the recording "happen" to them.

Anyone familiar with *In C* might note that Riley's piece "happens" with much more gusto than *Tintinnabulation*. Its lively, insistent piano pulse spurs the performance forward at a hasty 132 bpm clip, commanding listener attention far more readily than do *Tintinnabulation*'s unpulsed, languorous bells.[129] Through overdubs, *In C*'s performers and producers created what Carl calls a "thick, propulsive texture" of melodic yarns in which listeners could become involved and enmeshed.[130] By contrast, *Tintinnabulation*'s bells permit listeners time to observe their weirdly long sustains and decays, while the recording's relatively thin, arrhythmic texture surrounds listeners in airy reverberations rather than melodic layers. *In C*'s long melodic arcs to various modal centers (not just C) over the piece's course also produce a pitched purposiveness absent from the staid bell tones of *Tintinnabulation*;[131] while its bright, honking winds and percussion, jangling well into the track's "head space" above 5 kHz, assume a timbral presence lacking in *Tintinnabulation*'s dulled, mellow, low-mid metallic bell sounds. In sum, Columbia's *In C* offers a far more rousing, kaleidoscopic, and continually evolving journey than does *Tintinnabulation*'s meditative pool of sound—partly explaining why Teibel, unlike Riley or Williams, proposed that his record was entirely fit for ignoring.

At the same time, Williams and Teibel alike drew attention to their audiences' flexible awareness by imagining listeners noticing both the recorded sounds *and* their own sensory responses. "The assumption is that the listener is aware, to varying extents and in various ways," Williams writes of *In C*'s "fully embodied" listener. "The effort is to integrate this awareness, to ease the experiencer towards consciousness." As with Teibel's assertion that the *Environments* consumer *uses* sound rather than submitting to it, Williams posits listeners' holistic awareness of the record's arresting effects on the sensorium, affirming what might have otherwise been regarded, among highbrow listeners, to be an unenlightened or uncontrolled form of listening. Columbia's advertisers followed suit the following year in an ad for

129 Carl, *Terry Riley's* In C, 88.
130 Ibid., 82.
131 Fink, *Repeating Ourselves*, 152–53.

Riley's Masterworks follow-up *A Rainbow in Curved Air*, which announced that "you get to hear your own music while you listen to his."[132]

Intentionally or not, Teibel's realization of ambient audio in *Tintinnabulation* connected the dots rhetorically mapped out by recorded avant-garde minimalism's composers and promoters, while also adding a new promotional spin on this picture. As seen with *Come Out* and *In C*, proponents of recorded minimalism not only treated their repetitive, reliable, and consistent musical experiences as gateways to expanded forms of consciousness, but they also recognized the technological repeatability, reliability, and consistency inherent to recorded audio as facilitating this expanded self-awareness. Automated record playback, after all, offers users a certainty of continuity not unlike the cognitive security afforded by minimalist reduction and automation, with both permitting listeners to relax into a diffuse awareness of sound while appreciating the sound's "psychological" effects. Teibel's stroke of brilliance was to package these records as ambient audio by explicitly recommending *Environments*'s audiences freely direct their attention *away* from the recorded sounds and their effects altogether. Much as composers and listeners heard minimalism's hypnotic drones and loops as affecting their own perception, Teibel permitted that his own minimalist drones and loops, whether "heard" or "listened to," might also operate therapeutically as a "psychological" technology. With a "nature" design concept providing pretext, visual and aural design guiding users to its "functional" concept, and an emphasis on technological controllability, Teibel proposed his records' users reflexively loosen into a "loosely controlled" audio environment. *Environments*, in sum, innovated a new form of minimalism—without ever calling it such—while introducing the concept of ambient audio to an inchoate coalition of record markets across generations and taste cultures.

132 *Rolling Stone*, December 13, 1969, 53.

2

Pacifica Radio's *Music from the Hearts of Space* and the Spacious Sound of California's New Age

Preface: October 2, 1975, 11:47 PM

A deep, soft voice, comfortingly relaxed in delivery, reverberating with slight echo, intones a legal radio ID: "You're listening to *Music from the Hearts of Space* on KPFA and KPFB in Berkeley, and KPFC in Fresno, at 94.1, 88.3, and 88.1." Wet, frothy ocean waves—the beginning of Wendy Carlos's "Fall" from the 1972 *Sonic Seasonings* LP—fade in. A Moog flute-and-horn duo floats up and down around the ocean, sunny E major arpeggios flecked with E minor and A♭ major, occasionally ambling into blue patches of B♭ major/minor and F major/minor, dreamily adorning with wanderlust the waves mixed front-and-center. Seagulls caw; a Moog trumpet fanfare takes center stage amid sparkling pentatonic synth pads before the ocean takes over once more. A crossfade into wind and crackling campfire marks a second section in which distant synth flutes lazily improvise with gusting wind in mixed Phrygian-Aeolian. Minutes later, a "guitar" strums, wind rises, cows moo; then the synth flutes join in the folksy sonic conversation before being drowned by the sizzle of campfire. Sizzle cedes to wind and worry in the track's third section as low, brassy synths ponderously tie mixed chords into chromatic knots. Eventually, respite comes in a stretch of waves and seagulls, then the return of the B♭/F mixed-mode improvisation over the Moog trumpet fanfare. A series of impressions, realized scenically across an expansive twenty-two minutes, set adrift on the waves of an aural ocean . . .

. . . fading into the resonant, fat, close-miked blow of the bansuri, three looooong sturdy blows, each on the same pitch, each tenderly wavering, leaving trails of sound dissipating in the air like wisps of smoke. Silence, then a man's deep, swallowed chant over tambura drone. The mantra progressively explores the timbral and harmonic resonance of the voice ("ah . . . ") with

Turn On, Tune In, Drift Off. Victor Szabo, Oxford University Press. © Oxford University Press 2023.
DOI: 10.1093/oso/9780190699307.003.0003

tambura, the singer at times merging with its sound, capturing its overtones in his mouth, other times skating and swooping atop the tambura in a half-falsetto, or scraping below it at the lowest depths of his bass range. The singer is Bhagavan Das, the US American holy man of the Himalayas immortalized in Ram Dass's million-selling guide to cosmic consciousness, *Be Here Now*, as the inspirational wandering white sādhu. Listeners familiar with the 1971 album *Ah*, whose lengthy title track is playing, might know from the liner notes, or perhaps a previous airing of *Hearts*, that "AH is Seed Sound all pervading Ocean-Voice / roaring in Bliss and Emptiness / Mind-Body easily dissolves in Sound / as the quality of Ear Consciousness / is VAST like Sky at Dawn." They might also know that Bhagavan Das's controlled incantations, continuous as the ocean and sky are wide, manifest the Hindu *anahad shabd* or "unstruck divine melody," and that it may deeply affect listeners as either as subliminal "background music" or blissful "aesthetic experience." Ah . . .

. . . the chanting slowly fades out, and the announcer's steady voice returns: "As much as I hate to interrupt Bhagavan Das, who sings very deep and very beautiful, the requirements of laid-back FM nighttime radio being what they are, I should at least tell you why we're doing this." The host, who goes by "Timotheo," had persuaded some musicians to visit the studio: Henry Wolff and Nancy Hennings, whose 1972 album *Tibetan Bells*, Timotheo tells radio listeners, has become "a classic among those people who listen to inner music." He proceeds to converse with Wolff about the duo's travels through India and Nepal in the early '70s. Their conversation meanders drowsily from one misty speculation to the next about the spiritual "journeys" that accompany travel, about the "high level and rarefied treatment of the human mind" in Tibetan culture, and about the "surpassing beauty" of the bells, which seemed to Wolff from "another space and time."

Forty minutes in, Timotheo's co-host, "Annamystyq," chimes in to ask why the bells "affect the listener so deeply—what is it about the bell itself?"

"You hear the bell with more than your ears," Wolff responds. "It does something to the space between your ears, your brain I think, some people would call it chakras, I'm not particularly going to argue that, but . . . they do something inside the head which no other sound does."

"Okay. What?" asks Timotheo.

Wolff fumbles, then postulates that "the sound of bells is the only bridge between the mind and the greater world."

Annamystyq captures her metaphysical listening experience more vividly: "It seems like that bell sound is right at that point where vibration, which is the source of all, becomes manifest. It's like the first sound. I sat down last night with your record, in a very quiet space. And it almost seemed as if I were inside an atom. It took me to that place, and right on the edge of becoming manifest." Timotheo takes Annamystyq's description as occasion to invite Wolff and Hennings to play the bells, which they do, nearly fifty high-pitched bells all vibrating with intense presence, impossibly long trails of reverberation shimmering brilliantly in the air . . .

. . . about ten minutes later, Timotheo's echoing whisper returns: "Well, if you haven't all floated off totally into some other dimension, at least part of your physical vehicle is remaining in this plane"; and this part of this plane known as the Bay Area, the listener finds, involves some wonderful live performances happening this month . . .

Introduction

In October 1973, soft-spoken sound engineer Stephen Hill (aka "Timotheo") began producing and hosting a late-night radio program on community radio station KPFA-FM Berkeley—better known as Pacifica Radio—titled *Music from the Hearts of Space* (hereafter, *Hearts*). Co-produced and co-hosted by Anna Turner (aka "Annamystyq") starting in 1974, *Hearts* channeled rock, electronic, folk, jazz, art, and sacred musics from around the world into gentle airstreams of contemplative "outer and inner space music." Hill and Turner (Fig. 2.1) executed their spacious, synth-loaded vision of atmospheric music on community radio for nearly a decade before pursuing nationwide syndication through National Public Radio's satellite network. Starting January 1983, just as "new age" and "ambient" were catching on with a mass public as musical descriptors, thirty-five NPR-affiliated public stations, funded by local underwriters, paid annual subscriptions to air *Hearts*; by the time Turner left the show in 1987, *Hearts* reached over 200 stations around the United States; and one decade following syndication, *Billboard* magazine dubbed *Hearts* "one of the most successful and widely heard shows on public radio for the past 10 years," with an estimated quarter million listeners tuning in weekly.[1]

[1] Carrie Borzillo, "'Hearts of Space' Syndicated Show Breaks New Ground in New-Age Programming," *Billboard*, June 26, 1993, 82. Stephen Hill and his wife, Leyla Rael Hill, also launched a Hearts of Space record label in 1984, with albums regularly reaching *Billboard*'s "Top Adult Alternative" charts in the 1990s.

(a)

(b)

Figure 2.1. Stephen Hill and Anna Turner in the studio, 1981. Photograph by Steven Mangold. ©1981 Hearts of Space. Used by permission.

Still airing both terrestrially and as a streaming service in 2022, *Hearts* is, by most accounts, the longest running radio program of its kind in the world, and one of the best known.[2]

This chapter elucidates how *Hearts*'s space-based aesthetic and concept developed in tandem with the metaphysical ideals and material culture of the Bay Area's 1970s New Age counterculture. This grassroots "freeform spiritual community," as Hill today describes it, developed an alternative media praxis oriented around fostering subjective states of bodily transcendence and oneness with a transpersonal, transhistorical human unity, i.e., a "new consciousness" or "new age." *Hearts*'s space music found focus within this therapeutic and holistic material culture.

The first part of this chapter narrates the birth of *Hearts*, elucidating how *Hearts*'s expansive sonic vision of a cross-cultural, transhistorical "space music" anticipated and bridged the overlapping ideologies, genealogies, and aesthetic conventions that in the late 1970s and '80s became codified by the terms "new age" and "ambient." While industry professionals, listeners, and even Hill and Turner themselves eventually embraced "new age" and "ambient" as reference points, these stylistic labels were only two of *twenty-six* "flexible, organic" categories that organized Hill and Turner's selections.[3] The program's stylistic breadth was of a piece with the freeform and progressive rock radio formats that transformed FM radio in the late 1960s and early '70s United States; but unlike many freeform shows that preceded it, *Hearts* had a refined sound and clear concept that guided its curation: it offered slow, reverberant, hypnotic music for "psychological growth, inner healing and communion."[4] Here, I document the rise of *Hearts*'s space-based concept and sound that gave atmospheric music a formidable presence on community radio in its first decade on the air, from 1973 to 1982, at a time when more lucrative commercial formats like Top 40, AOR (Album-Oriented Rock), and Beautiful Music were largely eclipsing freeform FM programming in

[2] For example, *Hearts* is the sole "ambient and space music" radio program mentioned Thom Holmes's electronic music textbook; see Thom Holmes, *Electronic and Experimental Music: Technology, Music, and Culture*, 3rd ed. (New York: Routledge, 2008), 438–39.

[3] Anna Turner and Stephen Hill, *Music from the Hearts of Space: Guide to Cosmic, Transcendent and Innerspace Music* (San Francisco: Music from the Hearts of Space, 1981), xvii. Their twenty-six categories of space music: contemporary ancient, transcendental romantic, electronic space music, progressive infinite, cyclic, cellular wave music, ambient, sound space environments, organic nature music, etheric tropical, mystical vibratory experiences, mantra, meditative, raga and Eastern classical, world fusion music, new age, cosmic folk, spiritual pop, cosmic rock, psychedelic program music, space jazz, light etheric, restful and relaxing, Western classical, Western sacred, cosmiscellany.

[4] Ibid., xiv.

popularity. It also illuminates the heretofore underexplored relevance of the Bay Area New Age movement, whole-earth holism, and the rise of alternative media to the nascent space music aesthetic and its popularization on Pacifica Radio.

The second part of this chapter offers a style analysis of *Hearts*'s "space music" in its first decade on air. Based on Hill's own analysis of the style, I break down the *Hearts* sound by way of its slow, reverberant, resonant, gentle, hypnotic, and flowing properties, along the way illustrating these properties through records that received multiple spins during this time.

The third part of this chapter elucidates how Hill and Turner's *Hearts* put ambient audio in the service of what counterculture historian Theodore Roszak once called the "new ecological consciousness" of the 1970s: an awareness of one's oneness with one's many environments.[5] *Hearts*'s slow-moving reverberant sound channeled atmospheres that, in their free-floating diffusion, were meant to inspire awareness of the continuity of self with its surrounding spaces. The DJs' open, flowing sonic streams both aesthetically manifested and addressed the cosmic holism of the Bay Area New Age movement, which found value in this ecological awareness. Their sonic vision often had a universalist bent, ideally manifesting what composer/mystic Dane Rudhyar called "the planetarization of consciousness," or what composer Peter Michael Hamel dubbed the "new auditory consciousness," in which music puts the self in touch with essential transhistorical and transpersonal truths.[6] The central thematic of "space" hence captured multiple aspects both of the *Hearts* listening experience and its contemplative aims, including the program's simulations of atmosphere, musical globalism, links between outer and inner space exploration, and sense of historical timelessness and eternal presence.

In the chapter's coda, I outline how *Hearts* contributed to the popularization of the new age genre category, and how its DJs' "space music" appellation ultimately fell to the wayside of media discourses as the nascent hip high-middlebrow market for ambient audio became more popularly fragmented, conventionalized, and promoted according to the new age and ambient genre labels. Yet with *Hearts*'s first decade in hindsight, it should

[5] Theodore Roszak, *Unfinished Animal: The Aquarian Frontier and the Evolution of Consciousness* (New York: Harper & Row, 1975), 4.

[6] Dane Rudhyar, *The Planetarization of Consciousness: From the Individual to the Whole* (New York: Harper & Row, 1970); Peter Michael Hamel, *Through Music to the Self*, trans. Peter Lemesurier (Boulder: Shambhala, 1979), 7.

not be difficult to imagine an alternative history of ambient audio in which "space music," rather than "new age" or "ambient," guided this market to find common cause in the dissolution of self into space via atmospheric sound.

Hearts and the Bay Area New Age Counterculture

Welcome to the 1970s Bay Area Grassroots Spirituality Network

"They weren't calling it ambient, but—"
"—they were calling it new age."

Stephen and Leyla Rael Hill gently chime in to correct me when I suggest that *Music from the Hearts of Space* presented the concept of ambient music to the world before anyone ever called it "new age" or "ambient." The three of us have been spiritedly discussing the history of ambient music over coffee and toast in the spacious kitchen of the couple's San Rafael hillside home. The January weather seems a miracle as the salty bay air, beneficently warmed by a resplendent morning sun, wafts through the window. Though nervous about stumbling verbally around the razor-sharp couple, I am increasingly bemused at their tortoise-and-hare routine, with Leyla capping off Stephen's sentences at double the speed of his cucumber-cool delivery. "I got here in September 1970," Stephen continues calmly, "and I would say, within the first three months I was here I started hearing the term 'new age' used to describe not just music . . . " "That's what I'm telling you, it goes back to the late '60s, early '70s . . . " " . . . but the whole grassroots spirituality culture." "Right," Leyla instantly affirms. "The grassroots spirituality which took many, many, many forms."

These many, many, many forms of spirituality cropped up again and again in my archival research and conversations with the Hills during my weeklong stay at their home in 2016.[7] Ideas and practices deriving from occult theology; from westernized variants of Buddhism, Hindu, and Islam; and from

[7] In 2015, Hill invited me to his home upon my request to interview him for this book. He generously lent me access to his personal archive of notes, playlists, recorded shows, and assorted correspondence; in return, I cataloged his collection of *Hearts* programs that had been recorded on cassette prior to syndication. (As of this writing, the collection has not been digitized.) All uncited quotes attributed to Hill come from archival materials collected and interviews conducted during this stay, January 5–9, 2016, and from follow-up interviews on July 21, 2018, and December 8, 2019.

psychedelic communalisms around the globe blossomed within and around the burgeoning "New Age" culture's regional magazines, meditation groups, catalogs, conferences, classes, be-ins, bookstores, prayer retreats, tarot sessions, communes, cults, co-ops, physical therapy workshops, organic food shops—and music. The early years of *Hearts*, and the history of ambient music in the United States, is inextricable from this vibrant spiritual and material culture.

"Actually, there was a health food store on 9th Avenue called New Age Natural Foods," Stephen recalls in response to Leyla. (The store earned the name in 1966.) One could practically write a history of the Bay Area New Age counterculture by way of these early purveyors of whole foods and organic eating. When Stephen Hill first moved to California, he made many of his earliest connections with like-minded folk over "tantric cuisine" at the vegetarian Good Karma Café on Dolores St. in Noe Valley. As the '70s progressed, natural food stores and restaurants like the Good Karma played and sold independently released records and even homemade tapes by local new age musicians. Organic eateries also sponsored and hosted the occasional concert—including a series of shows assembled by Hill himself for *Hearts*'s inaugural month on KPFA-FM in October 1973.

Hill initially conceived of *Hearts* and started its airing as a broadcast of live concerts hosted at Berkeley's One World Family Natural Foods Center. The hub at Telegraph & Haste Streets, graced by a massive rainbow mural out front, included a performance space adjacent to the commune's vegetarian restaurant. (One in 2022 can still find the mural adorning Amoeba Records's flagship location.) A poster promoting the show's opening concert series illustrates some of the themes, sounds, and ideas in which *Hearts* trafficked around its inception (Fig. 2.2). Touting a month of "Celestial Sound" over a drawing of stars, comets, and planets by Haight-Ashbury cartoonist Wes Wilson, the poster not only advertised the name of Hill's recording studio at the time, but also tied into the beliefs of the One World Family community whose self-appointed "cosmic messiah" claimed to channel messages from aliens aiding the transformation of humanity. Over the poster's space-themed backdrop hovers majestically a Sufi winged heart, a symbol of receptivity to divine revelation, bearing Hill's own "Hearts of Space" calligraphy. The series's "intimate, meditative late nite explorations into the realm of inner sound" alternated nights of folk-based songs, such as by former Greenwich Village balladeer Judy Mayhan, and nights featuring

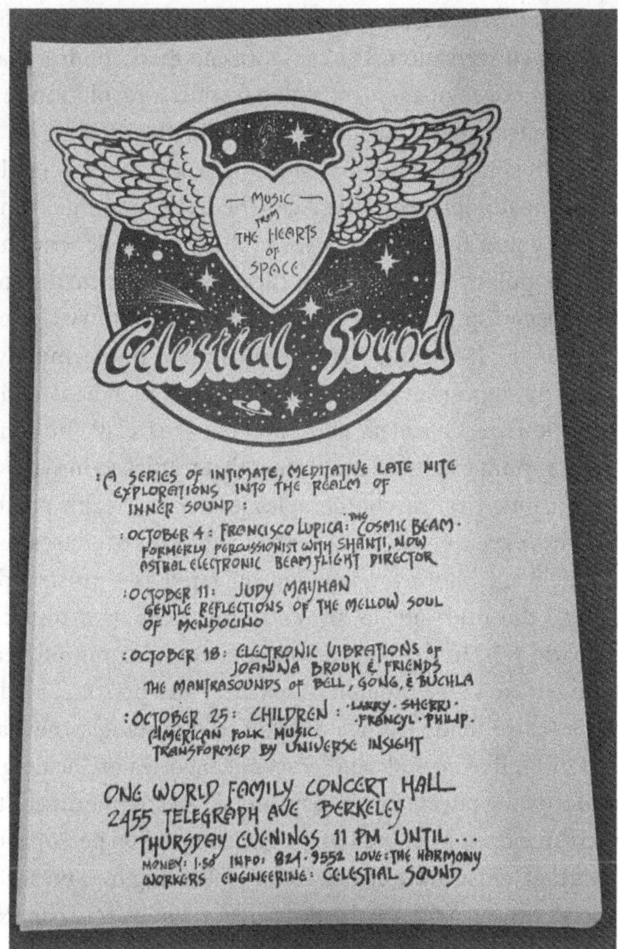

Figure 2.2. Poster for a concert series broadcast during *Music from the Hearts of Space*'s first month on air in 1973. Artwork by Wes Wilson; calligraphy by Stephen Hill. ©1980–83 Hearts of Space. Used by permission.

local composers Francisco Lupica ("astral electronic beam flight director") and Joanna Brouk (performing "mantrasounds" on bell, gong, and Buchla synthesizer). The phrase "new age" is nowhere to be found on the poster, but the One World Family connection and Sufi symbol suggest that *Hearts*'s gentle acoustic and mantric electronic sounds, although of an inward-facing "meditative" quality, portend a greater social transformation—a new age for humanity.

"At the time, it was a cause more than a market," Leyla recalls during our January morning conversation. The cause was no more modest than the evolution of human consciousness on a global scale, a revolution in personal and social awareness that took many names in the 1970s Bay: the New Consciousness, the Human Potential Movement, the Awareness Movement, and eventually most popularly, New Age. The term "new age" considerably predates *Hearts*, going at least as far back to the theosophic writings of Alice A. Bailey that popularized the term in the 1920s, if not further to various occult and neopagan spiritualities of the nineteenth-century United States.[8] Bay Area locals in the 1960s and '70s drew on diverse, but seemingly overlapping sources on human awareness, such as the writings of theosophist Helena Blavatsky, mystic G. I. Gurdjieff, and psychoanalyst Carl Jung in aligning "new age" with a countercultural movement that trafficked in syncretic "east-meets-west" spiritualities, psychotherapies, esoterica, health practices, and sounds, all in the service of sustaining expanded forms of consciousness.[9]

The label "new age," however, scarcely appeared as a musical descriptor in writing until the mid–late 1970s, and only arose as a music industry genre in the early '80s. In the United States, the rapid commodification and mainstreaming of New Age thought in self-help and personal media during this period has since made it since difficult to disentangle "new age" from commodity kitsch, like crystals and crackpot theories of "healing," sold by faux-gurus to trusting buyers for an easy dime.[10] As commodified "technologies of the self," media sold as "new age" often focused on personal therapies, a social praxis that leftists have criticized for embracing free-market thought, and that social conservatives have decried for its "narcissism."[11] But the

[8] Sarah M. Pike, *New Age and Neopagan Religions in America* (New York: Columbia University Press, 2004), esp. 39–65. Philip Jenkins identifies the popularization of alternative spirituality in California from 1910–35 as the "first New Age"; see Jenkins, *Mystics and Messiahs: Cults and New Religions in American History* (New York: Oxford University Press, 2000), 70–99.

[9] See Nicholas Campion, *The New Age in the Modern West: Counterculture, Utopia and Prophecy from the Late Eighteenth Century to the Present Day* (London & New York: Bloomsbury Academic, 2016); Nevill Drury, *The Elements of Human Potential* (Longmead: Element Books, 1989); Wouter J. Hanegraaff, *New Age Religion and Western Culture: Esotericism in the Mirror of Secular Thought* (Leiden, The Netherlands: E.J. Brill, 1996); Paul Heelas, *The New Age Movement: The Celebration of the Self and the Sacralization of Modernity* (Cambridge, MA: Blackwell, 1996); Pike, *New Age and Neopagan Religions*.

[10] Timothy Morton questions whether ambient aesthetics *should* be disentangled from kitsch; see Timothy Morton, *Ecology without Nature: Rethinking Environmental Aesthetics* (Cambridge, MA: Harvard University Press, 2007), 150–60.

[11] The phrase "technique of the self" is taken from Michel Foucault's widely cited work on the subject: Michel Foucault, *Technologies of the Self: A Seminar with Michel Foucault*, ed. Luther H. Martin, Huck Gutman, and Patrick H. Hutton (Amherst, MA: University of Massachusetts Press, 1988). For a leftist critique of new age, see Michael Rossman, *New Age Blues: On the Politics of Consciousness* (New York: E.P. Dutton & Co., 1979). For a socially conservative critique, see Christopher Lasch,

grassroots material culture of *Hearts*'s early days was initially more driven by pragmatism than profit, fueled by the desire to put transformative technologies and knowledge, not snake oil, in the service of a sustainable alternative culture and independent market for collective human flourishing.

Though they were hardly consistent in aims or beliefs, believers in the new consciousness largely held fast to a utopian and millenarian imagination of humanity's potential. Visions of universal peace and prophecies of impending human evolution, consistent with many found in theosophy and the psychedelic counterculture, fostered a culture devoted to personal enlightenment. Many practitioners displayed a ravenous, if oftentimes overly generous intellectual curiosity and eclecticism, particularly in the realms of Western psychology and Eastern religion. The movement encouraged ventures beyond scientific rationality into new forms of awareness, especially gnostic and epiphanic experiences of self-transcendence. Subjective states of boundlessness, ego dissolution, interpersonal communion, and mental transport were valued as departures from internalized sociocultural norms; as integrations of mind, body, and spirit; and as augury and noetic evidence of a forthcoming collective transformation. As prolific New Age author Nevill Drury wrote, "The new consciousness is very much an adventure of self-transformation which eventually takes us beyond self itself. It is a journey towards wholeness, towards totality of being."[12]

A concomitant discourse of holism sought to inspire awareness of humans' integration within, and dependence on, various environments—of human consciousness with the body, of individuals with culture, and of humanity with the planet. Counterculture historian Theodore Roszak described the "new ecological awareness" unfolding in the Bay as an ethical process of probing inner and outer space simultaneously: "Personal awareness burrows deeper into itself; our sense of belonging reaches out further. It all happens at once, the concentration of mind, the expansion of loyalty."[13] Confident that a new human culture would benefit from aligning the personal with the cosmic, the 1970s Bay Area grassroots spirituality network ardently designed and spread holistic media for developing the self beyond "oneself."

Culture of Narcissism: American Life in An Age of Diminishing Expectations (New York: W.W. Norton, 1978). For a critique that balances these perspectives, see Edwin Schur, *The Awareness Trap: Self-Absorption Instead of Social Change* (New York: Quadrangle/New York Times Book Co., 1976).

[12] Drury, *Human Potential*, 13.
[13] Roszak, *Unfinished Animal*, 4.

Despite most associated groups' concern with material transcendence, the Bay Area New Age network developed "alternative" media and retail markets to serve as resources for self-development. Through local vendors and distributors, proponents shared and sold techniques and technologies of mind-body integration and awareness-building—what author Marilyn Ferguson popularly called "psychotechnologies"—made to shatter each individual's illusion of the ego or "separate self," to reveal their partaking in a greater transpersonal collectivity and transcendent universality, and awaken a "new sense of caring and connectedness."[14] Music was just one psychotechnology among many promoted and sold within the movement; others included biofeedback, sensory deprivation or overload, self-help guides, hypnosis, meditation, psychotherapies like primal therapy, body disciplines like yoga or T'ai Chi, and seminars or retreats like Esalen in Big Sur.[15] In theory, this process would lead to collective transformation; in practice, however, the commodified media-orientation of the New Age movement circumvented questions of state politics and collective governance in deference to the governmentality of self-regulation and self-care.[16]

Today, we call this neoliberal ideology.[17] In 1980, however, Ferguson influentially called it the Aquarian Conspiracy, a purposeful process of change ushered in by a "leaderless but powerful network" dedicated to amassing the technological, scientific, social, spiritual, and political resources necessary for psychic transformation on a mass scale.[18] The "leaderless but powerful network," as it turned out, largely amounted to producers within a deregulated market, most of whom naïvely equated socially conscious consumption with collective action. The blinkered optimism of the New Age was, both politically and intellectually, the movement's Achilles heel; but this optimism also drove a rapid cultural, material, and creative flourishing that, with nigh unparalleled ambition, aspired to reorient human values around existential rather than material concerns.

Belief in contemplative music's mass-transformative potential certainly motivated Hill at first, as evidenced by a 1975 notebook in which Hill wrote

[14] Marilyn Ferguson, *The Aquarian Conspiracy: Personal and Social Transformation in the 1980s* (Los Angeles: J.P. Tarcher, 1980), 87, 100–101.

[15] Ibid., 86–87.

[16] I borrow "governmentality" from philosopher Michel Foucault, who defines it as "contact between the technologies of domination of others and those of the self." Foucault, *Technologies of the Self*, 19.

[17] For a definition of neoliberalism, see note 72 in Introduction.

[18] Ferguson, *The Aquarian Conspiracy*, 23.

that radio can be used to "fill people with the spirit" and provide a "live electronic connection between thousands of spirits to change consciousness *in that moment*."[19] Although his outlook shifted away from such New Age spiritualism as *Hearts* matured, Hill continued to find inspiration in the words of futurists like Barbara Marx Hubbard, who called on designers to proactively combine social innovations with "new techniques of group attunement and personal transformation."[20] As Hill mused in 1981, music media could assist with similar goals: "When enough hearts resonate together," Hill posited, "the game can change."[21] Elsewhere in the same notebook, a simple prophecy to guide his music-media practice: "The electromechanical technology of outer space exploration," Hill portended, "will be balanced by a psychotechnology of inner space exploration."

Hearts On Air

Stephen Hill had not always intended to work in radio. Although as a teenager he toyed with ham radio and volunteered at local stations in his native Atlantic City, Hill initially sought a career in architecture, completing a Master's in the field at the University of Pennsylvania in 1968. Yet two years and several internships later, tiring of East Coast cultural and aesthetic traditionalism, Hill swayed his first spouse, a devoted ex-Catholic Zen Buddhist, to chase the Zeitgeist with him in the Bay Area.

By Hill's arrival in 1970, the Bay Area New Age counterculture was well established and growing, and he and his wife quickly became enmeshed in various syncretic groups, causes, and institutions devoted to personal spiritual development and holistic health. Finding architecture opportunities scant, HIll began freelancing in sound, becoming over the course of the decade an increasingly vital signal booster for the many ideas, voices, and musical sounds cultivated within the community. Outside the radio station, Hill was there to assist when gurus needed PA systems, when singing swamis sought on-site field recordings, or when budding singer-songwriters wanted to cut a demo cassette. "I thought, they were trying to develop themselves, they were trying to evolve as ethical beings, and they were trying to cultivate these

[19] Stephen Hill, personal notebook, 1975.
[20] Barbara Marx Hubbard, "The Future of Futurism," *The Futurist* 17, no. 2 (April 1983): 58.
[21] Hill, personal notebook, 1981.

kinds of deeper value systems," as Hill recalls. "They just needed technical help." Hill's early years in the Bay, and the genesis of his radio programs in the early 1970s, quite vividly outline the contours of this New Age spirituality network.

Hill first broke onto community radio by way of the San Francisco Integral Yoga Institute. Its ashram at 770 Dolores St. coalesced around Integral Yoga popularizer Sri Swami Satchidananda, a proponent of interfaith dialogue who, just a few years after arriving on US shores, famously opened the 1969 Woodstock Music Festival with a speech calling music "the celestial sound that controls the whole universe."[22] Satchidananda and his followers held an hour-long Friday-night radio program called *Satsang* on the newly formed public station KQED-FM, one of the country's earliest National Public Radio affiliates. KQED, also home to a public access TV station, exemplified the sort of communications network that independent organizations and fringe movements in the 1970s like Integral Yoga were eager to use: noncommercial, publicly owned, and minimally regulated. Its FM station, managed by former NPR chairman Bernard Mayes, boasted at the time a "Tribal Radio" format that included almost forty different local minority groups and organizations, each of which paid $35 an hour to host its own program.[23] In late 1971 Hill tagged along with a friend in Satchidananda's group for a broadcast of *Satsang*, and finding that the station engineer needed help navigating the group's needs ("For him, it was like, who are these weirdos?"), he volunteered as a producer for that hour.

Shortly thereafter, KQED-FM hired Hill as an announcer and board operator. When *Satsang* sputtered out in early 1972, Hill and IYI ashramite Sudharshan (born Scott Virden Anderson) proposed a talk show called *Meeting of the Ways* to replace *Satsang*. *Meeting* provided a forum for divergent perspectives on interpersonal and divine consciousness, or in Hill's words a "rotating spotlight" for local spiritual groups, as well as meditation and music segments. In late 1972, following Sudharshan's departure, Hill recruited interfaith enthusiast and *Meeting* superfan Will Noffke to become the on-air moderator for the program. Noffke hosted programs of teaching, chant, music, and interviews with local spiritual groups that, despite their

[22] Integral Yoga is a school of yoga focused on entering, and becoming possessed and transformed by, "Divine Consciousness"; see Sri Aurobindo, *The Integral Yoga: Sri Aurobindo's Teaching and Method of Practice* (Twin Lakes, WI: Lotus Press, 1993).

[23] Bernard Mayes, "Tribal Radio in San Francisco," *Educational Broadcasting Review*, October 1971, 3–6.

multifarious religious associations, found common ground in mystical experience of "the Oneness uniting us all."[24]

When KQED-FM extended its broadcast day to midnight, Mayes gave Hill three hours on Saturday night for his own show. Hill dubbed his spot *The Adventure of Consciousness* after a book he admired on the lessons of Sri Aurobindo, founder of Integral Yoga and teacher of Satchidananda.[25] The program often included readings from *The Adventure of Consciousness*, as well as from *The Urantia Book*, an anonymously "channeled" Bible-like tome that combines Christian allegory with a cosmology of divine extraterrestrial beings. Following the readings, Hill would spin relaxing records for several hours as a way of blowing off steam, expressing himself, and assisting his own calm within a stressful urban environment. "The joke was, I needed it worse than anybody," recounts the self-professed Type A. *The Adventure of Consciousness* netted a wide listenership over KQED-FM's enormous broadcast range (most of Northern California) and eventually served as the blueprint for *Music from the Hearts of Space*.

Hill's musical treks migrated to Pacifica Radio in 1973 after Mayes left KQED-FM to preside over its TV wing and new management subsequently cut *The Adventure of Consciousness*. In response, Hill reached out to KPFA-FM Berkeley's music director, composer Charles Amirkhanian, in search of a new late-night slot. Pacifica Radio, Amirkhanian agreed, finely fit Hill's free-form vision.

Pacifica Radio had been a locus of nonconformity from its earliest days as a leftist "war-resistance" project in the 1940s, and soon after as the country's first listener-supported community radio station.[26] The station aired mostly Western classical, but also jazz, folk, and "ethnic" music shows, in addition to political and cultural commentary, radio dramas, poetry, and educational programs and lectures. But, most consequentially for *Hearts*, Pacifica in 1962 gave birth to the freeform radio format when DJ John Leonard took

[24] Will Noffke to Friends of Meeting of the Ways, September 15, 1973, The William 'Will' Noffke Papers, 1953–1998, 1:39–44, Graduate Theological Union Archives, University of California–Berkeley. In January 1975, *Meeting* merged with the program *Frontiers of Consciousness* by Michael and Justine Toms to create *New Dimensions*, a Human Potential talk show dedicated to "the broad spectrum of man's search and discovery of himself as a total being." Program Guide, *Focus: The Public Broadcasting Magazine of KQED, San Francisco*, February 1975, 34.

[25] Satprem, *Sri Aurobindo, or The Adventure of Consciousness*, trans. Tehmi. Lindisfarne (New York: Harper & Row, 1968).

[26] Jeff Land, *Active Radio: Pacifica's Brash Experiment*, Commerce and Mass Culture Series (Minneapolis: University of Minnesota Press, 1999); Matthew Lasar, *Uneasy Listening: Pacifica Radio's Civil War* (Cambridge, England: Black Apollo Press, 2006).

an unconventional artistic approach to sequencing, layering, and mixing live and recorded audio on his late-night program *Nightsounds*. Leonard's offbeat collages of jazz and folk music, poetry, literary criticism, and satirical commentary inspired DJs around the country to try similarly juxtapositional experiments in sound.[27] DJs like Chris Albertson and Bob Fass on Pacifica's New York station WBAI-FM, or KMPX-FM San Francisco's Larry Miller, crafted "freeform" sets of music, sound, and silence unified not by genre or popularity, but rather by theme, mood, and even loose and fleeting sonic and verbal associations.[28] While freeform radio morphed in the late '60s and early '70s into "underground" or "progressive rock" radio, a successful FM format in its own right, Pacifica broadened its musical offerings to feature contemporary Western avant-garde music as well as Asian musics such as Chinese opera, Japanese gagaku, and Hindustani raga.[29] Hill, well equipped to expand Pacifica's musical horizons further outward, was given Thursday nights from 11 p.m. until 6 a.m. to do as he pleased.[30] He divined the new program name, *Music from the Hearts of Space*, while meditating in his backyard, and was soon christened Timotheo by a spaced-out caller.

Anna Turner joined Hill as co-producer and co-host of *Hearts* in late 1974, around which time the program transitioned to late Sunday nights. A San Mateo native with a degree in journalism, Turner was working as a communications director and production assistant at KQED-TV when she and Hill met. Turner's work at NCET foreshadowed her zeal for broadcasting electronic music; the abstract televisual art broadcasted by the group, in Turner's words, explored "the vast uncharted reaches of electric dimensionality where few have ever traveled."[31] But Turner's artistic curiosity was never confined to the visual; as Hill recalls of their introduction at KQED, "She was the most avid music listener I had met." Turner, in turn, admired Hill's musical sensibilities, and they mutually bonded through aural exploration, offering one

[27] See Mark Fisher, *Something in the Air: Radio, Rock, and the Revolution That Shaped a Generation* (New York: Random House, 2007), 130, and Jesse Walker, *Rebels on the Air: An Alternative History of Radio in America* (New York: New York University Press, 2001), 73.

[28] See Fisher, *Something in the Air*, 130; Michael C. Keith, *Voices in the Purple Haze: Underground Radio and the Sixties* (Westport, CT: Praeger, 1997), 53–56; Michael J. Kramer, *The Republic of Rock: Music and Citizenship in the Sixties Counterculture* (New York: Oxford University Press, 2013), 73–74; and Christopher H. Sterling and Michael C. Keith, *Sounds of Change: A History of FM Broadcasting in America* (Chapel Hill: University of North Carolina Press, 2008), 130–31.

[29] Matthew Lasar, *Pacifica Radio: The Rise of an Alternative Network* (Philadelphia: Temple University Press, 2000), 117.

[30] Hill continued to work for KQED-FM for some time after moving his program to Pacifica.

[31] Ann Turner, "The National Center for Experiments in Television," *Radical Software* 2, no. 3 (1972): 46–47.

another listening recommendations and articulating experiential insights. Turner became so involved in the musical planning of *Hearts*, Hill regarded her as a co-producer of the program after its first year. Once on air, Turner became "Annamystyq," a name Hill affectionately dubbed the voracious reader and "sincere student" of New Age mysticism.

Although most every broadcast of *Hearts* predominantly featured music, Hill and Turner during *Hearts*'s earliest years (Fig. 2.3) infused utopian ideas from the New Consciousness movement into their shows through the occasional reading, lecture, or interview. Playlist entries from 1975, the first year documented fully by Hill, include readings from *The Urantia Book*; an

Figure 2.3. Anna Turner and Stephen Hill, hand-tooled Polaroid, ca. mid-1970s. Photograph credit unknown. ©1980–83 Hearts of Space. Used by permission.

interview with representatives of Lucis Trust, a nonprofit that prescribed occult meditation in the service of a one-world religion and new world order; and a 1974 speech by philosopher William Irwin Thompson advocating the supersession of global corporatism with a "cosmic consciousness" fostered through meditation and study of indigenous knowledge.[32] More frequently than these planetary missives appeared directives of personal development, including musical chants, prayers, mantras, and meditations of various origins; philosophical musings by Lao-Tzu, Ram Dass, and Carlos Castaneda; and fresh ideas from the Human Potential Movement such as a lecture by Frédérick Leboyer, an obstetrician who advocated "non-traumatizing" childbirth via soothing environments of soft lighting and music (e.g., Box 2.1).

Hill and Turner slowly phased out overtly spiritual and metaphysical messages around 1978 as they gave greater focus to ideas from the Human Potential Movement, as well as to local art exhibitions, films, and musical culture. Covertly, though, the prospect of a new cosmic consciousness motivated the contemplative body practices and New Age networks that *Hearts* continued to promote. For instance, listeners in 1978 might have heard interviews with Emilie Conrad or Susan Harper, representatives of the "Continuum Method" of exercise designed to break down cultural inhibitions and develop new physical habits around one's extracultural "cosmic anatomy."[33] Hill and Turner also played "hypergnostic meditation" and "relaxation" recordings by the Arica Institute, a New York–based school of spiritual development grounded in transcendental and transpersonal metaphysics; as well as soft musical and spoken word recordings by the San Francisco Medical Research Foundation, a "wholistic" health group focused on the "healing effects of music and color on the human organism."[34] They meanwhile continued to advertise festivals and conventions such as the New Age Awareness Fair and the International Cooperation Council's Rainbow Rose Festival that gathered psychics, musicians, healers, and Human Potential leaders under the New Age banner.

[32] William Irwin Thompson, "The Decline of International Civilization and the Rise of the New Planetary Culture," *Internet Archive*, https://archive.org/details/WilliamIrwinThompsonE1.

[33] Emilie Conrad, *Life on Land: The Story of Continuum* (Berkeley: North Atlantic, 2007), 5. As Edwin Schur documents, the Awareness movement involved such "somatopsychic" techniques that drew attention to the effects of one's bodily condition on one's mental state; Schur, *The Awareness Trap*, 24–27.

[34] Da Vid, "Artainment," *The Light Party*, https://www.lightparty.com/Artainment/Artainment_readmore.html.

BOX 2.1 ***Hearts*** **playlist: April 17, 1975 (Untitled)**

Paul Horn, "The Mahabutas (Elements)" (opening)
Joanna Brouk, *Conch Shell: The Sea at Sunset*
Radha Krishna Temple & George Harrison, "Bhaja Hure Mana"
Pete Townshend, "Content"
Excerpt of interview with Frédérick Leboyer
Elton John, "The Greatest Discovery"
Lecture by Frédérick Leboyer [raga playing underneath]
Kiki Dee, "Loving and Free"
Judy Mayhan, "Begin Again"
Buffy Sainte-Marie, "Nobody Will Ever Know It's Real But You"
Tomita, "Footprints in the Snow"
The Incredible String Band, "Mountain of God"
Bruce Cockburn, "You Point to the Sky"
Bruce Cockburn, "Life's Mistress"
Shawn Phillips, " 'L' Ballade"
[ocean waves]
Beaver & Krause, "By Your Grace"
Robin Trower, "Daydream"
Weather Report, "Milky Way"
Bruce Cockburn, "Shining Mountain"
[wind harp]
Bruce Cockburn, "High Winds White Sky"
Traffic, "Dream Gerrard"
[crickets]
Contraband, "Reverie"
Joni Mitchell, "Judgment of the Moon and Stars (Ludwig's Tune)"
Tomás Luis de Victoria, *O Magnum Mysterium*, perf. Choir of St. John's College, cond. George Guest
Judee Sill, "The Donor"
The Velvet Undergound, "Candy Says"
Les Paul and Mary Ford, "Vaya con Dios"

Yet while Hill and Turner were clearly responsive to the ideas of the New Age, Hill today describes himself more as an amplifier for these ideas than a transmitter or receiver. "I was a representative of the freeform spiritual community without actually being a member of any of those groups," as he describes his role. "I was essentially facilitating and reporting." Nonetheless, as Hill's notebooks from *Hearts*'s early years attest, the activities and ideas surrounding Hill in the '70s Bay Area strongly informed his worldview, inspiring him to foster what he now calls a "sonic spirituality" as a record engineer and radio DJ. This media-oriented artistic practice, enabled initially by Hill's study of architectural and audio design, found form on community radio and at Hill's recording studio, Celestial Sound. These avenues became key conduits within the alternative media ecosystem of the '70s and '80s Bay Area New Age technoculture, which sought, like other alternative media networks and independent media markets of the time, to spread information and tools that mainstream mass media did, would, or could not provide.[35]

The Bay Area's New Age Alternative Media Technoculture

When I ask Hill what brought him to San Francisco in 1970, he laconizes, "The Zeitgeist." When I then ask, after a beat, if he could be just a little more specific, he informs me that he had wanted to go to the place where Stewart Brand's million-selling *Whole Earth Catalog* of technologies for holistic living first emerged. Hill's mission, as he recalls, echoed Brand's reason for assembling the catalog of DIY technologies for empowered living—to bring old and new tools together in the service of human cultural evolution.

Brand himself had Promethean ecological ambitions for the *Whole Earth Catalog* when it was first published in 1968. As the *Catalog* mission statement read, in a formulation inspiring Hill, "We *are* as gods and might as well get good at it ."[36] The *Catalog* envisioned a technologically interconnected and integrated planet (represented by William Anders's famous *Earthrise* photograph of Earth from space on the front cover), and Brand instrumentalized that vision by accessibly distributing the print-based forum for readers to

[35] David Armstrong, *A Trumpet to Arms: Alternative Media in America* (Boston: South End Press, 1981), 21–22.

[36] Stewart Brand, *The Whole Earth Catalog: Access to Tools* (Menlo Park, CA: The Portola Institute, 1968), 1.

exchange ideas and materials in the service of earth-conscious everyday living.[37] Through radio, Hill likewise sought to produce an alternative media production dedicated to retooling the relationship between individuals and various wholes (the whole self; the whole earth; the whole of humanity; the whole universe).

The alternative media technoculture of the Bay Area New Age community facilitated material, informational, and affective exchanges that treated personal health, transpersonal coexistence, and natural conservation as matters of deep concern. Health food stores like New Age Natural Foods, bookstores like Shambhala or Earthsign, and record stores like Leopold's Records circulated not just magazines, pamphlets, directories, catalogs, newsletters, journals, and electronic databases devoted to New Age ideas, but also auditory media like wind chimes, nature sounds LPs, independent music, and even homemade cassettes that might cultivate in listeners a more contemplative disposition. As the 1970s progressed, mail order catalogs like Fortuna, Celestial Harmonies, Pacific Arts, Source Music, Rather Ripped Records, and Greenworld Records Ltd. also brought meditative music to listeners in the Bay and beyond. (Hearts of Space joined this list in 1981.) Pacifica Radio, with programs like *Hearts*, supplemented these outlets as a communitarian vehicle for spreading the new consciousness.

The Bay Area's New Age alternative media network partook in an overlapping and contemporaneous "appropriate" or "alternative technology" (AT) movement whose tech-friendly holism, as US environmentalism historian Andrew G. Kirk argues, was "perhaps the most significant and lasting contribution of the counterculture to American culture."[38] Raised to prominence by Brand's *Catalog*, and coined in E. F. Schumacher's 1973 book *Small Is Beautiful*, AT discarded the technophobia of 1960s conservationism and championed small-scale, affordable, simple, adaptable, and decentralized technologies like DIY solar panels, hand tools, wind machines, and greenhouses, as tools of environmental and collective integration. As written in *Rainbook*, an instantly popular 1977 AT guide, AT should "extend and

[37] Andrew G. Kirk, *Counterculture Green: The Whole Earth Catalog and American Environmentalism* (Lawrence: University of Kansas Press, 2007); .Fred Turner, *From Counterculture to Cyberculture: Stewart Brand, The Whole Earth Network, and the Rise of Digital Utopianism* (Chicago: University of Chicago Press, 2006).

[38] Andrew Kirk, "'Machines of Loving Grace': Alternative Technology, Environment, and the Counterculture," in *Imagine Nation: The American Counterculture of the 1960s & '70s*, by Peter Braunstein and Michael William Doyle (New York: Routledge, 2002), 355.

deepen our own capabilities and experiences and unify them with those of others and with our surroundings."[39]

Hill found himself drawn to alternative magazines and newsletters like *OMEN*, *Radical Software*, *Interrupt*, and *CoEvolution Quarterly* that, in line with AT philosophy, stressed the importance of grassroots media channels for transmitting personally freeing information, images, sounds, and code. "The media must be liberated, must be removed from private ownership and commercial sponsorship, must be placed in the service of all humanity," as video scholar Gene Youngblood declared in the first issue of *Radical Software*.[40] As AT philosophy found footholds nationwide, so did the idea that independent media "stress content over money," as touted a 1978 *New Age* magazine feature, making outlets like community radio, small-press publishers, film and video cooperatives, and regional record labels uniquely suited to nourishing "a far-flung holistic, life-affirming New Age culture." And community radio held special value for departing from the "safe format approach" of commercial radio, permitting new musical approaches to the new consciousness.[41]

By plugging listeners into an alternative information network, and doing so through a freeform musical aesthetic, *Hearts* presented a "conscious" alternative to what *Rainbook* called "plastic homogenized radio" and its "canned, prepackaged" sounds.[42] While underground rock radio had been going strong when Turner joined Hill on air in 1974, the format's heyday was waning. Revenues skyrocketed and competition had stiffened in the early '70s as teen-friendly Top 40 and MOR (Middle-of-the-Road) stations appeared on the FM dial. Underground rock stations, in response, rapidly transformed into AOR stations with tighter, more hit-oriented playlists.[43] Community radio and its college radio progeny became the only places on the FM dial where freeform shows like Hill and Turner's could survive.

Hearts thrived.[44] As with the light classical and pop marketed on the radio as "easy listening" since the 1940s, Hill and Turner's gentle space music found

[39] Lane deMoll, ed., *Rainbook: Resources for Appropriate Technology* (New York: Schocken Books, 1977), 2.

[40] Gene Youngblood, "Videosphere," *Radical Software*, Summer 1970, 16.

[41] Michael Haldeman, "Independent Media: Channels for a New Culture," *New Age*, October 1978, 53–54.

[42] deMoll, *Rainbook*, 119.

[43] Richard Neer, *The Rise and Fall of Rock Radio* (New York: Villard, 2001); Kim Simpson, *Early '70s Radio: The American Format Revolution* (New York: Continuum, 2011).

[44] The program mainly caught on with audiences via underground media, new age retailers, and word of mouth. Hill credits the Philadelphia music producer and radio dramatist Tom Lopez's ZBS Media program *Feed* with demonstrating how to execute freeform with a distinctive, well-defined sound and concept, something Hill saw as central to *Hearts*'s popularity.

widespread appeal in its applicability to deconcentrated states of listening.[45] Although the term "background music" does not do justice to the DJs' psychological, therapeutic, spiritual, and aesthetic aims, *Hearts*'s presentation and success on the radio resembled those of earlier easy-listening formats, particularly of the FM stations that in the 1960s began calling themselves "Beautiful Music." Beautiful Music took a cue from Muzak in sequencing "matched flows" of light-classical tunes with minimal variation in mood and tempo to provide unobtrusive ambiences for middle-class listeners.[46] These stations optimized musical flow by sticking to their motto, "more music, less talk," a credo that freeform rock DJs on San Francisco's KMPX-FM and KSAN-FM had likewise adopted to draw teenagers and hip listeners to the FM band.[47] As freeform stations fell by the wayside in the 1970s, Beautiful Music retained a substantial middlebrow and middle-aged-to-senior demographic, in part by shutting out rock and soul's groovy vibes.[48] *Hearts*, in turn, angled to hip and musically adventurous adults by pairing the psychedelic eclecticism of freeform rock with its own approach to matched flow. The program's spacey psychedelia and cross-cultural fusion sought to satisfy subversive and exploratory tastes while also fulfilling what Hill calls listeners' "internal need for a quiet, serene harmonic background." *Hearts*'s pleasures might have been easy and beautiful, but its DJs aimed to take listeners beyond mere "ease" and "beauty" into *extraordinary* states of meditative flow, inner space exploration, and adventures of auditory consciousness.

Hill also developed and spread his "alternative" audio as a recording engineer at Celestial Sound, his four-track recording studio, which he assembled using the money made doing service gigs in the early '70s. With the help of former Motown audio engineer Robert Olhsson, who shared technical knowledge with Hill while assisting in several projects, Hill took on various record production and sound editing jobs throughout the 1970s and beyond. Early clients included The New Troubadours, a local group of folk musicians transplanted from the budding international ecospiritualist community from Findhorn, Scotland. Hill's lush mixes of the band's *Winds of Birth* LP envelop audiences with constant sound, stereo fullness, and a rich, present low end, cocooning listeners in the Oneness dreamed in the

[45] Keir Keightley, "Music for Middlebrows: Defining the Easy Listening Era, 1946–1966," *American Music* 26, no. 3 (Fall 2008): 309–35.

[46] Joseph Lanza, "'Beautiful Music': The Rise of Easy-Listening FM," in *The Popular Music Studies Reader*, ed. Andy Bennett, Barry Shank, and Jason Toynbee (New York: Routledge, 2006), 157.

[47] Sterling and Keith, *Sounds of Change*, 133.

[48] See Lanza, "'Beautiful Music,'" 161.

lyrics: a "new world" of unity with nature ("I am the river running free") and a "new age" of love transcending time and space. Hill also worked with the Khalsa String Band from the Happy Healthy Holy Organization (3HO) whose founder, Yogi Bhajan, advocated for sonic practices of mantra and music (along with yoga and meditation) as alternatives to psychedelics.[49] The Khalsa String Band did not stick to traditional song, but rather developed their own singer-songwriter- and rock-inspired folk music, and tapped Hill and Olhsson in early 1975 to produce their second album *Sons of the Tenth Guru*.

Perhaps Hill's best-known production work from this period took place in 1976 when he recorded and produced Jordan De La Sierra's *Gymnosphere: Song of the Rose—Music for the Well-Tuned Piano* (originally released on Unity Records in 1977). Sierra (né Jordan Stenberg), a student of Terry Riley's, recorded the album in Berkeley on a rented Steinway D 9' concert grand piano specially tuned in E-natural just intonation. Like his teacher, Sierra played against a recycled tape delay that produced fractally multiplying trails of echo. Hill phase-shifted some of these dry recordings in mixing to create a shimmering timbre, then re-recorded all the tracks late at night in San Francisco's famous Grace Cathedral to capture the vaulted interior's famous seven-second reverb. The evanescent sounds of Sierra's piano became a favorite of Hill's in 1976–77, during which time listeners of *Hearts* could hear one of Sierra's extended improvisations nearly every week on the program.

What many of these productions shared with one another, as with the music played on *Hearts*, were rich, reverberant, immersive audio designs. Stylistically, Hill and Turner's musical interests were as inclusive, widespread, and syncretic as their intellectual and spiritual inspirations; but sonically and conceptually, they honed an appealing space-based aesthetic with which to embrace audiences and foster a holistic consciousness. Hill would later muse that he never left architecture; only now, he worked with an "architecture by other means," with *Hearts*'s programs as his "castles on the air."[50]

[49] On 3HO and music, see Nirinjan Kaur Khalsa, "When Gurbani Sings a Healthy Happy Holy Song," *Sikh Formations* 8, no. 3 (December 2012): 437–76.

[50] Stephen Hill, email to "The Hearts of Space—Stephen Hill," *Hearts of Space*, n.d., https://www.hos.com/shbio.html..

Hearing *Hearts*'s Space Music

The 1968 book *Sri Aurobindo, or The Adventure of Consciousness*, the eponym of Hill's pre-*Hearts* radio program written by Integral Yoga disciple Satprem, opens with a meditation on space. "The age of adventures is over," Satprem writes. "There is no longer any space on the swarming beaches, no space on the crushing roads, no space in the growing terminaries of our cities. We must open out elsewhere."[51] The exploration of outer spaces, including outer space itself, is a fool's errand: "Even if we go to the seventh galaxy we shall go there masked and mechanized, and we shall find ourselves once again such as we are" (iii). Fortunately, he observes, through psychedelics we have begun to face "the final adventure: ourselves" (iii). And yet, he continues, drugs are a dead end, not authentic experience but rather material bondage. What is needed, Satprem tells us, is a "technique of inner spaces" (iv) to guide us "into our own hearts as methodical, rigorous and clear-sighted explorers" (v).

In his subsequent exegesis of Integral Yoga founder Sri Aurobindo's teachings, Satprem explains that the fundamental technique of inner-space exploration is the silencing of the mind. One might, to get nearer this silence, imagine floating in an ocean and becoming one with its "tranquil vastness," an image through which "we get to know not only silence but a widening of consciousness" (34). As the inner explorer discovers this deep immobility within, their mind overflows the limits of their body, putting them in touch with the "infinite void" at the heart of "cosmic consciousness" (85–86). The integral mind—quiet, still, detached from sensation—learns to "universalize itself," to "englobe all and contain all in one's consciousness" (85, 186). The inner explorer, "having found the Transcendent" through techniques of self-dispossession, "can return upon the universe and possess it" (188).

What is the sound of cosmic consciousness? of a silent mind? of space? Are there sounds out there that can put people in touch with cosmic consciousness, with silence, with the infinite void in here? Do these sounds *sound* like an ocean feels? On *Hearts*, Hill and Turner floated answers to these questions in the form of soft, spare, spacious "space music" (sometimes spelled "spacemusic," as in Fig. 2.4). Show after show, the DJs carefully choreographed their musical selections, sequencing, and delivery to

[51] Satprem, *Sri Aurobindo*, iii.

Figure 2.4. "Spacemusic" art for Hearts of Space mail order catalogs, ca. 1980. Calligraphy by William Stewart. ©1980–83 Hearts of Space. Used by permission.

precipitate listeners' self-dispossession and imagined dissolution into atmosphere. With universalist aspirations, the pair designed *Hearts* to act as a vibrational and cultural transmission through which tuned-in selves might lose "themselves."

Why space? In short, space both motivated and metaphorized the expansion of consciousness enabled by *Hearts*'s music, like Sri Aurobindo's ocean image. As Turner once said of the program's contents, *Hearts*'s "inner and outer space music" does not merely represent space; it "opens, allows, and creates space."[52] These spaces figure into various aspects of *Hearts*'s sound and listening experience at once: in the music's atmospheric or reverberant quality; in the global breadth of the DJs' musical selections; in the sense of sonic presence evoked through sustained and repeated tones; and in the psychological depths to be plumbed by the listener. The program's unbounded aural vistas, often lovingly painted with warm harmonic hues and rich timbres, invite internalization, sonically synchronizing the listening imagination with untrammeled futures "far out" beyond itself.

[52] Turner and Hill, *Guide*, 134.

Hearts's presyndication program playlists, which Hill began meticulously documenting in April 1975, reveal decades of musical exploration that culminated in the notion of space music. Selections traversed genre—mostly contemporary US American and European rock, folk, experimental, and electronic music, but also classical, sacred, and traditional musics from around the world, especially from Europe, India, and Japan. Hill and Turner's selections were eclectic, a harbinger of the pluralist 1980s in which popular interest in "ethnic" music, once the domain of folklorists and ethnomusicologists, hastened the coinage of "world beat" and "world music" as genres. *Hearts*, however, never led with a global concept. At the heart of *Hearts* is space, a concept the show has long adhered to both thematically and architecturally in their musical selections. At once a metaphorical and design concept, space (and eventually "space music") strikes at the core of the DJs' distinctive style.

During the show's first several years, the DJs frequently evoked earthbound pastoral spaces through nature sounds (many culled from Syntonic's *Environments* series). Delicate acoustic music and the DJs' soft patter often overlapped with the sounds of the ocean, rain, wind, birdsong, wolves howling, crickets, and wind chimes, anchoring listeners to *terra firma*. (As Hill liked to remind listeners, "If you wanna keep your head in the clouds, you gotta connect with mama through your feet.") But around 1978, just as the otherworldly sounds of electronic instruments began to dominate *Hearts*'s musical selections, nature sounds largely disappeared from the program. This shift echoed and extended a parallel shift in psychedelic rock nearly a decade prior in which the subgenre's folkloric antimodernisms largely gave way to tropes of technology, outer space, and ambience. What music theorist William Echard calls the "space topic" of psychedelic rock, a musical topic linked to drone, motor rhythm, static harmony, reverb, and echo, became untethered from its tellurian associations while retaining the pastoralism of an "indifferent" and "timeless nature."[53] *Hearts*'s "space music" style prolonged this trajectory into the synth age, making mountains out of Minimoogs and oceans out of oscillators.

The use of the term "space music" to describe this post-psychedelic aesthetic precedes Hill and Turner's usage, which evidently started around the

[53] William Echard, *Psychedelic Popular Music: A History through Musical Topic Theory* (Bloomington: Indiana University Press, 2017), 201–3.

mid-1970s.[54] Hill recalls that synth musicians (and *Hearts* favorites) Michael Stearns and Kevin Braheny Fortune had described their own compositions as "space music" before he had; Stearns, for his part, remembers being inspired to use the term by Hill and Turner's program in the late 1970s, while Fortune recalls using it independently of *Hearts* in '75 to mean "a soundtrack for the 'space' you were in."[55] Before this, "space" had become affixed to a variety of experimental and electronic musics, including the compositions of Henry Brant ("spatial music") and Karlheinz Stockhausen ("*Raum Musik*") in the late 1950s, and of Sun Ra ("space music") in the '60s. Hill and Turner's use of the term, however, emerged more directly from the circulation of "space rock" in the late 1960s with reference to the open-ended improvisations of psych rock bands like The Grateful Dead, Hawkwind, and Pink Floyd, as well as the synth-friendly "cosmic music" (or *kosmische Musik*) of German artists like Tangerine Dream, Ash Ra Tempel, Popol Vuh, and Klaus Schulze, many of whom were commonly featured on the program in its early years.[56]

Today, thanks to *Hearts*'s popular influence, many associate "space music" primarily with the pastoral synthscapes commonly featured on the program (and on the duo's subsequent record label). Others identify space music as a style or US Western geographical variant of ambient or new age music. Hill himself, however, delineates space music along a few succinct sonic and experiential dimensions: the music is slow, reverberant, resonant, gentle, and hypnotic, and gives rise to experiences of journeying, floating, and dematerialization. Before further theorizing the relevance of this sound and these experiences to the New Age cultural imaginary, it may first be illustrative, if inherently reductive, to distill *Hearts*'s spacious sound to Hill's set of musical characteristics or "family resemblances" shared by the most frequently played recordings during the program's first decade.

Slow

Then as now, *Hearts*'s most notable feature is the supremely unruffled pace at which the music unfurls over the course of each episode. From the music's

[54] The genre term, as identified with the program *Hearts*, was already in circulation by 1978 as evidenced in David Simons, "Bay Area Free Music . . . Where Is It Coming From," *City Miner* 3, no. 2 (1978): 9–11, 47.

[55] Stearns, interview with author, February 1, 2019; Fortune, interview with author, January 17, 2019.

[56] On German cosmic rock, see Ulrich Adelt, *Krautrock: German Music in the Seventies* (Ann Arbor: University of Michigan Press, 2016), 83–109; David Stubbs, *Future Days: Krautrock and the Birth of a Revolutionary New Music* (Brooklyn: Melville House, 2015), 373–405.

drawn-out drones, surface rhythms, and tempos, to the accordingly lengthy recordings and pregnant silences lingering between tracks, each episode of *Hearts* takes . . . its . . . time. And a lot, especially prior to *Hearts*'s NPR syndication, when shows typically lasted 3–4 hours, often well past 3 a.m., with Hill and Turner (Fig. 2.5) easing into and matching the pace of life at its stillest. *Hearts*'s slowness cannot be separated from the late-night hours in which it originally aired; the DJs' musical and verbal attunement to the quiet of night created a restful or meditative experience in anticipation or lieu of sleep, rewarding listeners' willingness to enter hypnotic or dream-like states.

Hearts's eventual post-NPR tagline, "slow music for fast times," gives the impression that the program was meant to provide a calming antidote to the hectic pace of modern life. And indeed, as with Syntonic's *Environments* prior, ambient audio in the 1980s commonly hooked consumers with the promise to refresh their frazzled minds. Hill and Turner, however, rarely specified relaxation and ease as aims in their own mission statements. While Turner sometimes spoke of the music's healing powers, Hill has always remained vague about how listeners might "use" their slow music. "Relaxation is an outcome, but it's not a goal," Hill says. A listener too focused on relaxation, he explains, will easily miss the social, emotional, and psychological impact of the music. "What you want is it to be incidentally relaxing, only because it enables you to hear more deeply, if you put your attention into it."

Figure 2.5. Anna Turner and Stephen Hill, 1981. Photograph by Steven Mangold. ©1981 Hearts of Space. Used by permission.

Hearts's "incidentally relaxing" slowness can be partly, but not entirely, attributed to a preponderance of slow musical tempos. Many early selections with vocals (what the DJs dubbed "spiritual pop") were ruminative ballads like Judee Sill's "The Kiss" (1973), Essra Mohawk's "Looking Forward to the Dawn" (1970), Chi Coltrane's "The Wheel of Life" (1972), and Laura Allan's "Rest Assured" (1977). Western classical selections, too, tended to be slow-tempo movements of larger pieces, like the Adagietto from Mahler's Fifth Symphony (1901–02), or the Adagio assai from Ravel's Piano Concerto in G Major (1929–31). But *Hearts* just as often conveyed slowness through free-rhythm music, i.e., music without a perceptible regulating pulse or periodic organization,[57] as in orchestral selections like Charles Ives's *The Unanswered Question* (1908) and Morton Feldman's *Rothko Chapel* (1971), as well as cosmic rock and synthesizer improvisations like Tangerine Dream's "Birth of Liquid Plejades" (1972). The DJs also played tracks juxtaposing pulsed and free rhythms, tracks often moving from gentle pulsed flows to floating and back again, as with cosmic rock suites like Klaus Schulze's "Crystal Lake" (1977) or Edgar Froese's "Epsilon in Malaysian Pale" (1975), as well as the Hindustani ragas (Ali Akbar Khan's 1960 "Raga Bilashkani Todi" was a favorite) that gradually accelerated from a cool free-rhythm *alap* through ever quicker pulsed sections. In many of these cases, quick surface rhythms could still *feel* slow due to gradually progressing changes in articulation, harmony, phrase rhythm, timbre, texture, and instrumentation, as on Vangelis's 1975 "Entends-Tu Les Chiens Aboyer?," which begins with synths outlining a G major triad in free rhythm for over a minute before introducing a slightly lilting melody. The lilt gestures to an underlying mid-tempo pulse, yet the slow-moving melody suggests the metric downbeat as the most salient "pulse" of a serenely slow 24 hypermetric "beats" per minute—one "beat" every 2½ seconds. The performance, in its looseness, sounds assuredly unhurried.

Without a clear beat, what made many of *Hearts*'s pieces feel slow amounted to a concatenation of factors: slow surface rhythms, spaced-out melodic repetitions, extremely gradual textural and/or timbral change, and a low density of musical "events" or changes relative to the music's entire duration. Many of these recordings also had extreme lengths relative to most other music on the radio. Often, three-hour-long episodes of *Hearts* would feature only around 10–15 pieces simply because the DJs had no problem playing tracks lasting the full side of an LP (or longer): Keith Jarrett's "Runes (Dedicated to

[57] Martin R. L. Clayton, "Free Rhythm: Ethnomusicology and the Study of Music without Metre," *Bulletin of the School of Oriental and African Studies* 59, no. 2 (June 1996): 323–32.

the Unknown)" (1976), Stephen Micus's "As I Crossed a Bridge of Dreams" (1977), Iasos's "Angel Play" (1975), Kevin Braheny Fortune's "Perelandra" (1978), and the title track of Brian Eno's *Discreet Music* (1975), to name a few. Playing such slow music at great length could encourage listeners to relax expectations for musical "events" or arrivals along the temporal axis, and instead attend to the qualities of presently sounding sounds: their timbre, texture, and spatialization. *Hearts*'s slowness, in other words, permitted listeners to reorient their awareness from musical time to sonic *space*.

Reverberant

We hear space in reverberation; a sound's reverb informs us of the size, shape, resonance, and openness of the space in which the sound occurs. The reverberations of recorded sounds, however, through the magic of production, can be manipulated to suggest different sorts of virtual spaces, often by dint of association with the sound of real reverberant spaces. When sounds are recorded or produced to sound dry, or less reverberant, they sound sharply defined from their environments. Dry sounds appear starkly against reverberant sounds, sounding at their most extreme vacuum-sealed or artificially produced outside real space (like virtual images or holograms) or extremely up close and personal (like a fly in your ear). Very wet or reverberant sounds, by contrast, often lose definition and blend with other reverberant sounds to contribute to a mixed multitimbral ambience. A preponderance of such sounds in recorded audio may signal to the listener that the recording can itself be used as a contained space or stage for personal activity, and that one's personal space can be shaped and contained by the ambience of the recording.

Space music, by definition, sounds reverberant, usually conspicuously so due to acoustic and/or electronic enhancement. Many of Hill and Turner's favorite spins in the '70s featured little more than richly reverberant acoustic instruments, especially flutes, harps, bells, chimes, and gongs. Paul Horn's *Inside* (1968) and *Inside II* (1972) famously introduced the resonant jazz flute as a staple of the new age genre, as did Hōzan Yamamoto's shakuhachi on Tony Scott's *Music for Zen Meditation* (1965); these flutes were followed in later years by Swami Kriya Ramananda's *Song of the Golden Lotus* (1978), Larkin's *To the Essence of a Candle* (1978) and *O'cean* (1980), Zamfir's "Theme from *The Light of Experience*" (1971), and Jean-Pierre Rampal and Lily Laskine's *Sakura (Japanese Melodies for Flute and Harp)* (1969). The DJs also often played the lush, sparkling harps of Georgia Kelly's *Seapeace (Music for Harp)* (1978), Gail Laughton's *Harps of the Ancient Temples* (1969), and Joel Andrews's *The Violet Flame* (1977). Other favorite records drew attention to the overtones or upper partials ringing out from struck percussion, such as Henry Wolff and Nancy Jennings's *Tibetan Bells* (1972) and *Tibetan Bells II* (1979), or Bay Area composer and KPFA personality Joanna Brouk's *The Creative* (ca. 1972). In *The Creative*, Brouk strikes a handheld gong every few seconds, modulating each stroke as the overall density of sound grows and diminishes over time. The air sings as Brouk hits different parts of the gong, giving emphasis to different overtones at varying lengths and strengths over the course of the eight-minute recording. The gong's reverberations trickle outward as the overtones change, a naturally panning filter sweep. As with much space music, a quiet sort of drama ensues simply from filling space in different shades, colors, and intensities.

Richly reverberant synths and electronic keyboards also figured prominently in *Hearts*'s broadcasts, and increasingly so over *Hearts*'s first decade. Synth tones can muddy the seeming distinction between source sounds and their ambience, since synth performers can simulate reverberation by lengthening the "release" at the tail of the sound's ADSR (attack-decay-sustain-release) amplitude envelope. Although often noticeably (and often intentionally) artificial, this aspect of sound-sculpting in practice permits slow sonic dissipation to become a substantial compositional factor, as in the beloved solo synth/keyboard output of Iasos, Bernard Xolotl, Michael Stearns, and Kevin Braheny Fortune; as well as in group efforts featuring electronic keyboards like Mike Oldfield's *Hergest Ridge* (1974) and *Ommadawn* (1975), Cluster & Eno's self-titled LP (1977), or Steven Halpern and Georgia Kelly's keyboard-harp collaboration *Ancient Echoes* (1978).

As the latter title suggests, space music's practitioners sometimes imagined the enhanced reverberation of their recordings as echoes of ancient musical practices. For Hill and Turner, as with many New Agers, the mysterious transformations of space and mind made available by electronic reverberation revived the environmental animism of premodern musical rituals. The link, as media scholar Peter Doyle describes in his analysis of echo and reverb in pre-1960s recorded music, springs from "an ancient nexus between the reverberant spaces and the sacred or magical."[58] From preurban caves,

[58] Peter Doyle, *Echo and Reverb: Fabricating Space in Popular Music Recording, 1900–1960* (Middletown, CT: Wesleyan University Press, 2005), 42. See also Serge Lacasse, "'Listen to My

grottoes, and ziggurats to modern temples, shrines, mosques, and cathedrals, reverberant spaces have long played an important role in altering consciousness and amplifying song and speech in shamanic rites, religious rituals, and spiritual services. By way of these associations, Hill and Turner dubbed many of their favorite reverberant recordings "contemporary ancient," a category that also included Stuart Dempster's *In the Great Abbey of Clement VI* (1979), Steve Douglas's *The Music of Cheops* (1976), Stephan Micus's *Till the End of Time* (1978), Edward Larry Gordon's (aka Laraaji's) *Celestial Vibration* (1978), and Constance Demby's *Sunborne* (1980). Their use of an echo box for on-air announcements completed the link between space music and archaic magic, underscoring the DJs' shamanic roles while transforming even their own voices into misty ambience.

Resonant

Before meeting Hill, I had never seriously considered resonance an appreciable quality of recorded music production. Resonance, after all, is not easily quantifiable by objective standards; depending on the time, place, and perspective, certain sounds will resonate differently with different people and/or things. Hill, however, cites "resonant" as one common property of space music. As he describes it, music produced to sound resonant "adds harmonic complexity, volume, and sustain to tones." Such enhancements have the effect of drawing attention to and building on each tone's timbre, like an aural magnifying glass. To build resonance, individual tones may be combined and filtered to bring out their overtone structures, amplified and compressed to sound louder and more present, mixed with recirculated delays, and/or sustained (the "S" in the synth's ADSR envelope) to permit attention to their full, rich, dense materiality. Sonic resonances have heft; they contain multitudes.

Often, space music manipulates intonation and timbre to produce harmonic resonance, which is sometimes subjectively characterized in terms of tonal "consonance" or lack of "dissonance." However, many tonally dissonant yet nonetheless resonant harmonies abound in *Hearts*'s music, as in the opening of Deuter's *Haleakala Mystery* (1978). The recording opens with multiple singers laser-beaming their voices into a nonvibrato unison

Voice': The Evocative Power of Vocal Staging in Recorded Rock Music and Other Forms of Vocal Expression" (PhD diss., University of Liverpool, 2000), 30–70.

on "oh" and "ah," all building in intensity while gradually altering their combined timbre for the first minute through adjustments of volume and vowel shape. Thirty seconds in, an "oh" creeps in a major second below the opening tone, first faintly, then louder and louder as the singers adjust and balance their interpenetrating vocal timbres. A minute later, the lower tone fades, then rises a half step to (roughly) a minor second—the most dissonant possible tonal interval in equal temperament, yet here savored and tuned to build a tremulous composite resonance that lasts for nearly another minute. The close interval eventually melts into a near-unison, never "perfectly" matching the opening pitch, yet mixed into a mildly unstable resonant tone atop which the flute and synthesizer play.

As *Haleakala Mystery* illustrates, Hill and Turner never restricted themselves to the tonally hyper-consonant uplift that later became associated with the new age category. Softened and massaged through reverberance and resonance, *Hearts*'s space music included mysterious, even unsettling outer-realm and left-field ambiences. From its earliest days, Hill and Turner spun epically trippy space-rock freak-outs and synth experiments like Pink Floyd's unhinged "A Saucerful of Secrets" (1968), Folke Rabe's hypnonarcotic "Was??" (1970), and Tangerine Dream's woozy "Origin of Supernatural Probabilities" (1972). 1970s listeners might also have heard Lorq Damon's twisted, far-*outré*-space synth odyssey "Entry to the Land of Dreams" (1974) (a track prefiguring the "dark ambient" subgenre by a decade), or the aural aeromancy of the mammoth Aeolian harp's spooky ghost-tones on *Song from the Hill* (1972, credited to The Wind Harp). Hill and Turner also played and replayed Side A of Syntonic Research, Inc.'s *Environments: Disc 7* (1976), an "induced meditation" called *Intonation* full of richly resonant "oms" that swell and pool in odd, unearthly clusters.

But Hill and Turner did not strictly adhere to disorienting and isolationist head trips either, as some self-consciously ambient musicians later did; for *Hearts*, to achieve the *emotional* resonances the DJs sought, required heart. Warm sentiments coursed through *Hearts*, acting as its lifeblood and light source. Many of Hill and Turner's space music selections in the '70s openly courted feelings of love, joy, peace, and yearning, as in the tender-but-never-syrupy sentiments of Bhagavan Das and Amazing Grace's "Let My Heart Fly Open" (1974), Kiki Dee's "Loving and Free" (1973), or Shawn Phillips's " 'L' Ballade" (1970). In the early '80s, Hill and Turner's affectionate selections stretched to Charles Lloyd's "Koto" and "Pole Star" (1979), Schawkie Roth and Deborah Henson-Conant's *You Are the Ocean* (1979), and Don Slepian's "Rhythm of Life" (1982). Recordings like these exuded interpersonal feelings of kindness and compassion without the blithe cheer of Beautiful Music stations up the FM dial. As Hill reflected in his 1981 notebook, the emotional resonances of *Hearts*'s "new romantic" selections aligned with the program's "holistic" aims of "inner healing, opening the heart, and refining the emotions." And for Hill and Turner, the resonances of human feeling, to be effective, must tame listeners' hearts gently, not by force.

Gentle

Hill's 1970s notebooks boast an assortment of decorative and inspirational material among the playlists: poetry by Lao Tzu or Sri Chinmoy, quotes by Albert Einstein or Hazrat Inayat Khan, floral and geometric mandalas, prints of medieval Japanese and Persian paintings, and, in a 1978 notebook, a small white card with Hill's handwriting reading, "Together we make soft sweet music." Forget the hard, heavy, and harsh—*Hearts* coaxed listeners' hearts open with sensitive, gentle sounds.

In its earliest years, *Hearts* aired folk and rock ballads not too distant from those "softening" Top 40 and MOR (soon-to-be Adult Contemporary) stations in the early '70s, including those of singer/songwriters Bruce Cockburn, Judee Sill, Judy Mayhan, Joni Mitchell, Elton John, Cat Stevens, Shawn Phillips, and Sandy Denny, as well as soft rockers like Loggins & Messina, Dan Fogelberg, The Moody Blues, and Van Morrison.[59] Radio professionals typically heard such "soft" acts as housewife fodder, appealing to feminine sensibilities in their sonic intimacy, first-person delivery, introspective lyrics, and vocal displays of vulnerability.[60] But soft, emotionally nuanced pop also appealed to young educated liberal men like Hill, and undoubtedly many of *Hearts*'s male listeners, in displaying the sentimental sensitivity of the era's socially progressive, feminism-friendly Western man.[61] Psychedelic and feminist movements, after all, converged on the dictum that "the personal is political," and so it is no coincidence that space music's journeys into the self overlapped with the singer-songwriter and soft-rock boom of the 1970s. All such musicians sought to fully engage with a depth, nuance, capacity, and

[59] Simpson, *Early '70s Radio*, 55.

[60] Christa Anne Bentley, "Los Angeles Troubadours: The Politics of the Singer-Songwriter Movement" (PhD diss., Chapel Hill, University of North Carolina, 2016), 3–5.

[61] Emily Margot Gale, "Sounding Sentimental: American Popular Song from Nineteenth-Century Ballads to 1970s Soft Rock" (PhD diss., Charlottesville, University of Virginia, 2014).

range of individual feeling through an outwardly emotional sound, and most also did so nonaggressively, inviting fellow feeling with a delicate touch.

I mean *touch* quite literally—while quietness and sentimentality contributed to *Hearts*'s soft, sweet profile, so too did the restraint with which space musicians *touched* each soft, sweet sound. This restraint in musical articulation can be quantified in the amount of time between a sound's initiation and its peak amplitude, or the sound's attack. (There's the "A" in the synth ADSR envelope.) Whereas sharp, forceful, and/or percussive sounds have nearly instantaneous attacks, sounds with slow attacks, typically associated with winds and bowed strings, can take a while to achieve peak amplitude. Because the length of attack indicates, in part, the physical speed and force of the action used to produce the sound, sounds with slow attacks (like bowed strings) can feel gentler than sounds with fast ones (like percussion). Percussion in *Hearts*'s space music, if present at all, hence typically takes a quiet, unobtrusive backseat to other sounds, as in the gentle, reverberant ECM-label jazz of John Abercrombie's "Timeless" (1975), Terje Rypdal's "After the Rain" (1976), and Keith Jarrett's "Runes (Dedicated to the Unknown)" (1976). The association between slow attacks and gentleness also holds when sounds are produced synthetically, mechanically, or by other unorthodox means, as they so often are in space music. *Hearts*'s listeners would have heard one such approach to soft articulation in Ash Ra Tempel guitarist Manuel Göttsching's "Quasarsphere" (1975), which Hill and Turner used thematically as "sign-off" music toward the end of each episode starting in 1976. One would be forgiven for mistaking the piece's diaphanous, echoing tones as synthesizers; in fact, Göttsching used a volume pedal to circumvent the fast attack of the plucked electric guitar string and instead glide up to each plucked tone. Additionally, instead of using synths to create the airy harmonizing chords, which sound like synth pads, Göttsching used a Hawaiian steel bar to "bow" the guitar strings. The piece's solemn air never sounds grave, but rather contemplative in its billowy embrace.

The dominance of the synth pad in *Hearts*'s space music, and in much ambient music since, testifies to the soft power of the gentle attack. The synthesizer instrument characterized by its slow attack and propensity to sustainment, typically used in pop recordings to build ambience around a foregrounded melody (much like the string section of an orchestra), became a favored melodic and textural instrument in space music by the early 1980s (e.g., Box 2.2). Many ambient synth recordings of the time featured only synth pads, such as "Elysium Horizon," the opening track from Geoffrey Chandler's 1980 Moog classic *Starscapes*. The track begins with two minutes

BOX 2.2 *Hearts* playlist: June 27, 1982 ("Warm Dome of Clouds")

Bernard Xolotl, "Cometary Wailing"
Kevin Braheny Fortune, "Enchanter's Isle"
Kevin Braheny Fortune, "After I Said Goodnight"
Ojas, "Sunrise from 20 Miles Up"
Michael Stearns, *Planetary Unfolding* (Side A)
Michael Klostermann, "Die Morgenröte"
Emerald Web, "Von Aspen Shaden"
Emerald Web, "Stones of Precious Water"
Ojas, "Soundscape"
Bob Kindler, "Mystical"
Bob Kindler, "Devotional"
Bob Kindler, "Trance"
Alice Coltrane, "Jagadishwar"
Alice Coltrane, "Jai Ramachandra"
Alice Coltrane, "Rama Katha"

of free-rhythm synth-pad arpeggiation up and down a BMaj9 chord built on a rich, resonant, filter-swept bass note. From there, Chandler freely improvises chord-tone melodies over a moody BMaj9—D♯m9 Aeolian pendulum, gradually making his way up from the Moog keyboard's low-pass-filtered murky depths toward its bright upper limits. The gentle pads suggest not so much performed notes as coruscating beams of glowing light that pool in clusters as they gather into chords, dim as their upper frequencies are filtered out, and recede from view upon release.

Hill and Turner often favored versions of pieces featuring electronic instruments with smooth, gradual attacks and low-pass-filtered timbres over their brighter, more percussive acoustic counterparts. Debussy's piano music rarely appeared on *Hearts* as originally arranged, but Tomita's multitimbral Moog recreations on *Snowflakes Are Dancing* (1974) got multiple spins, especially the marshmallow-soft pitter-patter of "Footprints in the Snow" (based on Debussy's *Des pas sur la neige* [1909–10]). Similarly, while *Hearts*'s listeners in 1977 would not have heard Mozart's music for keyboard, they may well have heard Bruno Hoffmann's performance of Mozart's *Adagio in C Major* (K.356/617a, written 1791, performed 1987) for glass armonica, an instrument that requires players to rub moist fingers against rotating glass. Accordingly, the piercingly bright organ on Terry Riley's studio recording of *A Rainbow in Curved Air* (1969) appeared less frequently than the record's darker B side, *Poppy Nogood*, or the mellowed Vox Super Continental organ on Riley's live album *Persian Surgery Dervishes* (1972).

On the whole, Hill and Turner's gentle curation honored affective qualities and sonic attributes conventionally coded, and sometimes denigrated, as feminine,[62] articulating these qualities as necessary components in a holistically integrated musical world. At the same time, their commitment to gentleness did not preclude modernist weirdness, as evidenced by the eerily smooth glissandi of the ondes martenot in Olivier Messiaen's *Fête des Belles Eaux* (1937), or Morton Feldman's mysterious, ultraquiet, suspended cluster chords (*Piece for Four Pianos* [1957] and *Rothko Chapel* were favorites). Together, Hill and Turner played "soft sweet music"; but, as Hill reflected in a 1982 notebook, it ought never be so sweet as to "turn brains off." *Hearts* must be "musically complex and adventurous, moving, intense, explorative, intentionally beautiful, physcially [sic] soothing without being emotionally vacuous." Perhaps steeling himself against the deluge of sickly sweet new age music garnering industry buzz in the early 1980s, Hill wrote that "soothing and exploratory ≠ soothing and saccharine." One ought not assume gentle music amounts to empty calories.

Hypnotic

As with resonance, it can be difficult to quantify how hypnotic a piece of music sounds. What steady-state sounds send one listener into hyperfocused flow or aural ravishment might send another into an apoplectic fit of delirious boredom. No musical features intrinsically cause listeners to become entranced, as anthropologists of music and trance Gilbert Rouget and Judith Becker have shown, although some similarities can be drawn between types of music associated with hypnosis or trancing in different cultures: many involve both vocals and instruments, and many promote involvement through gradual acceleration of tempo and intensification of sound.[63] Yet

[62] See Elisabeth Le Guin, "Uneasy Listening," *Repercussions* 3, no. 1 (Spring 1994): 5–19; Rebecca Leydon, "The Soft-Focus Sound: Reverb as a Gendered Attribute in Mid-Century Mood Music," *Perspectives of New Music* 39, no. 2 (Summer 2001): 96–107.

[63] Judith Becker, *Deep Listeners: Music, Emotion, and Trancing* (Bloomington: Indiana University Press, 2004), 25; Gilbert Rouget, *Music and Trance: A Theory of the Relations between Music and Possession*, trans. Brunhilde Biebuyck (Chicago: University of Chicago Press, 1985), 73–91.

the dissociative state of consciousness known specifically as hypnosis was, during *Hearts*'s first decade, often prompted by the drones and cyclical repetitions of the avant-garde minimal music coming from California and New York.[64]

Hearts leaned heavily into sustained tones and cyclical repetition as triggers for hypnosis. Minimalist keyboard works, particularly when performed on electric organs, synths, or close-miked keyboards, found favor, as with Terry Riley's aforementioned *Persian Surgery Dervishes*, Peter Michael Hamel's *Nada* (1977), Margaret Fabrizio's *Holograms* (ca. 1976), or Jordan De La Sierra's *Song of the Rose* (1976). These pieces took differing approaches to sustaining listener interest through cyclical repetition, whether through raga-like improvisation (Riley's *Dervishes*), superimposition of cycles of different lengths (the title track of Hamel's *Nada*), augmentation or diminution of cycle length (Fabrizio's *Hologram #3*), or embedded sequences of shorter cycles within longer cycles (Sierra's "Sphere of Sublime Dances" from *Song*). Most of these pieces draw listeners deeper into trance through intensifications of energy, most often by adding rhythmic layers and/or accelerating tempo; although some, like Sierra's "Sphere of Sublime Dances," continue indefinitely at a supremely steady state, as though themselves slivers of infinity.

Gradual electronic modifications were also deployed on many *Hearts* tracks to hypnotic effect, especially resonant filters oscillating at low frequencies to create cyclically sweeping timbral modifications on sustained drones, as can be heard on Ashra's "Ocean of Tenderness" (1976), Steve Hillage's "Rainbow Dome Musick" (1979), or Swami Kriya Ramananda's "Devata" (1978). *Hearts* also gravitated toward rock and synth music that took advantage of newly available analog and digital sequencers to produce entraining and entrancing grooves, as in Klaus Schulze's "Floating" (1976) or throughout Michael Stearns's "Ancient Leaves" (1977). Like the minimalist keyboard works, these recordings often intensify energy over time as a way of drawing listeners deeper into musical hypnosis. For instance, Klaus Schulze's twenty-seven-minute-long "Floating" eases the listener in over the first few minutes with a sparkling layer of crystalline sounds, followed by an echoing vocal incantation, low synth bells, and mounting string and vocal synth pads around a B♭ drone. A little over five minutes in, a sequenced sixteenth-note

[64] Edward Strickland, *Minimalism: Origins* (Bloomington: Indiana University Press, 1993), 242–43.

arpeggiation alternating between D♭ and E♭m chords rises slowly in volume under the heavenly string pads. The piece slowly builds and transforms over time as Schulze introduces chord changes 8½ minutes in, followed by a drum kit chugging away alongside the sequencer arpeggio, then new synth pad layers, alterations of the sequenced patterns' timbre, and finally a melodic modal improvisation higher up in the keyboards. Like the best jam bands of the psychedelic rock era, or the ambient house and techno musicians to follow, space musicians like Schulze improvised with and around an involving groove to induce heady states of immersion in sonic flow.

Freeform Flow

The DJs' careful selection, sequencing, and mixing of tracks over the course of each full episode of *Hearts* also played a major role in orchestrating listeners' inner and outer space exploration. From start to finish, each program smoothly dipped and built in intensity, energy, and activity from recording to recording, tracing a flow meant to take listeners deeper into sound, into themselves, and/or into the activities they simultaneously undertook.

In *Hearts*'s first decade (and in many shows since), Hill and Turner typically looked to the seasonal, astrological, and meteorological moment for inspiration. As reflected in early episode titles like "Cool Mature Summer Night," "A Calm Night between the Storms," or "Smoky Night in Scorpio," the DJs selected music to match the mood set by the local weather or seasonal environment and then modulated this mood according to the energy flows suggested by the music (e.g., Box 2.3). As Turner described it in 1981,

> Each night is different. . . . [We] choose a piece to begin the program, that feels like the night—usually reflective of it, though sometimes a harmonic and sometimes another note entirely that makes a chord with it. And then we move—as it moves—staying on the edge of the moment, listening . . . waiting . . . responding . . . initiating . . . ."[65]

Turner's summary reflects how the feeling of the program rarely hovered statically, but rather ebbed and flowed in response to trajectories of energy and feeling suggested by the musical sequence. "Certain pieces do suggest

[65] Turner and Hill, *Guide*, xii.

BOX 2.3 ***Hearts*** **playlist: October 31, 1980 ("A Smoky Night in Scorpio")**

Laraaji, "Meditation #1"
Laraaji, "Meditation #2"
Joanna Brouk, *The Creative*
Michael Stearns, "Planetary Unfolding"
Jordan De La Sierra, "Pure Grace"
Harold Budd, *Madrigals of the Rose Angel*
Brian Eno, "2/1" (from *Music for Airports*)
Emerald Web, "Air Smith (Part 1)"
Emerald Web, "Air Smith (Part 2)"
Emerald Web, "Loosing the Shadow"
Emerald Web, "Reflecting Pool"
Emerald Web, "In the Eye of Jupiter's Hurricane"
Michael Stearns, "Picnic at Hanging Rock" (last half)
Michael Stearns, "Marriage Chords"
Constance Demby, "Darkness of Space"
Constance Demby, "Om Mani Padme Hum"
Constance Demby, "Peace of God"
Constance Demby, "Saint Ji"
Constance Demby, "God Is"
Aaron Copland, *Clarinet Concerto*, first movement, perf. Benny Goodman and The Columbia String Orchestra, cond. Aaron Copland
Manuel Göttsching, "Quasarsphere"

certain directions," she writes. "What we decide to consume and energize ourselves with is a moment-to-moment choice."[66]

Despite its improvisational nature, however, most every episode of *Hearts* in its first decade traced a similar arc, as Hill explains it, from induction, to deepening, to meditation. Through music, Hill and Turner choreographed for listeners a metaphorical retreat from the everyday realm of physical movement and social participation into a stiller, more contemplative, and more personal space, most often by beginning with rhythmically active

[66] Ibid., xii.

music (often prog or cosmic rock), then gradually easing over the first hour into gentler sustained sounds with simpler textures and fewer vocals (often soft jazz and classical selections, as well as nature sounds during the first few years). Hill describes this strategy as a process of taking listeners into "the deep zone" of contemplation, an "adjacent state of consciousness" that heightens concentration and creativity. Like an inverted electronic dance music set, which normally modulates intensity over time to reach peaks or climaxes of dance-trance energy, Hill and Turner would slacken the intensity of musical activity over *Hearts*'s first hour to usher in meditative "deep zones." From here, episodes could go in many different directions, often toward the end coming up for air with vocal music. Energies and moods throughout ideally flowed smoothly from one recording to the next, often through imaginative crossfades and cuts; but nothing too jarring or obtrusive, nothing to nudge the listener out of a contemplative state, especially not interruptive back announcements, which the DJs kept to a minimum. Hill even did (and still does) production work on the tracks themselves in preparation for each episode, including adjusting the music's EQ levels, adding reverb, cutting sections, and remastering records, all in the service of "improv[ing] the flow through the trajectory of the experience."

Yet while *Hearts*'s episodes followed a certain pattern, Hill and Turner always aimed to avoid the boring, predictable, or ordinary, seeking to "move" the listener into altered states of consciousness while steering clear of music that was vacuously "moving" without emotional complexity or sonic intensity. "We have made a choice to look for that which takes people away," writes Hill in a 1982 notebook. Episodes should be "extraordinary listening experiences which take people into new places"—that is, into new atmospheric worlds, through different levels of consciousness, and most profoundly, out of the individual self into a universal All.

Tuning In to the New Auditory Consciousness

Hearts's Unitive, Transpersonal, and Transhistorical Sounds

For Timotheo and Annamystyq, *Hearts*'s space music captured something of the boundlessness of space and time, and as such had the potential to awaken listeners to their own continuity with this spatiotemporal oneness. The

DJs' sound-spaces, in other words, made an opening for listeners to access what New Age thinkers, after Eastern mystics and theosophists, often called "unitive consciousness" or "unitive experience," a direct identification and merging with a nondualistic infinitude.[67] During the 1970s, the aspiration to unitive consciousness motivated what Human Potential scholars termed "transpersonal psychology," defined in 1968 as the methodical exploration of ecstatic, mystical, transcendent, and cosmic experiences and activities.[68] New Agers widely believed that the personal internalization of unitive experience could inspire social cooperation over competition; as *Yoga Journal* founder William Staniger wrote in a 1976 editorial, "It seems that one of the most important means of reaching [mutual] cooperation is through the individual experience of unitive consciousness. . . . [A]s the walls of division between the inner and outer, between oneself and others dissolve, the movement of life in one's environment is more and more experienced as oneself."[69] The internalization of "transpersonal awareness" involved dimensions of unitive experience such as a sense of transcending space, time, and personal identity; a perception of "deep stillness and peace" underlying everyday consciousness; and "an all-pervading aura or feeling of love and contentment for all that exists."[70] These ideals likewise motivated *Hearts*'s hypnotic atmospheric aesthetic, which afforded listener identification with a diffuse, disembodied, peaceful, and seemingly compassionate sonic field.

New Age practitioners in the 1970s often linked ambient audio like *Hearts*'s space music to unitive experience. Ambient audio's seemingly static nature, perhaps more so than science, largely explains why *Hearts*'s DJs and listeners associated space music with unitive experience, or at least something like it. "There is no regular beat, no continuous rhythmic skeleton," as one *Yoga Journal* reviewer noted of Steven Halpern's new age classic *Spectrum Suite* (1976). "This is part of what keeps you as a listener riveted to the 'hear' and now," as well as the means by which the music is "reflecting and

[67] The quest for unitive consciousness often motivated the sonic practices of New Age spiritual groups; 3HO founder, Yogi Bhajan, for example, described the goal of mantric chant as "a merge between the personal experience of you and the impersonal experience of Infinity beyond you and within you." Michael Stoeber, "3HO Kundalini Yoga and Sikh Dharma," *Sikh Formations* 8, no. 3 (December 2012): 355.

[68] Anthony J. Sutich, "Transpersonal Psychology: An Emerging Force," *Journal of Humanistic Psychology* 8, no. 1 (1968): 77–78.

[69] William Staniger, "Editorial," *Yoga Journal*, May–June 1976, 3.

[70] Ronald S. Valle, "The Emergence of Transpersonal Psychology," in *Existential-Phenomenological Perspectives in Psychology: Exploring the Breadth of Human Experience*, ed. Ronald S. Valle and Steen Halling (New York: Plenum Press, 1989), 259.

expressing a new consciousness."[71] Thankfully, Hill and Turner avoided the scientistic trappings of New Consciousness contemporaries like Halpern, who buttressed such experiential observations with spurious claims to the music's healing power. Perhaps more popularly than anyone at the time, Halpern marketed his and others' relaxing atmospheric music as "new age" on the basis of its therapeutic effects. "True New Age music," Halpern wrote summarily in the late '80s, "can deepen and regularize the breath, improve digestion, lower blood pressure, and balance the two hemispheres of the brain."[72] Credibly, Halpern linked these effects to the "non-anticipatory" nature of this music; but he also often linked such claims to uncited scientific "research" that "showed" that new age music "disengages" analytical "left-brain" thinking to make room for "right-brain" meditative states.[73] New Age writers on music commonly replicated the erroneous split-brain hypothesis; many also forwarded that energetic centers or chakras in the human body resonate at particular frequencies, and may thus be activated by musical sound.[74] Halpern, for example, wrote that individuals are "living bio-oscillators" that can be "tuned" by his music.[75] Hill and Turner smartly shied away from such explanations. "All that stuff is anecdotal, impossible to prove," Hill tells me. "I just never felt comfortable making wild, preposterous claims of therapeutic effect. It's much more effective to let people discover the value of it for themselves, and let them define that value in their own life and in their own terms."

Nevertheless, for Hill and Turner as for Halpern and many other New Agers, a vibrational ontology of the universe underpinned the notion that music could act as a personal gateway to unitive awareness. The theory that vibration, as a base fact of existence, could connect the personal to the universal was foundational to New Age spiritualities and philosophies of sound. Most believers developed some variant of the idea—borrowed from ancient and medieval European philosophies, North American spiritualisms, as well as Sufi, Buddhist, Taoist, and Hindu thought—that vibrations manifest something of an essential totality, bringing to life the "music of the spheres"

[71] "Music and Beyond," *Yoga Journal*, January 1977, 23–24.
[72] Birosik, *New Age Music Guide*, xx.
[73] "Music and Beyond," *Yoga Journal*, January 1977, 24.
[74] For a substantial rebuttal of new age musicians' claims to healing like these, see Lisa Summer, *Music: The New Age Elixir* (Amherst, NY: Prometheus, 1996).
[75] Steven Halpern, *Tuning the Human Instrument: An Owner's Manual* (Belmont, CA: Spectrum Research Institute, 1978), 10.

or a "universal mind." Vibrations were understood to mediate between the physical and metaphysical, between the micro- and macrocosmic; as Sufi teacher Hazrat Inayat Khan wrote, and as quoted Hill and Turner's 1981 space music guidebook, "All things and beings in the universe are connected with each other, visibly and invisibly, and through vibrations a communication is established between them on all planes of existence."[76] George Leonard, former president of Human Potential center the Esalen Institute, likewise wrote in 1978 of a "silent pulse" in each of us, a "complex of wave forms and resonances . . . which connects us to everything in the universe. The act of getting in touch with this pulse," he argued, "can transform our personal experience and in some way alter the world around us."[77] New age music writers in this manner invoked musical metaphors of vibratory resonance, intonation, and entrainment to characterize the harmonization of the self with the whole universe, a harmonization that many believed could develop out of lifestyle practices like music listening. Music, in the simplest versions of this theory, literally manifested and mediated the vibrations of the universe, its rhythms and harmonies biometaphysically intervening on the listener's energy field or "subtle body."[78] New age musical guides like Hal Lingerman's 1983 book *The Healing Energies of Music* hence spoke of the "proper" and "wise" use of music "to bring clearing and purification to the body, emotions, and thinking patterns," while musicians like Iasos described their music-making as using certain "frequency signals" to produce "harmonious emotions."[79]

While Hill and Turner never so overtly promoted specific healing effects of their program's music, their rhetoric nonetheless evoked the notion of vibration as an interface between the music listener and their environment. As Turner wrote in their space music guide, "We tune to the vibratory space of a particular night and improvise with it," for music "creates a way to enter a space that is always there, as close as the heart, a slightly different frequency . . .

[76] Turner and Hill, *Guide*, x.

[77] George Leonard, *The Silent Pulse: A Search for the Perfect Rhythm That Exists in Each of Us* (New York: E.P. Dutton & Co., 1978), xii.

[78] Jay Johnston, "Subtle Anatomy: The Bio-Metaphysics of Alternative Therapies," in *Medicine, Religion, and the Body*, ed. Elizabeth Burns Coleman and Kevin White, vol. 11, International Studies in Religion and Society (Leiden and Boston: Brill, 2009), 69.

[79] Hal A. Lingerman, *The Healing Energies of Music*, 2nd ed. (Wheaton, IL: Quest Books, 1995), 3; Elizabeth Kent, "Interdimensional Beings: Visions of the Invisible," *Yoga Journal*, January–February 1977, 17.

a breath away."[80] Through vibration, music could serve as a psychologically activating device, something that could expand and dissolve the receptive self into its local and global environments. "If you truly surrender to music, particularly this music," Turner continued, "it will take you somewhere."[81] And that "somewhere," as Turner's evocative conflation of outer and inner space suggests, was a unitive state of mind, one that put the personal self in touch with a universalized transpersonal and transhistorical humanity. Space music, in other words, would help usher in a new auditory consciousness.

Theorizing the "New Auditory Consciousness"

Hill today underscores that, of all books on music, the two that resonate most deeply with his understanding of space music's unitive power are Dane Rudhyar's 1982 *The Magic of Tone and the Art of Music* and Peter Michael Hamel's 1976 *Through Music to the Self* (*Durch Musik zum selbst*).[82] I was surprised when Hill named US avant-garde-composer-cum-astrology-guru Rudhyar's *The Magic of Tone* as a key tome through which to understand space music, since I had initially dismissed the composer and writer as trafficking in too vague notions about the "power" of sound and vibration. But Rudhyar, more deliberately and poetically than the average new age music promoter, charted a course around Western musical formalisms like tonality toward ineffable experiential truths that he had found in theosophy, Buddhism, and Asian musics.[83] This course pursued the "creative and transformative power" of what Rudhyar called "tone," a communication that, according to Rudhyar, in archaic times transmitted "mythological and vitalistic association[s]," and that may still be heard as "the descent of a current of cosmic or human energy (Sound) issued from a single source, a One."[84]

Unlike the abstract, singular "note," Rudhyar's "tone" is a living, organic, composite entity whose resonances accumulate and grow, filling and vibrating space. And unlike compositions that deal with the interaction of

[80] Turner and Hill, *Guide*, x–xi.

[81] Ibid., xii.

[82] The English edition of Hamel's *Through Music to the Self* was published in 1979 by Shambhala Publications, originally a Berkeley-based press dedicated to holistic health and Eastern spirituality.

[83] Carol J. Oja, "Dane Rudhyar's Vision of American Dissonance," *American Music* 17, no. 2 (Summer 1999): 129–45.

[84] Dane Rudhyar, *The Magic of Tone and the Art of Music* (Boulder: Shambala, 1982), chap. 6, https://www.khaldea.com/rudhyar/mt/mt_c6.shtml.

notes, music animated by tone—what Rudhyar calls "syntonic" music, best exemplified in the sacred music of bells and gongs—deals primarily with the enhancement of resonances of tones, and the interplay of these resonances in physical space.[85] Space, in turn, "can be experienced as a pleroma of interpenetrating and interacting tones, an immense and multitudinous resonance of the orchestra of cosmic existence."[86] Rudhyar's writing emphasizes how musical manipulations of tone may give impetus for listeners to reinterpret both themselves and their surrounding spaces as partaking in preexisting resonances, a "revelation" that, as he wrote in his 1970 book *The Planetarization of Consciousness*, links the individual to an existential, cyclical, and transcendental whole.[87]

Peter Michael Hamel, a German composer and writer, takes a less overtly metaphysical tack to describing the transpersonal power of syntonic sound. As a composer, he brought his study of Indian classical music and US minimalism to the fusion jazz group Between in 1970, and soon after to his own compositions and ambient audio productions. In *Through Music to the Self*, Hamel charts the development of "an entirely new form of world-music, now in its earliest infancy" that, over the course of the book, he variously describes as "contemplative music," "integral music," "meditative music," "world music," or "meta-music."[88] Throughout, Hamel describes the various contributions of Hindustani ragas, Tibetan tantric chant, Shango ceremonial drumming, Islamic muezzin calls, Indonesian gamelan, and from the United States and Europe spiritual jazz, cosmic rock, and minimalist music, to this new pancultural contemplative music. In integrating archaic conceptions of music with modern sensibilities, Hamel explains, contemplative music has the potential to revive in listeners an intuitive understanding of sound, inherited from antiquity, as a spiritual, ritual, psychological, and emotional transformer. In short, Hamel proposed, contemplative music testifies to the development of a "new auditory consciousness." As Hamel writes in a passage reproduced in Hill and Turner's space music guide:

> In all earlier world-cultures music stood at the service of ritual, of the holy cult, of consciousness-expansion and the deepest in human experience.

[85] Dane Rudhyar, *The Rebirth of Hindu Music* (orig. 1928; repr. New York: Noble Offset Printers, 1979), 21–23.
[86] Rudhyar, *The Magic of Tone*, chap. 6.
[87] Rudhyar, *The Planetarization of Consciousness*, esp. 63 and 235.
[88] Hamel borrowed the term "meta-music" (*Metamusik*) from his collaborator, Walter Bachauer.

> The intuitive understanding of this significance would be a precondition for a new auditory consciousness, capable of being applied to all today's varieties of music—whether Classical, Pop, Jazz, Avant-garde or non-European.[89]

Hamel's notion of a "new auditory consciousness," a holistic mode of aural awareness or "total mode of hearing," partook in the transhistorical universalism of New Age thought and its promise to carry in mind "living knowledge of the unity of visible and invisible, of physical and spiritual."[90] He had adopted this notion from Swiss philosopher Jean Gebser, whose key work, *The Ever-Present Origin* (1953), sought a "new consciousness" and a "new age" through the revival of ancient human psychology.[91] Humankind can be saved from itself, Gebser wrote, only if we integrate "archaic consciousness" into a (post)modern "integral" consciousness so that we may "constantly relive and re-experience in a decisive sense the full depth of our past."[92] Yet whereas Gebser discovered a "mutation toward integral awareness" in the "aperspectival" worlds of cubist painting and modernist art music, Hamel (as well as Hill and Turner) located a new consciousness in contemporary "contemplative music."[93]

Hamel's book, while skirting the rhetoric of the unitive or vibratory, nonetheless mirrors the contiguous language of transpersonal psychology to describe certain experiential ideals. The new contemplative or integral music, Hamel writes, may lead listeners into relaxed meditative states wherein, as commonly reported in psychedelic experiences of music, "one registers and perceives music no longer as outside oneself, but as inside one's own body."[94] As a "vehicle" for such experiences, Hamel explains, integral music renders drugs "superfluous"; so long as "the listener learns how to open himself totally to it," the music "carries him away—to himself."[95] Hamel repeatedly evokes "self-absorption" and "self-experience" as the ultimate aim of these musical experiences; most specifically, he speaks of the "primal experience of the spiritual non-ego," although he largely leaves vague the nature and value

[89] Hamel, *Through Music to the Self*, 7.
[90] Ibid., 8–9.
[91] Jean Gebser, *The Ever-Present Origin*, ed. Noel Barstad and Algis Mickunas, rev. ed. (Athens: Ohio University Press, 1991), 1–2.
[92] Ibid., 4.
[93] Ibid., 42.
[94] Hamel, *Through Music to the Self*, 38.
[95] Ibid., 142.

of such experiences.[96] True self-experience, for Hamel, is an experience of the universal, or "participation in the All," as he puts it; but this participation appears, based on his writing, quiet, passive, and featureless.[97] Indeed, the "self," the "body," and "consciousness" all rhetorically function very generally in Hamel's writing, as though contemplative music can speak to all selves, bodies, and minds regardless of any one's particular features.

Much like Hill and Turner's characterization of space music, Hamel's writings on the new auditory consciousness thus idealized modern meditative music as a universal gateway to a transhistorical and transpersonal essence. His rhetoric was typical of New Age writings on contemplative music as expressing something fundamental to humanity as an ancient whole. "For thousands of years," as Steven Halpern characteristically wrote, "people around the world have honored and acknowledged the healing, ceremonial, and uplifting role of music. From this perspective New Age music is really a return to roots, to a belief in the primordial power of sound."[98] Whether called contemplative, space, or new age music, atmospheric sound in the Aquarian Age was understood to be a phenomenon more biological than cultural, more vibrational than artistic. As Halpern once put it, new age music "can help put us in contact with our own biosymphony";[99] as catalogers of "holistic" music like The San Francisco Medical Research Foundation boasted, new age music puts listeners in contact with "the eternal verities of Love, Beauty, Grace, Freedom and Joy."[100] Or, as Hill and Turner simply wrote in their space music guide, "Some people have wanted to call *Music from the Hearts of Space* 'new age.' We think of it as universal."[101]

The Big Picture: "Ambient DNA" and New Age Universalism

> It probably began in the natural enclosures of the earth . . . our ancient musicians found a space where sound, once created, could sustain itself timelessly . . .

[96] Ibid., 93.
[97] Ibid., 7.
[98] Birosik, *New Age Music Guide*, xv.
[99] Steven Halpern, "Music and Beyond," *Yoga Journal*, March 1977, 55.
[100] Da Vid, "History and Evolution of Artainment," *The Light Party*, n.d., https://www.lightparty.com/Artainment/EvolutionOfArt.html.
[101] Turner and Hill, *Guide*, x.

> From the caves were born the sanctuaries. . . . The temples, the churches, the basilicas, the architectural enclosures . . . two thousand years of music reverberating in stone chambers . . . inspiring the mysterious emotions of spaces that sing.
>
> Today we are beginning to create spaces electronically, and a new music is emerging . . . bounded only by the infinite spaces of our imagination. We call it *Music from the Hearts of Space.*
>
> — Hill and Turner's introduction to *Hearts of Space*, Feb. 23, 1983 ("Moorish Dreams")

Today, Hill would like you to know that this book-length history of the ambient genre is just a small slice of the *real* story of contemplative sound. "The more you focus on ambient as a handle, and ambient as a genre, and ambient as a historical fact with chapters and verses that you can account for, the less you get the big picture," Hill tells me. The ambient label simply puts a convenient name to "a very very old approach to music."

How old?

"So, starting out with Paleolithic cave drawings . . . ." Hill takes me to his office to review his keynote address titled "Ambient Music: From the Caves to the Cosmos" from a 2014 ambient music conference. We are looking at a drawing of Kokopelli, the flute-playing deity depicted in Indigenous cave art around the Southwestern United States. "The first ambient musician?" the slide reads; Paul Horn's *Inside* plays in the background. Hill posits that cave dwellers made slow, contemplative music to enhance the sacredness and safety of the reverberant cave environment. "Slow, quiet, consonant sound tells your flight or fight response system to stand down," Hill explains as he shuffles through the next several slides: the dome of an Iranian mosque, the interior of a cathedral, and the Temple of Transition at the 2011 Burning Man, all designed for sonic reverberance to reinforce inhabitants' senses of safety and to support their experiences of transcendence.

Another slide presents stills from Stanley Kubrick's film *2001: A Space Odyssey* (1968) depicting the famous match cut of primitive man's weaponized bone with a satellite orbiting earth several million years later. As with Kubrick's flash-forward depiction of human technological achievement, Hill states, "We are now living out the cultural repercussions of the evolution in music, from primitive to cosmic. While hurtling into the future we've found it necessary to resurrect our deep past to understand ourselves." From here I get a snapshot history of the evolution of contemplative music, starting when "electronic instruments begin to break free of limits of acoustics." The juxtaposition of Kubrick's match cut with the history of electronic music brings Hill's cosmic perspective into focus, and for that matter the entire sensibility of *Hearts*, wherein electronic contemplative music appears as a space-age evolution within a vastly broader history of reverberant sound altering human consciousness.

Yet Hill's reference to Kubrick's *2001*, illustrative as it is of "big picture" thinking about human cultural evolution, also indexes the historical and cultural locality of transhistorical and universalistic thought about technology to the psychedelic imagination of the '60s and '70s. Indeed the film itself, released at the height of psychedelic culture's mass popularization in 1968, attempts to induce cosmic thought from the beginning by way of György Ligeti's fearsome, ravishing proto-ambient orchestral fantasia *Atmosphères* (1961). Densely woven micropolyphonies, dissonant chord clusters, and unearthly timbres billow over a black screen during the film's overture, intimating the glittering, formless space dust from which life emerged. Ligeti's dissonant, mercurial space music recurs during the kaleidoscopic Star Gate sequence that sends the protagonist careening into the void, destined to rebirth humanity anew. Leading up to this sequence, Pleistocene vignettes and space-age fables allegorize the promise and perilousness of human technological advancement. Posters advertised the film as "the ultimate trip."[102]

Kubrick may have spurned psychedelics, but his evolutionary vision could not have been more timely. As psychedelic drugs entailed visionary experience, psychedelic culture craved visionary art. Poets of the moment collapsed ancient and future, inner and outer through non-drug recreations of "eternal now" and "far out" infinitude, or what writer Aldous Huxley colorfully called the "perpetual present made up of one continually changing apocalypse."[103] More radically, New Agers aspired to an equivalent depth and breadth of empathy, carrying over from the psychedelic trip what literary critic R. A. Durr described as "a feeling of identity with the universe and love for all things."[104]

"Do you remember having been a cosmic being . . . nameless . . . formless . . . ethereal . . . made out of the substance of pure light?" reads the poem

[102] Dan Chiasson, "'2001: A Space Odyssey': What It Means, and How It Was Made," *New Yorker*, April 16, 2018, https://www.newyorker.com/magazine/2018/04/23/2001-a-space-odyssey-what-it-means-and-how-it-was-made.

[103] Aldous Huxley, *The Doors of Perception* (London: Thinking Ink Ltd., 2011), 7.

[104] R. A. Durr, *Poetic Vision and the Psychedelic Experience* (Syracuse, NY: Syracuse University Press, 1970), viii.

from Sufi leader Pir Vilayat Inayat Khan opening Hill and Turner's 1981 written guide to *Hearts*'s space music. "Do you remember all the festivities out of which you were born—of which you are a part? This is the meaning of the cosmic celebration in the heavens . . ."

" . . . And this," the authors respond, "is the inspiration for the *Music from the Hearts of Space*."[105]

For Californians approaching the "new consciousness" in the late 1970s and '80s, "New Age" was just one of many imperfect ways to refer to an irreducibly broad variety of cultural forms. As religion scholar Steven J. Sutcliffe observes, "New Age" was never a distinctive empirical entity, but rather a "codeword for the heterogeneity of alternative spirituality."[106] Within this alternative spirituality network, "new age music" coded a heterogeneity of styles and sounds from across cultures, histories, and genres as capable of fostering states of self-dispossession, unitive awareness, and ultimately a new holistic consciousness. What brought all these spiritualities and musical styles together, from the perspective of the New Ager, is their ability to hasten human evolution toward global unity in what Theodore Roszak called a "planet-wide mutation of mind."[107]

In Hill's big-picture perspective, then, "space music" is not a generic category so much as a way of talking about psychological sounds, sounds that could conceivably affect listening minds anywhere and at any time. Today, he proposes that space music resonates with a particular transhistorical and transcultural "ambient sensibility," a psychological profile that can be traced back to the dawn of humankind. "My contention is that this sensibility has been around for centuries, many centuries," Hill tells me. "If you can find it in as many ethnic music genres as we have found it . . . and if you find even within the Western classical canon slow, contemplative compositions, it proves that that sensibility has just migrated through time. And that's what we have now, whether it's interpreted by new age musicians, ambient musicians, or avant-garde musicians."

The observation that ambient music evinces a contemplative impulse within humans across history, geography, and culture is common among

105 Turner and Hill, *Guide*, iii.

106 Steven J. Sutcliffe, *Children of the New Age: A History of Spiritual Practices* (New York: Routledge, 2003), 11.

107 Roszak, *Unfinished Animal*, 4.

ambient's most studied historians. As David Toop writes in his genre-busting ambient history *Ocean of Sound*, "Ambient music is more a way of listening, an umbrella term for attitude, rather than a single identifiable style."[108] The claim that ambient is a personal "attitude" or "sensibility" is certainly a more inclusive and expansive construal of ambient than the claim that ambient constitutes "single identifiable style." What *Hearts* did and does, from this perspective, is tap into this long-standing sensibility.

Hill professes curiosity about the roots of this psychology when I ask why certain people prefer to make ambient music, and enjoy ambient music, over others. "I joke, well they've got ambient DNA," Hill says. "But I'm actually serious about it—ambient DNA means that you, internally, resonate to that sound. You definitely have it, I definitely have it, 100% of my audience definitely has it." In his presentation slideshow, a slide with the heading "Ambient DNA" reads: "Definition: a sensitivity to and preference for music and art that creates a sense of space, openness, calm and concentration. Genetic predisposition. May be shared by up to 35% of population."

"Where did you get the 35%?" I ask Hill.

"Made it up! Just based on anecdotal evidence."

"Do you think the psychology is in any way attached to the sociology?" I inquire. "The social background of the listeners?"

"No I don't. In fact, I've got major amounts of anecdotal evidence to prove that. Because we've now been a national show since 1983, so for 32 years now, going on 33, and we've heard from literally every kind of person you can imagine. Ages go from 14 to 80-plus, and they go from little old ladies to Charlie Manson, who, you know, was a *Hearts of Space* listener."

But *Hearts*'s universalism, from a historical and sociological perspective, was strongly rooted in—and structured by—the particulars of its place and time. In bringing sounds from around the globe into a smoothly flowing and electronically enhanced atmospheric aesthetic, the program gave expression to the technological optimism and universalist idealism of the visionary New Age imagination. Notably, this aesthetic indirectly drew on media theory of the 1950s and '60s that became popular with countercultural and Human Potential ideas such as Buckminster Fuller's "comprehensive design,"

[108] David Toop, *Ocean of Sound: Aether Talk, Ambient Sound and Imaginary Worlds* (London: Serpent's Tail, 1995), 62.

McLuhan's electrified "global village," and Stewart Brand's "whole earth."[109] Hill and Turner's space music presentations brought to life these writers' visions of an imploded, instantaneous, and integrated global media environment, microcosmically metaphorizing the electrified whole earth in which it presumptively existed. Transhistorical as the program was, it skewed toward the contemporary and the electronic in aestheticizing its own techno-atmospheric functionality. The gentle, almost translucent sounds of *Hearts*, with their sheer synthetic timbres and long reverb trails, brought to life the etheric sound of radio's electric embrace. The improvisatory nature of these electronically enhanced sounds, in their spontaneous, organic rhythmic arrangements, recreated audio in the image of nature—but a nature clearly infused with electricity and pliably integrated with what Stewart Brand liked to call "soft tech," personal tools more "alive, resilient, adaptive, maybe even lovable" than their infrastructural counterparts.[110] Often forsaking melody for chordal clouds, cascading tones, and drone zones, *Hearts*'s music could appear as non-hierarchical, spherical, and immersive as McLuhan's theoretical "auditory" or "acoustic space."[111] While stretching deep into the past, *Hearts*'s spacious sonification of futurity was distinctly shaped by the holistic technological optimism of its time.

Even more fundamentally, Hill and Turner's whole-earth sensibility was rooted in the flexible, cosmopolitan character of Cold War US American liberalism. As historian Fred Turner documents, US intellectuals and policy makers during and after the Second World War sought to nurture a nation that would be "united in heterogeneity" and globally empathetic.[112] Curators, artists, and designers in turn created what Turner calls "democratic surrounds," inclusive environments that permitted audiences to locate themselves within a differentiated world of individuals.[113] This mission extended to alternative media like Pacifica Radio, and to freeform programs like *Hearts*, that brought a remarkable array of musics from around the world together under a single umbrella. *Hearts*, to be sure, is resolutely Western in origin, with most programs during its first decade only occasionally venturing

[109] R. Buckminster Fuller, *Ideas and Integrities: A Spontaneous Autobiographical Disclosure* (1963; repr. New York: Collier Books, 1970), 79; Marshall McLuhan, *Understanding Media: The Extensions of Man*, 2nd ed. (New York: Mentor, 1964), 265, 46; Brand, *The Whole Earth Catalog.*

[110] J. Baldwin and Stewart Brand, eds., *Soft-Tech* (New York: Penguin Books, 1978), 5.

[111] Edmund Carpenter and Marshall McLuhan, "Acoustic Space," in *Explorations in Communication*, ed. Edmund Carpenter and Marshall McLuhan (Toronto: Beacon Press, 1960), 67.

[112] Fred Turner, *The Democratic Surround: Multimedia and American Liberalism from World War II to the Psychedelic Sixties* (Chicago: University of Chicago Press, 2013), 158.

[113] Turner, *The Democratic Surround*, 55.

outside the United States and Western Europe. But while US American and Western European artists dominated most of *Hearts*'s early playlists, Hill and Turner also drew on a range of sounds from across Eastern Europe and South Asia, and less commonly East Asia, the Middle East, and South America. Its slant toward Indian and Japanese music in its earliest years reflected the counterculture's fascination with Asian religions and spiritualities, which were often seen as antidotes to Western materialism (e.g., Box 2.4). Yet in broadly reaching out and finding continuities with nonwestern cultures, as well as in pulling together classical, popular, and traditional musics, Hill and Turner approached *Hearts* as a whole earth in itself, often immersing listeners in a diversity of the globe's music-media ecology.

BOX 2.4 *Hearts* playlist: September 17, 1976 ("The Night after Joya")

Wendy Carlos, "Fall"
Bhagavan Das & Amazing Grace, "Yah Devi"
Radha Krishna Temple & George Harrison, "Bhaja Hure Mana"
Bhagavan Das, "Ah"
Bhagavan Das & Amazing Grace, "Mother Song"
Radha Krishna Temple, "Gopinatha"
Radha Krishna Temple, "Govinda"
George Harrison, "Beware of Darkness"
Radha Krishna Temple, "The Sri Isopanisad"
Freelight, "Ancient Voices"
Siddha, "Lovely One"
The Senior Dagar Brothers, "Raga Asavari"
Bhagavan Das & Amazing Grace, "Raga Hemant"
George Harrison, "Be Here Now"
Donovan, "There Is an Ocean"
Ralph Vaughan Williams, *The Lark Ascending*, perf. New Philharmonia Orchestra, cond. Sir Adrian Boult
Frederic Mompou, "Damunt De Tu Nomes Les Flors," perf. Victoria De Los Ángeles
Jordan Stenberg, taped recording 8/17/76
Iasos, "The Angels of Comfort"
Donovan, "The Dignity of Man"

Hearts's universalism, like many universalisms as idealized by white westerners, also involved exceptions.[114] Most conspicuously, the hosts in the show's first decade often steered clear of Afrodiasporic sounds and expressions presented by black artists, excepting the occasional recording by Sun Ra, Weather Report, or Alice Coltrane. Although jazz and rock figured prominently in the programming, Hill and Turner opted for what music scholar George Lewis calls a "Eurological" construction of these genres in gravitating toward European labels like ECM and white rock acts like Pink Floyd, Tangerine Dream, and Ash Ra Tempel.[115] These exclusions perhaps rested on a binary association of blackness with urban noise and whiteness with pastoral quietude; relatedly, the cultural construction of whiteness as blank and invisible mapped onto the decorporealized spaces that *Hearts*'s DJs sought to produce.[116] The DJs' noninclusion of the soft soul and smooth R&B later popularized through the Quiet Storm format is especially confounding given the styles' aesthetic continuity with much of the singer-songwriter and soft rock they broadcasted during the early–mid 1970s.[117] In this sense, *Hearts*'s aural surrounds during the show's first decade were less reflective of US American social space than even the Top 40 stations of the time, which music scholar Eric Weisbard argues "channeled cultural democracy" through a commercially lucrative Black-positive pluralism.[118]

Such exceptions point to the ways *Hearts*'s aspiration to universality—always more a motivating ideal than description of its reality—belonged as much to its DJs' racial identities and social status as to their good intentions. As critical race theorist and geographer Arun Saldanha notes, Western psychedelic culture's commitment to self-transformation through mysticism, exoticism, drugs, music, and universalism fomented from white middle-class explorations of the "fringe possibilities" of modern bourgeois

[114] Richard A. Peterson and Roger M. Kern, "Changing Highbrow Taste: From Snob to Omnivore," *American Sociological Review* 61, no. 5 (October 1996): 900–907; Bethany Bryson, "Anything but Heavy Metal: Symbolic Exclusion and Musical Dislikes," *American Sociological Review* 61, no. 5 (October 1996): 884–99; Robin James, "Is the Post- in Post-Identity the Post- in Post-Genre?," *Popular Music* 36, no. 1 (2017): 21–32.

[115] George E. Lewis, "Improvised Music after 1950: Afrological and Eurological Perspectives," *Black Music Research Journal* 16, no. 1 (Spring 1996): 91–122.

[116] David Ake, "The Emergence of the Rural American Ideal in Jazz: Keith Jarrett and Pat Metheny on ECM Records," *Jazz Perspectives* 1, no. 1 (May 2007): 29–59, esp. 52, 59; Richard Dyer, *White: Essays on Race and Culture* (New York: Routledge, 1997), esp. 33–34 and 44–45.

[117] Jason King, "The Sound of Velvet Melting: The Power of 'Vibe' in the Music of Roberta Flack," in *Listen Again: A Momentary History of Pop Music*, ed. Eric Weisbard (Durham, NC: Duke University Press, 2007), 172–99.

[118] Eric Weisbard, *Top 40 Democracy: The Rival Mainstreams of American Music* (Chicago: University of Chicago Press, 2014), 6.

rationality, explorations made possible and enjoyable thanks to the versatility and viscosity racial whiteness has long afforded.[119] Although such self-transformations and transcultural explorations were and are not exclusively available to white middle-class westerners, Hill and Turner's whiteness and class status may reasonably be understood to have predisposed them to such pleasures.

Additionally, the musical "universalism" on display can be seen as a demonstration of Hill and Turner's elite tastes at a time when the terms of cultural sophistication were changing. As sociologists Richard Peterson and Roger Kern famously demonstrated, dominant status groups in the late twentieth century largely shifted from exclusionary snobbery to a "discriminating omnivorousness" as a mode of demonstrating taste.[120] This tendency toward selective omnivorousness, as later sociologists have shown, has been for decades most prevalent among upwardly mobile middle-class individuals.[121] And as philosopher Bernard Gendron has illustrated, popular music took on an elevated role in the struggle for cultural capital as standards of high and low began shifting in the 1940s, with the late 1960s becoming a high watermark in the critical legitimation of rock music.[122] From this perspective, *Hearts*'s high-low and east-west universalism, convergent on a new auditory consciousness as it may have seemed, was on another level a demonstration of the DJs' hip high-middlebrow sophistication.

That *Hearts* was and is a product of its founders' tastes does not escape Hill, who has since its earliest years sold the concept of the program in terms of its musical superiority to other new age and background music providers. Today, Hill argues *Hearts* compares favorably to music-based productivity apps like focus@will on the basis of its tasteful curation. "I believe that Ambient DNA is doing the work for me," as Hill tells me of his show's subscribers. "You know, they can tell the difference. One guy said, 'Well here's why I subscribe to *Hearts of Space*: the music's better, a lot better.' "

"So it's a taste thing, too?" I ask Hill.

119 Arun Saldanha, *Psychedelic White: Goa Trance and the Viscosity of Race* (Minneapolis: University of Minnesota Press, 2007), 6–12.

120 Peterson and Kern, "Changing Highbrow Taste," 904.

121 Bryson, "Anything but Heavy Metal"; Josée Johnston and Shyon Baumann, "Democracy versus Distinction: A Study of Omnivorousness in Gourmet Food Writing," *American Journal of Sociology* 113, no. 1 (July 2007): 165–204.

122 Bernard Gendron, *Between Montmartre and the Mudd Club: Popular Music and the Avant-Garde* (Chicago: University of Chicago Press, 2002), 1–2, 10–11.

"Taste is 100% of what I bring to the picture! Taste and experience, you know?" Hill goes on to tell me that he has demonstrated a "great deal" of taste since a young age, something that he says he probably picked up from his parents. "So maybe some of that rubbed off, I don't know. In the end, you're branded by your own proclivities and your enthusiasms. You evolve along those lines." In a follow-up interview, Hill was more circumspect. "In terms of taste, I had been essentially trained to be discriminating my parents, who were part of that generation of upwardly mobile, educated people. Things they bought identified them, so they were careful about it. They were people who bought Danish modern, because they thought it was good design. It was all about quality. . . . I kind of cut my teeth on those kind of judgments. So basically that's what's required of me on this program. To have judgment."

Hill and Turner's program in its first decade may have been as personal and sociocultural as it was universal—and, in effect, as white and high-middlebrow as it was global—but from the DJs' perspective, space music, selected and sequenced with deep care, also addressed something universal of *all* persons: their environmental embeddedness. Hill now attributes their program's success to his and Turner's remarkable ability to select and sequence music that draws listeners into contemplative and unitive states. Their program demonstrated that atmospheric music did not have to dull the senses; on the contrary, such sounds could make room and time for listening ears to wander, dwell, meditate, and awaken. Their thoughtful, timely musical sensibility attracted a remarkably wide audience for a late-night community radio program of mostly instrumental music, eventually leading to the program's syndication on National Public Radio in January 1983. In many ways, then, *Hearts of Space* did enliven and expand a new auditory consciousness that was spreading ever more rapidly from the New Age's "alternative" counterculture into the US middlebrow mainstream.

Coda: New Age Music, from the Margins to the Mainstream

Less than ten years after its national syndication on NPR, *Hearts* was spoofed on the B-movie-riffing cult cable TV hit *Mystery Science Theatre 3000*. On the episode, the human protagonist Joel, inspired by the synth score of their film-of-the-week, offers to teach his robot buddy Crow to make "great new new age music" on the spaceship's wall of keyboards. "Put your finger down, see?" Joel instructs Crow. A synth pad oozes out of the speaker. "You're playing a new age chord now, okay? Just like Yanni! Now put another finger down. . . ." Twinned synth pads flow out to Crow's delight. "See? Now you're playing a Yanni lick. Now hold it down for an hour, hold it down until you get a record contract from Windham Hill!"

"This music's kinda dull, isn't it?" asks Crow.

"Yeah," responds Joel, "but it's a good way to make a lot of money without a big initial investment."

The lights dim as the robot Servo emerges in front of a radio mic. "And now: *Music from Some Guys in Space*," announces Servo, delivering his best Stephen Hill impression. "Tonight on *Music from Some Guys in Space*, more fine new new age music and sounds from super progressive Bay Area new age keyboardist Joel Robinson. Joel will be accompanied on the wall of keyboards by veteran minimalist, Crow T. Robot. We invite you to sit back and enjoy more repetitive new age music as we cruise the space waves. Come along fellow travelers, and enjoy *Music from Some Guys in Space*." Under the spell of Joel's keyboards and Servo's velvety voice, Crow nods off.

The comedic sketch illustrates not just the prominence of *Hearts of Space* by the early 1990s, but also the web of associations around *Hearts* following space music's ascent to the cultural mainstream: the Bay Area, the perceived pretentiousness of the "progressive" music community, soporific musical minimalism, success stories like artist Yanni and record label Windham Hill, Hill's soothing invitations to take listeners on a musical journey—and, tying them all together, the tag "new age." By the time the program aired, major record labels CBS, RCA, A&M, MCA, and Capitol had all either started up or signed distribution deals with new age record labels; the Grammy Awards had a Best New Age Performance category; *Billboard* charted the week's top-selling "New Age Albums"; Windham Hill was grossing upward of $30 million annually; Yanni and Enya had albums with near-platinum RIAA certification in the United States; and *Hearts* was airing weekly on over 270 radio stations nationwide. Since its syndication, *Hearts* had a hand in popularizing ambient audio around the United States, as did the eponymous independent record label that Hill started in 1984. The program's expansively cross-generic and transhistorical "space music" anticipated the lush production aesthetics and freeform polystylism that became associated with the new age category, contributing to the genre's successful consolidation and popularization in the early–mid 1980s. Yet Hill and Turner remained committed to their distinctive sonic vision and the program's basis in alternative media as the 1980s pressed on, at a time when record and radio executives sold jazz, folk-pop, and light-classical fusion under the new age banner in attempts to cross over to an upwardly mobile middle-class adult audience via major record distributors and commercial radio.

By most written accounts, "new age" started gaining currency in Northern California as a catchall genre label between 1976 and 1978, during which time cosmic rock band and *Hearts of Space* favorite Ashra (formerly Ash Ra Tempel) released their *New Age of Earth* album (1976) and media distributor Pacific Arts produced a "New Age Music" bin to categorize otherwise hard-to-slot albums by such artists as Bhagavan Das and Swami Nadabrahmananda.[123] At the time, the genre tag found itself attached to most any recording sold through alternative lifestyle stores and festivals, which is why one 1977 *Yoga Journal* writer called the "new age music" idea "a contradiction in terms" and an umbrella for multiple musical categories.[124] By the time Hill and Turner published their space music guidebook in 1981 including twenty-six separate stylistic categories of space music (including "ambient" and "new age"), the Tower Records in Mountain View, California, had created a similarly eclectic "new age" bin devoted to a growing variety of records that were picking up in sales.[125]

Among these new "new age" records were those of San Francisco label Windham Hill, founded in 1976 by guitarist Will Ackerman, who at its inception marketed the label's folk-tinged music as instrumental jazz. The label had sold over 100,000 LPs during its first five years through independent record stores, alternative distributors, new age retail outlets, and mailing lists; by 1981, upstart pianist George Winston's mini-hit record *Autumn* (1980) accounted for nearly half of sales.[126] The apparent incoherence of such records sitting alongside synth-pop successes Jean-Michel Jarre and Vangelis, prog rockers Tangerine Dream and Mike Oldfield, classical minimalists like Steve Reich and Terry Riley, and the ambient records of Brian Eno rarely went unnoticed—not least by Ackerman himself, who hated the "new age" label—but all such records were nonetheless understood to cohere in their "atmospheric" instrumental aesthetic, in their ability to serve as background sound, and in their appeal to white baby boomers disenchanted with the

[123] "Longplay Shorts," *Variety*, October 25, 1978, 68.

[124] "Music and Beyond," *Yoga Journal*, January 1977, 23.

[125] Chris McGowan, "Instrumental Inroads: Outburst of Quiet Fusion Signals That New Age Has Arrived," *Billboard*, October 25, 1986, N-14.

[126] Sam Sutherland, "Offbeat & Creative, Windham Hill's Carving Its Niche," *Billboard*, May 16, 1981, 37 and 86; Sam Sutherland, "Pianist George Winston: He's Not Like You or Me," *Billboard*, September 5, 1981, 43 and 49.

heavy rock and dance-pop mainstream.[127] "The baby boomers are quite eclectic in their tastes," as Harvard business professor Michael Porter described new age music's audience in a 1985 *LA Times* feature. "They like rock if it's good, but they get tired of the noise."[128] Quiet smoothness and classical/pop crossover were becoming hallmarks of the unlikely new age genre as well as the source of its appeal for both record buyers and promoters. "We prefer to think of our music as 'eclectic,' but in the past it's almost been impossible to figure out where to merchandise our product," reported Michael Delich, marketing director of independent label American Gramaphone, in 1986. "Some stores put us with easy listening, some with rock, others with jazz, and we really didn't belong in any of those sections. So new age is a nice vehicle for us because at least there's a place for it now."[129]

The early–mid 1980s meanwhile saw "new age" expand its reach on the radio. By 1982, *Hearts* was no longer the only ambient audio program on the FM dial, with Steve Pross and John Diliberto having DJed *Star's End* on UPenn's WXPN-FM since 1976, and with Frank Forest heading the space-music show *Musical Starstreams* on progressive rock station KTIM-FM San Rafael. One year later, Hill and Turner launched the one-hour version of *Hearts of Space* through NPR's network (while still continuing the longer late-night program on KPFA well into 1984). By 1985, as *Hearts* spread from 35 to over 100 stations, Forest syndicated *Starstreams*, reaching fifteen different cities on launch.

Hill in the meantime walked a fine line between defending the ascendant new age genre against skeptics and affirming the superiority of his and Turner's curation over market calculations. He heard new age music as more listenable than other background musics, yet he also distinguished his and Turner's ability to sift through and recognize the finest of the genre. "The function of 'muzak' or 'easy listening music' is to *anesthetize* the consciousness of the listener and lead them into a nostalgic trance," jotted Hill in a personal notebook in 1983. "The function of 'new age' music is to *stimulate* consciousness and lead the listener into new states and conditions of awareness. That some 'new age music' fails to achieve the latter and therefore is only a superficially novel version of the former says only that as always, there is

[127] Jack McDonough, "Music for a 'New Age' Surfacing in California," *Billboard*, January 22, 1983, 63.

[128] William Knoedelseder Jr., "Quiet This Time: Baby Boom Rocks Music Scene Again," *Los Angeles Times*, January 1, 1985, 1.

[129] Geoff Mayfield, "The Independents: Oases of Individuality Offering Welcome Relief from Volume Wars," Billboard, October 25, 1986, N–20.

relatively 'good' and 'bad' music." Five years later, Hill denounced the clichéd "yuppie muzak" clogging new age bins while arguing that "the best of the genre invites substantial commitment and concentration from the listener." This form of concentration, he explains, is more "personal and 'holistic'" than other sorts of music listening—"an awareness of individual emotional response as well as the quality of the enveloping ambience being created."[130] As would be typical of ambient music's advocates from Brian Eno onward, Hill employed musical distinctions, as well as an expanded, multimodal notion of musical contemplation, to validate the idea of mood music for highbrow and high-middlebrow skeptics.

More and more record chains picked up the "new age" tag as time went on, and by 1986, a peak year for new age's industry boom, "new age music" for many seemed only tangentially related to alternative spirituality, meditative contemplation, or unitive consciousness. More popularly, it had become shorthand for '80s easy listening. Much as "easy listening" in the postwar years had developed from a radio format into a self-standing musical style and emblem of the professional-managerial adult "Establishment"—to the disdain of boomer rock fans—so the term "new age" reassembled the easy-listening concept for an omnivorous ("eclectic") and upwardly mobile boomer white middle class.[131] Will Ackerman in 1985 called his label's audience "the disenfranchised mainstream . . . mostly 25 to 35 years old, professionals, predominantly white, upper-middle-class and college-educated"—or in short, yuppies, as many articles covering new age music in the mid-1980s pointed out.[132] "New Age is the perfect music for washing one's BMW," read a prominent 1986 *Time* magazine feature on the topic, "which accounts for its stereotyping as yuppie Muzak."[133] Other radio DJs and record executives that same year noted new age's stereotyping by the public as "Beautiful Music of the rock generation," "Mantovani for baby boomers," "Music to consume Valium by," and music for "hip Yuppies waiting in a dentist's office."[134] The music's association with middlebrow affluence derived in large part from the folding

[130] Stephen Hill, "New Age Music Made Simple," *Hearts of Space* website, 1988, archived at Internet Archive, *Wayback Machine*, https://web.archive.org/web/19980128185008fw_/http://hos.com/simple.html.

[131] Keightley, "Music for Middlebrows," 321.

[132] Knoedelseder, "Quiet This Time,", 20.

[133] Michael Walsh, "New Age Comes of Age," *Time*, September 1, 1986, 83.

[134] Greg Mull, "Polygram Presents: Question of the Week," *FMQB*, July 11, 1986, 23; "A&M, Beggar's Banquet Campaign for New Age Music in England," *Variety*, January 29, 1986, 79; Ken Terry, "Major Labels Joining New Age Parade," *Variety*, August 20, 1986, 77; Ron Diaz, WYNF, "Polygram Presents: Question of the Week," *FMQB*, July 11, 1986, 24.

of the "smooth jazz" style into the new age bin, a style that, as musicologist Charles D. Carson details, was dismissed as "crossover" by '70s critics and jazz musicians for its luxe production values, as well as for its deemphasis of improvisation, an element seen as central to jazz's authenticity and blackness.[135] Such associations with middlebrow inauthenticity, perhaps as much as new age's alternative-spirituality origins, was a big reason industry executives in 1986 were equally eager as most musicians to replace the oft-derided "new age" label with tasteful alternatives like "contemporary instrumental."

That same year, influential programming consultant Lee Abrams told *Billboard* that he believed, based on the success of *Hearts* and *Starstreams*, that the country was ready for its first twenty-four-hour new age station. "It will appeal to two types of people," Abrams predicted. "Firstly, those who grew up with progressive rock in the late 1960s and early '70s and this is the next step in their personal musical evolution; secondly, to the person who may not have progressive rock roots and likes nice atmospheric music to relax to, but finds Mantovani awfully old and boring. And if you combine these two types of listeners, you have enough people to make the format viable commercially."[136] Abrams's predictions proved accurate; half a year later, Los Angeles's twenty-four-hour new age radio station, KTWV-FM The Wave, replaced the AOR-formatted KMET-FM in February 1987. Bearing "Music for a New Age" as its slogan, The Wave brought space music side-by-side with the similarly "smooth" sounds of light jazz and soft rock to create a more familiar, and hence more widely accessible, mélange of contemporary background-friendly music. A wave of "Wave format" stations soon swept the United States as the Satellite Music Network syndicated The Wave with over a dozen affiliates, the Progressive Music Network syndicated its own copycat "The Breeze," and nearly two dozen US radio stations independently programed Wave-formatted music.[137]

Most Wave-formatted stations did not sound quite like *Hearts*. Few featured nonwestern selections, while synth and minimalist music only occasionally bumped up against recognizable pop and R&B tunes from artists like Sting, Peter Gabriel, or Sade, as well as the "smooth" jazz-pop fusion of artists like Al Jarreau, Kenny G, or Andreas Vollenweider. As KTWV's

[135] Charles D. Carson, "'Bridging the Gap': Creed Taylor, Grover Washington Jr., and the Crossover Roots of Smooth Jazz," *Black Music Research Journal* 28, no. 1 (Spring 2008): 1–15.

[136] Ed Ochs, "New Age Radio: Syndicated Shows Blaze Cosmic Trail to Format of the Future," *Billboard*, October 25, 1986, N-8.

[137] Terry Wood, "Radio: Brighter Variety in Music Mix Lifts Format to Next Level" *Billboard*, October 29, 1988, N-10

director of programming Christine Brodie stated upon launch, stylistic categories cannot account for the station's "very eclectic" mixtures of music, only "mood."[138] But everything that made it onto The Wave was also specified by targeted audience testing, with playlists assembled based on adult research subjects' rankings of music recordings.[139] According to Frank Cody, vice president of programming at KTWV, this target audience overlapped most substantially with a 26-million-strong demographic segment that market researchers at Grey Advertising identified as "UltraConsumers," nontraditionalist urbanites who valued luxury goods and "the thrill of trying new things."[140] These initial audiences liked trying new things so much, they quickly moved on to other stations—by the end of 1990, most Wave-formatted stations had either died or flipped to a Smooth Jazz or AC format, entirely abandoning the space music associated with the new age genre. Promoters like Geffen Records' Christina Anthony likewise veered from "new age" to "New Adult Alternative" as a way of describing Wave-friendly music. "As long as we steer away from the term 'new age,'" she told *Billboard* in 1990, "more and more people will become interested in the format."[141]

The Wave was just one of many experiments in format fragmentation and narrowcasting since the 1970s—from Soft Adult Contemporary, Quiet Storm, and Eclectic-Oriented Rock before it, to Adult Top 40, Adult Album Alternative, and Urban Adult Contemporary after—designed to draw in advertising dollars by appealing to the tastes of middle- and upper-middle class adults seeking soft-yet-modern alternatives to youth-oriented Top 40.[142] The logic of "crossover" formats like these, as Eric Weisbard explains, was to "structure eclecticism rather than imposing aesthetic values," a strategy that Weisbard contrasts with the authenticity-oriented ideologies guiding genre formation in the 1970s.[143] Generic constructions like "space music," however, initially imposed the structuring of eclecticism *as* an aesthetic value, one originally based in the whole-earth mentality of the New Age movement, as well as in the themed freeform of radio programs like *Hearts*. What motivated

[138] Steve Sutton, "Industrial Noise," *The Hard Report*, February 20, 1987, 18.

[139] Simon Barber, "Smooth Jazz: A Case Study in the Relationships between Commercial Radio Formats, Audience Research and Music Production," *Radio Journal—International Studies in Broadcast and Audio Media* 8, no. 1 (2010): 56.

[140] Jon Pareles, "New Age Music Goes Nowhere Successfully," *Chicago Tribune*, December 3, 1987, 100.

[141] Devra Hall, "The Majors: In the Mainstream Game, New Age Today Is a Marketplace, Not a Genre," *Billboard*, November 3, 1990, N–4

[142] Sterling and Keith, *Sounds of Change*, 167.

[143] Weisbard, *Top 40 Democracy*, 9.

this value in the New Age network of the 1970s and '80s United States was not a democracy of tastes, but a rather a combination of the techno-utopian universalism and high-middlebrow omnivorousness that emerged from its largely liberal educated white upper-middle class adult demographic. As this eclecticism became commodified on a national scale as an "adult" alternative to the youth-oriented pop/rock mainstream, and as it concomitantly incorporated more conventionally MOR comforts, new age lost credibility with many omnivorous consumers—especially those on the younger side—who associated it with middlebrow yuppiedom. Just as quickly, new age fell out of favor with baby boomers who chafed at the music's associations with, well, actual New Agers and the lifestyle commodity culture that they spawned.

Indeed, what became nearly as mainstream as "new age music" by 1987 was hip and highbrow skepticism of the new age category as a marketing calculation, and the observation of hypocrisy in hip consumerism masquerading as transcendence of material culture. "New age fantasies often intersect with mainstream materialism," observed a *Time* magazine cover story on New Age, "the very thing that many New Age believers profess to scorn."[144] The criticism was hardly new—take, for instance, the scathing *Washington Post* satire nearly ten years earlier skewering the commercialism on display at the New Age Awareness Fair for offering new consciousness "at a discount"—but what had changed was how "new age music" had become so popularly synonymous with upper-middle-class comfort disguised as contemplation.[145] Even across the pond in England, where "new age" was just catching on as a tag in the late '80s, one London Tower Records employee sardonically described new age as "music for the muesli set with a positive ioniser in the corner who look at their Habitat furniture as they pay off the mortgage on their hi-fi."[146] The dreamy spaciousness associated with uplifting space music would be ever more widely (mis)understood, by way of the "new age" label, as an anodyne luxury good hypocritically deemed an "alternative" for the middlebrow masses, rather than as a catalyst of contemplation and technology of expanded consciousness.

What many listeners today forget, as a result, was the propensity for musicians associated with New Age spiritualities to embrace futuristic techno-utopianism, to experiment outside popular convention, and to

[144] Otto Friedrich, "New Age Harmonies," *Time*, December 7, 1987, 62.

[145] Cynthia Gorney, "Wares of Awareness: Psychic and Spiritual Necessities for the Enlightened Self," *Washington Post*, July 11, 1978, C1.

[146] Mark Prendergast, "The New Age Music Conundrum," *Sound on Sound*, January 1987, 66.

commit to independent production and distribution channels, as Hill did (and still does) before and after the mainstreaming of new age as a genre. As new age labels and Wave-format stations turned away from the electronic and minimalist in favor of more familiar idioms like jazz fusion and soft pop, Hill continued to approach his program according to the far-out atmospheric and flow-directed dictates of his contemplative space-oriented concept. The result, as from the beginning, is a bolder, more clear-eyed, and more exploratory aesthetic vision than those provided by labels like Windham Hill or stations like The Wave, one that neither shies from the extremes of stillness and quietude *nor* rejects soft comforts in pursuit of alignment of the inner self with the heavens. This aesthetic adventurousness was of a piece with the searching nature of the grassroots spirituality culture from which it came—for the visionary "universality" of the Aquarian consensus, as Theodore Roszak wrote, must aspire to "more than simple eclecticism; it must also be *convergence*. . . . Eclecticism sympathetically gathers together all the variations; universality hunts for the theme underlying them."[147] Top-down (or outside-in) approaches to music, like middlebrow marketing calculations—or sociological accounts of taste—cannot wholly account for why big-picture, universalist thinking has fueled the most lasting musical visions.

[147] Roszak, *Unfinished Animal*, 250.

PART 3

DRIFT OFF . . .

. . . to Ambient Music

3

Brian Eno's Ambivalent Ambiences

Introduction: Ambient against New Age

By 1989, Brian Eno had had enough of new age. "I generally find it too spineless and 'secure,'" he told an interviewer. "There is no thrill for the listener." He recounts the "torture" of having a sampler from the Private Music label "forced" on him by a driver overly interested in crystals and homeopathy. "Of course there is good and bad," he continued, but new age had fallen victim to the "mindless use of electronics."[1] Eno's negative assessment was actually a change of tone for the artist, who formerly did his best to apologize for a genre he had no great personal love for. "Of course, a lot of New Age music is bad," Eno had told an interviewer the year prior, "but so is most pop. I think it's an advance that people can listen to music without beats."[2] Eno's view of new age, however, as for many involved in rock, classical, and experimental music, soured on the torrent of unchallenging jazz-pop and formless synth doodles sold under the category. "It has become very easy for anyone to produce a tape of blurring noises mixed with 'pretty' sounds and call it New Age," he griped. "I realise I am partly responsible for this and regret the misunderstanding."[3]

Eno's presumed distance from the new age genre followed roughly a decade in which "ambient music," as coined by Eno, was widely recognized alongside new age and space music one of many emergent styles of ambient audio. Eno himself, according to Stephen Hill, attested in a fan letter that he could not have come up with anything closer to his own taste than the new-age-inclusive *Hearts of Space*.[4] As the decade progressed, many record

[1] Mark Prendergast, "Brian Eno: Thoughts, Words, Music and Art: Part Two," *Sound on Sound*, February 1989, 56–57.

[2] Divina Infusino, "For Brian Eno, Humor Helps, but Not Hype," *San Diego Union-Tribune*, September 11, 1988, E-1.

[3] Prendergast, "Brian Eno: Part Two," 57.

[4] Stephen Hill, interview with author, July 23, 2018; Eric Tamm, *Brian Eno: His Music and the Vertical Color of Sound* (London: Faber & Faber, 1988), 165–66 fn. 12. In their space music guide, Hill and Turner's recommendations under the "ambient" category have more of an avant-garde slant than

Turn On, Tune In, Drift Off. Victor Szabo, Oxford University Press. © Oxford University Press 2023.
DOI: 10.1093/oso/9780190699307.003.0004

catalogers, writers, and scholars recognized Eno as a prominent composer among new age artists, with ambient music described as a style or subgenre of new age or space music.[5]

Yet around the mid-1980s, several writers also begin describing Eno as a "visionary," "forerunner," and "first" of the new age genre, or at least the first to "legitimize" it as a genre.[6] As radio host and author John Schaefer wrote in a 1987 new music guide, Eno's *Ambient* series "remains a milestone in the evolution of 'space music' and its later offshoot, New Age."[7] Several that same year bolstered Eno's credibility by describing him as a studio "experimenter," including the *Chicago Tribune*'s Jon Pareles, who wrote that Eno's ambient work "inadvertently anticipated New Age music," and Joe Brown in the *Washington Post*, who asserted that new age "never caught up" to Brian Eno's "amorphous" and "nebulous" experiments.[8] Some, too, borrowed Eno's distinctions between ambient and Muzak to cleave aurally interesting ambient ("to be played quietly and half-heard," according to Pareles) from ignorable new age ("strictly nonstick, audio Teflon").[9]

The labels "ambient" and "new age," despite their shared association with atmospheric aesthetics and calming effects, had by decade's end acquired different meanings for hip and highbrow listeners across the anglophone world. Through new age's transformation from a scene- to industry-based genre,[10] new age music came to represent middlebrow Baby boomer quiescence disguised as alternativism, with its most popular artists heard, as US critic John Rockwell put it in 1986, as brashly imitating "third-world" and "folk" styles, more simplistic than simple, and too often confusing "meditation

most others: alongside the first three records of the *Ambient* series, they list the debut recording of Morton Feldman's *Rothko Chapel* (1976), Bay Area composer Alden Jenks's 1972 Buchla drone piece *Space (for Stephen Hill)* (1972), and California space-music performer's Kevin Braheny Fortune's unreleased *Tuned Wind/The Dragon Waits*. By contrast, the DJs solely categorized music with lyrics explicitly connected to the themes of the New Age movement as "new age." Anna Turner and Stephen Hill, *Music from the Hearts of Space: Guide to Cosmic, Transcendent and Innerspace Music* (San Francisco: Music from the Hearts of Space, 1981).

[5] See note 80 of the Introduction.

[6] John Rockwell, "The Pop Life," *New York Times*, June 20,1980, C30; Jim Washburn, "Visions of Eno," *Orange County Register*, November 6, 1987; Richard Garneau, "Ritual and Symbolism in New Age Music," *Pacific Review of Ethnomusicology* 4 (1987): 58; Ted Greenwald, "New Age Now: An Introduction," *New Age Musicians*, GPI Collectors' Edition, March/April 1988, 7.

[7] John Schaefer, *New Sounds: A Listener's Guide to New Music* (New York: Harper & Row, 1987), 12.

[8] Jon Pareles, "New Age Music Goes Nowhere Successfully," *Chicago Tribune*, December 3, 1987; Joe Brown, "Nine to Herald The "New Age,'" *Washington Post*, October 2, 1987, N19.

[9] Pareles, "New Age Music Goes Nowhere."

[10] On "scene-based" and "industry-based" genre forms, see note 12 in the Preface.

with relaxation, if not outright somnolence."[11] Critics increasingly adopted feminized terms to describe new age music's easy-listening blandness and pop inauthenticity from the vantage of highbrow and masculinist systems of aesthetic value.[12] "It's soft and sweet, smooth and unassuming," as Pareles mocked in a 1985 *New York Times* essay. "It turns up at better restaurants all around town. It's not the latest recipe for creme caramel—it's 'new age' music, a creditable idea gone awry."[13]

Ambient, by contrast, although once commonly identified as a subgenre or style overlapping with new age, was increasingly seen by critics and musicians as something different, something more affectively and aesthetically involving. As Sydney-based critic Lynden Barber wrote in 1987, "It's important to draw a distinction between 'ambient music' which, in the hands of people like Jon Hassell and David Sylvian, can accommodate a depth of expression, and the deliberate superficialities of 'New Age.' "[14] "Unlike New Age music's flawless emulsions," *Melody Maker* critic Paul Oldfield wrote correspondingly in 1990, "Eno's ambient is fabulously complex."[15] And Eno himself has continually reflected a dissatisfaction with new age's expressive range, whether describing the music as "rather watery," or expressing annoyance with its "cliché of everything being harmony and unity."[16]

In truth, the cliché of new age as wishy-washy harmoniousness was itself an oversimplification of the music's far-reaching psychedelic, contemplative, and universalist aspirations, an oversimplification calculated for the mainstream record market by promoters and distributors. Critics like Barber took offense to new age's apparent inoffensiveness, arguing that "the most

[11] John Rockwell, "New-Age Music Searches for Its Proper Niche," *New York Times*, June 22, 1986, 25, 29.

[12] On easy listening and feminized inauthenticity, see Keir Keightley, "Music for Middlebrows: Defining the Easy Listening Era, 1946–1966," *American Music* 26, no. 3 (Fall 2008): 309–35; Rebecca Leydon, "The Soft-Focus Sound: Reverb as a Gendered Attribute in Mid-Century Mood Music," *Perspectives of New Music* 39, no. 2 (Summer 2001): 96–107.

[13] Jon Pareles, "'New Age Music' Just Keeps Oozing Along," *New York Times*, September 29, 1985, 25.

[14] Lynden Barber, "Slowing Down the Airwaves," *Sydney Morning Herald*, May 18, 1987, 3.

[15] Paul Oldfield, "Eno: Patter of Life and Death," *Melody Maker*, October 13, 1990, 53.

[16] Stephen Hill, Brian Eno, Peter Gena, and Charles Amirkhanian, "Brian Eno Day," February 12, 1988, https://archive.org/details/AM_1988_02_12_c2/; Andy Gill, "Brian Eno: Towards an Understanding of Pop Past and Present," Q, November 1993, Rock's Back Pages, https://www.rocksbackpages.com/Library/Article/brian-eno-towards-an-understanding-of-pop-past-and-present.

contentious feature of New Age is its spineless and simplistic lack of contention."[17] Even artist and promoter Suzanne Doucet, perhaps Los Angeles's most active advocate for new age music at the time, decried the "exploitative music that imitates only the surface elements of new age music, yet calls itself by the same name."[18] In response to this oversimplification, critic Bruce Elder proposed distinguishing two ends of an ambient audio spectrum—on the one end, the "emotionally enriching and artistically satisfying . . . neoclassical ambience" of artists like Harold Budd, Daniel Lentz, or Pauline Oliveros, and on the other, the popular "folk-based ambience" of artists like Kitaro, William Ackerman, or Enya, a sound that Jon Pareles called "largely trivial and tranquilizing."[19] Mark Prendergast adopted a similar distinction in the UK mag *Sound on Sound* when contrasting Eno's " 'future' instrumental music, which breaks the boundaries of the past," from new age, the majority of which is just " 'old age' sound repackaged."[20] Ambient music, dismissed in the 1970s and early '80s by rock fans as too placid, and by classical critics as too pop, had by the end of the eighties gained clout internationally as innovative and expressively complex art, in contrast to placid, pop new age.

How did this happen? Some critics and scholars have characterized ambient music's distinction from other atmospheric genres like easy listening or new age as strictly taste-based, an elitist product of the cultural capital accrued from Eno's art-world authentications and critical backing.[21] And indeed, as this chapter illustrates, Eno credibly put ambient music into dialogue with key figures and movements associated with the avant-garde, at once demonstrating the relevance of atmospheric music to art-world canons and academic discourses while bolstering its credibility with tastemakers in the popular music world. Accordingly, no comprehensive study of ambient music can do without the insights of scholars like Bernard Gendron, who has illustrated how institutional and discursive processes of accreditation negotiated popular music's cultural value in the 20th century, or Sarah Thornton, who has shown how highbrow and masculinist systems of connoisseurship accorded certain styles of twentieth-century popular music,

[17] Barber, "Slowing Down the Airwaves."

[18] Suzanne Doucet, "Success Has Diluted New Age Music," *Billboard*, June 18, 1988, 9.

[19] Bruce Elder, "Budd Flowers with Help from Cocteaus," *Sydney Morning Herald*, February 7, 1989, 19; Pareles, "Oozing Along."

[20] Mark Prendergast, "The New Age Music Conundrum," *Sound on Sound*, January 1987, 65–69.

[21] Timothy Morton, *Ecology without Nature: Rethinking Environmental Aesthetics* (Cambridge, MA: Harvard University Press, 2007), 153–54; see also note 112 in Introduction.

like ambient music, hip subcultural distinction from a middlebrow and feminized "mainstream."[22]

But ambient music's eventual success cannot be reduced to a matter of institutional and discursive accreditation, either. As this chapter illustrates, the stylistic bent and technical acumen of Eno and his collaborators set the sounds of the *Ambient* records apart from a great deal of the mainstreamed new age of the 1980s. While the peddlers of the new age pushed music boasting affective uplift; familiar acoustic arrangements; and fusions of folk, world, jazz, and classical to the middle-class mainstream; Eno and his colleagues' more affectively ambivalent and overtly experimental atmospheric music provided an expressive framework for staking separate genre territory—while yet retaining the psychedelic cast of 1960s and '70s spiritual jazz, cosmic rock, space music, and, yes, new age.

This chapter examines the genesis, sound, and reception of five key albums between 1975 and 1982—Brian Eno's *Discreet Music*, and the four installments of Eno's *Ambient* series—that set the stylistic and discursive terms by which ambient music would later attain distinction from other genres of atmospheric music, especially new age. During this key period, Eno applied the lessons of his avant-garde training to the recorded medium—like many of his art-school-trained contemporaries translating "art into pop," as music writers Simon Frith and Howard Horne have described—and articulated the results of these applications with catchy conceptual concision.[23] Yet while Eno foregrounded the experimental provenance of these records in writings and interviews, he and his collaborators exuded pop sensibilities, filtering jazzy modal improvisations through sophisticated studio production and cutting-edge electronics. The products of this art-pop intermixture sonically and thematically conflated the technological with the natural while displaying a distinctive expressive slant toward the detached, dreamy, introspective, and mildly melancholy. These records' sensuous sounds, alongside Eno's erudite authentications, provided the aesthetic and conceptual latticework for future musicians, listeners, and critics to reconceive drifting, impersonal atmospheric music—as already established in such records as Irv Teibel's *Environments* series, or on Stephen Hill and Anna Turner's *Music from the Hearts of Space*—as hip and highbrow art.

[22] Bernard Gendron, *Between Montmartre and the Mudd Club: Popular Music and the Avant-Garde* (Chicago: University of Chicago Press, 2002); Sarah Thornton, *Club Cultures: Music, Media and Subcultural Capital*, U.S. Edition (Hanover, NH: University Press of New England, 1996).

[23] Simon Frith and Howard Horne, *Art into Pop* (New York: Methuen, 1987).

Discreet Music

Eno's Indiscreet Passivity

As Brian Eno tells it, his first album of ambient music, *Discreet Music*, was conceived by accident. The catalyzing incident occurred when a taxi hit the rock star as he was crossing the road in January 1975; a second accident, in consequence of the first, took place when a friend of Eno's, performance artist and punk musician Judy Nylon, gifted the convalescent artist a record of some "18th-century harp music."[24] As Eno recalls, he put on the record with "considerable difficulty" after Nylon left, but only upon reclining again did he realize he could barely hear the music, with one stereo channel dropped out and the volume too low.[25] Not wanting to get up again to adjust, Eno rested:

> So I drifted into this kind of fitful sleep, a mixture of pain-killers and tiredness. And I started hearing this record as if I'd never heard music before. It was a really beautiful experience, I got the feeling of icebergs, you know? I would just occasionally hear the loudest parts of the music, get a little flurry of notes coming out above the sound of the rain—and then it'd drift away again. And I began to think of environmental music—music deliberately constructed to occupy the background. And I realised that Muzak was a very strong concept and not a load of rubbish, as most people supposed.[26]

Eno latched onto the idea of music just barely surfacing in the listener's perceptual field, like the fraction of an iceberg seen from above.[27] Discreet music.

Eno later related this story of ambient's discovery-by-accident in the liner notes to *Discreet Music*. The anecdote has since become famed as ambient music's origin myth, told and retold by Eno, fans, journalists, and scholars over the ensuing years. Although recounted with varying details, it nearly always represents Eno as a passive conduit in the circuitry between a harp

[24] Brian Eno, liner notes to *Discreet Music*, Obscure 3, 1975, LP. Although Eno has not since specified the "18th-century harp music" in question, one likely candidate is a 1957 LP record by harpist Nicanor Zabaleta titled just that—*18th Century Harp Music*—whose appearance on a label called Esoteric Records might also have inspired the name of Eno's Obscure imprint.

[25] Lester Bangs, "Eno," *Musician, Player & Listener* 21, November 1979, 44.

[26] Ian MacDonald, "Before and after Science: Part One: Accidents Will Happen," *New Musical Express*, November 26, 1977, 33.

[27] Gene Kalbacher, "Profile: Brian Eno," *Modern Recording & Music*, October 1982, 50.

record, broken speakers, and his own busted body. Nylon, however, recalls events differently:

> I put the harp music on and balanced it as best as I could from where I stood; he caught on immediately to what I was doing and helped me balance the softness of the rain patter with the faint string sound for where he lay in the room. There was no "ambience by mistake." Neither of us invented ambient music; that he could convince EG Music to finance his putting out a line of very soft sound recordings is something quite different.[28]

According to Nylon, "discreet music" was not an accidental epiphany, but rather a coordinated effort. The narrative behind its creation, Nylon suggests, made for good promotional fodder—a way of selling the idea of "discreet music" to label Editions EG and potential buyers. And indeed, if a personal notebook from 1966 is any indication, the idea of discreet music had gestated for longer than Eno discloses in his origin myth: "Make some music to be heard and not listened to," the teenage Eno wrote, nearly ten years before *Discreet Music* came into being.[29]

This origin myth is not the only narrative in which Eno positions himself tangentially, as contingency rather than origin, in the realization of *Discreet Music*'s title track. The liner notes, for instance, describe how the track emerged from a sequencer and tape delay system that required "little or no intervention" on Eno's part. "I tend towards the roles of the planner and programmer, and then become an audience to the results," explains Eno. "It is a point of discipline to accept this passive role, and for once, to ignore the tendency to play the artist by dabbling and interfering." Eno elsewhere recounted how *Discreet Music*'s timbral modifications and half-speed playback came about almost "automatically" due to distractions during the recording process.

> Once I got it going the phone started ringing, people started knocking on the door, and I was answering the phone and adjusting all this stuff as it ran.

[28] Judy Nylon, "Live Now, Wise Up, Die Well: An Interview with Judy Nylon, Punk Legend," interview by Bart Plantenga, October 2001, http://www.3ammagazine.com/litarchives/oct2001/interview_judy_nylon.html. Thanks to Elizabeth Lindau for making me aware of Nylon's testimony.

[29] Michael Bracewell, *Re-Make/Re-Model: Becoming Roxy Music* (Cambridge, MA: Da Capo, 2007), 184.

> I almost made that without listening to it. It was really automatic music. The next day [Robert] Fripp came around and we were going through these things I'd made and I put that one on by accident at half speed and it sounded very, very good. I thought it was probably one of the best things I'd ever done and I didn't even realize I was doing it at the time.[30]

As with the harp music story, these statements illustrate the extent to which Eno rhetorically sidelined his own intentions in *Discreet Music*'s realization, purposively centering his "passive role" in the machinery of "automatic music."

Discreet Music's rhetorical making highlights the significance of Eno's foregrounded passivity to both the artistic legitimation and stylistic development of the ambient genre to come. While all sorts of background music and ambient audio preceded and informed the making of *Discreet Music*, Eno's rhetorical and technical depersonalizations endowed the ambient concept with both cultural authority and affective cool. Consistent with contemporaneous experimental music practices, Eno's engagement with automated systems credibly and explicitly aligned his work with an experimental avant-garde that was actively working out the consequences of composer John Cage's notion to excise personal intention from the compositional process. At the same time, Eno's techniques of self-effacement generated an impersonal atmospheric style and personal brand that helped distinguish ambient not just from Muzak, but also from other burgeoning genres of atmospheric and popular music. Ultimately, the detached minimalism, soft elegance, and conspicuous discretion of Eno's personal style served as an expressive means of making ambient audio attractive to a yet-untapped market of highbrow listeners and underground rock record consumers.

Eno's Experimental Education, 1964–69

Most of the manifold antecedents for Eno's depersonalized approach to audio production can be traced back to his postsecondary art education at Ipswich School of Art from 1964 to 1966, then at Winchester Art School until 1969. As music writers Simon Frith and Howard Horne have explained, these educational environments provided Eno the conceptual tools to "apply high art skills and identities to a mass cultural form."[31] In particular, Eno's

[30] Glenn O'Brien, "Eno at the Edge of Rock," *Interview*, June 1978, 31.

[31] Frith and Horne, *Art into Pop*, 2.

formative engagements with cybernetics, minimalism, and British systems music led the pop star, in Frith and Horne's words, "to eliminate himself from his work, to minimize his 'degree of participation,' to cleanse his art of the idea of the individual artist."[32] And ambient music specifically, as Eno himself attests, arose from his efforts "to use the perceptions and understandings acquired from the experience of experimental music . . . to make a new popular music."[33]

At Ipswich, the teenage Eno encountered the cybernetic theories and experimental art philosophies that fueled his interest in atmospheric sound. Cybernetician and department head Roy Ascott's "behaviorist" conception of art taught first-year students to regard artworks as "systems" of behavior with the potential to incorporate the actions of the audience.[34] Painter and composer Tom Phillips handed Eno John Cage's influential philosophical treatise *Silence*, and later introduced him to experimental composers of the New York School as well as British experimentalists like Cornelius Cardew, John Tilbury, and Howard Skempton.[35] Eno discovered that, much like behaviorist artists, these composers permitted unplanned events and actions to enter into the work's realization. Through techniques of "indeterminacy" like chance procedures, tape splicing, and graphic scores, experimental composers, in Cage's words, explored "ways and means to remove themselves from the activities of the sounds they make."[36] A decade later, Eno theorized experimental music in cybernetic and behaviorist terms, explaining that experimental compositions plan for a "variety" of outcomes in performance and build in feedback mechanisms for participants to respond behaviorally to any environment.[37] "A music score," as Eno summarized in 1974, "is by definition a map of a set of behaviour patterns which will produce a

[32] Ibid., 118.

[33] Brian Eno, foreword to *Experimental Music: Cage and Beyond*, 2nd ed., by Michael Nyman (New York: Cambridge University Press, 1999), xiii.

[34] On Eno's experience of Ascott's tutelage, see Brian Eno, Russell Mills, and Rick Poynor, *More Dark Than Shark* (London: Faber & Faber, 1986), 40–41. On Ascott's own theorization of behaviorist art, see Roy Ascott, "Behaviourist Art and the Cybernetic Vision," *Cybernetica: Revue de l'Association Internationale de Cybernétique* 10, no. 1 (1967): 25–56.

[35] The New York School broadly refers to a network of visual, literary, and sound artists based in New York between the late '40s and early '60s, including Cage and composers Morton Feldman, Earle Brown, Christian Wolff, and David Tudor; see David Nicholls, "Getting Rid of the Glue: The Music of the New York School," in *The New York Schools of Music and Visual Arts*, ed. Steven Johnson, Studies in Contemporary Music and Culture (New York: Routledge, 2002), 17–56.

[36] John Cage, "Experimental Music," in *Silence: Lectures and Writings* (Cambridge, MA: MIT Press, 1961), 10.

[37] Brian Eno, "Generating and Organizing Variety in the Arts," *Studio International*, vol. 192, no. 984 (November–December 1976): 279–83. Eno's definition, it should be noted, does not apply to much music still widely considered to be experimental, including many of Cage's works.

result—but on another day that result might be entirely different."[38] For Eno, experimental music *was* behaviorist art.

Because Cage's prominent concern with "ambient" sound shaped Eno's interest in sonic ambience, Cage's music is often cited as a forerunner of ambient music. It bears pointing out, however, that Cage's and Eno's sonic visions were fundamentally incompatible. In his writings, Cage usually ascribed "ambient" to the sounds of silence, not music. "People often ask what music I prefer to hear," Cage once remarked in a typical formulation. "I enjoy the absence of music more than any other, or you could say silence. I enjoy whatever ambient sounds there are to hear."[39] What we typically call silence, Cage emphasized, if one listens to it, is a "sound-space" shot through with "ambient" sounds.[40] Accordingly, Cage's writings on ambience normally connoted the absence or bracketing of expressive intent from sound. Eno's later concept of a "discreet" or "ambient music" that is intentionally crafted to be added to the environment, and integrated with ongoing sounds, would have for Cage only detracted from an already-musical sonic ambience.

Cage's corresponding disinterest in Eno's music may be extrapolated from a 1985 *Musician* magazine interview with the two composers in which Cage largely refrained from commenting on Eno's work, only remarking politely that he was "struck" by the incorporation of silence into Eno's *Ambient 1: Music for Airports* (1978).[41] Given a second opportunity to comment, Cage instead marveled at how audiences of his 1982 piece *Instances of Silence* could not distinguish between the music and the ambient sounds of the environment.[42] Cage's silence regarding Eno's obtrusively musical sounds, intentionally or not, communicated that he had little interest in music like Eno's that was composed with expressive intentions. Eno, by contrast, seemed uncompelled to listen to ambient sounds without lovely music to attract his attention to them. While acknowledging Cage's "liberating" influence as an artist, Eno in the same interview admitted, prior to Cage's arrival, "I now disagree with nearly everything he said."[43]

By the time Eno departed for Winchester in 1966, based on his continued engagement with post-Cagean experimentalism, Eno's conception of what

[38] Eno, text for a lecture to Trent Polytechnic, 1974; quoted in Eno et al., *More Dark Than Shark*, 41.

[39] John Cage, *I–VI* (Cambridge, MA: Harvard University Press, 1990), 444.

[40] Eric De Visscher, "'There's No Such a Thing as Silence . . .': John Cage's Poetics of Silence," in *Writings about John Cage*, ed. Richard Kostelanetz (Ann Arbor: University of Michigan Press, 1993), 129.

[41] Rob Tannenbaum, "A Meeting of Sound Minds: John Cage & Brian Eno," *Musician*, September 1985, 68.

[42] Ibid., 69.

[43] Ibid., 66.

counted as "art" encompassed everyday activities and mundane processes.[44] At Winchester, Eno executed process-based compositions, happenings, and "sound sculptures" that allowed environmental sounds to be observed with special intensity, including the tape-loop delay systems that undergirded his later collaborations with King Crimson guitarist Robert Fripp, and ultimately *Discreet Music*. These experiments involved passing a single loop of tape through at least two tape recorders, with (at least) one recording the ambient sounds of the environment, and (at least) one playing back the recording within the same environment. Eno imagined the tape delay system as a "participation piece" in which listeners could take on the role of performers, and vice versa.[45]

Eno's time at Winchester also entailed his first revelatory exposures to US American minimalism. La Monte Young's *X for Henry Flynt* (1960), a composition calling for the performer(s) to repeat X times a loud sound or sound-cluster as uniformly and regularly as possible, made a particularly strong impression on Eno who, upon sinking his arm into a block of piano keys 3,600 times, came to realize that minimizing the means of sound production could form the basis of unexpected sonic variety over time.[46] Steve Reich's *It's Gonna Rain* (1965), a predecessor to *Come Out* that gradually phases two near-identical tape loops of a street sermon out of sync with one another, also led Eno to discover "whole worlds of sound" within seemingly minimal material.[47] As Eno describes his first encounter with the piece on Reich's *Live/Electric Music* LP (Columbia Masterworks, 1968),

> Since the material is common to both tapes, what you begin to notice are not the repeating parts but the sort of ephemeral interference

[44] The art writer Richard Kostelanetz summarized the post-Cagean experimental milieu of happenings, conceptual art, Fluxus, performance art, and total environments as the "theatre of mixed-means"; see Richard Kostelanetz, *The Theatre of Mixed Means* (New York: RK Editions, 1980). On happenings and total environments, see also Fred Turner, *The Democratic Surround: Multimedia and American Liberalism from World War II to the Psychedelic Sixties* (Chicago: University of Chicago Press, 2013), 261–83; on Fluxus, see also Hannah Higgins, *Fluxus Experience* (Berkeley: University of California Press, 2002).

[45] Brian Eno, "Decay and Delay," *Clare Market Review*, Summer 1968, 32–33, http://www.moredarkthanshark.org/feature_clare_summer-1968.html. Although Eno's tape delay systems bore some similarity to Terry Riley's "time lag accumulator" and Pauline Oliveros's tape delay systems created at the San Francisco Tape Music Center earlier in the decade, Eno claims to have derived the idea independently, which is plausible given Riley's and Oliveros's somewhat obscure status in England at the time. See Bracewell, *Remake/Remodel*, 185.

[46] David Sheppard, *On Some Faraway Beach: The Life and Times of Brian Eno* (Chicago: Chicago Review Press, 2009), 51.

[47] Jim Aikin, "Brian Eno," *Keyboard*, July 1981, 60. For an extended analysis and interpretation of *It's Gonna Rain*, see Sumanth S. Gopinath, "Contraband Children: The Politics of Race and Liberation in the Music of Steve Reich, 1965–66" (PhD diss., Yale University, 2005), 125–93.

> pattern between them. Your ear telescopes into more and more fine detail until you're hearing what to me seems like atoms of sound. That piece [*It's Gonna Rain*] absolutely thrilled me, because I realized then that I understood what minimalism was about. The creative operation is listening. It isn't just a question of a presentation feeding into a passive audience.[48]

That the listener could create a "thrilling" auditory experience out of the automatic playback of a mostly automated process—an experience one might expect to be totally mundane and predictable—fascinated Eno.

It's Gonna Rain reoriented Eno's existing interest in recorded sound. Prior to this experience, Eno's tape delay systems generated unpredictable interactions between sounds occurring at the time of audition; the final recording was simply the "residue" of this process.[49] *It's Gonna Rain*, however, showed Eno that a recording of a process, even a severely delimited one, could serve as the *starting* point for unpredictable moments of audition. The piece raised for Eno the possibility that recordings, like pieces of experimental music, could create a variety of interactions between the recorded sounds' playback and the listener's psychology and environment. Eno, once drawn to music for its ephemerality, came to appreciate how tape made music a "plastic art" and thus available to further uses and hearings beyond the initial recording process.[50] Through *It's Gonna Rain*, the young artist had received what he later called experimental music's most "lasting message": that "music is something your mind does."[51]

Eno's Ambient Antecedents, 1970–75

Throughout the 1970s Eno, a self-described "non-musician," primarily honed his skills and identity as a recording artist and producer, rather than as a composer of notated music or performer of live music. Although interested in unpredictable outcomes, Eno also enjoyed the control and precision permitted by tape and studio editing. The recording artist enjoys "a whole set

[48] Brian Eno, "Aurora Musicalis," interview by Anthony Korner, *Artforum* 24, no. 10 (Summer 1986): 79.

[49] Eno et al., *More Dark Than Shark*, 41.

[50] Stephen Demorest, "The Discreet Charm of Brian Eno: An English Pop Theorist Seeks to Redefine Music," *Horizon*, June 1978, 83.

[51] Eno, foreword to *Experimental Music*, xii.

of freedoms that you don't have as a performer," Eno reflected in 1978, "and those freedoms interest me."[52]

Eno's first forays into music production took place following a serendipitous invitation in early 1971 by his friend and woodwind player Andy Mackay to cut some demo tapes for a new band. Eno ended up acting as technical assistant and VCS3 synth player for said band, Roxy Music, the outfit that would launch him into rock stardom. Roxy Music reinvented '60s Mod dandification through flamboyant, ostentatious costuming, with Eno playing the eyeshadowed, long-haired peacock to frontman Bryan Ferry's coiffed and pressed playboy. Their overt emphasis on glamor subverted the heavy-blues earnestness and symphonic prog pretensions prevailing in the United Kingdom at the time. The band's music reflected a similarly camp sensibility with Ferry's arch, melodramatic vocals delivered over a cheeky, dance-friendly amalgam of bubblegum pop, rhythm & blues, psych rock, and free jazz, with the alienesque Eno supplying spacey synthesizer strangeness.

But Eno's entry into the world of pop was hardly happenstance: like many of his British art school peers inspired by pop art and rock music, Eno had aspired since his time at Winchester to work with pop styles, codes, conventions, and points of reference, and to enjoy the artistic and financial fruits of that move.[53] It was especially the Velvet Underground's coy visual presentation, gritty proto-punk minimalism, and art-world straddling that suggested to Eno pop music could be a fruitful arena for experimentation. As Eno recalls, he and Ferry "very much liked the idea of a band sitting on that line between fine art and performance art and happenings, yet co-opting the pop audience—we thought that was a very good position to be in."[54]

Much like the visionary psychedelic "heads" across the pond, Eno imagined rock as a system that could be invigorated by the ideas and sounds of "serious" music. "Pop looks like / becoming my container, / not to mention contingent," gushed Eno cybernetically in a July 1969 journal, just as his formal education was drawing to a close.[55] For Eno, rock provided a cultural and semiotic environment wherein the heady conceits of experimental art could bump against and thrive alongside pop music's pleasures. As he later reflected in 1972, "We [Roxy Music] regard the rock idea as a system that

[52] Lee Moore, "Eno = MC Squared," *Creem*, November 1978, 68.
[53] Frith and Horne, *Art into Pop*, 103–4.
[54] Bracewell, *Re-make/Re-model*, 347.
[55] Ibid., 343.

can be programmed in many different ways—we choose to program it with not only the jazz, rock, blues tradition, but also with the less familiar 'serious' music tradition. We want to handle the visceral/physical as well as the spiritual and conceptual."[56] Experimental composition, after all, was full of "ideas there that were ripe for plucking," and pop musicians plucked. Popular conventions of borrowing afforded the self-described "non-musician" leeway to import the lessons and ideas of experimental music into his own works. "In pop nobody has any embarrassment about copying," as Eno once remarked. "In fact, that's how it works: 'That's a good sound. How do we do that?' They don't chuck one sound out to take another. They let it in."[57]

At the same time, Eno regarded pop musicians to be more artistically advanced than the avant-garde in some respects—especially in the art of audio production.

> [Pop musicians] knew that listening to a record was a different experience to a live performance. They realised that the record had to be a distinct, separate and satisfactory experience; it couldn't just be a memento of a performance. So pop musicians were way ahead of the avant-garde in terms of thinking how do you make a successful work of art on a piece of vinyl. You had Steve Reich for example—who made both a record that changed my life [*It's Gonna Rain*] and some really bad ones, as well—I think through not understanding what recording was about. Some of those very diagrammatic pieces of his, like *Drumming* (1971), just didn't work as a record. It was like seeing a sketch of a musical event; you didn't really want to listen to it more than once.[58]

Pop musicians were "ahead of the avant-garde" because they crafted recordings not only to document musical events, but also to enable unique listening experiences that worked independently of these original musical events, potentiating a variety of outcomes from playback to playback. To use the words of musicologist Albin Zak, pop producers in the hi-fi era came to treat recordings not as reproductions of a "real" event so much as "realities in themselves."[59]

[56] Ibid., 348.
[57] Eno, "Aurora Musicalis," 79.
[58] Bracewell, *Re-make/Re-model*, 241.
[59] Albin Zak, *The Poetics of Rock: Cutting Tracks, Making Records* (Berkeley: University of California Press, 2001), 21.

Eno first applied experimental approaches to recorded music production while working with Roxy Music, during which time he developed a list of verbal heuristics to inspire lateral thinking and improvisation in the studio. His friend Peter Schmidt, a painter, had developed a similar list, and in January 1975 the artists jointly published a set of "oracular" cards titled Oblique Strategies, with phrases like "Repetition is a form of change" and "The tape is now the music" providing a means of conditioning behavior and sidelining personal intention.[60] Eno later explained the value of such studio improvisations as a means of generating unplanned sonic events to work with as audio material. These events, as audio, become familiar over repeated listenings, permitting the recording artist to "become very fond of details that weren't intended by the composer or the musicians"—and to manipulate such details.[61] Eno would elsewhere describe studio composition as, like gardening, an "accretion of processes" wherein the creator manages rather than controls the outcome: "What you've done is partake in a process, you haven't really *controlled* the process . . . you didn't *make* the flower."[62] Planning and management, however, were still key for Eno, whether in devising the Oblique Strategies deck, in using tape and studio equipment, or in working with a selected group of musicians. Commenting in 1974 on the process of assembling improvisers for his first solo album, Eno explained, "I'm interested in chaotic situations if I've established the parameters for the chaos sufficiently. But I'm not interested in loose situations. But it is organized with the knowledge that there might well be accidents, accidents which will be more interesting than what I intended."[63] The happiest musical accidents, for Eno, occurred in an organized, planned framework. Inside the studio, Eno's passivity was always thoroughly prepared; his surrender of rational control, rationally controlled.

Eno continued to fuse avant-garde and popular approaches in his solo work (as simply "Eno" at first) after he left Roxy Music in July 1973 following a souring of his relationship with Ferry. The first two solo LPs, *Here Come the Warm Jets* (1974) and *Taking Tiger Mountain (by Strategy)* (1974), took experimental approaches to lyrics, but musically gave little hint of the

[60] O'Brien, "Eno at the Edge," 31.

[61] Brian Eno, "The Studio as Compositional Tool," *Downbeat*, July 1983, More Dark Than Shark website, http://moredarkthanshark.org/eno_int_db-jul83.html.

[62] Alan Jensen, "The Sound of Silence: A Thursday Afternoon with Brian Eno," *Electronics & Music Maker*, December 1985, 22.

[63] Cynthia Dagnal, "Eno and the Jets: Controlled Chaos," *Rolling Stone*, September 12, 1974, 21.

ambient aesthetic to follow.[64] Not so with the third. *Another Green World*, released in September 1975, not only brought to full fruition many of Eno's concerns in cybernetics and experimental music, but also included instrumental tracks that foreshadowed the style Eno would call ambient.[65] On "Becalmed," heavily chorused piano and synth strings lazily cycle through an unmetered, variable four-chord progression in A major. "Zawinul/Lava" loops a bright, reverberant rising piano motif that distinctly foreshadows "1/1" on *Music for Airports*. The final track, "Spirits Drifting," features Rhodes, synth strings, and winds oscillating between the tonic and various dominant substitutions, peppered with added ♭6 and ♯11s that anticipate the floating extended chord tones of later ambient works. All such tracks foster contemplative moods through relaxed pacing, harmonic predictability, and gentle timbres, much as would his forthcoming records of "discreet" and "ambient" music.

Eno also developed a drifting ambient aesthetic in his collaborations with guitarist Robert Fripp. In 1972 Eno enlisted Fripp to join him and a tape delay system in the recording studio, with one tape machine recording Fripp's electric guitar, and the other playing the recording back at times of Eno's choosing. These playbacks would then get recorded as echoes by the first machine at progressively lower volumes. Fripp took quickly to the method, providing licks on his Gibson Les Paul that Eno would weave into fuzzy, thickly layered beds of droning delay echoes upon which Fripp could improvise further. This method resulted in the two sides of the *(No Pussyfooting)* LP (released November 1973), recordings far more like Terry Riley's late '60s pieces or Hindustani classical music than they were like any of Eno or Fripp's previous work.[66] The record cover shows the pair sitting in a hall of mirrors, reflecting visually the smooth continuity of the musicians' dronescapes, as well as the fading repetitions of the loops therein. *Evening Star*, the duo's follow-up album released shortly before *Discreet Music* in late 1975, took this loop-based approach in even lovelier directions, including the brilliantly shimmering live excerpt "Wind on Water," the lullaby-like proto-post-rock title track, and even a brief outtake from the *Discreet Music* tapes. Side B,

[64] For an extended look at these albums, see Tamm, *Brian Eno*; Elizabeth Ann Lindau, "Art Is Dead. Long Live Rock! Avant-Gardism and Rock Music, 1967–99" (PhD diss., Charlottesville, University of Virginia, 2012), 127–69; Eno et al., *More Dark Than Shark*.

[65] The impact of Eno's study of cybernetics on the making of *Another Green World* is detailed in Geeta Dayal, *Another Green World*, 33⅓ Series (New York: Bloomsbury Academic, 2009).

[66] Hear, for instance, Terry Riley, *Poppy Nogood and the Phantom Band*, from *A Rainbow in Curved Air*, Columbia Masterworks MS 7315, 1969, LP.

the mysterious twenty-eight-minute-long drone odyssey "Index of Metals," ventured into the darker side of ambient audio, its dissonant atonal swirls recalling not just bands like Popol Vuh or Tangerine Dream at their most mysterious, but also the outer edges of György Ligeti and Morton Feldman's uncertain atmospheres.

Making *Discreet Music* Experimental

Eno released *Discreet Music* in November 1975 as the third of four albums on his Obscure series and label. (More on Obscure to follow.) The thirty-plus-minute-long title track took up Side A; on Side B appeared three "variations" on Johann Pachelbel's *Canon in D.* Composer Gavin Bryars, credited with arranging the Pachelbel variations for strings, played a significant role in its realization; as Bryars now remembers, "I composed the music from the rules and processes suggested by Brian. He would come 'round to my house in Ladbroke Grove and I would play through what I was doing so that he could hear it."[67] Eno was inspired to use Pachelbel's *Canon*, as Bryars recalls, by the Jean-François Paillard Chamber Orchestra's 1968 record, itself a rather reverberant rendition that launched the piece's popularity as background music staple.

Eno created *Discreet Music*'s title track in May 1975 while making tapes for Fripp to solo over in some upcoming shows. He devised a tape delay system using an EMS Synthi AKS as his sound source and a digital sequencer to loop simultaneously two programmed sequences of four melodic snippets (Ex. 3.1). These sequences, around thirty seconds each, had slightly different lengths, leading to unpredictable alignments of the sequenced snippets in recording. Eno looped them simultaneously for about fifteen minutes, then slowed the recording down to half speed, doubling the total length of the piece. Eno's delay system also included a Gibson echo unit, a graphic equalizer, and two Revox A77 tape machines. The audio signal passed through the echo unit and equalizer, with the echo unit's dirty playback heads adding a pleasant wooliness to the synthesized sounds.[68] These sounds were recorded as audio by the first of the two tape machines before moving, after several seconds, to the playback head of the second, creating echoes of the recorded

[67] Bryars, email message to author, October 22, 2014.
[68] Prendergast, "Brian Eno: Part Two," 61.

Example 3.1. Melodic snippets used in *Discreet Music.* Snippets 1–4 comprise the first sequence; snippets 5–8 comprise the second sequence.

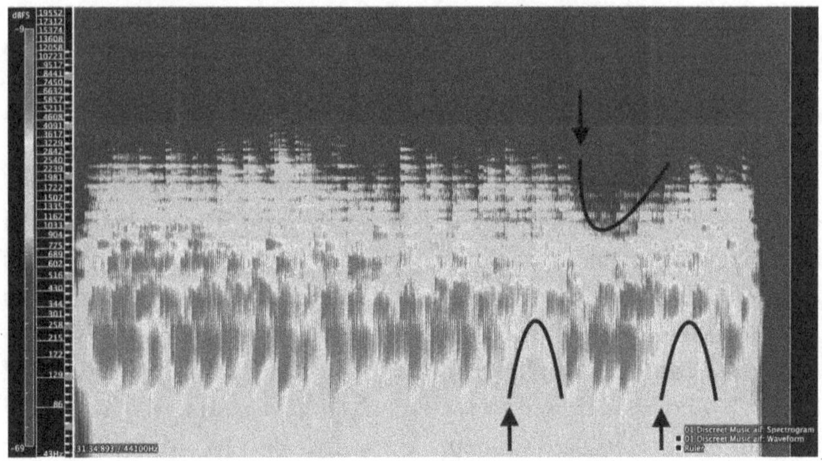

Figure 3.1. Spectrogram of *Discreet Music*, marked to indicate filtering.

audio. Once more recorded, these echoes would then reach the playback machine again, reecho, become recorded yet more softly, and so on. As echoes multiplied and faded, fragments newly emerged from the sequencer at a higher volume, resulting in eight interweaving melodic strands that, depending on one's focus, might also sound like a single unfolding chord (A♭6/9add11 or mixed B♭m/A♭).

As the piece was recording, Eno changed the synth's output by continually manipulating the waveform mix, resonant filters, and graphic equalizer. The waveform adjustments altered the timbre of the synth sounds over the course of the recording, with fragments transmorphing from faux English horn to alto saxophone, oboe, alto flute, and space-age clarinet. High- and low-pass filtering of the sonic composite (marked with curved lines and arrows in Fig. 3.1) created some significant global changes in the second half of the piece as well, introducing a subtle dramatic narrative arc into the composition. The analogy of the natural circadian cycle (day-sunset-night-sunrise-day) seems especially apt given the alterations of timbral brightness, as well as the associations of woodwinds with pastoral scenes.

Discreet Music, as I elaborate in the following section, took on many features of the English experimental "systems" music that accompanied it on the Obscure record series, including its radical reduction of pitched material, melodic fragmentation, tonality without functional harmony, and uncoordinated modular repetitions. All such techniques, as composer Michael Nyman notes of minimalist music generally, can result in a "flattening out" or "de-focusing" of the listener's perspective.[69] In the terms of Eno scholar Eric Tamm and music theorist Jonathan Kramer, Eno produced "vertical music," which, as Kramer explains, may be understood as a "bounded sound-world" that defines its limits early on and "stays within the limits it chooses."[70] Kramer compares vertical music to sculpture, in that the perceiver may at any time decide on their own sequence of observational postures toward, or away from, the music; in Eno's words, this music creates a "solid block of interactions" that listeners might enter into and leave at any point.[71] This notion of a multiperspectival "vertical music" not only had analogues in preexisting space, minimalist, and systems music, but also in the static, nondevelopmental minimalist films of Andy Warhol such as *Sleep* (1963) and *Empire* (1964), which Eno has acknowledged as similar in conception.[72]

As his interest in producing vertical music progressed beyond *Discreet Music*, Eno began comparing his solo releases to visual art, particularly painting. Likening pop vocals to the "figure" in a recording's "landscape" ("all questions of scale and depth are related to it"), Eno sought to collapse the landscape into a unified sound picture by removing the figure.[73] Doing so, he reasoned, would "create many different foci of attention" for the listener, including such aspects as texture, timing, color, production effects, mood, or even the ways sound interacts with nonmusical factors both external and internal to the listener.[74] "I like the idea of my music being treated like sound pictures," Eno later explained. "You don't sit and stare at paintings for three

[69] Michael Nyman, *Experimental Music: Cage and Beyond*, 2nd ed. (New York: Cambridge University Press, 1999), 30.

[70] Jonathan D. Kramer, *The Time of Music: New Meanings, New Temporalities, New Listening Strategies* (New York: Schirmer, 1988), 54; Tamm, *Brian Eno*.

[71] Kramer, *The Time of Music*, 57; Frank Rose, "Scaramouche of the Synthesizer," *Creem*, July 1975, 70.

[72] Rose, "Scaramouche of the Synthesizer," 70.

[73] Eno, "Aurora Musicalis," 77.

[74] Gregory Miller, "The Arts: Video," *Omni*, June 1980, 111.

minutes, you can turn your back. Painters are not insulted by lack of attention, why should composers be?"[75]

As Eno's commentary suggests, vertical music does not only permit perceptual drift within the piece to different aspects of the sound, but also allows for attentional drift away from the music altogether. *Recorded* vertical music, moreover, can foster different experiences from playback to playback, or place to place, since it permits listeners to treat it as a backdrop or atmosphere in various sorts of situations. Because of its relatively underdetermined form, as Eno noted in a 1985 interview, "You can use recordings as a way to generate unpredictability rather than repetition."[76] And because these recordings accommodate and exploit the variety of their possible listening environments, Eno conceived of them as behaviorist art.

Eno's liner notes for *Discreet Music* also deftly situated the record's production as experimental, or contingent to his own artistic intentions, while at the same time guiding audiences to treat the record as ambient audio. His description of the title track's production emphasizes his own passivity in the act of recording, rather than the significant decisions he made in planning and execution. The subsequent narrative of *Discreet Music*'s conception unfolds in parallel fashion, with Eno's bedridden body exceptionally passive ("confined," "stiff and static," lacking the "energy to get up"). The analogous breakdown of the stereo equipment gives rise to a situation in which recorded harp melds seamlessly, and seemingly without human intervention, into the perpetuity of environmental sound, light, and color. Together, these framing narratives set up a circuit of identification between the consumer (the record's buyer, programmer, and listener) and Eno (the recording's planner, producer, and audience). Once you program *Discreet Music*, they tell the consumer, take advantage of its automation, and treat it passively as though the music were part of the place in which you listen. Such a message might be especially instructive for the serious rock or avant-garde music listener who might find something so delicate and antique as 18th-century harp music—or so sweet and unassuming as *Discreet Music*—an unnatural environmental presence. Resist the urge to turn the volume up (or the stereo off), the narratives tell the listener; avoid trying to "improve matters" by "dabbling" and "interfering," and you may find yourself able to appreciate it as discreet music.

[75] Anthony Denselow, "Over and Over," *Observer*, February 23, 1986.
[76] Tannenbaum, "A Meeting of Sound Minds," 69.

The "New Consonance" in 1970s British Experimentalism and Obscure Records

Perhaps because of the narratives of accident surrounding *Discreet Music*, remarkably little attention has been paid by scholars to the influence of the UK experimental music scenes with which Eno remained involved in the early '70s on his approach to the album.[77] Several of Eno's colleagues during this time gravitated toward a semi-sweet, semi-ironic embrace of melodiousness, leading Michael Nyman in 1975 to declare a "new consonance" and "cult of the beautiful" dominating British avant-garde experimentalism.[78] Unlike the consonance of US American minimalists, who reacquainted the avant-garde with tonality through radical reduction, English experimentalists defamiliarized tonality by applying amateur performance and "systemic" process techniques to simple, familiar-sounding melodies. As composer Howard Skempton later summarized the trend, English experimentalists of the time were interested in "making the overfamiliar sound strangely beautiful" by approaching classical conventions and canonic works with unfamiliar sounds, techniques, and mistakes.[79] The radical reduction of pitched material, fragmented and scrambled melodicism, tonality without functional harmony, and uncoordinated loops of *Discreet Music* drew on, and contributed to, this trend.

Composer Gavin Bryars, co-creator as he was of *Discreet Music*'s side B, attests to this influence. Bryars himself had for years taken interest in the repetition of simple lyrical melodies which were often quoted directly from older tunes, as in *The Sinking of the Titanic* (1969), wherein a small string ensemble repeats and slowly stretches out the Episcopal hymn "Autumn" as wind and bass string drones grow, ebb, and swirl around it. Bryars became well known in experimental circles for this piece, as well as for *Jesus' Blood Never Failed Me Yet* (1971), in which Bryars looped a tape of an elderly vagrant singing a religious song over a slowly thickening orchestral arrangement. (Nyman in 1975 declared *Jesus' Blood* a shining example of the "new consonance" dominating British experimentalism at the time.)[80] Other

[77] Cecilia Sun has documented the influence of Eno's participation with the Portsmouth Sinfonia and the Scratch Orchestra on *Discreet Music*; see Sun, "Brian Eno, Non-Musicianship and the Experimental Tradition," in *Oblique Music*, ed. Sean Albiez and David Pattie (New York: Bloomsbury Academic, 2016), 29–48.

[78] Michael Nyman, "As the Titanic Went Down," *Music and Musicians* 21 (December 1972): 14.

[79] Nyman, *Experimental Music*, 160.

[80] Nyman, "As the Titanic Went Down," 14.

English experimentalists also approached the overfamiliar by repeating again and again simple melodies with predictable chord progressions in homophonic textures. Skempton, for example, developed what musicologist Virginia Anderson calls a "sweet" style of minimalism in repeating square, banal tonal melodies with rudimentary accompaniment at great lengths.[81] As Bryars explained the impact his and his colleagues' music had on Eno, "[Eno] told me that the performances that I gave at the Purcell Room and the Queen Elizabeth Hall with John Tilbury had a profound effect on his musical development. His idea of ambient music grew out of the non-assertive nature of much of English Experimental Music, which was quite happy to stay in the background in an understated way."[82]

The Promenade Theatre Orchestra (PTO), likewise contributors to the understated English "new consonance," also hinted at Eno's breezy experimentation with background-friendly discretion. Composer-performers John White, Christopher Hobbs, Hugh Shrapnel, and Alec Hill starting in 1969 performed weekly concerts at London's New Arts Laboratory with a toy piano, a reed organ, and their own wind instruments. As White explains their motivation, "There was something sort of rebellious about the PTO writing non-harrowing, pleasant consonant music on, from a concert point of view, substandard instruments."[83] Hobbs recalls that this rebellion wasn't just a matter of avoiding dissonance or complexity, but also about deflating the seriousness of new music ensembles such as the Steve Reich Ensemble—"highly trained professionals playing slick, difficult music"—with ease and humor.[84] Humor not only came about in their music, but also through satirical promotions: one advertisement devised by White announced that the group would play "Live Muzak!!!!"; another described the PTO's gentle sound with ironic flair: "Restful reed-organs, tinkling toy pianos, soothing psalteries, suave swanee whistles, jolly jew's harps—NO noisy electronics! (Just the job for that lazy Sunday afternoon!)."[85] PTO composers also frequently toyed with preexisting music. Hobbs for instance, in homage to

[81] Anderson, "Systems and Other Minimalism," 90.

[82] Gavin Bryars, email message to author, October 22, 2014. The Purcell Room performance to which Bryars refers took place on October 9, 1970. The performance at Queen Elizabeth Hall took place in 1972, and featured the premiere performance of *The Sinking of the Titanic*.

[83] Virginia Anderson, "British Experimental Music: Cornelius Cardew and His Contemporaries" (Master's thesis, University of Redlands, 1983), 128.

[84] Christopher Hobbs, email message to author, October 13, 2014.

[85] V. Anderson, "British Experimental Music," 132; Michael Nyman, "Believe It or Not Melody Rides Again," *Music and Musicians* 20, no. 2 (October 1971): 28.

Marcel Duchamp, created "readymades" like *The Remorseless Lamb*, which shuffles around bits and pieces of J. S. Bach's *Sheep May Safely Graze* according to chance procedures; and *MacCrimmon Will Never Return*, which has performers simultaneously playing different slowed-down versions of a *piobaireachd* (bagpipe) tune on reed organs.[86]

Several UK experimentalists called their processes of jumbling pleasant sounds "systems" or "systemic" music.[87] While "systems music" later referred generally to minimalist or repetitive music, in the 1970s the term referred more specifically to this cohort's application of random- and fixed-number algorithms to the genesis of sequential musical processes; as Hobbs defined it, systems music is "music in which the structure and note-to-note procedure are dictated by a numerically expressible construct."[88] Nyman's description of the results of these processes indeed calls to mind *Discreet Music*: "The sounds tend towards a sort of ragged consonance, the procedures usually involve much repetition with changes happening almost imperceptibly over large spans of time, and the atmosphere is usually pretty calm and unruffled however fast the pace of the music."[89] As composer Michael Parsons explains, repetition and sustainment in systems music were not meant to entrance listeners, or enhance their perceptual disorientation, as they did in US minimalism, but rather acted as a "ground for the creation of perceptible oppositions."[90] Composer Brian Dennis summarized the experience of hearing systems music as follows:

> For the listener the note-to-note experience of the music is impossible to define. The sounds are pleasant and the "content" subdued. It is a music of discovery: from a myriad possible forms, structure and texture are interfused; new images are defined. Only the listener with a blissful disregard for all the numbers, structures and permutations which concern the composer can assess the quality of the image: the actual effect of the music.[91]

[86] V. Anderson, "British Experimental Music," 132.

[87] The use of the term "systems" to describe this music arose in response to the development of "systems art" in 1960s British painting; see Virginia Anderson, "Systems and Other Minimalism in Britain," in *The Ashgate Research Companion to Minimalist and Postminimalist Music*, ed. Keith Potter, Kyle Gann, and Pwyll Ap Siôn (Burlington, VT: Ashgate, 2013), 99–100.

[88] Brian Dennis, "Repetitive and Systemic Music," *The Musical Times* 113, no. 1582 (December 1972): 1037.

[89] Nyman, "Believe It or Not," 27.

[90] V. Anderson, "Systems and Other Minimalism," 100.

[91] Dennis, "Repetitive and Systemic Music," 1038.

The uncoordinated temporal cycles of harmonious sounds in systems music, in short, gave listeners the freedom to notice subtle coincidences and juxtapositions in the "pleasant" musical "image"—or as Eno would later put it, in the "sound picture."[92] As John White described it elsewhere, the systems music listener, habituated by the music's "happily indulged sentimentality," encounters the possibility of "delight in finding happy accidents among the numbers."[93]

In early 1975, Eno sought a happy home for these happy accidents in the pop market by proposing to his home label Island Records a sublabel devoted to the unabashedly pretty experimentalism flowering around him. He sold the idea to A&R department head Richard Williams as an inexpensive investment in research and development; the purpose of this new label would be to record and release music otherwise difficult to find commercially.[94] Eno called the label Obscure Records, and upon approval he took up the roles of label manager and producer for ten LPs, released between 1975 and '78, of music by English systems minimalists Bryars, Nyman, Hobbs, and White, among a handful of other avant-pop composers and groups.

In November 1975, Eno put out the first four Obscure records simultaneously, including pieces by Bryars, Hobbs, David Toop, and Max Eastley in addition to *Discreet Music*. Eno's album fit comfortably with the reverb-drenched gorgeousness of Bryars's pieces and the melodic deconstructions of Hobbs; together, these recordings helped establish an Obscure "sound." Nyman characterized this first batch of releases as "typically English" in their "gentle, casual, slow, unassertive" restraint.[95] Eno believed pop audiences would better appreciate this restrained loveliness than did the international avant-garde; as he wrote of Nyman's piece in 1976, *1–100* is "extremely beautiful to listen to—a factor which seems to carry little critical weight at present."[96] As Eno saw it, this music represented an attractive path out of the complexity and asceticism of the avant-garde and the virtuosic bombast of heavy and progressive British rock—in part because it retained the possibility for the listener to "turn it down and let it sit in the background."[97] In a

[92] Denselow, "Over and Over."

[93] Nyman, "Believe It or Not," 28.

[94] Adrian Jack, "'I Want to Be a Magnet for Tapes,'" *Time Out*, 1975, Hyperreal, http://music.hyperreal.org/artists/brian_eno/interviews/timeo75a.html.

[95] Michael Nyman, "Music [Obscure Records]," in *Michael Nyman: Collected Writings*, ed. Pwyll Ap Siôn (Burlington, VT: Ashgate, 2013), 260–61.

[96] Eno, "Generating and Organizing Variety," 282.

[97] MacDonald, "Before and after Science," 42.

self-penned 1975 essay, Eno submitted that Obscure records could breathe new life into the concept of "muzak."

> I believe that we are moving towards a position of *using* music and recorded sound with the variety of options that we presently use colour—we might simply use it to "tint" the environment, we might use it "diagrammatically," we might use it to modify our moods in almost subliminal ways. I predict that the concept of "muzak," once it sheds its connotations of aural garbage, might enjoy a new (and very fruitful) lease of life. Muzak, you see, has one great asset: you don't *have* to pay attention to it. This strikes me as a generous humility with which to imbue a piece of music, though it is also nice to ensure that the music can offer rewards to those who do give it their attention.[98]

This passage, one of Eno's first public articulations of his ambient concept outside of *Discreet Music* itself, sketches the terms by which Eno would later define ambient music as a sort of mood music "as ignorable as it is interesting."[99]

Although the composers represented on Obscure were, from Nyman's perspective, part of England's "experimental mainstream," few had such an opportunity for broad market exposure as their US avant-garde peers (recall Columbia's Music of Our Time series). A project like Obscure Records, as Nyman wrote at the time of its release, could only have been instantiated on the backing of someone with such considerable cultural capital as Eno: "It's obviously because he's a rock star that Island agreed to entrust him with a project like [Obscure]."[100] "No ordinary record company would have touched [our music]," Hobbs now corroborates.[101] Obscure Records represented the possibility of connecting with listeners who might not otherwise encounter it, and so the composers leapt at the chance when Eno presented the idea; as Bryars once told Nyman, *Jesus' Blood* "could go out on Radio 2 if they'd put it out for 30 minutes."[102] Eno himself, inspired by John Peel's radio show

98 Brian Eno, "Shedding Light on Obscure Records," *Street Life*, November 15–28, 1975, 55.

99 Brian Eno, "Ambient Music," liner notes to *Ambient 1: Music for Airports*, Editions EG, AMB001, 1978, LP.

100 Nyman, "Music [Obscure Records]," 259.

101 Hobbs, email message to author, October 13, 2014.

102 Nyman, "As the Titanic Went Down," 14. More recently, both Bryars and Hobbs told me that they had no particular audience in mind for these releases ("That was entirely Brian's domain," Bryars says); Gavin Bryars, email message to author, October 22, 2014; Hobbs, email message to author, October 13, 2014.

The Perfumed Garden, saw the label as an opportunity to enrich the popular mainstream with experimental sounds.[103] Island, however, hardly promoted Obscure's records, and so the sublabel, and the music on it, remained obscure for its duration.

Art into Pop: *Discreet Music*'s Socioaesthetic Pleasures

For Eno in the mid-'70s, *Discreet Music*—and the entire Obscure series of LPs it appeared on—represented the latest experiment testing his hypothesis that the concepts and compositions of experimental art, enhanced with the techniques of pop record production and sold through the pop market, could flourish on a social level. As he put it in 1977, "I know a lot of people think that I'm trying to elevate rock into the Fine Arts. . . . Well, in fact I'm actually more interested in doing the opposite. I'm more interested in relegating the Fine Arts from their sanctified position into something that people enjoy doing and seeing, something which forms a part of their social behaviour and social discourse."[104] As Eno saw it, the pop market could better accommodate the visceral and relational pleasures of his and other experimentalists' music than could the fine arts establishment. And bringing the ideas of experimental music into pop, for Eno, meant producing and framing it as something that could produce pleasure and thereby carry social agency or power.

Eno at times has explained this importation as a process of massaging the strict intellectualism and conceptualism of experimentalism into sensuous beauty. In 1975, for instance, he attested to producing *Discreet Music* with the intention of creating a luscious sonic invitation, rather than an "uncomfortable" avant-garde experience:

> I must say that I'd always go for a sensuous sound when making a piece. In *Discreet Music* I was very concerned to make something that wasn't uncomfortable. It's intended as music you don't have to concentrate on. It's like adding to your ambience, changing the condition of the room a little bit. If you want to focus on another level, there's a set of ideas that are interesting in terms of systems working like Steve Reich's piece *It's Gonna Rain*. And to stop it being monotonous—and, I suppose, completely ignorable—I did

[103] Eno, "Shedding Light on Obscure," 55.

[104] Caroline Coon, "The Brian Eno Interview," *Ritz*, 1977, Rock's Back Pages, http://www.rocksbackpages.com/Library/Article/the-brian-eno-interview.

> make changes during the piece. This touching up is very much a philistine idea in the experimental composer's terms; it's wanting to entertain. But I think that borderline area is a very interesting one.[105]

Eno has often defended his abandonment of strict process in this way, commenting that "if something doesn't jolt your senses, forget it. It's got to be seductive."[106] Eno regarded this stance as a revolt against the antisentimental abstractionism of most experimental composition. "I think the trouble with almost all experimental composers is that they're all head, dead from the neck down," he said in 1979. "They don't trust their hearts, I think, and tend to take themselves with a solemnity so extreme as to be downright preposterous. I don't see the point, really. I've always abandoned pieces which succeeded theoretically but not sensually."[107]

Such statements as this might seem strange coming from one of rock's most notorious eggheads. Eno, however, has explained that his own interest in minimalism arose as much out of personal taste as it did from conceptual intrigue. He has surmised, for instance, that the music of Young and Reich "produced in me a taste for simplicity, I think, rather than complexity, a taste for repetition rather than variation."[108] In fact, Eno's taste for sensuous simplicity seems to have predated his encounters with Young and Reich; he has mentioned, for instance, how he wanted to be an artist as a child at the sight of a Piet Mondrian painting.[109] Such taste for simplicity was also observed by one of Eno's interviewers in 1977, who noted that Eno's living space "breathes a kind of sensuous asceticism. The colors are quiet blues and browns. Objects are at a minimum. Records and books are assigned three shelves. . . . Everything else is pallid, unobtrusive, and mutable."[110] For Eno, minimalism across visual art, decoration, and music alike offered a style, a way of projecting a sense of self, through elegant, subtractive simplicity.

Yet despite Eno's many reflections on, and investments in, avant-garde minimalism's tasteful sound and pop potential, it was not until the 1980s that

105 Jack, "'Magnet for Tapes.'"

106 Steven Grant, "Brian Eno against Interpretation," *Trouser Press*, August 1982, 29.

107 Lester Bangs, "Brian Eno: A Sandbox in Smallville," 1979, republished in *Perfect Sound Forever*, August 2003, http://www.furious.com/perfect/bangseno.html. This stance sparked controversy when Eno "arrogantly" articulated it at the New Music, New York festival in 1979; see Tom Johnson, *The Voice of New Music: New York City, 1972–1982* (Eindhoven, The Netherlands: Het Apollohuis, 1989), 398.

108 Aikin, "Brian Eno," 60.

109 Sheppard, *On Some Faraway Beach*, 24.

110 Rose, "Scaramouche of the Synthesizer," 70.

Eno outwardly reflected on minimalism's *social* appeal as an aesthetic. By then, Eno had taken considerable flak from rock musicians and journalists who found the pacifying nature of ambient records like *Discreet Music* unnerving. Rock critic Lester Bangs, for instance, wrote that the music's calmness "makes you sometimes wonder if [Eno] couldn't go merrily along creating his pleasant little ambient tapes under the most totalitarian regime, which leads you to further speculate that it might have been amoral in the first place."[111] Eno, in response, justified his musical style as an antidote to the self-importance and narcissism he perceived guiding the political orientation of rock's critical darlings. He explained that ambient music resulted from his own principled anti-individualism, a concerted effort to understand the self as more as a product of the environment than point of origin. Working with one's environment "has political resonances," argued Eno in 1982. "The decision to stop seeing yourself as the centre of the world, to see yourself as part of the greater flow of things, as having limited options and responsibility for your actions—the converse of that 'me' generation, 'do your own thing' idea—that is political theory, and it's what the music grows from."[112] But when less on the defensive, Eno's desire to melt into the environment seemed to emerge more from personal instinct than political consideration. "One of the nice things about the kind of music I'm doing now," as he put it in 1985, "is that it makes me feel quite unimportant. I like that feeling."[113]

Music to make you feel unimportant . . . discreet . . . obscure . . . environmental . . . could this have been the sort of sensuous social appeal Eno was importing into the pop world with *Discreet Music* and the rest of Obscure Records? Consider how so many of the compositions featured on the sublabel, including *Discreet Music*, featured the machinations of impersonal systems. Consider also how Eno conceived of his "vertical" music as all ground, emptied of overt subjective presence. And consider the many narratives of accident surrounding *Discreet Music*'s conception and execution in which Eno appears as passive as the automated technologies that brought the recording into being. Eno, it seems, had been working out "that feeling" for a while.

For someone who so often downplayed his own importance, it may appear fortuitous that Eno developed into one of 1970s pop music's leading auteurs. But Eno's star rose, nonetheless, as he quite audibly made self-effacement a hallmark of his musical style and artistic persona. Critics noticed; *Downbeat*

[111] Bangs, "A Sandbox in Smallville."
[112] Mick Brown, "Life of Brian According to Eno," *Arts Guardian*, May 1, 1982, 10.
[113] Jensen, "The Sound of Silence," 25.

reviewer Gilmore, for instance, wrote admiringly of Eno's "ideal of passivity" as displayed in *Discreet Music*, while Lester Bangs keenly observed that Eno's 1978 album *Before and after Science* "bespeaks a certain yearning for passivity, a desire to let some nameless Other take creative control and dictate the resultant piece through its own mysterious processes."[114] These authors' fascination with the gorgeous results of Eno's passivity illustrates just how well Eno manipulated the "mysterious processes" he set up, and just how sensitively he "touched up" the results. Facility with cutting-edge production technologies that were unavailable to many avant-garde composers, as well as a keen ear for timbre and mixing, allowed Eno to guide with precision what he now calls "surrender situations," or situations that require sharing agency with the environment.[115] Although the genesis of his sounds was and is often environmentally distributed, Eno's authorship over these situations would never be doubt.

The popularity of Eno's passivity has also intertwined with his remarkable ability to guide the narratives of production surrounding his musical output. The stories surrounding *Discreet Music*'s genesis, in particular, emphasized personal circumstances and accidents over Eno's considered, controlled engagement with preexisting and contemporaneous musical practices. As already observed, such narratives served a didactic purpose for listeners unaccustomed to liking feeling unimportant; at the same time, they buttressed Eno's claims to authoring a piece whose conceptual, technical, and stylistic underpinnings came from cybernetics and experimental music. Yet an additional benefit may be noted for both Eno and other minimalist artists who, as art critic Anna Chave has observed, commonly positioned their work as "self-evident" rather than authored, a commonality calling into question "what partisans of minimalism have had to gain by denying the art's identity as a private statement."[116] What else might Eno have gained in framing *Discreet Music*'s genesis as impersonal, unintended, and environmental as the music sounds?

To start, one might note that the "minimalist" repetition and reduction featured on *Discreet Music*, as well as the title track's tape-, synth-, and sequencer-based automated processes, had by 1975 opened up similar

[114] Lester Bangs, "Eno Sings with the Fishes," in *Mainlines, Blood Feasts, and Bad Taste*, ed. John Morthland (New York: Anchor, 2002), 243.

[115] Brian Eno, *Red Bull Music Academy*, interview by Emma Warren, 2013, http://www.redbullmusicacademy.com/lectures/brian-eno.

[116] Anna C. Chave, "Minimalism and the Rhetoric of Power," *Arts Magazine* 64, no. 5 (January 1990): 52.

sound worlds in psychedelic space rock, Californian new age, and German cosmic rock. *Discreet Music*, presented not as an offshoot of these contemporaneous popular practices, but rather as (accidental!) experimental music, conveyed the heady conceptualism of the avant-garde instead of the trippy psychedelicism of the counterculture. Its detached, indirectly compassionate beauty also stylistically set *Discreet Music* apart from the caprice, vividness, and grandeur so often conveyed by contemporaneous psychedelic excursions in technomusical drift. Emotionally poignant and lovingly crafted as it is, *Discreet Music*, as writer Frank Rose summarized Eno's oeuvre in 1977, has a "bloodless sound." Sweet but distant, Eno's music, Rose wrote, "reflects warmth but does not seem to generate it."[117] Eno's conceptual and stylistic distinctiveness, compared to most of the popular field's engagement with "minimalist" techniques and automated technologies, comes as much from its carefully crafted impersonality as from its comforting lifelikeness.

Art critics and music writers have long observed impersonal detachment as a mood pervading minimal art more broadly. Barbara Rose, in her 1965 essay on minimalist painting and sculpture—she then called it "ABC Art"—took note of the movement's exsanguine "blandness" and "neutrality," and argued that the pieces' outright "denial of content" indeed constituted their content.[118] As critic Edward Strickland put it, minimalist visual art and music strike a "tone" of impersonality by "simulat[ing] an autonomy from the human will."[119] Musicologist Richard Taruskin has similarly observed that US minimalist music, in conspicuous contrast to the political turbulence of the 1960s, exudes "coolness" throughout.[120] And indeed, "impersonality" appears as a refrain across Steve Reich's own writings, in particular the essay "Music as a Gradual Process," in which he claimed that gradual processes give the listener "direct contact with the impersonal."[121] Not all audiences, of course, find the impersonality of minimal art appealing; as Anna Chave observes, museum patrons have commonly regarded minimalist visual art as arrogant, cruel, and impenetrable due to its evident disinterest in human life.[122] The repetitions and drones of minimal music, although imperfectly

[117] Frank Rose, "Four Conversations with Brian Eno," *Village Voice*, March 1977, 72.

[118] Barbara Rose, "ABC Art," in *Minimalism: A Critical Anthology*, ed. Gregory Battcock (New York: Dutton, 1968), 281.

[119] Edward Strickland, *Minimalism: Origins* (Bloomington: Indiana University Press, 1993), 7, 292.

[120] Richard Taruskin, "A Harmonious Avant-Garde?," *Music in the Late Twentieth-Century*, Vol. 6 of *The Oxford History of Western Music* (New York: Oxford University Press, 2005), 354.

[121] Steve Reich, "Music as a Gradual Process," in *Writings on Music, 1965–2000*, ed. Paul Hillier (New York: Oxford University Press, 2002), 35.

[122] Chave, "Minimalism and the Rhetoric," 55.

analogous to visual art's techniques of depersonalization, have likewise famously led many audiences to boredom, if not outright anger or frustration. But whereas some may be put off by minimal music's coldness, or irritated by its lengthy drones and loops, it seems plausible that listeners who aspire to impersonality might conversely find this quality of minimalism an affective means of relation, attachment, and even self-recognition.

One of the spiky charms of impersonal presentation, as Chave explains of both people and art, is its simulation of objectivity. Impersonal appearance does not merely display "neutrality" and "unfeelingness," Chave notes; it also, by dint of this unfeelingness, carries the authority of "masculine" rationality (51). As an ideal of human feeling, impersonality is the legacy of the Enlightenment, the modus operandi of the experimental scientist, and hegemonically assumed of light-skinned educated men. Minimalist art that demonstrated success in gaining institutional support within the fine art world in and around the 1970s typically assumed impersonality's authority in the repetition of simple forms, in clean and clear sense of proportion, and in austere design, all in keeping with the norms of classical architecture as promoted by European intellectuals (53). Yet by disavowing the social life of these forms, authors of minimalist art have been able to hide "the mechanisms by which [minimalism] has been elevated or empowered as a public statement of the first importance"—mechanisms that, as Chave's essay reveals, are not only financial and institutional, but also affective, experiential, and gendered (52). And what better way to enhance an art piece's authoritative veneer of impersonality, its affective coolness, than to say it simply happened of its own accord?

Discreet Music's impersonal cool, along with Eno's rhetorical emphasis on its depersonalized creation, presented both an authoritative mood and validating narratives for audiences who might have bristled at the album's feminized "sensuousness" and subordination of form to function typical of low- and middlebrow pop. As the late twentieth century saw a shift from snobbish to omnivorous listening habits among highbrows, pop exuding the calm detachment traditionally appropriate to aesthetic discernment may have retained special appeal for consumers aspiring to or embodying disembodied "rationality." As preeminent sociologist of taste Pierre Bourdieu observed in the 1960s, an attitude of detached ease had long been the sine qua non of highbrow consumption, a bodily *habitus* that demonstrates the freedom from desire and distance from economic necessity.[123] And while the

[123] Pierre Bourdieu, *Distinction: A Social Critique of the Judgement of Taste*, trans. Richard Nice (1979; repr. Cambridge, MA: Harvard University Press, 1984), 53–54, 256.

tastes of high-status cultural producers and consumers have since diversified, the display of disinterestedness has remained integral to the communication of cultural status in Europe and North America.[124] Eno's passivity, and the technologized accidentalism of *Discreet Music* on the whole, confirms the listener's "rational" distance from passion, even as the music simultaneously invites facile "surrender to immediate sensation" outlawed in classical bourgeois norms.[125] Eno intended the album's knowing aloofness, it seems, to be a byproduct of converting experimental art into minimal pop—a mood that would carry, along with it, the distinction of avant-garde art.

Even beyond this, the music's easy discretion not only makes available highbrow and masculinist identifications with rational authority; it also takes on the social invisibility and bodily transcendence presumed of racial whiteness in the anglophone world. *Discreet Music*'s sensuous emptiness might provide an appealing route of identification for subjects whose racial identity, as cultural studies scholar Richard Dyer writes of the white westerner, "may readily be felt as being nothing in particular."[126] This understanding resonates with musicologist Lloyd Whitesell's charge, rooted in Dyer's and Toni Morrison's pathbreaking analyses of white cultural representation, that the stylization and interpretation of twentieth-century avant-garde music as empty, blank, and neutral, a trend most purely represented in art-house minimalism, "echoes a white perspective" in its symbolic negation of subjectivity.[127]

All of which is to say that Eno's passivity, and the passivity of *Discreet Music*'s listeners in turn, was thoroughly prepared to be taken as a virtue, rather than a flaw, by the assurance of Eno's personal authority as a white male avant-pop auteur, and by the demonstration of social authority conveyed in his personally expressive impersonal musical style. Given the white, male, and college-educated demographic skew of the genre culture over the following decades, ambient music's minimalism also proved an attractive means of hooking consumers who already discreetly commanded sociocultural authority. The instinct to surrender to Eno's staid ambiences, in other words, may be primed by the passive assumption of social power, a rather

[124] Josée Johnston and Shyon Baumann, "Democracy versus Distinction: A Study of Omnivorousness in Gourmet Food Writing," *American Journal of Sociology* 113, no. 1 (July 2007): 197–99.

[125] Bourdieu, *Distinction*, 486.

[126] Richard Dyer, *White: Essays on Race and Culture* (New York: Routledge, 1997), 80.

[127] Lloyd Whitesell, "White Noise: Race and Erasure in the Cultural Avant-Garde," *American Music* 19, no. 2 (2001): 184.

particular consumer trait for sounds commonly assumed to be universal, neutral, ambient.

Interlude: In the Spirit of Satie?

Eno's liner notes to *Discreet Music* contained one conspicuous reference that would reverberate throughout ambient music's written histories from then on: "I was trying to make a piece that could be listened to and yet could be ignored . . . perhaps in the spirit of Satie who wanted to make music that could 'mingle with the sound of the knives and forks at dinner.'" Of course, French composer Erik Satie (1866–1925) didn't just "want" to compose *musique d'ameublement* ("furnishing music," or, as it's more commonly translated, furniture music), but did in fact compose four such pieces between 1917 and 1923.[128] None of Satie's own *musiques d'ameublement*, however, ever actually mingled with the sounds of silverware; at least, not in Satie's lifetime. Although, as David Toop writes, furniture music is "cited often as a visionary precursor of ambient music, Muzak, dinner party music, interval music, Walkman music, elevator music and all the other functionary fill-ins and backgrounds, highbrow and lowbrow, that now accompany our lives," Satie's furniture music compositions have rarely been realized in performance, then or since.[129] Their "visionary" status, moreover, can be overstated given that background music for everyday use, from *Tafelmusik* to light music, both preceded *and* animated Satie's invention. To this point, Eno learned of furniture music indirectly from John Cage's account of artist Fernand Léger's remembrance of Satie's early conception; and, as Léger recalled,

> We were having lunch, Satie and some friends, in a restaurant. The music was so loud we simply couldn't stand it and left. But Satie said:
>
> "Even so, there's room for a 'musique d'ameublement,' that's to say, music which would be part of the noises around it and would take account of them. I think of it as being tuneful, softening the noise of knives and forks without overpowering them or making itself obtrusive. It would fill in the

[128] For a richly detailed historical account of Satie's *Musiques d'ameublement*, see Caroline Potter, *Erik Satie: A Parisian Composer and His World* (Woodbridge, UK: Boydell & Brewer, 2016), 138–76.

[129] David Toop, *Ocean of Sound: Aether Talk, Ambient Sound and Imaginary Worlds* (London: Serpent's Tail, 1995), 197.

> silences which can sometimes weigh heavy between table companions. It would banish the need to make banal conversation. At the same time it would neutralise street noises, which can be tactless in their behaviour." It would, he said, be responding to a need.[130]

Satie's idea for furniture music, hardly ex nihilo, distinctly responded to the live music becoming ever more ubiquitous as an accompaniment to dining, shopping, and other public activities in the first decade of the twentieth century.[131]

Given the obscurity of Satie's actual furniture music compositions, Eno had probably taken more inspiration from the concept of furniture music than from its actual sound, and name-checked Satie chiefly in the spirit of avant-garde conceptualism. As ambient media scholar Paul Roquet writes, "Satie's image as an idiosyncratic and solitary genius from Montmartre allowed him to serve as an ideal ancestor for later generations of ambient musicians attempting to envision a more artistic and independent heritage for atmospheric music."[132] And given Satie's and Eno's frequent joint appearances in subsequent histories of twentieth-century art music, sound art, and background music, the historiographic connection worked.[133] Still, there is something more to the commonly made link from Satie to Eno than cultural accreditation; for several pieces of Satie's furniture music, like Eno's ambient music, reinterpreted extant atmospheric music practices through an aesthetics of minimalism and mechanism. Automatic repetition, and the resulting impersonality of the

[130] Fernand Léger, "Satie Inconnu," *La Revue Musicale* 214 (June 1952): 137–38: "Nous déjeûnions, des amis et lui dans un restaurant. Obligés de subir une musique tapageuse, insupportable nous quittons la salle et Satie nous dit: 'Il y a tout de même à réaliser une musique d'ameublement, c'est-à-dire une musique qui ferait partie des bruits ambiant, qui en tiendrait compte. Je la suppose mélodieuse, elle adoucirait les bruits des couteaux, des fourchettes sans les dominer, sans s'imposer. Elle meublerait les silences pesant parfois entre les convives. Elle leur épargnerait les banalités courantes. Elle neutraliserait en même temps les bruits de la rue qui entrent dans le jeu sans discrétion.' Ce serait, disait-il, répondre à un besoin." Translation reprinted from Robert Orledge, *Satie Remembered*, trans. Roger Nichols (London: Faber & Faber, 1995), 74–75.

[131] Although I have not located any similar studies of Paris, Daniel Morat details the growing ubiquity of popular music in public space in Berlin around 1900, which can likely be extrapolated to Paris; see Morat, "Music in the Air—Listening in the Streets: Popular Music and Urban Listening Habits in Berlin ca. 1900," in *The Oxford Handbook of Music Listening in the 19th and 20th Centuries*, ed. Christian Thorau and Hansjakob Ziemer (New York and London: Oxford University Press, 2018), 335–53.

[132] Paul Roquet, *Ambient Media: Japanese Atmospheres of Self* (Minneapolis: University of Minnesota Press, 2016), 39. Cultural studies scholar Ryan Hibbett has similarly posited that Eno probably saw in Satie, as with Cage, a persona who could sustain his "artistic aura"; see Ryan Hibbett, "The New Age Taboo," *Journal of Popular Music Studies* 22, no. 3 (2010): 302.

[133] See, for instance, Alan Licht, *Sound Art: Beyond Music, between Categories* (New York: Rizzoli, 2007), 276–77.

sound, not only became a stylistic marker for both artists, but also threw the aesthetic and social validity of contemporaneous atmospheric music practices into question.

Much as Eno would later deride Muzak for papering over the idiosyncrasies of the playback environment, Satie decried light music's mispurposing of other genres.[134] "It is habit—custom—to make music on occasions with which music *has nothing to do*," Satie wrote in 1920. "And so one plays 'waltzes,' operatic 'fantasies,' and other such things written for another purpose."[135] In a diatribe unpublished during his lifetime, Satie riled against "grotesque arrangements" of such music piped into places like the Grands Magasins Dufayel, a popular Parisian department store that specialized in furniture.[136] "In many places," Satie groused,

> sweet and excellent silence has been replaced by bad music. It is thought smart by most people to hear falsely pretty things, and listen to silly, vaguely churchy ritornellos, while they drink a beer or try on a pair of trousers; to appear to appreciate the sonorous tribute of basses and bassoons, and other ugly-pipes, while thinking of nothing at all.[137]

Satie, evidently (or possibly sarcastically) just as irritated by the loss of silence as with the "falsely pretty" music replacing it, and with the so-called appreciation this nauseating musical "Dufayelization" inspired in ordinary shoppers, advertised furniture music as a corrective.[138]

Ironically, Satie's first two *Musiques d'ameublement* between 1917 and '18, *Carrelage phonique* (Acoustic Tiles) and *Tapisserie en for forgé* (Iron-Wrought Tapestry), do not sound custom-crafted for their explicitly stated

[134] On the sounds of light music in nineteenth-century France, see Derek B. Scott, *Sounds of the Metropolis: The 19th-Century Popular Music Revolution in London, New York, Paris, and Vienna* (New York: Oxford University Press, 2008).

[135] Ornella Volta, *Satie/Cocteau: Les Malentendus d'une Entente* (Bègles, France: Le Castor Astral, 1993), 112. "L'habitude—l'usage—est de faire de la musique dans des occasions où la musique n'a *rien à faire*. Là, on joue des 'Valses,' des 'Fantaisies d'Opéras,' & autres choses semblables, écrites pour un autre objet."

[136] Erik Satie, *A Mammal's Notebook*, ed. Ornella Volta, trans. Anthony Melville, Atlas Arkhive Five: Documents of the Avant-Garde (London: Atlas, 1996), 106.

[137] Erik Satie, *Écrits*, ed. Ornella Volta (Paris: Editions Champ Libre, 1977), 24–25: "Dans beaucoup de lieux, l'excellent et doux silence a été remplacé par de la mauvaise musique. Il est bien vu, par le commun, d'ouïr de fausses belles choses, d'écouter de sottes ritournelles, vaguement pieuses, en prenant un bock ou en essayant un pantalon; de sembler apprécer les dûs sonores des basses, contrebasses & d'autres vilains flûteaux, tout en ne pensant à rien." Translation reprinted from Satie, *A Mammal's Notebook*, 105.

[138] Satie, *A Mammal's Notebook*, 106.

purposes, but rather sport the bland facelessness of functionalist design.[139] In contrast to the "moneyed glamor" sounding at the Grands Magasins, Satie's austere approach to his music stylistically aligned with the functionalist principles of contemporaneous design and architecture movements such as Bauhaus, Constructivism, De Stijl, and the International Style, all of which commonly eliminated "the ornaments and imitations typical of the democratization of luxury."[140] Not all of Satie's pieces of furniture music reflected this sensibility: *Chez un "bistrot"* and *Un Salon*, for instance, instead rearranged the "marches" and "fantasias" that Satie advertised furniture music as replacing.[141] Yet *Carrelage* and *Tapisserie* displayed functionalist economy, with each comprising a single four-bar melody to be looped ad infinitum (and/or ad nauseam). Satie instructed players to repeat the phrases over and over, like a vamp, so that the music at length would come to resemble the repeated patterns of wallpaper, floor tiles, or tapestry.[142] The pieces, in their modularity and sheer melodic contouring, reflected the composer's own interest in rendering music architecturally.[143] As the twentieth century progressed into its second decade, composers and music critics across Europe likewise began to shun ornamental complexity in music, with some holding up Satie's sparer musical designs as aesthetic ideals.[144]

Carrelage and *Tapisserie*'s neutered affect and dumb monotony clearly detract from their humanness, making them ostensibly fit for ignoring. But considering Satie's comments on light music, satirical intentions may too have been at play. Might their mechanization represent the unthinking deployment of charming dances for atmospheric use? Could it represent the stereotypically blank, undifferentiated, lumpen masses, *le commun*, for whom Satie imagined furniture music produced? Does the music's expressive emptiness also give the lie to the artificial demonstrations of care by bourgeois audiences, like the one that famously tried to listen respectfully to

[139] Performance instructions for the score of *Carrelage* read, "For a luncheon or marriage contract"; on *Tapisserie*, "To greet the arrival of guests at a grand reception. To be played in a lobby."

[140] Rosalind H. Williams, *Dream Worlds: Mass Consumption in Late Nineteenth-Century France* (Berkeley: University of California Press, 1982), 164. Williams notes that the term "functionalism" didn't arise in France until much later. On the history of functionalist aesthetics, see George H. Marcus, *Functionalist Design: An Ongoing History* (Munich and New York: Prestel-Verlag, 1995).

[141] Satie, *A Mammal's Notebook*, 200.

[142] Satie employed a similar strategy of melodic looping in composing film music for his final work, the "Entr'acte" of *Relâche* (1924).

[143] James Graham, "*Musique en fer forgé*: Erik Satie, Le Corbusier and the Problem of Aural Architecture," *AA Files*, no. 68 (2014): 6.

[144] Gurminder Kaur Bhogal, *Details of Consequence: Ornament, Music, and Art in Paris* (New York: Oxford University Press, 2013), 313.

a 1920 performance of Satie's other furniture music?[145] To this day, it seems impossible to resolve the ambiguity Satie's *Musiques d'ameublement* set at the intersection of elegant, *moderne* functionalism and mass culture send-up.

Eno, like Satie before him, rejected popular conventions of background music by replacing it with something more affectively removed, blandly consonant, and formally economical. With *Discreet Music*, Eno developed a charming aesthetic of monotony by combining handicraft and technological design elements and presenting them in an understated manner. Eno's next major ambient release, *Music for Airports*, even better embodied the contrarian spirit of Satie in its titular satire of the mood music LP, which echoed Satie's own *blague* sloganeering of furniture music that parroted contemporaneous advertising practices.[146] Perhaps most significantly, neither Eno nor Satie heeded high-art avoidance of the popular marketplace, instead seeking consumer viability even while slyly lampooning consumer culture.[147]

The comparison, however, has its limits, since Satie's and Eno's ambient musics expressively refract their fundamentally distinct conditions of musical transmission and reception in different ways. Whereas Satie's hard-edged, insistent patterns would have been performed by live musicians, ironically heightening the music's monotony, Eno's soft-lit, lazy, randomized audio repetitions lend naturalness and warmth to the automatic playback situation. *Discreet Music*'s layers are not coordinated by a unified beat structure or meter; melodic fragments recombine and overlap, generating constant interactional variety; their timbres and tone also change at whim. The irregularity of the texture, although mechanized, makes Eno's recording more akin to a living, buzzing ecosystem than Satie's rigid, dead-eyed repetitions. This also makes close, or even intermittent listening to *Discreet Music* more rewarding than *Carrelage* at length. Unpredictable, subtle shifts within the static limitations of the piece suggest a human touch behind the tape system's automatism; the piece's intertwining tendrils of synthesized and taped sounds approximate nature-sound organicism. While Eno's tape loops technically embed the automation of record playback into the piece itself, their soft-lit A♭ Major glow reflects kindly on this mechanism. With rhythmic looseness,

[145] Robert Orledge, *Satie the Composer*, Music in the 20th Century (New York: Cambridge University Press, 1990), 160.

[146] Steven Moore Whiting, *Satie the Bohemian: From Cabaret to Concert Hall* (New York: Oxford University Press, 1999), 102.

[147] Caroline Potter, *Erik Satie: A Parisian Composer and His World* (Woodbridge, UK: Boydell & Brewer, 2016), 19–21; Jerrold Seigel, *Bohemian Paris: Culture, Politics, and the Boundaries of Bourgeois Life, 1830–1930* (New York: Viking, 1986), 334–35.

timbral handicraft, and patient unfolding, *Discreet Music* prepares a personal playback situation in which listeners may settle into a homey sonic embrace. Heard at home, the feeling fits; Eno's happy outcomes reflect favorably on the comforts of domestic record consumption.

Contrast this with Satie's *Carrelage*, for which close listening does not reveal any spontaneous nuance, but only amplifies the inscrutable, unwavering automatism of the performance. Satie's choice to employ performing musicians rather than the popular pianola, as architecture historian James Graham argues, harkened to his own employment in the cafés of Paris, and rendered his furniture music more a "wrought-iron" artisanal product than "cast-iron" mass reproduction.[148] Yet his choice not to automate the playback of mechanical music also draws attention to the alienation of musicians' labor when used as decoration or status symbol. The pieces' upbeat and upright pleasantries orchestrate the industrious human production of empty decoration, a performatively absurd, if discreet, spectacle of dehumanization. As Roquet aptly summarizes, "Furniture music hints at environmental mood regulation, but only while ironically distancing itself from its own instrumentality."[149]

Given furniture music's original design and advertisement as a stripped down and custom-built *alternative* to the light classical arrangements heard in public places, and given its satirical two-facedness, it would be off the mark to say, as art historian Hervé Vanel writes, that "Satie invented muzak, and muzak realized Satie's idea."[150] Nor did Satie anticipate the use of radio in the home as background, as his compatriot composer Darius Milhaud mused:

> Nowadays, children and housewives fill their homes with unheeded music, reading and working to the sound of the wireless. And in all public places, large stores and restaurants, the customers are drenched in an undying flood of music. Is this not "musique d'ameublement," heard, but not listened to?[151]

No, it is not—for neither Muzak nor easy-listening radio were crafted in the ironic, contrarian spirit of Satie's furniture music compositions, nor did they come close to these pieces' angular, aloof compositional style. Eno's

[148] Graham, "*Musique en fer forgé*," 6–7.
[149] Roquet, *Ambient Media*, 40.
[150] Hervé Vanel, *Triple Entendre: Furniture Music, Muzak, Muzak-Plus* (Urbana: University of Illinois Press, 2013), x.
[151] Orledge, *Satie Remembered*, 153–54.

ambient music far more precisely updated Satie's elegant ironization of conventional easy-listening. Yet in 2022 as in the 1970s, recordings of Satie's furniture music, or of anything like it, rarely appear in public spaces outside of art galleries and exhibitions; live performances are practically nonexistent. Ambient music listening, at least in private, remains popular as ever. Furniture music, a historical curio, is scarcely heard.

The spirit of Satie nevertheless haunts Eno's early ambient records, not only because these records, like Satie's furniture music, realized an alternative to standard background music, but also because their ostinato figures, nonfunctional harmonies, *douloureux* mood, and enervated drift are redolent of Satie's most commercially successful music: the *Gymnopédies*, written many decades prior his furniture music compositions. In fact, when Satie's piano music enjoyed a revival in the 1970s and '80s on the recorded medium, commentators noted that their simplicity made them "well suited to domestic consumption," a facet eventually exploited by the many relaxation and "stress relief" albums from the 1990s that often included *Gymnopédie no. 1*.[152] As both Joseph Lanza and Paul Roquet acknowledge, Satie's *Gymnopédies* stood as a model, in contradistinction to Debussy's more sentimental impressionism, of atmospheric music at once relaxing, impersonal, and mildly melancholy.[153] This air of detached moodiness, it turns out, would become a primary means of making ambient music "seductive" for popular music listeners—and a distinctive genre among popular genres of ambient audio.[154]

The *Ambient* Series

Ambient 1: Music for Airports

As Eno has told it—both in spirit and manner of Satie—the inspiration for *Music for Airports* arose during a stop at Flughafen Köln/Bonn (the Cologne/Bonn Airport) on a clear, sunny Sunday morning in late 1977:

> The light was beautiful; everything was beautiful, except they were playing awful music. And I thought, there's something completely

[152] Allen Hughes, "New Releases Highlight Music in the French Manner," *New York Times*, May 23, 1982, 27.

[153] Joseph Lanza, *Elevator Music: A Surreal History of Muzak, Easy-Listening, and Other Moodsong* (New York: Picador, 1995), 19–20; Roquet, *Ambient Media*, 44–46.

[154] Grant, "Brian Eno against Interpretation," 29.

> wrong that people don't think about the music that goes into situations like this. You know, they spend hundreds of millions of pounds on the architecture, on everything, except the music. The music comes down to someone bringing in a tape of their favorite songs this week, and sticking them in, and the whole airport is filled with this sound. So, I thought, it would be interesting to start writing music for public spaces like that.[155]

Over the next several months, Eno produced four solutions for what he perceived to be a naïve or thoughtless approach to the use of music for airports. Using synthesizers and tape loops of improvised material, Eno created four tracks of invariant instrumentation and texture, with each establishing a contained repertory of pitches, gestural shapes, and motivic content throughout its entirety. With each recording also sitting within a narrow dynamic range and avoiding timbral distortion, the atmospheres on *Music for Airports*, like those on *Discreet Music*, were made to facilitate assurance of their consistency and discretion—a novel approach, at the time, to designing music for public spaces of commerce and transit, as such music typically employed familiar popular songs and styles to assure listeners that they were "at home" in public.[156]

Ignorable musical consistency and discretion might not seem to make for especially "interesting" at-home listening; and yet, today, *Music for Airports* sits atop several lists of "great" ambient albums, and even stars as the subject of a book published as part of a series dedicated to the musicological canon that calls Eno's album "seminal," "transformative," and a "masterpiece."[157] The album's early reviews, however, scarcely identified a future musical

[155] Brian Eno, interview by Martin Large, "Opening Holland Festival," NOS (Netherlands Broadcasting Foundation), June 5, 1999, TV. It is unclear whether Eno's characterization of airport music as a tape of someone's "favorite songs" captures what he heard on that date in 1977, or what he was commonly hearing in 1999 when the interview took place.

[156] Ronald M. Radano, "Interpreting Muzak: Speculations on Musical Experience in Everyday Life," *American Music* 7, no. 4 (Winter 1989): 456. The media scholars Tia DeNora and Jonathan Sterne have explained, along these lines, how musical styles map and regulate retail space by marking out areas in which consumers may find their identities recognized and affirmed; see Tia DeNora, *Music in Everyday Life* (New York: Cambridge University Press, 2000), 109; Jonathan Sterne, "Sounds Like the Mall of America: Programmed Music and the Architectonics of Commercial Space," *Ethnomusicology* 41, no. 1 (Winter 1997): 29.

[157] Andy Beta et al., "The 50 Best Ambient Albums of All Time," *Pitchfork*, September 26, 2016, http://pitchfork.com/features/lists-and-guides/9948-the-50-best-ambient-albums-of-all-time/ ; Tony Marcus, "The 20 Greatest Ambient Albums Ever Made," *FACT Magazine*, June/July 2008, https://www.factmag.com/2011/07/19/20-best-ambient/; John T. Lysaker, *Brian Eno's "Ambient 1: Music for Airports,"* Oxford Keynotes (New York: Oxford University Press, 2018).

"masterpiece," save *Music Journal*'s Robert Henschen, who presciently, if tentatively, surmised that Eno's record "may truly represent one profound direction for electronic music in the future."[158] Other positive reviews offered milder praise for the music's "lulling" functionalism, with *Audio* magazine's Michael Tearson, recalling *Environments*'s early advertisements, calling *Airports* "better than Valium, and completely without undesirable side effects."[159] Most reviewers, however, derided the album as bland. *Rolling Stone*'s Michael Bloom called the album "unfocused . . . aesthetic white noise," while *New York Times*'s Ken Emerson quipped that its "hues are as faint as the flavor of those Japanese teas so delicate you're never quite sure you aren't just simply sipping hot water."[160] *NME*'s Lynden Barber suggested that the "simply ignorable" album's "white-tiled atmosphere" could have earned it the title "Music for Toilets"; and Robert Christgau registered it, pointedly, "a bore."[161]

Ironically, while these at-home listeners found in *Airports* an "ignorable" bore, air travelers and airport employees found the album a little too "interesting" when *Airports* was installed at various airports in the early 1980s. At New York's LaGuardia Airport in 1980, some airport workers and travelers complained that the music induced unease.[162] As one remarked, "It sounds like funeral music."[163] The album's later installation in Pittsburgh International Airport allegedly garnered requests for the usual background music to be restored.[164] And in 1984 the music sparked protest from employees at Berlin's Tegel Airport who were annoyed by the acoustic "interference."[165] Perhaps these listeners heard *Airports* exuding, as mood music aficionado Joseph Lanza describes it, "a kind of sonic ambivalence that encourages grave contemplation of feelings of impending doom. . . . Behind all of Eno's cold, metallic engineering is a frightening and moody world that is anything but emotionally neutral."[166] Lanza's dramatic descriptions

158 Robert Henschen, "Review," *Music Journal*, September/October 1979, 62.

159 David Sargent, "Recordings," *Vogue*, July 1979, 26; "Album Picks," *Record World*, April 21, 1979, 19; Michael Tearson, "The Column," *Audio*, September 1979, 89.

160 Michael Bloom, "*Ambient 1: Music for Airports*," *Rolling Stone*, July 26, 1979, 80; Ken Emerson, "Brian Eno Slips into 'Trance Music,'" *New York Times*, August 12, 1979, D22.

161 Lynden Barber, "Atmospheres in the Home," *New Musical Express*, 1982, http://music.hyperreal.org/artists/brian_eno/interviews/rvonland.html; Robert Christgau, "Brian Eno: *On Land*," *Village Voice*, August 31, 1982.

162 Sheppard, *On Some Faraway Beach*, 279.

163 George Rush, "Brian Eno: Rock's Svengali Pursues Silence," *Esquire*, December 1982, 28.

164 Lanza, *Elevator Music*, 198.

165 Ursula Frohne, "Brian Eno: Tegel Airport, Institute Unzeit, Berlin," *FlashArt*, May 1984, 43.

166 Lanza, *Elevator Music*, 196.

of Eno's music, along with the comments of the airport listeners, contrast starkly with the lukewarm assessments of *Airports*'s reviewers. Even more ironically, they align with Eno's intentions—*Airports*, as Eno later attested, needed to reflect the fact that traveling by plane always carries an element of "flirting with death."[167]

To understand how these intentions developed, it helps to hear how Eno keyed in on certain stylistic parameters for ambient music during his formative studio partnerships in the three years between *Discreet Music* and the *Ambient* series. Most notably, while in Berlin in 1976 and '77, Eno collaborated on a then-unreleased studio album with krautrock trio Harmonia (Hans-Joachim Roedelius, Michael Rother, and Dieter Moebius), two LPs with duo Cluster (Harmonia *sans* Rother), and various studio sessions with David Bowie. Eno's teaming with *kosmische* rockers Harmonia and Cluster, themselves explorers of a pop idiom based in improvised plateaus of electronic minimalism, resulted in unhurried, sumptuous sound-paintings like "Sometimes in Autumn," "Schöne Hände," and "Wehrmut." Eno's collaborations with Bowie during the *Low* and *Heroes* sessions also resulted in vivid, melodious proto-ambient sketches like the limpid "Moss Garden" and the foreboding "Sense of Doubt." Tying all such work together were the delicate balances struck between constancy and mystery, with each track progressing cautiously, but certainly, into hazy musical futures. Eno, in his *Airports* essay, captured this expressive penchant in a turn of phrase pseudonymous with his Bowie collaboration: "Whereas conventional background music is produced by stripping away all sense of doubt and uncertainty (and thus all genuine interest) from the music, Ambient Music retains these qualities."[168]

This "sense of doubt," on *Airports* as elsewhere in Eno's early catalog, established certain thematic and affective coordinates that surveyed ambient music's later expansion as a genre. With *Airports*, Eno shaded the theme of air travel ambivalently with both calm and apprehension. The album's containment of certain musical uncertainties within dependably stable parameters, as the forthcoming analysis illustrates, not only functions to contain the anxiety of air travel, but also captures aesthetically something of how infrastructures of air travel attempt to do the same. Ambivalently both embracing and ironizing, at once, airports'

[167] Brian Eno, *A Year with Swollen Appendices* (London: Faber & Faber, 1996), 295.

[168] Eno, "Ambient Music."

technocratic human management, the record's aesthetic and cultural significance today has less to do with the way it improved upon "conventional background music," and more to do with the ways it expressively, with a "sense of doubt," addressed its own place in an increasingly planned and programmed world.

A closer examination of *Music for Airports*'s four recordings illuminates the sources of the music's uncertain undercurrent. While these tracks promote an overarching stability by constraining the parameters of global or long-term change, local or short-term variabilities keep the music from resting on certain ground. Although the sounds in each recording remain within a single modal pitch collection, the irregular, seemingly unmotivated oscillations between major and minor sonorities within each collection lend the music an emotional mercuriality. And although the nonperiodicity of repeated sonic iterations relieves listeners of expecting their metric placement, these sound events also overlap indiscriminately, and dissipate into indefinitely long echoes, creating a bounty of microvariations in timing and timbre. Within the tracks' overall stable texture, such irregularities generate just enough light turbulence to keep those on board with the music from nodding off. Seemingly weightless and placid at a distance, the music remains astir and amiss, possibly fostering an uncanny sense that the music's stability is a ruse.

Of *Airports*'s recordings, the ghostly "2/1" probably contributed most to the discomfort expressed by airport workers and patrons. For this track, Eno recorded onto tape three women singing "ah," unison and *nonvibrato*, within an F Aeolian pitch collection. Eno then treated each of these tones with reverb and synthesizer, and separated them into tape segments, with long gaps of blank tape about twice the length of each pitch following end of each note. The final recording is almost entirely automated, with eight total tape segments of lifeless-sounding vocals looping simultaneously (see Ex. 3.3).[169] Due to the loops' irregular, uneven lengths, the voices overlap in slightly different configurations over the course of the piece (see Table 3.1). At times, this results in silent gaps arising unpredictably, and somewhat solemnly, between sounding patches of voice. The pitch content also gives reason for the "funereal" associations of one airport listener: while

[169] I say "almost entirely automated" because of Eno's editing in postproduction. In addition to added effects (slow decays, reverb), he occasionally enhances overtones (often an octave above the F3 or A♭3) and drops notes (e.g., the C5 that should sound around 2:55).

Example 3.2. Transcription of "2/1" [0:00–1:40] from *Ambient 1: Music for Airports.*[170]

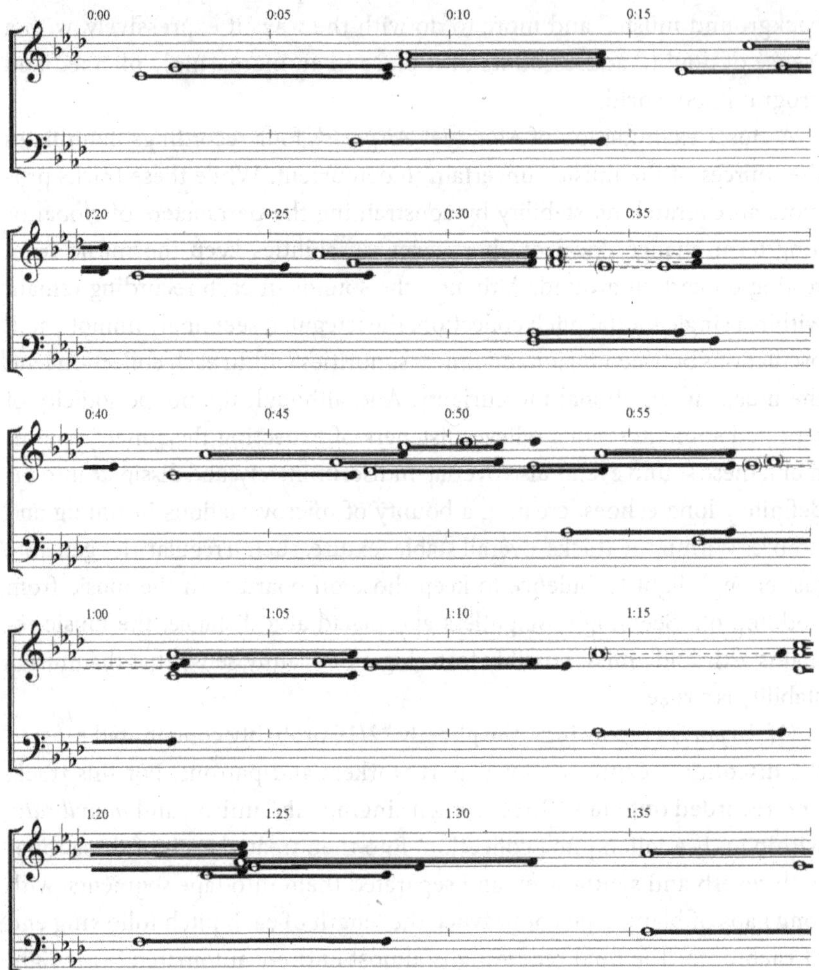

Table 3.1. Approximate Length of Each Voice Loop in "2/1" from *Ambient 1: Music for Airports*

F3	A♭3	C4	D♭4	E♭4	F4	A♭4	C5
24½″	21″	20″	31½″	16½″	19″	18″	31″

Source: Adapted and corrected from Eric Tamm, *Brian Eno: His Music and the Vertical Color of Sound* (London: Faber & Faber, 1988), 133.

170 Open noteheads indicate the notes' initiations; closed noteheads indicate the notes' endings; the bars in between indicate the length of the notes' sustains. Open noteheads in parentheses indicate overtones or "ghost" notes; dotted lines indicate the length of the notes' sustain.

the composition tends toward F Aeolian due to the bass F3's, the occasional appearance of the D♭4 in the absence of the F3 implies a major subtonic triad or seventh chord (VI or VI^7) before proceeding back to an implied tonic (e.g., 0:48; 1:20). This i-VI Aeolian pendulum, as Philip Tagg has found, is often associated with ominousness, resignation, or death in much European and North American music (for instance, an Aeolian pendulum famously starts Chopin's *Marche funèbre*).[171] Music theorist Scott Murphy has more recently illustrated a corollary to Tagg's finding, as he has found the mirror-image triadic pairing of I-iii frequently accompanying scenes of loss or grief in film and television scores; this pairing might be observed in the slow reversions from D♭ major back to F minor, with D♭ heard as a temporary tonic.[172]

On all of *Airports*'s tracks, sixths, sevenths, ninths, and elevenths above the bass also create mild harmonic dissonance and melodic irresolution, leading to an overarching soft sense of tension. In "1/1," for instance, two similar-sounding melodic themes in D Mixolydian melodically elaborate a D major triad, with nonharmonic tones G and E operating as incomplete neighbors or passing tones. These melodic lines alternate with shorter melodic fragments and chords that occasionally include the G4 eleventh above the D bass. These uses of G4 do not necessarily call for a resolution to the third below—elevenths in popular music are common enough—but given their regular resolution to F♯ in the main melodic themes, the appearance of the G4 outside these themes (e.g., 1:45) can seem expectant and unresolved.

Given their divergent criticisms, *Airports*'s naysayers likely found different aspects of the music discomfiting against different backdrops of expectation. For a rock critic, *Airports*'s generally dispassionate pleasantness and overarching predictability could have been cause for offense. By contrast, for listeners expecting extraverted, peppy, or familiar background music,

171 Philip Tagg, "'Universal' Music and the Case of Death," *Critical Quarterly* 35, no. 2 (1993): 54–98. Tagg borrowed the term "Aeolian pendulum" from Alf Björnberg, "On Aeolian Harmony in Contemporary Popular Music" (Department of Musicology, University of Göteborg, 1984), English translation available at http://www.tagg.org/others/othxpdfs/bjbgeol.pdf.

172 Scott Murphy, "Scoring Loss in Some Recent Popular Film and Television," *Music Theory Spectrum* 36, no. 2 (2014): 295–314. Murphy gives some explanation for why I-vi does not carry similar associations, but barely comments on the more closely related harmonic transposition, i-VI.

Example 3.3. Pitch repertories used on *Music for Airports*.

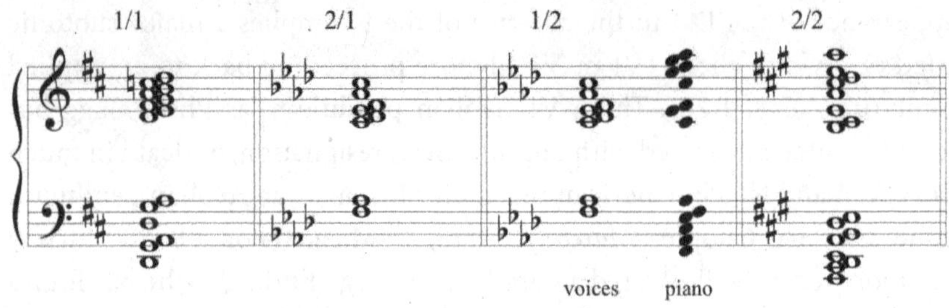

Table 3.2. Timbral Characteristics of *Music for Airports*'s Recordings

Track	Temperature	Luminance
"1/1"	Warm & Cold	Bright
"2/1"	Cold	Dark
"1/2"	Cold	Bright & Dark
"2/2"	Warm	Dark

Note: My use of "temperature" and "luminance" as axes of timbral description are adapted from R. L. Pratt and P. E. Doak, "A Subjective Rating Scale for Timbre," *Journal of Sound and Vibration* 45, no. 3 (1976): 317–28.

Airports might have come off as icy, eerie, or depressed. These different critics might also have responded chiefly to different tracks, taking their particular global affects to be representative of the whole album. Tracks "1/1" and "2/2" imply global D Mixolydian and A Ionian modal areas, respectively, while tracks "2/1" and "1/2" globally imply the more dour F Aeolian modal area (Ex. 3.3). Each track also enjoys different combinations of timbral characteristics (Table 3.2). Generally, "1/1" and "2/2"'s combination of more uplifting global modes with warmer timbres can seem more inviting than "2/1" and "1/2"'s glummer global modes and cold, dark timbres. Whatever the case, *Airports*'s ambivalent moods appear to counteract the moods its critics would prefer to sustain—whether from antagonistic to complacent, or from assured to uncertain.

Eno has in interviews described his compositional activity as a process of discovering musical textures that might bring out in the listener a predetermined mood or feeling: "A composer, or any artist really, is a kind of curator of feelings," as Eno once stated.[173] The connection between musical texture and mood might seem too mysterious or subjective to substantively qualify; but these analyses of Eno's *Airports* designs provides a concrete basis for pondering their ambivalent mixtures of assurance and doubt. If doubt involves the perception of instability in some assured statement, thing, or state of affairs, then a musical evocation of doubt would either have to create a musical or lyrical "object" or state-of-affairs about which it conveys uncertainty (thereby expressing a doubtful emotion), or it would somehow capture uncertainty's affective shape or gist without the content (setting a doubtful mood).[174] As the earlier analyses indicate, *Airports*'s recordings do the latter by establishing global stabilities (through use of a limited range of melodic gestures, a narrow dynamic range, etc.) while remaining inconstant on the local level (through unpredictable entrances, shifts in color, changes in harmonic quality, and so on), essentially conveying assurance while also hinting that this assurance might be a false pretense.

In a 1999 interview, Eno explained why maintaining a musical sense of uncertainty would be desirable in the context of air travel:

> When you went into an airport, or an airplane, they always played this very happy music, which is sort of saying, "You're not going to die! There's not going to be an accident! Don't worry!" And I thought that was really the wrong way around. I thought that it would be much better to have music that said, "Well, if you die, it doesn't really matter." You know? And so I wanted to create a different feeling that you were sort of suspended in the universe, and your life or death wasn't so important. So, rather than trivialize the thing, I wanted to take it seriously: the possibility that you *were* actually, now, going to sit in space. Which is what you do when you travel on an airplane.[175]

As Eno conceived it, *Airports* should enable nothing less than an existential epiphany for the anxious air traveler. Not unlike the prospect of flight delays,

[173] Robert Palmer, "Brian Eno, New Guru of Rock, Going Solo," *New York Times*, March 13, 1981, C17. See also Moore, "Eno = MC Squared," 67; O'Brien, "Eno at the Edge," 31.

[174] On the difference between emotion and mood in art, see Noël Carroll, "Art and Mood: Preliminary Notes and Conjectures," *The Monist* 86, no. 4 (2003): 526–30. For more on the musical conveyance of mood, see Eldritch Priest, "Felt as Thought (or, Music Abstraction and the Semblance of Affect)," in *Sound, Music, Affect: Theorizing Sonic Experience*, ed. Marie Thompson and Ian Biddle (New York: Bloomsbury Academic, 2013), 45–63.

[175] Eno, "Opening Holland Festival."

lost baggage, and plane crashes—but certainly less consequentially—the unpredictable soundings and silences of *Airports*'s recordings leave listeners' immediate futures unknown. This constant transience, instead of distracting or shielding listeners from their anxiety, maintains tension while diminishing the stakes at doubt. Rather than dispelling uncertainty, their frictionless musical worlds perpetuate and contextualize irresolution within a broader stability that renders the unknown "not so important" in the grand scheme. For Eno, musically preserving this modicum of uncertainty was a way of "taking seriously" the existential suspension and loss of control intensified and literalized by air travel; at the same time, this irresolution is cushioned within a stable musical space wherein feelings of doubt might detach from any specific object.

For this reason, *Airports* should not be understood as strictly utilitarian: a metaphorical suggestiveness *about* the reality of air travel, however idealized, persists throughout. Mobility studies scholar Christopher Schaberg, along these lines, contends that Eno's airport installations sparked protest because they "enhanced the peculiar feel of airport life: being in between."[176] The music, in generating localized rhythmic and tonal tensions within a static global framework, paradoxically conveys both movement and hesitation, and in doing so evokes what Schaberg calls the "elimination of speed" produced by airports, where one travels "even when standing in barely moving lines, or waiting for baggage to appear."[177] Airplanes similarly suspend passengers' physical agency, even as they move these passengers over great distances at great speeds. Much like air travelers, the sounds of Eno's album seem inert while being yet carried along, both suspended and adrift, neither at home nor at their destination, but sitting in space somewhere in between.

In addition to its mixtures of stability and irresolution, *Airports* evokes a sense of airport space by conveying an impersonal, functionalist distance from human affairs. It relates this distance in a number of ways. For one, the incidental interactions of sound events on its recordings replicate the transient sociality of airport travelers; rather than consorting cooperatively through chordal harmony and commonly held meter, the motives and pitches of *Airports* loop independently of one another, a loose aggregate rather than unified assembly of sound events. Second, rather than summoning familiar popular song forms and tunes, *Airports*'s recordings anchor listeners in

[176] Christopher Schaberg, *The Textual Life of Airports: Reading the Culture of Flight* (New York: Continuum, 2012), 90.

[177] Ibid., 102.

internal consistencies of musical material (pitch repertory, amplitude range, etc.) and of technological origin (sequence lengths, looping system, synthesizer, etc.). And third, *Airports*'s electronic timbres, whether sterilized by the synthesizer, or clouded and delicately mixed in postproduction, exercise an alien, uncanny mimesis of acoustic instruments and natural voices. These elements place *Airports* at a windowed remove from Western music's most familiar musical conventions, supplanting this familiarity with the music's smoothly manufactured internal consistencies.

Eno's design of the album's front cover (as with the remainder of the *Ambient* covers) likewise conveys this sense of abstraction and distance from the familiar world (Fig. 3.2). The drawing depicts a magnified square section of a map framing topographic regions and a river system, with one letter from the map intruding upon the landscape. At the scale drawn, its beige, pale yellows, greenish browns, and light blues recall the view of a landscape from an airplane window. Yet while replicating the perspective of the

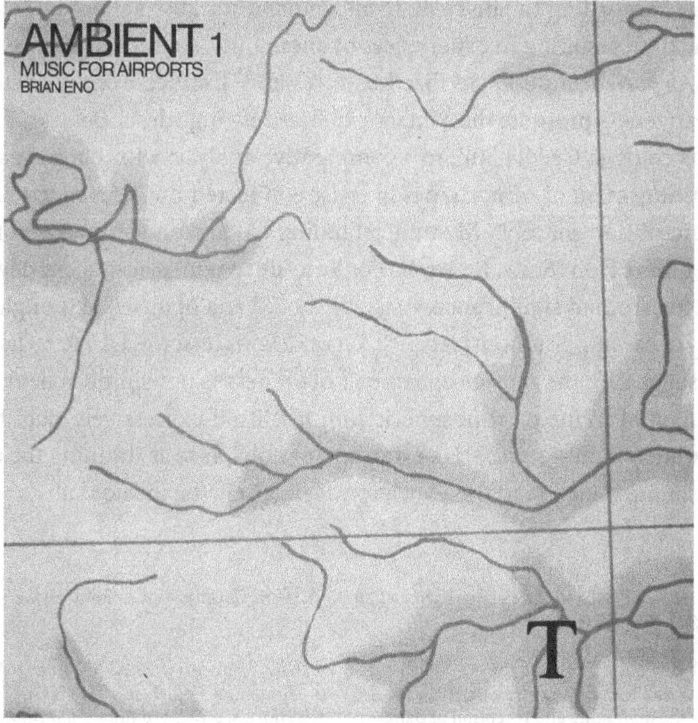

Figure 3.2. Album cover for Brian Eno's *Music for Airports* (Editions E.G., 1978).

airplane traveler hovering off the ground, the absence of color gradation and the serifed "T" reveal this perspective as that of a map viewer, and the viewed "ground" as human artifice. The ambiguity of perspective enhances the sense of a map viewer's dislocation from authentic emplacement above the landscape, while the air traveler's perspective too involves an abstracting distance from earth. As when listening, *Airports*'s cover viewers might imagine or recall what it is like to travel by air—including the sense of disconnection from grounded living air travel produces.

Through such conveyances of distance from nature and human sociality, the recordings of *Airports* evoke something of what anthropologist Marc Augé calls "non-place": "A world surrendered to solitary individuality, to the fleeting, temporary and ephemeral."[178] Functionalist architecture, vehicles of transport, and commercial venues comprise this "evacuated world" of globalized circulation, consumption, and communication. The transitory spaces of non-place, Augé explains, disperse the social relations or collective histories that would otherwise be embedded in what he calls "anthropological place."[179] This scattering or smudging of personal and collective pasts operates according to late capitalism's demand for abstraction and efficient transaction, resulting in experiences of anonymity, solitude, and empty passage. *Airports*'s smooth, sterilized textures and distance from conventional expressiveness promote the solitary experiences Augé describes.

Musicologist Cecilia Sun, in a comparative analysis with Bang on a Can's live arrangement of *Airports*, has likewise connected Eno's *Airports* to Augé's concept of non-place.[180] My understanding of *Airports*'s evocation of non-place differs from Sun's, however. For Sun, since non-places seem devoid of collective human significance, *Airports* should analogously be thought of as empty of meaning, a "non-piece."[181] Yet as various unsettled *Airports* listeners have suggested, the music's ephemeral blankness is not simply a neutral environmental frame or atmospheric tint; it is itself expressively rich. Rather than understanding *Airports*'s evocation of non-place as draining the album of meaning, then, I read this evocation as precisely the music's substance.

[178] Marc Augé, *Non-Places: An Introduction to Supermodernity*, trans. John Howe, 2nd ed. (New York: Verso, 2008), 64.

[179] Ibid., 102.

[180] Cecilia Sun, "Resisting the Airport: Bang on a Can Performs Brian Eno," *Musicology Australia* 29, no. 1 (2007): 152; Bang on a Can, *Music for Airports—Brian Eno*, Point Music, 314 536 847-2, 1998, CD. On the marketing and reception of Bang on a Can's effort, see William Robin, *Industry: Bang on a Can and New Music in the Marketplace* (New York: Oxford University Press, 2021), 157–60.

[181] Sun, "Resisting the Airport," 152.

With this in mind, it appears *Airports* scripts listening experience not just according to its utilitarian aims or imagined reception locations, but also according to the sort of airport space it seeks to conjure, the sense of movement through space it proffers, and the moods it brings into the journey. One might connect *Airports*'s virtual airport space to the open-ended designs of Eno's architectural muse, the Cologne/Bonn Airport, which exert what John Allen calls "ambient power," a "soft" power that works through seduction rather than domination, and inclusion rather than exclusion.[182] Conveying an aura of detachment through visual transparency and spatial accessibility, such designs appear to offer many choices for movement while being yet limited in broadly scripted ways.[183] *Airports*'s sparse textures, long silences, and heavy reverb likewise convey spaciousness and evoke transparency, even while minute timbral and harmonic shifts gently impose an emotional agenda. Each recording promotes feelings of stillness and solitude in open space, virtually manifesting a "space to think" via long and distant echoes. *Airports* invites listeners to dwell serenely and alone in a sleek and luminous limbo where, as Eno's collaborator David Byrne once described heaven, "nothing ever happens."[184] It locates listeners within the experiential architecture of the airport, and of air travel more generally, while yet providing more "room" to breathe and reflect than does your average modern airport or airplane.

In this way, *Music for Airports* idealizes airports and airplanes as spaces conducive to calm and contemplation. As Eno himself recalls, he created *Airports* while imagining "this ideal airport where it's late at night; you're sitting there and there are not many people around you: you're just seeing planes take off through the smoked windows."[185] Yet Eno's designs neither contradict the anxiety-inducing reality in which inhabitants' immediate futures are suspended between architecture, automated machinery, ground control, and their own thoughts. Rather, the recordings subtly acknowledge this reality while also aestheticizing it, smoothing its intensities, and diminishing the stakes of its consequences.

[182] John Allen, "Ambient Power: Berlin's Potsdamer Platz and the Seductive Logic of Public Spaces," *Urban Studies* 43, no. 2 (February 2006): 443. Helmut Jahn, the architect who designed Allen's chief case study, the Sony Center on Berlin's Potsdamer Platz, incidentally also designed the terminal extension to Flughafen Köln/Bonn completed in 2002.

[183] Ibid., 445.

[184] Talking Heads, "Heaven," *Fear of Music*, Sire, SRK 6076, 1979, LP.

[185] Aikin, "Brian Eno," 62.

The tracks on *Airports* might hence be understood as mimicking the "softer" ways in which modern institutions of human management, such as airports and airlines, manage risk and anxiety on a large scale. Their virtual arrays bolster listeners' cognitive sense of "safety" by predictably remaining within a constrained framework of possibility, a feature that allows the recordings to recede outside listeners' attentional fields. This technique mirrors the manner in which institutions like airports attempt to stabilize individuals' experiential horizons. As sociologist Anthony Giddens has theorized, vast institutional systems like public transportation, global capitalism, and public health aim to "bracket" and defer the possibility of high-risk consequence outside individuals' subjective worlds, buttressing the positions from which each person "orders contingent events in relation to risk and potential alarms."[186] On the face of these institutions' façades of safety and invisibility, however, openly lurks the reality that these systems regulate both a heightened intensity and widened scope of disaster, the prevention of which lies outside any one individual's control.[187] The contingency of one's own security within these operations, Giddens asserts, results in a generalized unease pervading the modern experiential world: "Radical doubt," he writes, "filters into most aspects of day-to-day life. . . . Living in a secular risk culture is inherently unsettling."[188]

Giddens's analysis gives insight into another parallel between airport experience and the recordings of Eno's *Airports*: even as sonic monotony assures listeners of future stability, their reductionism can seem uncannily facile—*over*certain, even, in light of their variably fortuitous internal permutations. This may be considered a reiteration and extension of the reductionism enacted through airports' slick architectural designs, with the hints of estrangement running through Eno's album giving the lie to the security airports promise. Shades of loss and longing undercut the music's ongoingness, almost as if the recordings themselves felt melancholy over the impermanence of their own playback. Anxiety hangs in the balance.

In the context of personal regimes of record programming, then, *Airports*'s "sense of doubt" carries associations with airport space and the experience of air travel. And yet Eno's liner notes also less specifically assert that ambient music in general, without this sense of doubt or uncertainty, would lose

[186] Anthony Giddens, *Modernity and Self-Identity: Self and Society in the Late Modern Age* (Cambridge, UK: Polity Press, 1991), 128.

[187] Ibid., 130.

[188] Ibid., 181.

any "genuine interest." So what makes doubt and uncertainty more "genuinely interesting" than their absence, anyway? One could chalk the sentiment up to the composer's personal preference. Eno has admitted on a number of occasions his predilection for affectively ambiguous or unsettling art experiences, especially those tinged with melancholy.[189] Any departure from certainty, he mused in one interview, calls "partly for celebration and partly for melancholy. It's both exciting and unnerving."[190] At the same time, Eno has proposed that art by definition creates a "safe space" for both artists and audiences to deal with disorientation. "Good art," he summarizes, "forces people to either accept disorientation or to retreat. If they retreat from life as they do from art, they eventually come to live in the past."[191] *Airports*'s sonic invariances reinforce this sense of safety, ideally permitting listeners to accept the disorienting contingencies therein, and perhaps also to apply this sense of stability to the anxieties of the everyday.

Eno's assertions that ambient music should retain a sense of doubt, and that art should provide a space for disorientation, also offer insight into how Eno might have imagined ambient music's ambivalent moods as providing personal enhancement for the record consumer.[192] His insistence on the primacy of art's disorienting function recalls a range of aesthetic techniques and theories, from Victor Shklovsky's остранение (*ostranenie* or defamiliarization) to Berthold Brecht's *Verfremdungseffekt* (estrangement effect), Sergei Eisenstein's montage theory, Walter Benjamin's "profane illumination," and Guy Debord's *détournement*, all of which advanced the modernist avant-garde goal of shocking art's audiences out of habitual perception, and into an enhanced or altered awareness of everyday life.[193] Eno's ambient

[189] Bangs, "Eno" (1979), 39; Demorest, "Discreet Charm," 85; Ian MacDonald, "Another False World: Part 2: How to Make a Modern Record," *New Musical Express*, December 3, 1977, 33.

[190] MacDonald, "Another False World," 34.

[191] Rose, "Four Conversations with Brian Eno," 69.

[192] On the social uses of background music for personal enhancement, see Steven Brown and Töres Theorell, "The Social Uses of Background Music for Personal Enhancement," in *Music and Manipulation: On the Social Uses and Social Control of Music*, ed. Steven Brown and Ulrik Volgsten (New York: Berghahn Books, 2006), 126–60.

[193] Viktor Shklovsky, "Art as Technique," in *The Critical Tradition: Classic Texts and Contemporary Trends*, ed. David H. Richter, 3rd ed. (1917; repr. Boston & New York: Bedford/St. Martin's, 2007), 775–84; Berthold Brecht, "A Short Organum for the Theatre," in *Brecht on Theatre: The Development of an Aesthetic*, ed. and trans. John Willett (1947–48; repr. New York: Hill and Wang, 2001), 179–208; Sergei Eisenstein, "A Dialectic Approach to Film Form," in *Film Form: Essays in Film Theory*, ed. and trans. Jay Leyda (1931; repr. Orlando, FL: Harcourt Brace & Co., 1977), 45–63; Walter Benjamin, "Surrealism," in *Walter Benjamin, Selected Writings*, ed. Marcus Bullock and Michael W. Jennings, vol. 2 (1929, repr. Cambridge, MA: Belknap, 2004), 207–18; Guy Debord, "A User's Guide to Détournement," in *Situationist International Anthology*, ed. and trans. Ken Knabb, rev. ed. (1956; repr. Berkeley, CA: Bureau of Public Secrets, 2006), 14–20.

Table 3.3. Documented Airport Installations of *Music for Airports* prior to the Year 2000.

Year	Airport	City
1980	LaGuardia Airport	New York City, USA
1980	Minneapolis-Saint Paul International Airport	Minneapolis, USA
1982	Greater Pittsburgh International Airport	Pittsburgh, USA
1984	Tegel Airport	Berlin, Germany
unknown	Guarulhos International Airport	São Paulo, Brazil

music, as sound artist Daniel Barbiero puts it, "sublimates" this alienating shock of modernist art "into a nuanced undertone."[194] In the form of music for personal enhancement, this undertone may slip quietly into that realm of habit, home, and routine called "everyday life" in which listeners might wake up to uncertainty on their own time.[195] Ambient's ambivalence, moreover, might also provide a resource for self-identity, a process that Tia DeNora calls music's "identity work."[196] By producing moods involving melancholy, alienation, and uncertainty, ambient recordings offer their listeners the unconventional pleasure of electing to feel ambivalent—a more appealing sort of mood enhancement for the hip and high-middlebrow, for social critics, and for other skeptics of the idea that musical listening should be entirely "easy."

Airports eventually did find public programming in airports, but not for over a year after its commercial debut. The documented instances of airport installations in the decades following make up a short list (Table 3.3). In the meanwhile, Eno popularized *Airports* through the pop record market, with the album publicized and reviewed in newspapers and periodicals, especially anglophone rock magazines in which Eno's name had commercial traction. It did not sell particularly well at the time, but the album's popularity, of course, grew with its canonic status. Given the record's quarter-million sales numbers and exceeding number of streams today—Spotify in 2022 puts "2/1" in excess of *25 million* plays—one can now soundly assume that far more people

[194] Daniel Barbiero, "After the Aging of the New Music," *Telos* 82 (Winter 1989–90): 148. Thanks to Sumanth Gopinath for this reference.

[195] This description of everyday life comes from Rita Felski, "The Invention of Everyday Life," *New Formations* 59 (1999): 15–31.

[196] DeNora, *Music in Everyday Life*, 62–74.

have listened to *Airports* intentionally than have had it imposed on them in public. Of course, since 1978 and the era of the Sony Walkman, many air travelers may have now also *chosen* to listen to *Airports* in airports, fulfilling Eno's original vision. But the album's evocation of air travel, and its mixtures of assurance and doubt, would make the biggest impressions outside of airport space, as Eno admitted in a 1984 interview when asked where he imagined his ambient music being heard. "Initially public places," he answered, "but when you make a record you are making it for a living room."[197]

Ambient 2: The Plateaux of Mirror

Harold Budd (1936–2020), the composer and performer behind the second installment of the *Ambient* series, despised genres. "I don't think about genres," he stated in 2016. "I don't think about labels, they don't have meanings."[198] Genre labels, maintained Budd for most of his roughly sixty-year career, short-circuit an essentially ineffable communication between musical creator and listener. "If someone likes a piece of music," as he told critic Mark Prendergast in 1986, "and the person who created it likes it as well, I have to presume that there is something fundamental that is agreed upon, and it can't be analysed or stated. That to me is *immensely* important."[199]

But blanket genrephobia notwithstanding, no label bothered Budd more than "new age." "When I hear the term 'new age,'" the composer often quipped, "I reach for my revolver."[200] During new age's peak popularity in the 1980s Budd was equal parts embarrassed and infuriated at his music's frequent "new age" tagging, at times begging record store clerks to move his records out of the new age bin. New age's biometaphysical, spiritual, and meditative claims, he believed, amounted to "lightweight mysticism" and a "marketing ploy."[201] As a musical style, Budd understood new age to sound "wholly vacuous"; it was music with "absolutely no evil in it." His own music,

[197] Eno, "Aurora Musicalis," 77.

[198] Paul Rigby, "Budd Heavy," *Record Collector*, November 25, 2013, https://recordcollectormag.com/articles/budd-heavy.

[199] Mark Prendergast, "The Sound-Painted World of Harold Budd," *Sound on Sound*, December 1986, 56.

[200] Jon Pareles, "The Pop Life," *New York Times*, February 18, 1987, C21.

[201] David Snow, Interview with Harold Budd, Opal Information no. 19, 1991, reprinted in Harold Budd, liner notes to *Budd Box*, All Saints Records, WASTBOX1X, 2018, CD, 32; Prendergast, "The Sound-Painted World," 48.

Budd hoped by contrast, would convey "an element of danger and a kind of unsettled quality. Unresolved issues. I don't find it meditative at all, just the opposite."[202]

Yet despite the seeming resonance of Budd's "evil" and "danger" with Eno's "sense of doubt and uncertainty"—and despite Budd's prominent collaboration with Eno on 1980's *Ambient 2: The Plateaux of Mirror—and* despite today being regarded a forefather of the ambient aesthetic—Budd too rejected "ambient." The categorization frustrated Budd, who once called the genre label "a preposterous and juvenile term."[203] When asked in 2012 about his relationship with the ambient genre, Budd was even blunter than his usual deadpan self. "I feel like I've been kidnapped, you know what I mean? Kidnapped into something that I don't know anything about, and have no interest in, at all."[204] As spoken by Budd, these comments sound less surly than they read, more breezy and matter-of-fact. I gather, from listening to several interviews, that his distaste for the genre label stemmed from an honest perplexity about the concept of ignorable music, which seemed to him fundamentally misguided. "I feel that all music can be listened to at many different levels and one cannot pigeon-hole it," he once attested.[205] Music made for passive consumption in a regime of flexible listening, it stood to reason, must not be worth much in the first place.

Upon hearing his deceptively simple, quiet, and abstract music, one might reasonably imagine Budd had felt otherwise. Most of his records, often made in collaboration with other performers and producers, feature unabashedly pretty modal keyboard improvisations based on short motifs and extended chords. Impeccably crafted pillows of reverb typically hover around Budd's heavily filtered and processed keys, which animate a coloristic play of sonority and timbre in deft flurries, sweeps, and clusters. The results are almost always immediately lovely, if also somewhat impersonal and moody; Budd's keystrokes at once gestural and skeletal, withdrawn and expressionistic.

Brian Eno supposedly once called his collaborator "a great abstract painter trapped in the body of a musician"—high praise coming from someone who admittedly "think[s] a lot of in terms of color of sound" and described his own

202 Holmes, *Electronic and Experimental Music*, 401.

203 Colin Buttimer, "How Dark the Response to Our Slipping Away," *Signal to Noise*, Spring 2005, 15.

204 "Harold Budd Interviewed by Jason Hoffer," *Little Darla Has a Treat for You, Vol. 28: Lucky 2013*, Darla Records, DRL280, CD.

205 Prendergast, "The Sound-Painted World," 56.

work as aspiring "to the condition of painting."[206] Although in late life Budd discouraged comparisons between his music and visual art ("They are two different disciplines. There is no one-to-one relationship."), Eno's alleged compliment aptly captures the painterly nature of Budd's keyboard smears, splotches, and washes.[207] Budd himself acknowledges a long-standing fondness for abstract expressionist and color field painting, paintings that "went strictly for the surface— brilliant blasts of colour that simply engulfed you."[208] He cites Jackson Pollock and Mark Tobey as early influences, and Mark Rothko, Ellsworth Kelly, Robert Motherwell, Serge Poliakoff, and Hans Hartung as making an impact in the late 1950s and '60s, just as the budding composer was turning on to John Cage and Morton Feldman. Such paintings "were so attractive to me that I thought, 'I wonder if there's a place for that feeling in music?' "[209]

In the 1960s Budd had followed lines of conceptualism and radical drone minimalism parallel to those drawn by fellow West Coaster La Monte Young, leading him to create written compositions like *Intermission Piece* (1968) (in which the performer makes "barely audible" sounds in the concert space during intermission), *The Candy-Apple Revision* (1970) ("D-flat major," the score reads alone), and *Lirio* (1971) ("Under a blue light, roll very softly on a large gong for a long duration"); as well as the nearly-twenty-minute recordings "Coeur D'Orr" (1969) (a Coltranesque sax solo cascading over a shimmering sustained organ cluster-chord) and "Oak of the Golden Dreams" (1970) (a raga-like modal improvisation performed on the Buchla Box). Such routes of radical reduction led to an impasse: "I had minimalized myself out of a career," as Budd once recalled.[210]

Eighteen months of silence later, Budd composed *Madrigals of the Rose Angel*, a piece for harp, piano, celesta, percussion, and wordless female choir that was written to be, in Budd's words, "simply *pretty*: mindless, shallow and utterly devastating."[211] His turn toward the purely gorgeous spurned the received wisdom of the avant-garde that "serious" music could not entertain

[206] Blair Jackson, "In the Room with Harold Budd," *Mix*, May 1, 2001, https://www.mixonline.com/recording/room-harold-budd-372801; Kalbacher, "Profile: Brian Eno," 50; Mark Prendergast, "Brian Eno: Thoughts, Words, Music and Art: Part One," *Sound on Sound*, January 1989, 25.

[207] Harold Budd, interview by BD, *The Mouth Magazine*, January 2, 2014, https://themouthmagazine.com/2014/01/02/the-confessions-of-harold-budd/.

[208] Prendergast, "The Sound-Painted World of Harold Budd," 52.

[209] Andrew Fleming, "Unknown Spins: Lost in the Humming Air: An Interview with Harold Budd," *Ceasefire Magazine*, April 29, 2012, https://ceasefiremagazine.co.uk/unknown-spins-2-harold-budd/.

[210] Harold Budd, liner notes to *The Pavilion of Dreams*, Editions EG, EEGCD 30, 1992, CD. Originally released in 1978.

[211] Budd, liner notes to *The Pavilion of Dreams*.

beauty-for-its-own-sake; it was a stylistic revolt that, for Budd, also constituted a political statement.[212] In England, Gavin Bryars, upon hearing a tape of the piece, noted its potential appeal to Eno and passed the tape on. The music's angelic *ahhs*, tinkling keyboards, and gentle major-seventh-chord drift reportedly "struck something very personal" in Eno, who immediately summoned Budd to London to make a record.[213] Budd was nothing short of thrilled to find fellowship with Eno, Bryars, Nyman, and the budding British "new consonance." His resulting *Pavilion of Dreams* was an artistic rebirth according to Budd, with the cycle of works, including *Madrigals*, appearing as the tenth and final Obscure record in 1976.

Revealingly, also on *Pavilion*: "Two Songs," a stripped-down alto and harp rearrangement of Pharaoh Sanders's "Let Us Go into the House of the Lord" that melts into a languid rewrite of John Coltrane's "After the Rain."[214] Budd's delicate interpretations bear witness to the composer's early growth rooted in 1950s and '60s cool, modal, and free jazz. Thelonious Monk, Stan Getz, Lennie Tristano, and John Coltrane drew the teenage Budd deeply into jazz; he went on to play drums alongside Albert Ayler while training in the US military. Although academic experimentalism tugged the composer away from jazz, Pharaoh Sanders's rippling pools of luminous, undisguised consonance pulled him back with a "paradisiacal lyricism" that was pure "magic" to his ears.[215] "It wasn't fancy, it was just there," Budd recalls of Sanders's music. "It was 100% there. Loud. There. And there . . . so that's where I'm meant to be. I wanted to be there without innuendos. I wanted to go right for the jugular."[216]

Following *Pavilion*, Budd took an intuitive approach to composition and improvisation that, as with Sanders's undulating chordal washes, bathed listeners in sparkling and uncomplicated beauty. His slack, viscous modal improvisations drew on the harmonic and formal conventions of rock, which by the end of the 1970s he found more artistically vital than either avant-garde or jazz experimentalism.[217] Budd often composed using little

[212] Paul Tingen, interview with Harold Budd, *Sound on Sound*, January 1997; reprinted in Budd, liner notes to *Budd Box*, 52.

[213] William Shaw, "Harold Budd: Budd in May," *The Independent*, May 8, 2015, https://www.independent.co.uk/arts-entertainment/music/features/harold-budd-budd-in-may-490088.html.

[214] Lonnie Liston Smith arranged Sanders's version of "Let Us Go into the House of the Lord," and later released a version with the Cosmic Echoes in 1973.

[215] Budd, liner notes to *The Pavilion of Dreams* (reissue), Editions EG, EEGCD 30, 1992, CD.

[216] Christina Gubala, "Harold Budd: Show Me Where I Belong," *L.A. Record*, August 21, 2016, https://larecord.com/archive/2016/08/21/harold-budd-interview.

[217] "Forum: Improvisation," *Perspectives of New Music* 21 no. 1/2 (Autumn 1982–Summer 1983): 56.

more than jazz/pop chord changes, harmonic grounds that in most rock music would serve as melodic background, but in Budd's music buoys the flotsam of "pulverized" melodies.[218] Quite often, Budd simply lingers on tonally underdetermined extended chords, occasionally discovering and elaborating on snatches of melody within the tetratonic, pentatonic, or hexatonic pitch collections comprised by those chords. Within this seeming simplicity, Budd welcomes the vicissitudes of his intuition and musical circumstance. "There's a whole world fraught with possibilities in consonant music," as Budd has attested. "In Beethoven, a consonant chord had a function, but in my music the focus has shifted to consonance as a thing in itself. It's completely free, complete anarchy. What you hear in the music is just a hunch. It's intuition telling me that this works and this doesn't. I hear an absolute whole life in consonant chords."[219]

In interviews, Budd never hesitated to point out how a lack of formal piano training informed his uncomplicated approach to studio improvisation. He also rarely failed to credit Eno, and their collaboration on *Ambient 2: The Plateaux of Mirror*, for apprising him of the manifold possibilities contained in the studio environment. Whereas *Pavilion* saw Budd executing a preexisting work, with Eno and recording engineer Rhett Davies supplying the final production touches, Budd and Eno began recording *Plateaux* without set preconceptions of what the music would ultimately sound like. "You play the way that you do," Budd recalls Eno saying, "and I'll play around the way I do."[220] Budd quickly inherited the lessons that his fellow "non-musician" had been developing for nearly a decade. "Things start coming together, accidents happen, just as they happen in live performance," Budd relays. "What do you do then? Well, you take advantage of it."[221] From then on, Budd remembers, "recording and composition became equal members of the creative process" rather than separate entities.[222]

For most of *Plateaux*, Budd improvised based on a loosely composed idea or schema of his own while responding from moment to moment to Eno's atmospheric touches and keyboard "treatments." Eno's layered "sound-worlds" had become even more fine-grained since *Airports*, with the producer

[218] Kuniko Watanbe, interview with Harold Budd, Opal Information No. 3, November 1986; reprinted in Budd, liner notes to *Budd Box*, 6.

[219] Pareles, "The Pop Life," February 18, 1987.

[220] "Harold Budd Interviewed by Jason Hoffer, Goingthruvinyl.com, May 3, 2012," Darla Records, 2013, Spotify, https://open.spotify.com/track/1dGu6CfwHpy3wdHGsWSxnl.

[221] "Forum: Improvisation," 59.

[222] Tingen, interview with Harold Budd, 52.

splitting Budd's piano signal into multiple frequency bands and applying various filters, types of reverb, and other effects across different audio bands. "I started to get really atomic about sound and analyse it carefully to see what could be sucked out of it," as Eno recalls of the recording of *Plateaux*. "I wanted to use the studio like a microscope for sound, which is what good engineers do."[223] Budd improvised based on the sound of Eno's treatments, with Eno sometimes adding additional synthesizer flourishes in post.[224]

Eno's "atomic" approach is clearest on the elegiac "Among Fields of Crystal," an improvisation reminiscent of Chopin's E-minor *Prelude*, in which a lonesome ghost of a melody pirouettes pensively over a chromatic-step chordal descent. Eno's application of a chorus effect to the mid-range gives Budd's melody more presence than the supporting chords, as do the shorter attacks in the upper range, rendering the melody's highest notes a brittle porcelain. A resonance filter applied to the mid- and upper ranges also causes a perfect-fifth overtone to ring prominently over the melody, with a lengthy reverb decay giving the overtones a vocal quality. Budd's improvisation responds sensitively to Eno's treatment as he modulates his volume and articulation according to register, at times introducing octave tremolos or large upward leaps to create brilliant mists of singing reverb.

"Above Chiangmai," "The Chill Air," and "Failing Light" display a similarly understated approach by Eno, with a mixture of various filters, reverb types, and chorus and delay effects treating a lone acoustic piano. (Occasional distant bird-like hooting or chirping also augments "Chiangmai"). Eno's contributions come more to the fore on other tracks, particularly on the richly evocative "Wind in Lonely Fences," with Eno supplying the bulk of sound, including chimes and animal sounds, as well as synthesizer chords, licks, and wind-like pitch bends layered over Budd's electric piano arpeggios. The swirling tapestry of mysterious nighttime sounds is one of Eno's most virtuosic displays of production on the album, previewing the sort of heavily textured sound worlds that would later appear on *Ambient 4: On Land* (compare, for instance, "The Lost Day").

Some tracks display a more traditional songwriting approach that eludes the expectation for flatness and nondirectionality set for ambient music on *Music for Airports*. The charming title track, for instance, bears the skeleton of a verse-refrain AABA song form. The introductory "verse" is more

[223] Mark Cunningham, "From Jams to James," *The Mix*, September 1994, 102.
[224] Sheppard, *On Some Faraway Beach*, 325.

freeform than the refrain, with Budd drifting up and down the keyboard in sixths over a drone in G♯ Phrygian. The E-major refrain with F♯-major bridge, although performed freely with unmetered arpeggios in the bass, displays regular melodic phrasing. Eno's scattered touches produce a pastoral ambient counterpoint to Budd's song, with animal-like chittering and clicking occurring at irregular intervals, and with pedal-steel strums adding loosely timed flourishes to the beginnings and endings of phrases, belying the song's relaxed regularity. Eno's timbral treatment of the electric piano likewise dissolves the song into atmosphere, with a Lexicon Prime Time digital delay system creating a wobbly out-of-phase amplitude oscillation in the keys, as well as a self-propagating echo that, as Eno puts it, creates a "halo of ringing sound" around Budd's playing.[225]

"Not Yet Remembered" sets up an even more conventional song arc, with Budd's piano dirge building to Eno's sexless synth choir in the bridge, then an additional bass guitar and vocal layer as the opening returns, and finally a sung descant over the last repetition of this material. The vaporous, reverb-thick "First Light" also uses textural elements to dramatic effect as Eno, six minutes into Budd's subdued minimalistic arpeggiations, floods the stereo field with warm, woodwind-like synths climbing up a CMaj7 chord to greet the sun. As with Eno's collaborations with Fripp, as well as various solo tracks outside of *Discreet Music* and *Airports*, the tracks on *Plateaux* blend atmospheric and nonlinear constructions with trajectories that reward sustained involvement.

Budd and Eno also collaborated on the album and track titles that would link, poetically and descriptively, to the sounds and moods inside. In some cases the titles took several weeks to devise, with the composers occasionally calling each other up suggesting names or alterations. "Since it's the only literary aspect of the album," Eno recalls, "we put a lot of energy into it."[226] Titular words like "Light," "Air," "Wind," "Crystal," and "Mirror" generate associations with clarity and transparency while linking sonically to the tinkling and shimmering luminance of Budd's piano; "Air," "Doves," "Above," and "Wind" meanwhile lend associations with height and flight, resounding with the album's open-air tails of echo and reverb. "Mirror," "Chill," "Crystal," and "Wind" contribute a sense of coldness, while "Not Yet,"

[225] Charles Amirkhanian, interview with Brian Eno, "Morning Concert," KPFA, March 13, 1980, YouTube, https://www.youtube.com/watch?v=Sg1zx4d3iN4.

[226] Amirkhanian, interview with Brian Eno, "Morning Concert," March 13, 1980.

"Lonely," and "Failing" gesture to the forlornness and futility suggested by Budd's minor-mode flirtations. In sum, the titles convey a sense of luminousness, transparency, reflectivity, and openness—all qualities through which space as such is perceived, poetically proffering instruction to regard the sounds as atmosphere—but also pensiveness and solitude, inviting moody introspection.

Unfortunately, while *Plateaux*'s overarching reserve makes the album fit for background use, the music is not very well served by the suggestion to ignore it. Whereas *Airports* delivers timbral profiles, styles, and moods distinctive enough to be memorable, regardless of concentration level, *Plateaux*'s poetic charms lay more in the details of the craft than in their gestalt. Absent attention to the music's measured design, exquisite production details, and Budd's sensitive improvisations, the album can register as merely pretty, a wispy, translucent sonic fabric forgettable as linen sheets. Early critics, attentive or not, did not take kindly to it—perhaps more because of its "ambient" designation and association with Eno than anything. The *New York Times*'s John Rockwell for instance, after identifying the album as an experiment in "discreetly faceless avant-garde Muzak," called *Plateaux* "too sweet for comfort" and "too often just cloying."[227] Rafi Zabor, writing for *Musician, Player, and Listener*, found that the album neither sustained "real interest" nor provided a "luminous background."[228] *NME*'s Ian Penman derided the album, as with Eno's career more broadly, as shallow and apolitical.[229] And even Gavin Bryars, in a retrospective on Budd, indirectly takes a dig at Budd's collaborations with Eno, noting that not until after *Plateaux* and their follow-up collaboration *The Pearl* (1984) did Budd rise above "the sloppy contemplative vacuity" of new age.[230]

Budd, it seems, had good reason in the 1980s to reject the ambient and new age labels, which possibly overemphasized his music's atmospheric or healing potential while underselling the music's considerable improvisational lyricism, expressive nuance, and formal economy. A listener looking for "ambient" or "new age" might never think to observe the ways Budd manipulates diatonic tonality, producing novel configurations of the simplest harmonies and melodic motives while exploiting ambiguities of

227 John Rockwell, "The Pop Life," *New York Times*, Jun 20, 1980, C30.

228 Rafi Zabor, "Record Reviews," *Musician, Player, and Listener*, November 1, 1980, 70.

229 Sheppard, *On Some Faraway Beach*, 326.

230 Gavin Bryars, encyclopedia entry for Harold Budd, *Contemporary Composers*, eds. Brian Morton and Pamela Collins (London: St. James Press, 1992), 137.

mode and key. Nor might such a listener notice the ways Budd, like his jazz forebears, often circles pensively, with the minutest of continual changes, around a hint of a melodic idea. Budd, although appreciative of his ambient-adjacent avant-pop contemporaries like Jon Hassell, Hans Roedelius, and Michael Brook, spurned common association with them by way of the assumption that all their music invites passive listening. (Tasked with categorizing his own music, Budd has noted that "avant-pop," though imperfect, comes closest.)[231] Each composer's music, he felt, represents each composer's unique voice, and should be respected as such rather than treated as anonymous wallpaper.

At the same time, however, Budd's slow-moving, soft-focus music, particularly from *Plateaux* on, often bore more than superficial similarity to contemporary ambient and new age music—in part because the *Ambient* series established *Plateaux* as a founding document of the ambient genre, with self-described "ambient" musicians taking cues from Budd. The composer's efforts to escape the inevitability of genre now seem to have been for naught—against his wishes the artist has been, and continues to be, regularly referred to as one of the definitive ambient artists. As John Schaefer wrote in 1987, Budd's records "practically define the term 'ambient'"; and as his present-day artist biography on AllMusic and Spotify states, Budd's training in composition makes him "one of the very few who can very rightly be called an ambient composer."[232] Although impossible to say whether Budd would be so closely associated with ambient had he not released *Plateaux* under the *Ambient* banner, *Ambient 2* wedded Budd's misty sound-paintings to Eno's understated cool, and linked his music's undertow of melancholy—his penchant, as he puts it, for "the darker side of musical experience"—to Eno's introspective sense of doubt.[233]

Budd has more successfully, although not entirely, cast off the "new age" appellation, largely thanks to ambient music's evolution in the 1990s into an alternative to new age. Some of his improvisations, however, particularly in his early career as a recording artist, recall even some of the most starry-eyed musings of new-age keyboardists like Iasos or Steven Halpern. Budd's special ire for "new age" surely stemmed not from familiarity with the music so much as the term's increasingly indiscriminate usage in the United States as a

231 Prendergast, "The Sound-Painted World," 49.
232 Schaefer, *New Sounds*, 41; John Bush, artist biography of Harold Budd, *AllMusic*, https://www.allmusic.com/artist/harold-budd-mn0000186927/biography.
233 Pareles, "The Pop Life," February 18, 1987.

catch-all for reverberant easy-listening instrumentals. As a marketing term, "new age" rose precipitously to the US mainstream just as Budd was finding his footing as a recording artist, particularly between 1981 (Tower Records's first "new age" bin) and '86 (the addition of "Best New Age Album" to the Grammy Awards). His intense disdain for the genre label was of a piece with the exasperation of other West Coast minimalists and future self-professed ambient artists who, defending their own work against charges of shallowness and selling out, heaped scorn upon their commercially popular counterparts. New age music on the whole, however, was never quite so distant from West Coast minimalism as these composers insisted, while Budd's music at times could just as easily fade into blandness. Although Budd exhibited musical sensitivity, ingenuity, and at times also a sinister sound rare among his peers, his recorded improvisations could meander on occasion into drab new-age and faceless ambient, particularly when overreliant on atmospheric concerns like timbre and production effects. Less distinctive as a record producer than composer, Budd has from time to time (mostly early on) minimalized himself out of an individual voice, and right into ambient anonymity.

Yet in his prolific forty-plus years as a recording artist, Budd amassed nearly forty studio albums in a variety of styles and modes, including sixteen solo studio LPs, altogether attesting to his inventive and idiosyncratic artistic vision. The "ambient" label, as defined by Eno in 1978 as an "atmosphere" or "tint," not only belies the stylistic and conceptual variety of Budd's considerable output, but also betrays his long-standing artistic intentions. It only stands to reason, then, that an ambient genre now firmly associated with Budd cannot be reduced to atmospheric functionalism, however attentive the listener—it also identifies a *sound*, a popular style, and a range of expressions through which other record producers have found their individual voice, and with which listeners continue to find musical resonance. That ambient aesthetic, from the jump, has continuously expanded thanks to the lovely contributions of Harold Budd, whose musical freedoms, against his wishes, have informed a genre that has always eluded mere atmosphere.

Ambient 3: Day of Radiance

Laraaji (1943–) had fallen into a trance. It was a serene late summer evening in 1979; the musician was sitting in the lotus position, eyes closed, improvising rhythms on an electrified zither in the northeast corner of Lower Manhattan's Washington Square Park. He had been playing for several hours—exactly how long, Laraaji could not say, having been ushered by the modified autoharp out of mundane time into a hyperpresent state of consciousness. He did not know it at the time, but the universe, as Laraaji would later put it, had "divinely orchestrated" a professional connection during his musically induced hypnosis.[234] Following his meditation, collecting the money in his autoharp case, he came upon a note:

> Dear Sir, please excuse this ragged piece of paper. I am working on a project, if you would be interested in hearing about it.[235]

The paper included a local phone number, and a signature by Brian Eno.

Eno, at this point a New York resident, had been rather busy since the release of *Airports*. His projects during this time included the release of *Music for Films*, a collection of soundtrack work and studio outtakes reimagined as a soundtrack to imaginary films; record production for Talking Heads and David Bowie; and the beginnings of his video explorations. Eno also collaborated with composer and trumpeter Jon Hassell on an album of electronic music with prominent jazz and nonwestern elements called *Fourth World vol. 1—Possible Musics*. The ambient-abutting "fourth world" style—"an idealized interbreeding of 'first' (technological) and 'third' (traditional) world influences," as Hassell later described it—surrealistically reinterpreted African, Middle Eastern, and South Asian styles and sounds through Hassell's Terry Riley-esque digital-delay-based improvisations.[236] Projects such as this, Eno explained in a May 1980 interview, attested to his recent boredom with Western rock, and to his newfound interest in producing cross-cultural polystylistic hybrids. Eno not only identified his collaborations with Budd and Hassell in this vein, but also *Ambient 3: Day of Radiance*, which Eno produced for Laraaji in late 1979 and released through Editions EG the following year. "You would not be sure where they came from if you listened to them," claimed Eno of these records. "If you didn't see my name there, you

[234] "Blissing Out with Laraaji," *New Commute*, January 19, 2018, https://www.newcommute.net/feed/2018/1/16/laraaji.

[235] John Shand, "Outside the Square," *Sydney Morning Herald*, May 23, 2009, 10.

[236] Jon Hassell, "*Possible Musics—Fourth World, Vol. 1*," May 20, 2006, https://jonhassell.com/1980-2/.

wouldn't even assume that they were from this culture or had anything to do with rock."[237]

Laraaji, for his part, hadn't even assumed that the sounds coming from his zither were his own. "At that time," he now reflects, "I was very much attracted to the idea of channeling, being a channel, being a medium, being a conduit for an intelligence or an emotional field that vibrates beyond my mundane personal identity . . . a self that's bigger than the mundane personal self."[238] The man born as Edward Larry Gordon (known as "Larry G," to some) had reinvented himself as Laraaji that same year, with the name's incorporation of the Egyptian sun god "Ra" and the Indian honorific "-ji" signaling a sense of higher musical calling.

By this time, Laraaji had left far behind his schooling in musical performance, theory, and composition at Howard University, as well as his career as a comedian, actor, and freelance pianist, in pursuit of meditative music and music-based meditation. Nearly a decade prior, Mr. Gordon appeared in the proto-blaxploitation feature film *Putney Swope* with only partial knowledge of the film's content, leading him to question the ethical implications of mass-media representation. For answers, he looked to psychedelics and meditation, making sure to set an intention to surrender to the guidance of his heart along the way. He took counsel in Richard Hittleman's popular 1969 *Guide to Yoga Meditation*, especially Hittleman's interrogation of the concept of "self." Seeking, as Hittleman wrote, to "dissolve" the ordinary mind into "Universal Mind," Larry G made a mantra of casting aside all earthly titles and identifiers.[239] "I'm not a musician," he would tell himself; "I'm not a composer; I'm not a negro; I'm not male; I'm not an American citizen; I'm not a Christian. . . ." Through these practices, as well as through deep breathing exercises, Mr. Gordon discovered a cocoon-like "present-time bliss" outside of worldly identity and linear time. He also discovered that piano improvisations simply "poured through" him following these meditations, and soon decided to devote his entire being to channeling the vibrations of the cosmos through the combination of meditation and music.

Laraaji today identifies three specific experiences in the mid-'70s that led him to the style of zithering destined to capture Eno's ears. In the first,

[237] David Hajdu, "A Talk with Brian Eno: Newer Than New Wave," Music Supplement to *The Real Paper*, May 17, 1980, 8.

[238] Laraaji, interview with author, November 20, 2018. Any uncited quotes from Laraaji in this section come from this interview.

[239] Richard Hittleman, *Guide to Yoga Meditation* (New York: Bantam Books, 1969), 116.

Laraaji, meditating, received a "sound-vision" with no perceptible origin, a vibrational field that he likens to a large brass orchestra. "It was uncontainable, the roar of the infinite present moment," he recollects.[240] When I spoke with the artist in 2018, he described the event as a unitive rather than solely aural experience. "One of the emotional pictures I got," Laraaji said, "was that this was the soundtrack for a cosmic reunion of all conscious beings, a simultaneous unified moment, feeling the truth of eternal unity." The affective epiphany has stuck with the musician, serving as a source of inspiration for all musical endeavors since. His interest in effects pedals and synthesizers, for instance, developed out of an effort to realize the fluidity and spontaneity he perceived in his sound-vision. "I can't play the music I heard in that moment," avers Laraaji, "but that vision still informs the kind of music I reach for on this side of reality."[241]

Laraaji had another cosmic hearing experience not long after. Barely scraping by as a freelance musician, the Brooklyn resident went to a pawnshop to sell his Yamaha six-string guitar. The clerk offered him $25. "Following that," as Laraaji tells it, "a very clear and very present sort of ethereal voice suggested, or commanded, or advised, that I not take money but swap the guitar for the autoharp in the window."[242] Laraaji listened (Fig. 3.3). He brought home the autoharp (plus $5) and removed the bars to use open tuning, as he had enjoyed doing on his guitar. He soon added a pickup, and later also delay pedals, phase shifters, flangers, and reverbs to better approximate the liquid roar of infinity.

His third experience occurred while cleaning one morning after a jam session at the Aquarius Coffeehouse in Park Slope. He put on some music—maybe the radio, or perhaps a cassette sitting around, he doesn't quite recall—and noticed, after a while, two nuns standing outside, listening through the window. This heightened his own attention to the sound, and he soon became engrossed, feeling his spirit lift and soar in response. Steven Halpern's *Spectrum Suite* (1976), a series of electric keyboard recordings, was doing the lifting; and the album, along with the later-discovered Iasos's

[240] Steve Smith, "Laraaji: Ambient Music, Laughter, and the Infinite Present Moment," *National Sawdust*, October 28, 2016, https://nationalsawdust.org/thelog/2016/10/28/laraaji-new-age-music-laughter-and-the-infinite-present-moment/.

[241] T. Cole Rachel, "Musician and Mystic Laraaji on Meditation and Creativity," *The Creative Independent*, November 8, 2018, https://thecreativeindependent.com/people/musician-and-mystic-laraaji-on-meditation-and-creativity/.

[242] Harley Brown, "Laraaji: A Life in Music and Meditation," *Red Bull Music Academy Daily*, October 16, 2017, http://daily.redbullmusicacademy.com/2017/10/laraaji-a-life-in-music-and-meditation.

Figure 3.3. Laraaji and his autoharp. Photograph by Laraaji. Used by permission.

Inter-Dimensional Music (1975), gave him a sense of musical direction, signaling "to be less concerned about clear-cut form of stopping and starting, and more in the moment of drifting and floating and feeling."

Laraaji toyed with a few different names for the style of music he began performing at concerts, parties, meditation groups, yoga groups, and psychic fairs in the mid–late 1970s. Ethereal music, mind travel music, spiritual music, groovy music, even space music arose as options—but "celestial music" became a favored descriptor. Sometimes listeners would ask Laraaji if he had a cassette of the stellar sounds they had just witnessed. "I would say no," recalls Laraaji with a laugh, "but I'll have it by next week!" The zitherist took personal requests as opportunities to sit in a quiet place with a tape recorder and "dream up a new cassette, just dream it out of the sky."

One such listener at a holistic healing lecture, Stuart White, offered to finance the recording and release of an LP record; and so in 1978 White's record label SWV released a limited pressing of Gordon's beguiling first album, *Celestial Vibration*. Each roughly twenty-minute side showcased the wild range of sounds the musician could coax out of his instrument, from rapid-fire hammered patterns to glistening washes of reverb and refreshing mists of strummed strings, all inviting listeners to bask in the brilliance of overtone-rich drones. The sleeve notes on the back of the album extolled the "healing force" of Gordon's zither; the front cover announced an album performed "through Edward Larry Gordon."[243]

As with the music of Iasos, Steven Halpern, and many other New Agers, Laraaji's drone- and repetition-based improvisations attested to their maker's cosmic worldview. What Laraaji today calls his "vertical music" aims to guide listeners toward awareness of the permanence of the Now, an unbroken continuity that cannot accommodate temporal boundaries. "That is strong inspiration for a large body of my music," Laraaji tells me, "that is, using music to celebrate, honor, and embrace a continual present time-ness, so that there's no official beginning or official end but every moment is the wholeness of the universe, every moment is the wholeness of eternal time." With each plucked string contributing to and dancing within a cloud of sustained overtones, Laraaji's zither continuously produces a sonic wholeness in which each moment partakes.

No wonder, then, that Laraaji was confused by Eno's concept of ambient music upon meeting him after that fateful day in Washington Square Park. "I was challenged to grasp what Eno was talking about," Laraaji recalls, unable to fathom being anything but fully present to the enveloping overtones of his modified autoharp. Like Eno's other *Ambient* collaborator, Harold Budd, the artist had trouble imagining his own music functioning as an ignorable space. "For me," Laraaji continues, "I played beautiful, trance-meditative music."[244]

[243] Linda Cousins, liner notes to *Celestial Vibration* by Edward Larry Gordon, Universal Sound, US LP30, 2010, 33 rpm. Originally released in 1978.

[244] Andy Beta, "From Stand-Up Comic to Master of Trance Music," *Wall Street Journal*, August 21, 2015, A15.

It is not difficult to understand Laraaji's confusion given *Day of Radiance*'s effervescent, sparkling side A. Inspired by his experience with dance as a form of meditation and musical study, Laraaji poured out streams of lively, joyful pulse-pattern zither hammering in major pentatonic and hexatonic tunings for the three movements of "The Dance." Within these streams, embedded rhythmic patterns and melodic motifs emerge and subside in rolling waves, with subtle differences emerging from iteration to iteration. The interlocking rhythmic cycles of the first two dances bound forward at a swift eight strums per second; the third dance, filtered and slowed down to enhance the tinny inharmonic clattering of the hammers against the strings, especially begs comparison with the Indonesian gamelan musics that had fascinated the zitherist since the '60s. Laraaji's vibrant, energetic improvisations do not in any obvious way sound crafted to induce "calm and a space to think," as Eno's ambient music manifesto would have it—in fact, just the opposite, with their zestful rhythms and metallic timbres brightening and adding stimulus to the listening environment. (Their unambiguous major-key tuning and steady pulsations also leave little reason for doubt.)

But side A's awkward sonic fit with Eno's original ambient concept was not Laraaji's doing alone. Its vivid, difficult-to-ignore brightness, for instance, would not have been possible without Eno's decision to use highly sensitive microphones to record Laraaji's zither. Formerly, Laraaji used direct line-ins to record the electrified autoharp, but Eno showed Laraaji how high-quality microphones could bear witness to the "juicy, therapeutic brilliance" of the acoustic instrument.[245] The presence and audile tactility of each hammer stroke resounds on this side of the record, with brilliant high-frequency sounds dominating the mix in a way rarely heard elsewhere in Eno's output. Partly thanks to the Eventide Harmonizer, a digital processor capable of lush delay and feedback effects, stereo delay and phasing add psychedelic appeal as echoes sweep wide across the stereo field like a hand disturbing a pool of water, producing coruscating waves within the immersive rush of sound. Entrancing, yes; discreet, not so much.

On *Day of Radiance*'s side B, two tracks titled "Meditation" more obviously match Eno's ambient definition and sound than do the dances on side A. These gentler, calmer improvisations had to be recorded at a later date, since Eno's extraordinarily sensitive mics during the original take picked up machine noises bleeding in from elsewhere in the building. It took Eno

[245] Laraaji, interview with author.

six months to find a studio suitable for recording Laraaji's softly strummed meditations. Both improvisations are in free rhythm, with Laraaji modifying his strokes and toying with silence in response to Eno's treatments. Much like the *Discreet Music* title track, Eno alters his treatments gradually over time, with lengthy decays trailing ever more impossibly long beyond Laraaji's strums, and with multiband filters modifying the color of reverberation throughout. The first meditation has Laraaji easing in and out of an unmetered strumming pattern in A Mixolydian, with its A5-E5 descending-fourth melodic motif recurring over a constantly reconfigured mid-range texture for nearly twenty minutes. Laraaji purportedly recorded the second, moodier meditation based on a mental image of New York's Central Park Reservoir on a winter day.[246] Whereas the A5-E5 melodic motif returns periodically here as well, it takes on a bluer tint within this improvisation's D-Aeolian tuning. The mix is also far less weighted toward the high end of the frequency range than the dances, with the top curved off to render the recording overcast. In its dimness, the second "Meditation" recording remains a relative rarity within Laraaji's now considerably expanded discography; as Laraaji reflects, "My choice has been to bring music that is uplifting, soothing, and positive into the world. I'm capable of doing other kinds of music, but I haven't chosen to make that part of my performing style."[247]

Yet despite his general disinterest in exploring doubt and darkness musically, Laraaji has ever since *Day of Radiance* remained open to the applicability of the ambient label to his music—even if this application meant that some listeners, like the *New York Times* critic John Rockwell, would dismiss Laraaji's metaphysical aspirations as "pretentious" while confusingly deeming *Radiance* "a background record with class."[248] Unlike Harold Budd, who throughout his life rankled at the genre's implications of ignorability, Laraaji today sees the value in the term, particularly with regard to its spatial implications. For example, he now describes his epiphanic "sound-vision" of an infinite vibratory embrace as a glimpse of the universe's "cosmic ambient" music. The term has also given Laraaji a sonic language to work with and fine-tune as other artists stepped into the ambient fray starting in the 1990s, with the musician finding interest in others' interpretations of the style.

[246] Simon Reynolds, "Brian Eno: Taking Manhattan (by Strategy)," *Red Bull Music Academy Daily*, April 25, 2013, https://daily.redbullmusicacademy.com/2013/04/brian-eno-in-nyc-feature.

[247] Rachel, "Musician and Mystic Laraaji."

[248] John Rockwell, "The Pop Life," *New York Times*, August 29, 1980, C14.

From this time until the 2010s, however, ambient music's critics, fans, and historians largely sidelined Laraaji while yet embracing the reticent Budd. Whereas Budd's high-art background and aspirations consistently appealed to ambient's tastemakers, Laraaji's orientation toward personal uplift, meditation, healing, and vibrational metaphysics led many to dismiss his music's relevance to ambient while associating it more closely with new age. As critics Matthew Weiner and Tom Burns wrote for *Stylus Magazine* in 2004, *Day of Radiance*'s embrace of natural acoustics and "relentless prettiness" made it more new age than ambient, creating "not a space to think, but space out. In other words, Muzak for hippies."[249] *Pitchfork*'s retrospective review of Eno's *Ambient* series that same year, evidently in agreement, simply skipped Laraaji's album altogether without once mentioning it.[250] Only more recently, following new age's critical rehabilitation in the early–mid-2010s, has Laraaji's music been reconsidered as ambient canon, with *Radiance* appearing in *Pitchfork*'s 2016 "Top 50 Ambient Albums of All Time," and with the *New York Times* in 2019 calling Laraaji an "ambient-music giant."[251]

Laraaji's music, in truth, is neither here nor there, but rather in-between and beyond, a fascinating border study on par with *Tintinnabulation*, *Hearts of Space*'s space music, and other such celestial sounds. Indeed, Laraaji himself has since the 1970s participated in explicitly New Age activities and practices, from his days performing at Harlem's esoteric Tree of Life bookstore, to his fleeting associations with groups in the Northeast like the Spiritual Frontier Fellowship and the Sound Healers Association, to his performances at New Age expos like the Mind Body Spirit Festival, and his studies with Shri Brahmananda Sarasvati at Ananda Ashram. The musician, however, disavows entirely belonging to New Age culture then and now. "My sense of calling at that time was more universal," Laraaji tells me of these activities. "I didn't feel like I was part of a community, I felt like I was sharing music beyond the boundaries of community lines." And while Laraaji never wholly rejected the new age label, which he says freed him early on to explore

[249] Matthew Weiner and Tom Burns, "Brian Eno and the Ambient Series, 1978–82," *Stylus*, September 29, 2004, More Dark Than Shark, http://www.moredarkthanshark.org/eno_int_styl-sep04c.html.

[250] Liam Singer, "Brian Eno / Harold Budd: Discreet Music / Ambient 1: Music for Airports / Ambient 2: The Plateaux of Mirror / Ambient 4: On Land Album Review," *Pitchfork*, October 7, 2004, https://pitchfork.com/reviews/albums/11731-discreet-musicambient-1-music-for-airportsambient-2-the-plateaux-of-mirror-with-harold-buddambient-4-on-land/.

[251] "The 50 Best Ambient Albums of All Time," *Pitchfork Magazine*; Giovanni Russonello, "An Experimental Music Scene Grows in Gowanus," *New York Times*, April 3, 2019, https://www.nytimes.com/2019/04/03/arts/music/public-records-gowanus-music-scene.html.

alternative forms of musical expression, he also acknowledges that a good swath of new age music is "a little too passive and peaceful."[252] I detect in most of the artist's music an impulse to push past cozy contentment, whether in early recordings like his 1981 electric-piano-and-zither odyssey *Unicorns in Paradise* and his sumptuous 1982 synth-drone symphony *Trance Celestial*, or in more recent collaborations with artists like Audio Active, Bill Laswell, Blues Control, and Sun Araw. All such adventures point to a sonic restlessness and hunger for experimentation not typically associated with new age, all clear evidence of Laraaji's willingness to wander off the beaten path toward sonic comfort into the weeds of electronic happenstance, patches of tonal ambiguity, and wormholes of amorphous sonic weirdness.

When I asked the zitherist to reflect on the use of the term "new age" to describe his music, Laraaji responded with a thoughtful meditation on his music's relationship to time, a reflection equally capable of addressing all sorts of music beyond his own. It is worth quoting at length:

> I've always respected music as a way of controlling and managing time. And so new age, for me, is the use of music to manage time in such a way that the listener can stay in present time. A person will say, I don't have time for the present time! [Laughs] I've got things to do! But certain music, if you put it on, will keep them in present time. It wasn't always called new age music, it could be called trance, mood music, or atmospheric music. Sometimes jazz can do that for somebody. But music that has a continual drone, and that expresses a fluidity, and that allows for the listener to be present with their breathing, and to be in present time, and to drift away from mundane thoughts, and to feel an emotional sense of connection to the universe, or to the all-that-is—to me, that's getting into nowness. So *now age* music would be my way of rephrasing new age for my purposes.

What Laraaji expresses here is a desire to bring his listeners, straightjacketed by expectation and tethered to labels, into the unbounded, uncontainable present. In its consistency and continuity, Laraaji's ambient audio beckons the listener to recognize the ongoingness of present time and stay with it; in its constant flux, his music demonstrates a human sensitivity and emotional responsiveness to the now-and-forever. As he told me, nowness is available

252 S. Smith, "Infinite Present Moment."

for anyone willing to "trust and explore and open," which is exactly what his "now age" music permits listeners to do.

To varying degrees and in varying ways, countless Western musicians in the twentieth century have shared Laraaji's concern with ushering listeners into consciousness of the ongoing present, from jazz improvisers to Cagean composers, minimalists to muzak-makers, psychedelic rockers to mantric mystics, new agers to ambient aficionados. Laraaji's searching, capacious music and philosophy attest to the unity in this musical diversity, a sonic commitment to present-time awareness that goes beyond any one genre, community, or culture. His music's inclusion in the *Ambient* series likewise attests to the possibility of stylistic multeity within seeming genre unity—a possibility that should be, for listeners seeking enlightenment, far more interesting than ignorable.

Ambient 4: On Land

Eno's work with Budd and Laraaji on *Plateaux* and *Radiance*, far from mismatching or falling short of the ideals he laid out in his *Airports* manifesto, expanded and remolded the parameters of his landmark ambient music conception. An ambient record, it seemed, neither had to be "for particular times and situations" (even just "ostensibly") nor "as ignorable as it is interesting."[253] Its creators need not anticipate any one place's "atmospheric idiosyncracies [sic]." They might even pursue enticement over enhancement. Muzak's "canned music" became an increasingly irrelevant point of comparison and contrast; indeed, the music on display in *Ambient 2* and *3* appeared less concerned with functionalism per se—atmospherics—than with exploring *atmosphericity*, the quality of atmosphere as filtered through human perception and feeling, distanced from action, and reconstituted as diffuse sonic moods.

This conceptual drift away from ambient's initial site-specificity, not incidentally, coincided with the release of the Sony Walkman and the popularization of the personal stereo. Portable music had long existed before the

[253] Although most of Eno's ambient albums were not composed explicitly for certain spaces, Opal Records has issued limited releases of music that Eno originally made for site-specific audiovisual installations, including *Extracts from Music for White Cube* (1997), *Lightness: Music for the Marble Palace* (1997), *I Dormienti* (1999), *Kite Stories* (1999), *Music for Civic Recovery Centre* (2000), *Compact Forest Proposal* (2001), and the compilation *Music for Installations* (2018).

Walkman's release in July 1979, but as *Personal Stereo* author Rebecca Tuhus-Dubrow points out, the isolated and cocooning nature of stereophonic headphone listening made the Walkman equally as mentally transportive as the device was physically portable.[254] And in the years following its release, Eno's mind flew regularly by tape as he darted between his New York base and such far-flung locations as Ontario, California, England, and Ghana. Walkman in hand, headphones on head, the jet-setting avant-pop producer gained appreciation for recordings' ability to produce and confer an "instant sense of location" wherever he went. "When I was traveling a lot, I used to carry four or five cassettes that I knew could reliably produce a certain condition for me," Eno recalled in 1984. "I realized that while I was living this nomadic life, the one thing that was really keeping me in place, or giving me a sense of place, was music."[255] He began conceiving audio recordings as "landscapes," a metaphor by which Eno mapped the "places, times, climates and the moods that they evoke."[256]

Eno reinforced his revised conception of ambient music in the liner notes to his fourth and final release of the *Ambient* series, *On Land*. The record, recorded primarily in early 1981 and released April 1982, brought to fruition a possibility only hinted at in earlier *Ambient* records by exploiting recorded music's ability to generate, for individual listeners, a "sense of place that complements and alters your environment."[257] Although functional as an atmospheric tint, *On Land* also stages virtual spaces intricate and spatially immersive enough to transport listeners out of time and space into "more desirable" places, regardless of the listener's immediate surroundings. "This is escapism in a sense," Eno reflected, "but it isn't retreating from one world so much as advancing on another."[258]

Eno's *Ambient* productions, to be sure, all proffer escapism unto elsewhere. But unlike the sterile, smooth-tiled spaces of *Airports*, the skylit, high-ceiling rooms of *Plateaux of Mirrors*, or the shimmering, ethereal no-man's land of *Day of Radiance*, *On Land* conjures the feel of natural landscapes with both

[254] Rebecca Tuhus-Bugrow, *Personal Stereo*, Object Lessons (New York: Bloomsbury Academic, 2017), 5. See also Shuhei Hosokawa, "The Walkman Effect," *Popular Music* 4 (1984): 165–80; Michael Bull, *Sound Moves: iPod Culture and Urban Experience* (New York: Routledge, 2007). Karin Bijsterveld et al. similarly emphasize the isolated and cocooning nature of car audio; see Karin Bijsterveld et al., *Sound and Safe: A History of Listening behind the Wheel* (New York: Oxford University Press, 2014).

[255] Eno, "Aurora Musicalis," 78.

[256] Brian Eno, liner notes to *Ambient 4: On Land*. Editions EG EEGCD 20, 1987, CD. Originally released in 1982.

[257] Grant, "Brian Eno against Interpretation," 30.

[258] M. Brown, "Life of Brian," 10.

its track titles and thickly textured recordings. Synthesizer *portamenti* and spectral filtering evoke the whimsy and warp of wind and earth, from the hollow moans of "The Lost Day" to the swampy gurgles running through "Tal Coat." The album tracks' multilayered productions buzz and heave with synthesized and sampled animal cries; canines howl amid a creaking din of drones in "Lantern Marsh," while "Shadow" resounds with the chirping of night animals bouncing off a forest canopy. The album displays a wider variety of timbres than most of Eno's earlier ambient recordings, from recognizable musical instruments to unpitched noises and more overtly synthetic sounds. The wealth of timbral nuance presented in these soundscapes rewards high-volume, headphone, and surround-sound listeners with detail enough, as Eno later summed of ambient music broadly, "to swim in, to float in, to get lost inside."[259]

According to this summation, immersing listeners in a musical environment was always "the point" of making ambient music, a point Eno underscored by including in *On Land*'s original liner notes a diagram for a quadraphonic speaker setup. This surround-sound arrangement would augment the immersive textures and stagings already inherent to the album's audio productions, which position the listener as a subject enveloped by mutually unrelated sounds.[260] *On Land*'s production philosophy is continuous with *Airports* and *Plateaux* in this sense, albeit with crisper focus. Its recorded environments stage a nonlinear first-person perspective amid quasi-familiar sounds occurring at variable distances from the listener. These sounds, by appearing uncoordinated yet endemic to the same listening space, nestle listeners inside richly detailed virtual environments without offering strong attentional guidance toward any one feature.

Eno was initially inspired to create such multilayered virtual spaces by hearing Miles Davis's 1974 recording "He Loved Him Madly," a slack, heady thirty-two-minute elegy to Duke Ellington that gave Eno a "glimpse of another world, almost like a sci-fi story."[261] The recording became a touchstone for Eno throughout the *On Land* production process, in part by way of producer Teo Macero's space-making experimentation with hard

[259] Eno, *A Year with Swollen Appendices*, 294.

[260] On recorded audio "staging," see William Moylan, *The Art of Recording: The Creative Resources of Music Production and Audio* (New York: Van Nostrand Reinhold, 1992); Serge Lacasse, "'Listen to My Voice': The Evocative Power of Vocal Staging in Recorded Rock Music and Other Forms of Vocal Expression" (PhD diss., University of Liverpool, 2000).

[261] Paul Tingen, "Brian Eno: Recording Another Day on Earth," *Sound on Sound*, October 2005, https://www.soundonsound.com/people/brian-eno.

panning, reverberation, and delay on different instruments; and in part due to its brooding air, an atmospheric bleakness that, according to session percussionist James Mtume, permeated the recording process. "We were playing off a mood," he recalls. "Forget the chords, forget everything, it is all ambience."[262]

Eno's inspiration was bolstered by a visit at the end of 1980 to Accra, Ghana, where Eno listened, alone, to the amplified acoustic sounds of the night. Although he had brought his audio equipment with the intention of recording music and speech, he spent time instead "sitting out on the patio in the evenings with the microphone placed to pick up the widest possible catchment of ambient sounds from all directions, and listening to the result on my headphones. The effect of this simple technological system was to cluster all the disparate sounds into one aural frame; they became music."[263] Eno became interested in how the amplification captured, as he wrote in the re-release liner notes, "a large field of loosely-knit sound," a dynamic stereo image wherein various sounds occurred at different distances from himself and one another.[264] With *On Land*, he fabricated similarly dynamic sound-spaces through panning and generous stereo delay, which push the stages' expanses wide and open. To add depth, Eno rendered the tracks' constituent sounds variously distant or occluded through individual adjustments of volume, reverb, filtering, and envelope shape. These sonically heterogeneous worlds afford listeners the pleasures of surprise at subtle and unpredictable sonic reconfigurations, what Paul Roquet calls (after psychologists Stephen and Rachel Kaplan) ambient art's "soft fascinations."[265]

"Unfamiliar Wind (Leeks Hills)" bristles with such allurements. Throughout the track, seven brief synthesizer tones of five pitch classes (A♭, C, D♭, E♭, and F) continuously loop independently of one another at various time intervals between one and three seconds. Their unpredictable rhythmic patterning is more or less apparent depending on listener attentiveness, environmental noise, and audio playback equipment; in less focused or less immersive scenarios, a humming, undulating mid-range F-minor breeze emerges from the texture, while with more attention and/or bass-friendly equipment, an airy E♭-D♭ dyad can also be heard continuously oscillating out of sync with itself. These patterns suggest interweaving streams of

262 David Stubbs, *Mars by 1980: The Story of Electronic Music* (London: Faber & Faber, 2018), 158.
263 Sheppard, *On Some Faraway Beach*, 351–52.
264 Eno, liner notes to *Ambient 4: On Land*.
265 Roquet, *Ambient Media*, 111.

outdoor air that, overlaid with unpredictable and slow-fading bug and bird chirps, conjure an open-skied, uneven, and indifferent terrain. As the track progresses, pitched animal cries, melodic riffs, and timbral treatments refract the air with feeling, shading the environment with what may be heard as a single extended chord or, with more sustained attention, various chordal and modal configurations within a modally ambiguous pitch collection. As elsewhere on the album, amplitude modification, filtering, timbral changes, and expansions of register may shift perceptions of local chord roots or the overarching modal center, while fleeting melodic figures, acoustic sounds, and chromatic inflections fleck and smear these shifting moods.

In aurally fabricating three-dimensional spaces that recall outdoor landscapes, Eno intended to make *On Land*'s recordings "like figurative painting, but without referring to the history of music—more to a 'history of listening.'"[266] Mimeses of everyday sounds like animals, bells, or wind contribute a sense of strangeness, not only by way of the modal and harmonic ambiguity of their shading, but also in Eno's processing or synthetic mimicry of these sounds to place them "on the borderline of familiarity."[267] Smooth, periodic waveforms betray the music's unnatural provenance, while impossibly thick reverberation clouds and muddies the depicted landscapes. Take the blue-gray nostalgia of "Dunwich Beach, Autumn, 1960," for instance, wherein scattered electric-piano clangs, murky bass drones, barely-there crickets, and faraway seagull cries conjure a ragged coastal landscape. An obscure whirring suggests whooshing wind; a building and receding layer of tape hiss intimates a softly churning sea. Droopy, detuned synth warbles meanwhile lend the atmosphere palpable gloom. In delivering these timbral contortions through muted, bittersweet moods and, of course, the abstraction inherent to recorded audio, *On Land*'s worlds do not just stimulate memory; they simulate remember*ing*, their indistinctness reproducing pale reminiscence through the gauzy haze of temporal distance.

For Eno, these techniques of defamiliarization simulate the vagueness of sound-based memories, summoning the sensation of déja vù that natural environments so readily spark. To capture this feeling, Eno harvested his own childhood memories of the Suffolk countryside. He composed "The Lost Day," for instance, based on a recollection of a day spent during his youth, in his town of Woodbridge, alongside a stretch of the River Deben that opened

[266] Franck Mallet, "In the Enosphere," *Artpress*, September 2001, http://music.hyperreal.org/artists/brian_eno/interviews/artpress01.html.

[267] Eno, "Aurora Musicalis," 79.

into a harbor. "Throughout my childhood it was an evocative place for me. It was always empty, so whenever you went there, you were lonely. I got to like that feeling rather a lot."[268]

Eno could well have stuck with the album's working title, *Empty Landscapes*, not only because of its unoccupied soundscapes but also because of the estrangement suggested in the album's musical moods.[269] As with *Airports*, *On Land* blends feelings of calm and unease, but here the darkness goes from undertone to undertow, with tracks often stirring a sense of haunting or dread through ominous bass drones and figures: "You get the pastoral prettiness on top," Eno explains, "but underneath there's a dissonance that's like an impending earthquake."[270] From one moment to the next, tracks waver and wander from staid wonderment to mild melancholy and vague anxiety through chromatic inflections, octave doublings, shifts in register, and transient noises. "The Lost Day," for example, begins with a whirring sub-bass rumble that unsettles the track; a subdued din of crickets suggests night. At 0:27, metallic sheets of sound (light gong tremolos, perhaps) evoke the sound of wind howling through a tunnel-like space. The wind rises, then eerily recedes into the distance through a pronounced downward pitch bend. (The sonic trope of the downward pitch bend—common in horror and suspense films—reemerges periodically over the entire track.) Amid clattering chimes and tinkling bells (in fact, a greatly attenuated Fender Rhodes), a recurring synthesized string melody of C♯–D–G♯–B rises from the deep (e.g., 1:39) lending the track a C♯ Phrygian modality. As with "Unfamiliar Wind," differing modal interpretations emerge, for instance with the clanging bells at 2:30 suggesting G♯ Locrian, or the bubbling electric piano around 6:30 alternately suggesting F♯ Aeolian. These modal inflections inevitably return to the unstable Phrygian, which in the nighttime setting lends a sinister mood.

"On the whole," Eno reflected in 1989, "*On Land* is quite a disturbed landscape."[271] As first suggested by *Airports*'s "sense of doubt," and since confirmed by much of Eno's catalog, ambient music's affective topography as Eno envisioned it often contained at least a hint of darkness, balancing light with shadow, presence with distance, warmth with chill, contentedness with fear. Even occasional exceptions—the iridescent, serene 1985 LP *Thursday Afternoon* for one, or most of Laraaji's *Day of Radiance*—suggest, in Eno's

[268] Kalbacher, "Profile: Brian Eno," 47.
[269] Sheppard, *On Some Faraway Beach*, 355.
[270] Don Watson, "Man out of Time," *Spin*, May 1989, 42.
[271] Ibid., 42.

words, a "strange connection of familiarity and mystery embodied in the same source."[272] Eno's ambient productions almost always retained something of the shadowy side of retreat into nature, calm, self.

From Eno's perspective, this was a melancholy without sadness, disturbance without upset. Ambient-assisted solitude, as he sought it, should manifest feelings of "luscious silence" and "aloneness," not a hollow emptiness or deprived loneliness.[273] Recall that for Eno, art provided a "safe space" for encountering feelings of unimportance, melancholy, and disorientation, affects buffeted by aesthetic distance and sonic invariance.[274] Through poignant mixtures of the familiar and strange, of the predictable and unknowable, Eno's ambient landscapes offer listeners frames for feeling alone and uncertain in the world.

For the self-described sonic painter, sonic and affective variegation assisted in conjuring realistic, transportive times and places through sound. "I think a lot in terms of color of sound," Eno mused shortly after the release of *On Land*. "I've always been moved by the moment when a piece suddenly has a geography to it. I suddenly feel that this piece is located somewhere."[275] Undoubtedly seeking to "move" listeners similarly, in the double sense of both spatial and emotional transport, Eno pulled together timbral and textural details to render vivid aural snapshots of distinct elsewheres and -whens, while at the same time entertaining multivalent sonic and affective mixtures that convincingly recall and replicate the complexity of life as lived. *On Land*'s psychogeographic spaces cast this familiar world in a new light, manifesting "a more desirable reality" to disappear into and eventually emerge from reconstituted.[276] "I guess the feeling I always want from my own music is to be able to get lost in it and find myself again in different ways," as Eno reflected in 1982. "I think that's what everyone wants."[277]

And yet not all critics easily lost themselves in *On Land*, at least initially. As with previous *Ambient* efforts, several rejected the record's seeming softness. The *New York Times*'s John Rockwell in 1982 perceived *On Land* as merely "pleasant," and wished Eno would take a break from "restful,

272 M. Brown, "Life of Brian," 10.
273 Miller, "The Arts: Video," 28; Kalbacher, "Profile: Brian Eno," 51.
274 Rose, "Four Conversations with Brian Eno," 69.
275 Kalbacher, "Profile: Brian Eno," 50.
276 Ibid., 52.
277 M. Brown, "Life of Brian," 10.

lulling art-background music" to "assert himself" more forcefully.[278] Robert Christgau, with a compliment about as backhanded as they come, calls *On Land* "an undeniable pleasure so mild I'm not sure anyone would want to pay for it."[279] Others, though, found sympathy with Eno's goals. The *Washington Post*'s Richard Harrington, comparing the album to Irv Teibel's *Environments* records, praised *On Land* for its versatility in commanding "total involvement . . . under the influence of headphones," and in alternatively acting as a "perfect tranquilizer."[280] *NME*'s Lynden Barber came out with even fuller praise, noting that *On Land* offers an "embarrassment of atmospheric riches, sometimes evoking the familiar in a strangely unfamiliar way."[281] Record buyers, too, took greater notice of Eno's ambient records around this time. Although Eno, around the time of *On Land*'s release, no longer expected much of a monetary return on his ambient investments, by 1984 his ambient records sold equally well as his rock ones—partly thanks to the ballooning new age market in the United States, but also surely helped by *On Land*'s maturation of the ambient concept.[282] (*Hearts of Space*'s Stephen Hill, in a letter to Eno, called the record "superb" and "something very new," praising especially Eno's innovations in sound mixing and staging.)[283] The record has since the 1990s ranked high on fan and critic all-time "best ambient albums" lists, despite some writers disputing its ambient status based on Eno's original manifesto.[284] Simon Reynolds in 1995, for instance, noted a sharp distinction between Eno's original concept of ambient as "decor" and *On Land*'s presentation of "psychogeographic music."[285] Pitchfork's Mark Richardson in 2002 similarly marked *On Land* "simply not ambient music as Eno originally defined it. It's a dark piece of music with a serious sense of tension, interesting

[278] John Rockwell, "Using Records to Sample New Music," *New York Times*, April 25, 1982, 19.

[279] Robert Christgau, "Christgau's Consumer Guide," *Village Voice*, August 31, 1982, https://www.robertchristgau.com/xg/cg/cgv9-82.php.

[280] Richard Harrington, "Laurie Anderson's Brave New Art," *Washington Post*, May 6, 1982, B23.

[281] Lynden Barber, "Atmospheres in the Home," *Hyperreal Archives* (orig. *NME*, probably 1982), http://music.hyperreal.org/artists/brian eno/ interviews/rvonland.html.

[282] David Sterritt, "The 'Furniture Music' of Rock Star Brian Eno," *Christian Science Monitor*, May 3, 1984, 1.

[283] Stephen Hill, personal notebook, undated.

[284] Darryl Steven Roy, "Recommended Ambient Albums," *Hyperreal*, September 1, 1996, http://music.hyperreal.org/epsilon/info/1996_recommended_ambient.html; Kevin Renick, "Classic Ambient Recordings: The 2001 Survey," *Hyperreal*, January 2002, accessed October 15, 2015, http://music.hyperreal.org/epsilon/info/2001_classic_ambient.html; Kevin Renick, "Ambient Favorites: The 2015 Listeners' Survey," *Ello*, March 2015, accessed October 15, 2015, https://ello.co/johnkochnorthrup/post/ed2z9oc_bcq1hq09ifgxta; Marcus, "The 20 Greatest Ambient Albums"; and "The 50 Best Ambient Albums of All Time," *Pitchfork Magazine*.

[285] Simon Reynolds, "Muzak of the Fears," *Artforum* 33, no. 5 (January 1995): 61.

as hell but in no way ignorable."[286] As with *Music for Airports*, the range of responses to *On Land* speaks to its affective and functional ambivalence, to the uncertainty it poses between stability and instability, background and foreground, between sheltering environment and transportive vehicle, between the listening here and the recorded there.

But a break with the past, *On Land* was not. Rather, the record developed the ideas, reinterpreted the themes, and continued the aesthetic expansions set forth in earlier *Ambient* records. Not only did *On Land* deepen and refract the "sense of doubt" first entertained on *Airports*, it also expanded the ways in which ambient records might be either interesting or ignorable, producing a wide array of timbral and textural fascinations while also summoning outdoor settings like a nature sounds record, a large landscape photograph, or an open window. The production of outdoor scenes, and the impressionistic track titles, followed from Eno's experiments in this area on *Plateaux*. Like Budd, Eno also drew on languorous modal jazz as a prototype for the sound he wished to achieve. And as with Laraaji, Eno seemed determined to produce sounds that could not be easily categorized by genre, ethnicity, or culture; hear especially the pan-pipe-like trumpeting in "Shadow" (courtesy of Jon Hassell) and the peaceful pentatonic meditation of "A Clearing." Ultimately, as Eno reflected in the liner notes to *On Land*'s reissue, *On Land* was not his first "landscape" record, nor the first to convey a sense of place or location. "In retrospect," Eno writes, "I now see the influence of this idea, and the many covert attempts to realise it, running through most of the work that I've released like an unacknowledged but central theme."[287]

Ambient Music's Ambivalent Places of Passage

Eno's *Ambient* series, in sum, explored several ways in which ambient audio might provide personal enhancement for listeners via a sense of place or space associated with their sonic designs and moods.[288] Listeners need not consciously process these evocations in terms of place to enjoy these audio

[286] Mark Richardson, "As Ignorable as It Is Interesting: The Ambient Music of Brian Eno," *Pitchfork*, October 16, 2002, https://pitchfork.com/features/resonant-frequency/5879-resonant-frequency-17/.

[287] Eno, liner notes to *Ambient 4: On Land.*

[288] For further discussion of ambient music's evocations of place and space in the context of electronic music aesthetics, see Joanna Demers, *Listening through the Noise: The Aesthetics of Experimental Electronic Music* (New York: Oxford University Press, 2010), 113–19.

atmospheres, and such associations might often be beside the point of their affective operation. Yet the intricate production, clean visual and conceptual designs, and expressive range of these records make the ambient audio of the *Ambient* series well worth returning to as virtual "places" in themselves: medial locations in between the workaday and transcendent; places in time for reflection or gathering energy, or what Eno calls "the dream time, in your daily life, times when things get sorted out and reshuffled."[289]

Since the series, media scholars have detailed how consumers use many kinds of audio, not just ambient audio, as ignorable environments that proffer comfort and occasion alterations or enhancements of mood.[290] Moreover, ambient music is not alone in its ability to conjure a sense of place or space; many audio recordings find association with real spaces by dint of their conceptual frames, aesthetic designs, and affective qualities. Even when they do not, as media scholar Jody Berland has theorized, recorded music's temporal designs may be understood to operate within a "sociomusical 'third space'" or "time-outside-of-space" as their playback disembeds listeners from local space and "places" listeners in the "affective and topographic worlds" of their temporal designs.[291] Indeed, consumers use all sorts of audio to program and "colonize" their own futures much in the same way that modern institutions and infrastructures—like airports, say—plan, organize, and manage human experience to make it more reliable.[292]

Personal audio's mediating function may hence be understood according to Henri Bergson's concept of the *place of passage*: "A connecting link between the things which act upon me and the things upon which I act—the seat, in a word, of sensori-motor phenomena."[293] As philosopher Edward

[289] Kristine McKenna, "Eno," *Wet*, July/August 1980, 44. Elisabeth Le Guin has likewise affirmed the value of ambient music along these lines as a feminist resource; Elisabeth Le Guin, "Uneasy Listening," *Repercussions* 3, no. 1 (Spring 1994): 5–19.

[290] Sam Binkley, *Getting Loose: Lifestyle Consumption in the 1970s* (Durham, NC: Duke University Press, 2007); Bijsterveld et al., *Sound and Safe*; Michael Bull, *Sounding Out the City: Personal Stereos and the Management of Everyday Life* (New York: Berg, 2000); Bull, *Sound Moves*; DeNora, *Music in Everyday Life*; Giddens, *Modernity and Self-Identity*; Anahid Kassabian, *Ubiquitous Listening: Affect, Attention, and Distributed Subjectivity* (Berkeley: University of California Press, 2013); Andrew Williams, *Portable Music and Its Functions*, vol. 6: *Music [Meanings]* (New York: Peter Lang, 2007).

[291] Jody Berland, "Locating Listening," in *The Place of Music*, ed. Andrew Leyshon, David Matless, and George Revill (New York: Guilford, 1998), 131 and 138–39. On the "disembedding" function of electronic media, see also Bull, *Sound Moves*; Giddens, *Modernity and Self-Identity*, 146–47; Holly Watkins, "Musical Ecologies of Place and Placelessness," *Journal of the American Musicological Society* 64, no. 2 (Summer 2011): 408.

[292] Giddens, *Modernity and Self-Identity*, 133.

[293] Henri Bergson, *Matter and Memory*, trans. N. M. Paul and W. S. Palmer (New York: Doubleday, 1959), 145; as quoted in Edward S. Casey, *Remembering: A Phenomenological Study*, 2nd ed. (Bloomington: Indiana University Press, 2000), 195.

Casey theorizes it, a place of passage simultaneously acts as an *intra-place*, an environing place (or mood) within which things move, and as an *inter-place*, or a transportive place (or mood) that sends masses into motion.[294] Audio, like the listening bodies it contains and is contained by, affectively stabilizes physical spaces of reception at the same time as it unsettles them, disposing inhabitants to cognitive and emotional displacements and arrivals. These medial places style, structure, and orient the terrain of the personal and social everyday along spatiotemporal corridors, vectors, passages, and paths.

Eno's *Ambient* series, with these theories in mind, invites interpretation as an ambivalent reflection on the spatial and transportive mediations provided by personal audio. As metaphors for their own affordances, *Music for Airports* and *On Land* present especially elegant conceptual counterpoises to one another. Both produce virtual spaces reminiscent of those of the physical world, recalling places and times peripheral to social life and workaday time, symbolic asocial zones that effectively afford listeners the withdrawal they represent. Their aesthetics jointly concern the disengagements from the physical world that they provide listeners, with both depicting detachment from the social and the human through presentations of locations largely indifferent to human presence. Yet with *Airports* representing modern spaces of transport, and with *On Land* immersing listeners in pastoral retreats, these albums' respective places of passage metaphorically bookend the spectrum between inter-place and intra-place, between the transportive and environing, or between the mobilizing and stabilizing, functions of recorded ambience. At the same time, both records flexibly mix these functions, and in doing so ironize their atmospheric functionalism, with *Airports*'s hyperminimalist, static sonic façades overcompensating for the fragility of technologized (audio) transport, and with *On Land*'s quasi-familiar and unsettlingly transient mimeses of nature reflecting uncertainly on the naturalization of (audio) technology as personal environment. Ambient music's evocations of space and ambivalence may accordingly be understood not just as atmospheric, or as bundles of affects and effects; they might also cast doubt on the stability of their own mediations.

Perhaps Eno's *Airports* now enjoys its prominence in the ambient canon not just because it introduced "ambient music" to the world, but also because it so elegantly interprets, metaphorizes, and aestheticizes the everyday transportations that ambient audio promotes. The record may not (yet) have

[294] Ibid., 196.

inspired a trend in programmed music for public spaces, but it did establish a novel conceptual and aesthetic framework for ambient audio design and programming. Then as now, recordings described as "ambient" often revive the impersonality, transience, and social alienation of modern transportation through ambivalent mixtures of the inviting and alienating, connective and isolating, futuristic and nostalgic, moving and grounding. Indeed, ambient music recordings might even themselves be understood as vehicles of modern transportation—and with this in mind, one could equally well regard airport experience, and the experience of vehicular transport more broadly, as metaphor for the equally pacifying and unsettling experience of ambient music listening.

At the same time, as I hear it, *On Land* not only manifests more arresting audio landscapes than does *Airports*, but it also poses a more piquant symbolic irony in undercutting its ostensible "naturalism" via sonic markers of technology. Synthesized sounds, periodic waveforms, production effects, loops, and sustained tones translate the recording's "hidden nature" as a disembodied, dehumanized, and discreet electronic mechanism into musical sound. Sustained tones and drones double the automated constancy of electric currents and synthesized sounds. Looping aurally reproduces the music's underlying materiality in circuits and oscillators. Such production techniques make the album playback's automaticity audible, elevating the very factors that allow consumers to program audio themselves and treat it as if it were "naturally" part of their listening environment.

Compared to a great deal (but certainly not all) of contemporaneous ambient audio, what made Eno's *Discreet Music* and *Ambient* series especially "interesting" were, more than anything, their unusual affective mixtures—the hints of impersonality, infinity, distance, and danger they injected into the production of cozy, soothing personal audio—and the potential for reflexive interpretation embodied therein. Across their affective axes of ambivalence, these albums hinted at a distinctive musical style with a promising range of unconventional pleasures: to feel uncertain within calm, to register alienation from both nature and culture, to contemplate the fullness of the immediate present, and to take a disorienting trip inward. And as the preceding history of ambient audio suggests, such pleasures of disaffiliation, defamiliarization, and introspection resonated especially strongly with both countercultural and highbrow listeners—which helps to explain the allure of the ambient label for a new generation of "mental" British electronic voyagers at the turn of the 1990s, the peak of psychedelia's second coming.

4

Ambient EDM, or Dance Music That Isn't Dance Music!

Preface: "It Must Be Obvious (UFO Mix)" by the KLF vs. The Pet Shop Boys (1990)

L: A studio-miked man conversing with a woman via telephone— perhaps a call-in radio show?	R: A staticky signal. A distant jazz trumpet. A TV announcement.

Center: A hollow, bassy rumble rising—
the engine of an aircraft, as heard from inside.

The rumble and radio voices continue as the Pet Shop Boys' "It Must Be Obvious" fades up loud and center. As Neil Tennant croons of unrequited love, the engine rumble fades—airplane sounds whoosh from left to right to left—video-gamey synths drop like bombs from overhead. Telephone chatter. The Pet Shop Boys' song, largely untouched itself, has a strange new ambience.

The bass rumble reemerges, and soon overwhelms Tennant's voice, which fades into the distance. "What am I supposed to do now?" asks a man, from the right, via some sort of transmitter. Radio voices appear and disappear all over the stereo field. Planes enter and exit. What happened to the Pet Shop Boys? The rumble fades.

A synth tone with volume controlled by a low-frequency oscillator (LFO) wobbles up from below. The throats in the radio voices disappear, leaving only sibilants and fricatives. A percussive ringing in the left. A raft of filter-swept white noise floats up. "Are you ready for this, Julia?" asks the radio man. The engine rumble reenters, far right. Is that a distorted telephone ringing, or an alarm going off? [loud transmitter static] "HELLO? WH-WH-WHERE ARE YOU?" Where *am* I? (A spacecraft, it seems—but why?)

Turn On, Tune In, Drift Off. Victor Szabo, Oxford University Press.
DOI: 10.1093/oso/9780190699307.003.0005

Another LFO-controlled synth flutters in from left, lands right. Echoing from the left, only the highs audible: "Even when the darkest clouds are in the sky / You mustn't sigh and you mustn't cry . . ." (Sting, "Spread a Little Happiness" [?!]) A sharp intake of air. Revving, or zipping, or something. The aircraft rumble keeps fading in and out. Sting dies; a little girl speaks; more zipping; more radio voices; more aircrafts shooting across the stereo field. "HELLO? WH-WH-WHERE ARE YOU? WH-WH-WHERE ARE YOU?"

The engine rumble exits fully, and the texture thins. Floating in outer space. The fluttering signal exits—and a robot speaks—there's a faint static hiss—a radio dial searches for the right frequency, which turns into a synth portamento—more radio voices. Another aircraft zooms left to right. [loud transmitter static] "WH-WH-WHERE ARE YOU?" "WH-WH-WHERE ARE YOU?" The fluttering signal returns. Radio man: "Just a word." Synth beeps and bloops. A robotic voice. The static hiss fades—(I forgot it was there)—and now I am in some vacuum-sealed space, disembodied noises fluttering and beeping and buzzing intermittently from all around. . . . "PREPARE TO ACTIVATE." . . . The LFO wobble wanders aimlessly around the stereo field. . . . A "power-down" pitch sweep intrudes; a screeching synth skitters in; a pulsating beeping floats in from the left. . . . Robotic voices appear, disappear, reappear all around the stereo field. . . . "PREPARE TO ACTIVATE." . . . More bleeps and bloops, a modular synthesizer poem . . . or maybe a dial-up modem? . . . A rising Shepard tone joins in. . . . Pulse-wave sputters, and sine sweeps too . . . my focus floating somewhere between these sounds and my thoughts; or, rather, wandering through where my thoughts should be, but where instead strange sounds are floating in and out ("Where are my thoughts right now?," I wonder as I wander). . . .

And then, unexpectedly, the space shuttle ambience drops out: birdsong.

Then, also unexpectedly, a drum machine in the left channel . . . a man singing, "Tell me why" . . . . It's distant, tough to make out amid the birdsong. (It is, in fact, "So Hard" by the Pet Shop Boys—the single's A-side!)

. . . and then the Shepard tone returns, as does, unexpectedly, a FURIOUS engine rumble. Birds become whirs; I am HURTLING through space, zzzzzzzZIP, wwwwWHOP—radio voices return again then disappear—revving—the bass rumble fades in, then out, then in again, rising and rising as alarm-like synth tones and zzzips and radio voices and static hiss pile up, wind RUSHING by—

And then, about the least expected sound of all: "It Must Be Obvious" by the Pet Shop Boys, fading up, loud and center. Of course! Its return should have been obvious—but it was not at all until now, having returned. The effect is startling, funny. But as the pop song continues, unabated, a slight melancholy sets in, not dissimilar to the feeling of returning to earth at the end of a roller-coaster ride. Is it over already?

"It must be obvious," Neil Tennant deadpans, unremixed. The song fades out.

Introduction

September 1989: The "Second Summer of Love," also known as the "Summer of Rave," has been raging in England for well over a year. Working- and middle-class youth in London and Manchester, mostly straight white teens formerly predisposed to genres like punk, new wave, or soul, are turning on to ecstasy, an MDMA-based drug, while tuning in and letting loose to electronic dance music (EDM) at parties, clubs, and raves.[1] They are finding house and techno's sample-and-drum-machine-powered locomotion, once chiefly popular among African American partygoers, gay clubbers, and Ibiza vacationers, to be moving, transportive, a trip. Especially in combination with ecstasy: together, they summon euphoria, stimulate motion, dissolve inhibition, and intensify sensation, sometimes to the point of synesthesia and hallucination.[2] Strangers are suddenly friends; peace, love, unity, and respect blur into PLUR, a guiding principle for the new countercultural matrix crystallizing around music, psychedelics, and the dissolution of personal boundaries.[3]

And now, at the crest of rave's wave, DJ Paul Oakenfold and pals have just launched Land of Oz, a Monday night party at Heaven in Trafalgar Square. Upstairs from where Oakenfold and others are spinning acid

[1] Simon Reynolds, *Energy Flash: A Journey through Rave Music and Dance Culture* (Berkeley: Soft Skull, 2012). See also Matthew Collin, *Altered State: The Story of Ecstasy Culture and Acid House* (London: Serpent's Tail, 1997). Here as elsewhere, I use "EDM" as an umbrella term for electronic dance music of all styles, and not (as it is sometimes used) to refer to a specific style of festival-friendly electronic dance music that rose to the US mainstream around 2010.

[2] Reynolds, *Energy Flash*, xxx–xxxi.

[3] On the fluidity of personal boundaries and "liquidity" of togetherness in club culture, see Luis-Manuel Garcia, "Crowd Solidarity on the Dance Floor in Paris and Berlin," in *Musical Performance and the Changing City*, ed. Fabian Holt and Carsten Wergin (New York: Routledge, 2013), 227–50.

house, select clubgoers enter the VIP bar to relax on couches and beanbags, rehydrate, hang with friends, and come down from their ecstasy-and-adrenaline highs while spacing out to the sounds. And in this particular "chill-out room"—reportedly the first—DJs LX-Dee (Alex Paterson) and Rockman (Jimmy Cauty), together calling themselves The Orb, mix house and techno with such disparate styles as psych and cosmic rock, soft soul, new wave, and dub, as well as animal and nature sounds, spoken children's stories, and other assorted oddities. They, along with friends like DJ Youth (Martin Glover), call this heady brew "ambient house," partly in reference to the music of Brian Eno, whose floaty synth recordings also make their way into the duo's mixes.[4]

Over the following years, "ambient" will become shorthand for the music associated with chill-out rooms and areas, which become semiregular features of underground clubs and raves in the United Kingdom. Parties more devoted to chilling than dancing will also emerge, begetting a bohemian electronic music scene driven by young DJs' transgeneric musical curiosity. Synergistic swirls of space music, downtempo jazz, hip-hop, dub, and echoing samples will overlap with a swath of new house and techno tracks with slower tempi, lusher arrangements, and/or deemphasized percussion—all under the ambient banner.

But why the term "ambient" to describe this corner of EDM? It doesn't much resemble the music of Eno's *Ambient* series; it doesn't even much sound like Eno's ambient with a dance groove; and its artists, unlike Eno, are not especially invested in the music's ignorability. Ambient EDM does, however, introduce spacious, body-mellowing, and mind-expanding "psychological sound" to the Gen-X counterculture, and with it the expectations of, and associations with, the world of ambient audio that had come before.

The chapter outlines the reemergence of ambient between the late 1980s and mid-1990s first as a stylistic marker of EDM, and eventually as a self-standing popular genre. It describes the interchange and imbrication of scene-based and industry-oriented concerns as the ambient genre tag at once became attached to distinct scenes, sounds, affordances, and markets within British EDM subcultures, while simultaneously circulating as a style

[4] Cressida Bowyer, at the time Jimmy Cauty's wife, originally came up with the "ambient house" tag, according to Adam Morris. See Morris, "The Racist Spin of Adam Morris," May 7, 2021, https://racistspinofadammorris.life/.

descriptor within a transatlantic market for electronic music records. This recounting illustrates how the ambient genre's formation, far from a linear trajectory out of Eno's records and chill-out rooms, drew on a wide assortment of pop and electronic styles while taking shape through distinctions from these styles' genre forms and cultures.

In the first half of this chapter, I trace the discursive emergence of "ambient house" both in connection with UK chill-out rooms, and as the term usurped "new age house" and "deep house" as a media descriptor for heady, chilled-out EDM records coming from producers like The Orb. A comparative analysis of ambient house albums illustrates the thematic motif of "traveling without moving" that linked such records to the psychoactive musical trip as explored in earlier ambient audio such as the *Environments* records, *Music from the Hearts of Space*, and Eno's *Ambient* series. Through this self-reflexive theme, ambient house's travelers rooted their work in ambient's psychedelic lineage while bringing focus to the combination of mental transport and bodily stillness that distinguished ambient listening from other uses of EDM. As the cover of a 1993 issue of *DJ Mag* stated, ambient EDM artists made "dance music that isn't dance music!" (Fig. 4.1).

In the second half, I chronicle how the ambient genre label in 1992 found new life through a second wave of popularization as "ambient" EDM styles proliferated in the European market, and as a growing audience of non-raver home listeners in North America caught on to these styles. From 1992 to 1995, ambient's stylistic dalliances and market contexts multiplied as the concept drew interest across dance, rock, and experimental music scenes. Throughout these discourses, the label continued to imply lush melodics, echoey effects, deemphasis of percussion, and a privileging of the mix's high end; and concomitantly, it implied the music's suitability for home listening and applicability to bodily ease and mental drift. Yet as ambient "followed the well-trodden route from the underground to the overground," as The Orb originator Cauty put it, ambient's adherents explicitly negotiated the boundaries of the genre as a highbrow expression relative to other EDM styles.[5] These negotiations centered and canonized the contributions of

[5] Matt Anniss, "Ambient House: The Story of Chill Out Music, 1988–95," *Red Bull Music Academy Daily*, February 17, 2016, archived at Internet Archive, *Wayback Machine*, https://web.archive.org/web/20190327060903/https://daily.redbullmusicacademy.com/specials/2016-ambient-house-feature.

Figure 4.1. Front cover to August 26–September 3, 1993 issue of *DJ Mag* featuring Ultramarine. Photograph by Paul Hammond. Used by permission.

white male DJs and producers within the ambient genre formation, racializing and gendering the genre according to the persistence of a mind/body dualism associating relaxed embodiment and highbrow status with hip white masculinity.

Traveling without Moving through Ambient House

From New Age House to Ambient House

Before "ambient house," there was "new age house," a niche subgenre invented by UK promoters toward the end of 1988 to describe chill-out-friendly, jazz-fusion-fueled, nature-sound-tinged instrumental house music.[6] The term cropped up most prominently in connection with quartet 808 State's "Pacific State," a sunny cut layered with warm synth strings, trilling loons, and faux-kalimbas jamming over a funky syncopated bass, as well as a signature gooey minor-triad soprano sax riff drizzled atop a lightly swinging Roland 909 groove. 808 State's producers had cobbled together the track's elements from jazz fusion (Pharaoh Sanders's *Thembi* was a particularly potent influence), Latin EDM, and the deep house that had infiltrated the "Madchester" dance scene that year.[7] DJs spinning at Manchester's famous Haçienda club first drew attention to "Pacific State" by closing out their sets with the track; and the recording, released commercially in early 1989, became a summer club hit, making the dance charts with extensive BBC Radio 1 play. By the end of the year UK music mags like *Record Mirror* and *Melody Maker* were dubbing the band and their music "new age house."[8]

Like the industry-based "new age" genre formation before it, "new age house" was more of a media construction than artist-driven term, and it at first did not mark any intentional stylistic choices so much as recode relaxed, nature-inspired house music in terms of earthy hippie chill. Ecstasy had, after all, revived countercultural idealism among urban British youth; why not conceptualize this idealism in a familiar way? "People I'd known for years were suddenly dressing all ethnic and getting spiritual," attests DJ and producer Mark Moore. "The whole New Age thing surged forward."[9] Fashion magazines spoke of the rise of "new age clubbers" and "nouveau hippies," while declaring that "the Me Generation has been replaced by the

[6] The term appeared on occasion in the United States, as on the New York–based house producer L.B. Bad's "New Age House," released as a 12" B-side in 1989.

[7] Becca Antoon, "Game Changer: 808 State 'Pacific State,'" *DJ Mag*, November 21, 2018, https://djmag.com/content/game-changer-808-state-'pacific-state'.

[8] Paul Oldfield, "A Guy Called Gerald, ULU, London," *Melody Maker*, February 24, 1990, http://homepages.force9.net/king1/Media/LiveReviews/1990-02-09-LiveReview-ULU-London-England.htm; Tim Jefferys, "Back in the DHSS," *Record Mirror*, March 25, 1989, 34; Simon Reynolds, "808 State: New Bold Dreams," *Melody Maker*, November 18, 1989, 42.

[9] Reynolds, *Energy Flash*, 47.

We Generation."[10] But Martin Price, a member of 808 State, bristled at the tag as an attempt of "big business" to promote their music in familiar terms:

> A lot of people are looking to bracket it, and they think that if they take it down the Sixties' road, you know—coming down music, a sound for when the sun's coming up and the trip's near its end—then they make the scene to be more important than the actual music. I think there's music for all moods, and why can't it just be left as dance music? To me, all the "new age" thing boils down to is that there's a gentler sound available.[11]

The "new age" tag, in this context, had a racial dimension as well, marking the music in terms of the overwhelming whiteness of the hippie, New Age, and British rave movements. "We realize that we're all white," 808 State's Martin Price told *Spin* in 1990, but the new-age appellation, he continued, dishonestly "takes the blackness out" of house.[12] The feature nonetheless ran with the headline "New Age Soul Boys" under a photograph of the four white bandmates, inviting reinterpretation of "new age house" as the "blue-eyed soul" of rave.

The "new age" on display with "Pacific State," in truth, was not all that new, nor all that white, given the music's roots in Ibiza-based Balearic Beat and Chicago-based deep house, both of which had emerged several years prior. "Balearic Beat" was itself a media-driven promotional tag that originally specified a mood and attitude rather than unified style. The term was based on the hodgepodge of laid-back new wave, Italo disco, soul, Europop, tropicalia, and house introduced by DJ Alfredo to the open-air club Amnesia in the mid-'80s. Various London DJs brought these low-key Balearic vibes back to London in '87 and '88, providing a mellow counterpoint to the hard-driving acid house ragers, and eventually a more intimate and classed-up scene set in opposition to the mainstreamed and increasingly working-class club culture.[13] As big singles like Sueño Latino's "Sueño Latino," The Grid's "Floatation," and Innocence's "Natural Thing" continued the Balearic vibes into 1989 and '90, British observers interpreted the breezy, slow-house serenity on display as "new age."

[10] Sheryl Garratt and Lindsay Baker, "Clubland after Acid," *The Face*, December 1989, 62.
[11] Reynolds, "808 State: New Bold Dreams," 42.
[12] Bob Mack, "Flash: New Age Soul Boys," *Spin*, March 1, 1990, 18. 808 State originally included Gerald Simpson (best known as A Guy Called Gerald), a Black British DJ/producer who programmed the drums for "Pacific State" (among other contributions) before leaving the group in 1989.
[13] Reynolds, *Energy Flash*, 50–53.

"Deep house" had meanwhile come to the United Kingdom from across the Atlantic, where it first circulated mainly in underground gay clubs in Chicago, New York, and New Jersey. As DJ Ron Trent recalls, the term "deep" in its original context specified attitude over style, namely anything slanted toward the "obscure or weird or mysterious."[14] Yet around 1986–87, the term began to identify a softer, more jazz- and R&B-influenced house sound than the heavily percussive body-jackin' beats ruling dance floors. Most associated with the productions of Larry Heard (aka Mr. Fingers or Fingers Inc.), Marshall Jefferson, and Frankie Knuckles, Chicago deep house came to entail soft drum pads, soulful vocals, rolling bass gallops, and luxuriant extended chords played on synth pads or strings in a minor mode. Deep house's mild melancholy, bluesy soulfulness, and lush jazz harmonies more obviously drew on Quiet Storm R&B and soul than on, say, Eno's experiments or *Hearts*'s space music, but its sonic profile and affective mixtures would conceivably make "ambient house" or "space jazz" equally apt descriptors. The sounds of deep house gained some promotion in the United Kingdom as "new age" in 1989; an advertisement in the British magazine *Blues & Soul* for instance, perhaps putting the blackness back in "new age house," called the deep house album *Ammnesia* by Mr. Fingers "New Age house with the jazz touch."[15] David Toop, in a July 1989 feature for UK pop-culture magazine *The Face*, linked "new age" to Chicago deep-house duo Virgo (aka Virgo Four) whose self-titled album, he noted, "can drift by without necessarily making any strong impression on the listener."[16] 808 State member Graham Massey now attests to attempting to recapture in "Pacific State" the "tropical warmth" of Marshall Jefferson's 1988 cut "Open Our Eyes," a fine contender for the first distinctly "new age house" track with its digitally sampled shakuhachi licks and rippling forest stream ambience.[17] The Orb's Alex Paterson, too, acknowledged the atmospheric element latent in deep house, in 1990 recommending to "listen to Fingers Inc.'s 'Washing Machine' or 'Can You Feel It,' minus the beats. Very ambient."[18]

[14] Piotr Orlov, "Songs We Love: Ron Trent Shares Some Deep House 'History,'" *NPR*, February 21, 2017, https://www.npr.org/2017/02/21/516393834/songs-we-love-ron-trent-shares-some-deep-house-history.

[15] *Blues & Soul* no. 532, April 4–17, 1989, 19.

[16] David Toop, "Noise in the New Age," *The Face*, July 1989, 75.

[17] Richard Buskin, "Classic Tracks: 808 State 'Pacific State,'" *Sound on Sound*, April 2014, https://www.soundonsound.com/people/classic-tracks-808-state-pacific-state.

[18] Push, "Ambient House: The Ecstasy Fantasy," *Melody Maker*, March 10, 1990, http://www.808state.com/various/interview/1990-03-10-MelodyMaker-Article.html.

It was in this context that The Orb, who had been toying with spacey, eclectic mixtures in Cauty's home studio for months, committed in October 1989 to the "ambient house" tag. "I was really frightened that we might get called 'New Age house,'" as Paterson later explained, and so he and Cauty, at the suggestion of Cauty's wife at the time, copped Eno's term to avoid any association with "new age rubbish."[19] The duo's improvisations in Land of Oz's VIP lounge (later known as The White Room) produced musical mixtures far more surrealistic than 808 State's Balearic tropicalia or Mr. Fingers's deep-house mellow. Using three turntables, a DAT machine, a tape recorder, and a mixer, The Orb layered bizarre sound effects, vocal samples, and bits of classical music over house tracks like DTR's "Journey into a Dream," prog rock jams like Steve Hillage's "Rainbow Dome Musick," Lee Scratch Perry's dub reggae, and even Led Zeppelin's "When the Levee Breaks," often isolating and looping nonpercussive sections and/or cutting the bass. Their experimental improvisations, like Eno's, were driven by the pair's nothing-to-lose amateurism, a willingness to try anything in absence of musical training.[20]

The first recorded production The Orb put out in this freewheeling style was a remix of "3 A.M. Eternal," a hip-house track originally produced by Cauty's other outfit, the KLF.[21] The Orb's "Blue Danube Orbital" remix of the track appeared, uncredited, on a 12" single in September 1989. The track opens with a din of delay-echoed birds and bugs, a woman singing wordlessly, and a synth chorus, followed a minute and a half in by a light shuffling groove and melodic lead. Two minutes later, the groove fades out to a delay-echoed treatment of Strauss's "By the Beautiful Blue Danube" waltz, likely in allusion to the tune's spacey use in the film *2001: A Space Odyssey*. A chorus sings the "eternal" hook from the original track; a man then announces, through heavy echo: "Our space cadets have finished their nap, and have one hour before landing." The percussion, synth chorus, and wordless vocals over

[19] Don Crispy, "Alex Paterson," *Metropolis*, 2005, archived at Internet Archive, *Wayback Machine*, https://web.archive.org/web/20091227105436/http://archive.metropolis.co.jp/tokyo/590/clubs.asp; Jack Barrow, "The Orb," 120–21, in accompanying booklet, *Trance Europe Express*, various artists, Total Record Co. via BMG (UK) Ltd., TEEX 1, 1993, CD. See also note 4 on the origins of "ambient house."

[20] As Cauty's partner in the KLF, Bill Drummond, joked of the duo's experimentalism in a press release, "[The Orb] make no claims that the results of their efforts can be considered music, or has any relevance to the outside world, or contains any elements of a tune, or tracks of anything vaguely memorable." Ian Shirley, *Turn Up the Strobe: The KLF, The JAMS, The Timelords: A History* (London: Cherry Red Books, 2017), 162.

[21] According to the KLF, the first ambient house recording was in fact the "minimal" mix of their 1988 track as The Timelords, "Doctorin' the Tardis," released on the 12" B-side. Ian McCann, "Profile: The KLF," *The Face*, September 1990, 73.

the next several minutes float back into the mix and proceed effortlessly, a groove without sweat, until the final fade.

The Orb first promoted the style as "ambient house" the following month with the release of a monster 12" single titled "A Huge Ever Growing Pulsating Brain That Rules from the Centre of the Ultraworld." The nineteen-minute sample-rich odyssey, originally titled "Loving You (Orbital Mix)" based on the sampled Minnie Riperton song, was a curiosity not only due to the track's extreme length, but also for its almost total lack of percussion. The duo had recorded the track following a Brighton rave; as Paterson in 1989 told *NME*, Cauty had a headache, hungover from too many house beats. "We wanted to capture the warmth of the day, the sun and the sea's sound. Initially we started recording the piece with a drum beat—we built the track around that but it felt wrong. So we took out the drums and it was perfect. It was the chill out music we'd always been trying to find."[22] The press release, and later the back of the single, prominently announced the arrival of "ambient house for the e generation" (Fig. 4.2).

But beats, it should be said, were not entirely absent from the original mix of "A Huge Ever Growing Pulsating Brain." In what would become a signature element of the ambient house sound, The Orb continually hint at, then pull away from, a full-blown dance groove, conveying the pulsating headspace of a listener drifting light years away from a party right around the corner. The track opens with synth pads arpeggiating an E♭ minor pentatonic collection, soon layered with a stuttering choir sampled from Grace Jones's "Slave to the Rhythm"; these elements become interspersed with eighth-note drum-machine cymbal taps, rippling water, and ocean waves crashing over a i-III-iv-v cycle implied by the bass. The choir, cymbal, and waves flow in and out; the arpeggios are slowly filtered; a few synth pads fill out the texture. Four minutes in, almost all falls away but the arpeggios, and the sound of cascading water rises to the front of the mix. Only once the water recedes, and after another choral interlude, does a drum emerge—a snare lightly hit a few times, soon followed by a cymbal tapping out the eighth-note pulse with the arpeggio. A muted tom joins half a minute later, and it sounds like a groove will finally land once the tom rises in volume . . . it rises . . . but instead, at about 6:40, a heavily delay-echoed a cappella sample of Riperton's "Lovin' You" enters the mix. Faint birdsong. The tom exits, Riperton sings, and then the introductory synth material enters once more. The track continues in

[22] Shirley, *Turn Up the Strobe*, 163.

(a)

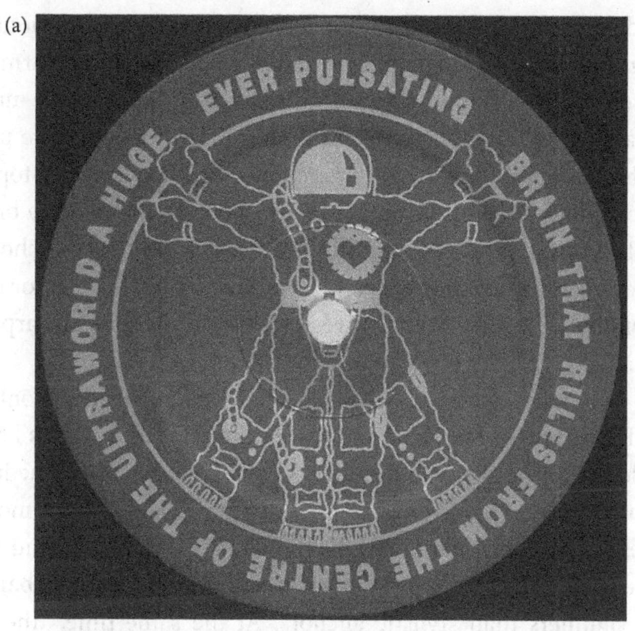

(b)

Figure 4.2. Vinyl disc sticker and back cover to the 12" single for The Orb's "A Huge Ever Growing Pulsating Brain . . . " (WAU! Mr. Modo Recordings, 1989).

this gradually surging fashion for the next six minutes, with various samples entering and exiting—an engine rumbling here, a clock alarm there, a rooster crowing—all appearing and disappearing around the undulating filtered arpeggios. Finally, fourteen minutes in, a sixteenth-note percussive groove builds—and then a funky percussion track syncs over top, climactically matching the propulsion with body-shaking energy for a brief thirty seconds!—but then the kick cedes to the synth arpeggios and choir . . . the sounds of planes whoosh overhead . . . a minute later, the clamor of church bells clanging . . . then ocean waves crashing . . . the synth arpeggiation slows . . . the track fades out . . . .

"The Orb have achieved what Marshall Jefferson could only begin," Cauty's KLF partner, Bill Drummond, concluded in the single's half-jesting press release for the single; but unlike, say, "Open Our Eyes," the imprint of deep house on "A Huge Ever Growing Pulsating Brain" is hazy, more absent than present, a fading memory of the night before.[23] Soft soul and new wave are present by way of the Riperton and Jones samples, but just barely, more floating signifiers than stylistic anchors. At the same time, "the soothing sounds of Eno" referenced in the same press release are similarly distant touchstones. Whereas Eno's ambient tracks float by untethered from groove, enveloping listeners in timbral nuance within predictable musical parameters, "A Huge Ever Growing Pulsating Brain" gathers momentum from underlying rhythmic pulsation—more directly recalling 1970s Kosmische, Eurodisco, and pulse-pattern minimalism—while also adopting the often unpredictable collage aesthetics of 1980s synthpop. The Orb's track, in light of its formal innovations, well warranted a new stylistic descriptor; but the "ambient" label, at face, more directly communicated the music's affordances of bodily stillness and mental drift than anything.

The music press, while enthusiastic about the "ambient house" moniker, did not at first distinguish it from "new age house" like The Orb did. Paul Lester, in a December 1989 *Melody Maker* review, combined the two in describing 808 State's "Pacific State" as "ambient New Age House."[24] In February 1990, Paul Oldfield described the music of A Guy Called Gerald as " 'New Age,' aka 'ambient' house, the phenomenon that emphasises the trance in trance dance, and should reconcile House music with 'head' rock."[25] And

[23] Wau! Mr. Modo Records, "Ambient House for the E Generation," Bad Moon Publicity press release, 1989.

[24] Paul Lester, "Review: *90* by 808 State, *90*," *Melody Maker*, December 9, 1989, 34.

[25] Oldfield, "A Guy Called Gerald, ULU, London."

Lindsay Baker, one month later, called Innocence's "Natural Thing" an "ambient" track with "a new age feel."[26] Overseas that same month, *Spin* reviewer Frank Owen referred to "New Age house" as "highly energized, ambient Muzak," and in May, he introduced the music of Larry Heard with a litany of descriptors: "New age house, ambient house, abstract house, whatever you call his music, Heard . . . has created a distinctive body of work characterized by an eerie, environmental feel."[27] The *Chicago Tribune* in July similarly redescribed ambient house as "New Age house," calling the genre "house with a mellower melody."[28]

Yet by the end of 1990, the term "new age house" had largely disappeared. In an end-of-year dance music roundup, for instance, *Spin* identified The Orb as inventors of ambient house, called 808 State "ambient-house masters," and gestured to Manuel Gottsching's 1984 "E2E4" as "one of the earliest ambient house records."[29] As a substyle of house, "ambient" had stuck, while "new age" largely fell to the wayside. Where did it go?

Paul Oldfield's 1990 *Melody Maker* feature on ambient house gives some hints. The emergent style, as Oldfield explained it, shares various themes with new age music—nature, space, technology—but should be distinguished on the basis of its listenability, its "progressive" lineage, and its techno-utopian futurism.[30] "Although it's been called New Age house," writes Oldfield, "the best cuts aren't background music, aren't the anodyne aural equivalent of a Radox bath."[31] Oldfield connects ambient house's propensity for creating womb-like sonic sanctuaries not to the Private Music catalog nor to Californian limited-press cassettes, but rather to ECM jazz, the "galactic rock" of Tangerine Dream and Tomita, Eno's ambient records, and the "oceanic" dream-pop of The Cocteau Twins.[32] Although ambient house, like new age, "fetishises . . . mother Nature," the freshest of the genre foregoes "caring" traditionalism for "a high-tech future" that's more about starting anew rather than conservation. And while its techno-futurism thematizes outer space, this theme "doesn't

[26] Lindsay Baker, "British Lions," *The Face*, March 1990, 20.

[27] Frank Owen, "Big Beats," *Spin*, March 1990, 78; Frank Owen, "Environmental House," *Spin*, May 1990, 84.

[28] Marla Donato, "A Lesson on House Music," *Chicago Tribune*, July 11, 1990, sec. 7, 20.

[29] Bob Mack, "Flash: House Music Map of the Western World," *Spin*, December 1990, 33.

[30] Paul Oldfield, "Ambient House: The Ecstasy Fantasy," *Melody Maker*, March 10, 1990, http://www.808state.com/various/interview/1990-03-10-MelodyMaker-Article.html.

[31] Oldfield, "Ambient House: The Ecstasy Fantasy."

[32] Oldfield's "oceanic pop"-oriented genealogy of ambient house anticipates Simon Reynolds and Joy Press's; see Reynolds and Press, *The Sex Revolts: Gender, Rebellion, and Rock 'n' Roll* (Cambridge, MA: Harvard University Press, 1995), 191–227.

just correspond to New Age's drift into tranquility and boundlessness" but also gestures to evolutionary enlightenment and the drug trip. Never mind that musical progressivism, visionary technological futurism, and outer-space psychedelia were all endemic to the grassroots New Age subcultures of the 1970s and '80s—"ambient house" by 1990 was poised to reclaim holistic techno-utopianism from a mainstreamed, industry-bought new age genre, and to rescue atmospheric immersion from the middlebrow aesthetic conservatism and feminized regime of care it seemed to represent. In short, the term defined a new, hip style of high-middlebrow head music for Generation X.

In addition to increasing media attention, the "ambient house" tag also found a foothold in The Orb's mounting popularity and record sales in 1990. "A Huge Ever Growing Pulsating Brain" quickly gained exposure thanks to its positive reception by influential BBC Radio One DJ John Peel, who regularly spun the track on his program and invited the duo to record a remixed version at BBC's Maida Vale Studios, eventually sending the track to #78 on the UK singles chart in July 1990. The single had also gotten a boost from the Italian label DFC's *Ambient House* compilation, which found popular distribution throughout Europe and Japan, further spreading the "ambient house" tag in association with The Orb. Although most other tracks in the collection were largely indistinguishable from Balearic-style "new age house" (aka "dream house" in and around Italy), The Orb's track appeared prominently on the B-side, with DFC promising in the sleeve notes "a revolutionary new form of dance music that mixes moody atmospheric sounds of new age and ambient music with pulsating house beats."[33]

As The Orb and the "ambient house" tag quickly garnered attention in the press and on air, various record labels leapt at the prospect of promoting album-friendly electronic music and sought to sign the duo. Cauty, who wished to release The Orb's album-in-progress on his own label, clashed with Paterson, who wanted to sign to Big Life Records, and so the duo split in April, with Paterson retaining the band name and Cauty retaining the session recordings. Paterson soon after teamed up with Martin Glover (DJ Youth) and Kris "Thrash" Weston to assemble "Little Fluffy Clouds," a blissed-out acid-house anthem boasting samples from a Rickie Lee Jones interview, Steve Reich and Pat Metheny's *Electric Counterpoint*, Ennio Morricone's "The Man with the Harmonica," and Henry Nilsson's "Jump into the Fire." The single,

[33] Claudio Collino, Cutmaster G, and Ricky Persi, liner notes to *Ambient House: The Compilation by DFC*, BCM Records, BCM 50422, 1990, CD.

which also sported a drumless "ambient" mix, landed at #87 on the UK singles chart, fueling anticipation for The Orb's debut album. By the time *The Orb's Adventures beyond the Ultraworld* debuted in April 1991, reaching #29 on the UK album charts, the group had proved there was a wide market for similarly "ambient" EDM records.

The staying power of "ambient" in EDM circles, proved somewhat surprising given that "ambient house" was conceived in equal parts as a promotional fad and piss-take.[34] The idea of dance music "without a beat" easily read as an oxymoronic, self-conscious gimmick, especially given the stylistic penchant for overtly kitschy, "new agey" nature sounds. The revival of unhip prog-rock pretentiousness in The Orb's samplings of Steve Hillage, visual references to Pink Floyd, and "symphonic" length recordings exuded irony in the context of a scene built around ego loss. Cauty, moreover, already had a widespread reputation as a prankster, having had reached #1 on the UK singles chart in 1988 with the KLF's novelty song "Doctorin' the Tardis," a satirically bone-headed mash-up of Gary Glitter's "Rock and Roll" with the *Doctor Who* theme. Cauty, in a February 1990 interview, affirmed that the "ambient house" moniker was made of mischief:

> We're dead serious about the music, but the name was a joke. It was never intended to be played in a club—it was for when you got home afterwards. But then suddenly everyone wanted to interview us about it. I don't know what it is they're latching onto, because there isn't a "scene." There isn't anything at all. People keep ringing me to ask if I want to DJ at their New Age night, but I've only got four records![35]

When the KLF released their ambient house album *Chill Out* that same month, their own Pink Floyd–referencing album cover—sheep lounging in a typically English pastoral field—not so subtly suggested an analogy between the album's listeners and the compliant animals depicted on the cover (Fig. 4.3). And yet, as a 1993 *Wire* feature later observed, even though the KLF's album was thrown together partly in jest, its concept nonetheless "caught on when it turned out that irony was not after all a raver-characteristic."[36]

[34] As Paterson himself reflected in 1994, "We're just chuffed that our albums sell 100,000 copies; not bad for a group which started as a joke." Neil Spencer, "Pilots of Inner Space for Ecstasy Kids," *The Observer*, June 5, 1994, 5.

[35] Sheryl Garratt, "Welcome to the *Hippydrome*," *The Face*, February 1990, 49.

[36] "An A–Z of Ambient," *The Wire*, July 1993, 10.

(a)

(b)

Figure 4.3. Album covers for the KLF's *Chill Out* (Wax Trax!, 1990) and Pink Floyd's *Atom Heart Mother* (Harvest, 1970).

Enter the Ambient Room

As a style tag for recorded EDM, "ambient" largely signaled the music's suitability for laid-back home listening. "We want The Orb to be a Sunday afternoon experience," as Paterson told the *Toronto Star* in 1991. "It's a relaxation period in our very, very rushed lives. It's primarily not for dancing; you should deal with it sitting down."[37] Ravers, however, sought solace in ambient audio at parties as at home. The "ambient" tag appropriately captured the music's aptness for use in chill-out rooms, aka "ambient rooms." As with earlier space rock and concurrent "ambient house" records, chill-out-room DJing did not necessarily divert sonic focus so much as diffuse it, permitting one's attention to wander from one sonic element to another, or to and from the music entirely. The music in these areas also permitted conversation better than did the thunderous dance beats outside. Yet perhaps even more than deconcentration or ignorability, what the ambient name advertised for the "E generation" was the music's calming, immersive, mind-expanding, and style-traversing potential.

Excursions in ambience persisted through the first years of the '90s European rave underground in tandem with, and partly as a counterbalance to, the rise of hardcore techno (aka hardcore or 'ardkore). At the time, big-room UK DJs frequently favored British, Belgian, and Dutch tracks with thudding four-on-the-floor kicks, dubwise and subbass-heavy basslines, and distorted, body-pummeling hip-hop drum breaks ("breakbeats"). As tempos increasingly sped over the first half of the '90s, reaching 160 BPM and up around 1993–94, ambient became the antidote. "Everything was just getting faster and faster and more intense," recalls DJ/producer Jonah Sharp (SpaceTime Continuum) of the early '90s UK rave scene. "That's how the ambient or chill out room came about. You had to have it, because the music was so fucking intense that you had to go and chill out somewhere."[38]

By most clubgoer accounts, "chilling out" was synonymous with coming down. The ambient room gave ravers a space to ease out of the ecstasy or amphetamine highs that prolonged and fed the manic dance-floor intensity. "The role of drugs in this can't be overestimated," as Chicago rave organizer David Prince reflected in 1994. "As the beats per minute would accelerate to about 180 or so, you'd pop something to keep going in the middle of the

[37] Peter Howell, "Ex-Bandmates Finally See Eye to Eye on Orb," *Toronto Star*, November 20, 1991, B1.

[38] Anniss, "Ambient House."

night. At some point, the legs just stop, but your brain is still going. So the answer to that became the ambient room."[39] The combination of exhausted bodies and buzzing brains was conducive to absorbed musical exploration, as Kevin Foakes, DJ/producer and party organizer, emphasizes. "If you're raving all night on whatever drugs, you really do want to chill out at some point, and you can find yourself quite happily in one place for hours, as time can be elastic, soaking up new music."[40]

In contrast to the relentlessness of hardcore, ambient room DJs took the opportunity for freeform stylistic and technical exploration. The music played in ambient rooms was scarcely reducible to a singular "ambient house" or "chill-out" style, but rather showcased a variety of downtempo and melodic electronic styles from deep house to dub, cosmic rock to trip-hop. "It was an opportunity as a DJ to get creative with genres and bring in musical elements from outside the dance music world," recalls Sharp, whose recounting of the chill-out room palette is nearly indistinguishable from some *Hearts of Space* playlists: "Terry Riley, Quincy Jones, dub reggae, new age, world music, Krautrock, Tangerine Dream, and so on."[41] Experimentation with unusual, off-the-grid sounds was key. "Ambient gave people permission to play weird records that didn't have heavy 4/4 beats," as Foakes remembers. "People would go off and find their own way, their own path. It was very random, experimental. There weren't really any rules."[42]

Exemplifying the cross-generic experimentation of the ambient room were the DJ sets of Mixmaster Morris (aka The Irresistible Force), who quickly became a central node within the UK's expanding chill-out circuit. Formerly a DJ on pirate radio and on tour with psychedelic electronic jam band The Shamen, Morris found inspiration in The Orb's pathbreaking sets at Land of Oz. In 1991, Morris made a name for himself through various ambient compilations and singles, eventually taking over as The White Room DJ for Heaven's new Monday night, Madlands. Over the next several years, Morris would become an outspoken champion of electronic-experimentalism-in-the-name-of-ambient, piecing together marvelously left-field trips using curious spoken-word samples and cutting-edge tracks by the likes of Carl Craig, William Orbit, Move D, The Black Dog, B12, Global Communication, and Pete Namlook, as well as '70s and '80s space music from Paul Horn,

[39] Greg Kot, "Subversive Sound Sculpture—with a Beat," *Chicago Tribune*, June 5, 1994.
[40] Kevin Foakes, interview with author, July 23, 2019.
[41] Jonah Sharp, interview with author, August 23, 2019.
[42] Foakes, interview with author.

Popol Vuh, Tomita, Kraftwerk, Terry Riley, Laraaji, and Tonto's Expanding Head Band.

Yet despite ambient DJs' mantra of "no rules, no limits," there were trends. The sampledelic cross-genre experimentation of chill-out sets, as the following sections illuminate, became conventionalized by ambient house records in particular musical ways, including a general avoidance or muting of obtrusive low-frequency features like bass leads or kicks, deemphasis of percussive sounds, slower (or nonexistent) tempi, and/or plateaus of sustained sounds and samples with no underlying percussion. This consistent deemphasis of the drum-and-bass "beat" implied a difference in sonic purposing from other EDM, since ambient house, without a banging groove to make you move, invited states of dreamy relaxation, immersed contemplation, or detached chill.[43] Alongside this redefinition, a thematic of psychic transport contrasted with EDM's thematizations of bodily motion. The body may have stilled, but the head could keep on tripping.

Traveling without Moving through Ambient House Records

Ambient house producers of the early 1990s regularly adopted the self-reflexive themes of nature and transport extending back through Eno's *Ambient* series and earlier ambient audio by sculpting and metaphorizing records in terms of "traveling without moving" through natural and outer spaces. These vehicular trips send listeners through uninhabited geographical and celestial dreamscapes, symbolically affirming the utility of recorded music as a vehicle of social and somatic disengagement. The recurring motif of "traveling without moving" represents as it configures the private pleasures of physical relaxation and free-floating deconcentration. Fluctuating synth lines and sundry samples, alternately connected to and disconnected from motoric grooves, thematize the roaming departures into "head space" that listeners' audio devices enable in real time. In this section, I pull together some common technical elements, narrative techniques, and stylistic threads that conventionalized ambient's traveling topic in some of the best-known ambient albums of the 1980s and early '90s.

[43] Marc Weidenbaum, *Selected Ambient Works Volume II*, 33⅓ Series (New York: Bloomsbury Academic, 2014), 23.

Figure 4.4. Album cover for the KLF, *Space* (KLF Communications, 1990).

After The Orb's initial split, Jimmy Cauty gathered the remaining material he and Paterson composed in earlier sessions, removed Paterson's contributions, and released this material on the album *Space* in July 1990 under the Space alias (Fig. 4.4). Described in the press release as a "roller-coaster ride around the solar system," *Space*'s eight tracks, named after the planets (excepting Earth), soar on Cauty's Oberheim OB-8 synth out from Mercury toward Pluto.[44] Mid-tempo rhythmic arpeggios intermittently propel the tour forward over *Space*'s sparse thirty-eight minutes; but long stretches of vacuum-sealed silence, or gentle whooshing and whirring sound effects, occupy nearly as much time on the album, not so much killing momentum as relinquishing it to drift. The muffled sound of a rocket blasting as heard from inside recurs throughout, as do angelic soprano and operatic mezzo-soprano vocalises echoing wildly from a distance. Airborne

[44] KLF Communications, "K.L.F. Communications Info' Sheet Nine," June 1990, https://klf.fandom.com/wiki/KLF_BIOG_009.

spoken-word samples careen from one side of the stereo field to the other, bumping up against clips from a Morricone soundtrack, Snap!'s hip-house hit "The Power," loops of Holst's *The Planets* suite, and "Twinkle Twinkle Little Star" creepily pitch-shifted up to sound like *The Wizard of Oz*'s Lullaby League, all curious attractions dotting *Space*'s bounding voyage. Nature sounds, at last, follow the rapid, intense plunge back to Earth: winds bellow, birds caw, waves churn.

Paterson likewise maintained a connection with outer-space travel as The Orb. With a huge roster of co-producers, engineers, and writers to the project name, The Orb released the double album *The Orb's Adventures beyond the Ultraworld* to broad critical acclaim in April 1991. Poppier than *Space*, but similar in concept, *Ultraworld* sails outward from home to the galaxy unknown. The excursion lasts for nearly two hours, blasting from Earth's "Little Fluffy Clouds" into lunar orbit and beyond: through tabla-laced spiritual jazz ("Back Side of the Moon"), soothing fusion reminiscent of Mark Isham or David Sylvian's jazz-pop ("Spanish Castles in Space," "Star 6 & 7 8 9"), hyped-up hip-hop-meets-dancehall dubtronica ("Perpetual Dawn"), and slowed acid-house funk ("Earth (Gaia)," "Outlands"). *Ultraworld* also flies high on looping synths strung together with heavenly choirs, snatches of dissimilar tunes such as Kraftwerk's "Europe Endless" and Gregorio Allegri's *Miserere*, and NASA-derived samples of space travel—many of which came from a documentary film about the Apollo moon missions, *For All Mankind* (1989), for which Brian Eno composed a soundtrack.

Eno's film soundtrack, although not itself an ambient house record, bears mention for its similarities to, and influence on, these early ambient house records. *Apollo: Atmospheres and Soundtracks*, an LP composed with the assistance of Eno's brother Roger Eno and producer/guitarist Daniel Lanois, emerged in 1983 when the release of the film (originally titled *Apollo*) became indefinitely stalled. According to the album's liner notes, the music sought to capture the "grandeur" and "strangeness" that Eno imagined of the moon missions, qualities he felt got obscured by the chattery news coverage of the event.[45] The music's airy, glassy string pads; gentle harp and piano; and distant echoes of uncertain origin evoke weightlessness in vast space. The second half of the LP also prominently features pedal steel guitar licks and glides, pitch-shifted and processed heavily with reverb and delay to create, in

[45] Brian Eno, liner notes for *Apollo: Atmospheres & Soundtracks*, Brian Eno, Roger Eno, and Daniel Lanois, EG, EGCD 53, 1990, CD. Originally released in 1983.

Lanois's words, a "celestial twang."[46] Eno had found it appropriate that many of Apollo's astronauts took country records with them for their exploration of the so-called final frontier, and so he sought to create a "frontier space music" to accompany this pioneering space exploration.[47] This associative link was not circumstantial; throughout the twentieth century, the US West served as a popular metaphor for both sky and outer space, zones of increasing travel and prospective settlement by humans.[48] The eerie echoes swirling around Lanois's pedal steel also recall the reverberant productions of midcentury country-western music that, as Peter Doyle has detailed, often connoted the mystical or dream "inner" space of the lone outlaw cowboy.[49]

Eno's use of pedal steel on *Apollo* evidently made its mark on Cauty, who did the same on the KLF's ambient house album, *Chill Out* (1990). Recorded with Bill Drummond in a live take at Cauty's South London studio, *Chill Out* depicts an imaginary journey from the southern tip of Texas up the Gulf Coast to Louisiana. Yet unlike the spacebound manifest destiny of *Apollo*, *Chill Out*'s prominent pedal steel is connected specifically to earthbound terrain. Many of the album's other sonic signifiers are only occasionally specific to the US American West and South, and usually not by way of Texas or Louisiana: "Dream Time in Lake Jackson" showcases heavily echoed Tuvan throat singing, "Elvis on the Radio, Steel Guitar in My Soul" includes a sample of Tennesseean Elvis Presley singing "In the Ghetto" over Graham Lee's pedal steel, and "3AM Somewhere Out of Beaumont" goes from birds singing and ocean waves crashing to sheep bleating and . . . Fleetwood Mac's "Albatross"? "I've never been to those places," Drummond reflects, referring to Texas and Louisiana. "I don't know what those places are like but in my head, I can imagine those sounds coming from those places, just looking at the map."[50] The results are fanciful and eccentric, a hallucinatory US South with a musical history only conjecturally connected to its spatial and cultural makeup.

[46] Steve Ciabattoni, "Daniel Lanois: My Life in 15 Songs," *Rolling Stone*, September 19, 2016, https://www.rollingstone.com/music/music-lists/daniel-lanois-my-life-in-15-songs-108584/.

[47] Andy Gill, "To Infinity and Beyond," *Mojo*, June 1998, archived by Hyperreal, http://music.hyperreal.org/artists/brian_eno/interviews/mojo98a.html.

[48] David T. Courtwright, "The Routine Stuff: How Flying Became a Form of Mass Transportation," in *Reconsidering a Century of Flight*, ed. Roger D. Launius and Janet R. Daly Bednarek (Chapel Hill: University of North Carolina Press, 2003), 209.

[49] Peter Doyle, *Echo and Reverb: Fabricating Space in Popular Music Recording, 1900–1960* (Middletown, CT: Wesleyan University Press, 2005), especially 105–19.

[50] Ian Roullier, "Spotlight: The KLF, Chill Out," *Clash Magazine* 2, no. 5 (November 2006), http://www.ianroullier.com/interviews_and_features/klf_chillout.htm.

An even more eclectic musical sourcing came together on *Air II*, a 1994 release by producer and owner of the independent German ambient label FAX +49-69/450464, Pete Namlook. The second album of five released under Namlook's pseudonym Air, *Air II* showcases an eleven-song suite titled *Travelling without Moving*. The LP's eleven "Trips" marry synth drones and loops with sounds from around the globe: throat singers (Trip 1), tabla (2), gamelan (6), mbiras (7), didgeridoo (8), oud (9), and various other musical signifiers unspecific to a single geographic locale. As with *Chill Out*, Namlook conveys movement across vast space by assembling the music of distant places, with abstract synths suturing a fluid global totality. Like his British predecessors, Namlook also plays on visual tropes of space travel, with the album cover depicting an astronaut floating in outer space, apparently hovering above Earth's atmosphere, gazing down. The Air compilation album art invites an analogy between this space-borne astronaut on the back cover and a young clubber, lying prone in what appears to be a domestic setting, perhaps after a night out, on the front (Fig. 4.5).

As with *Music for Airports* and *Apollo*, these ambient house albums thematize passage not just in the titles and visuals, but also by sonically simulating the experience of transport. Combinations of synths, samples, and aural signifiers create metaphorical zones of vehicular dwelling and outward movement. Consistent synthesizer drones, pulsations, and arpeggios contain listeners in predictable, contained musical vehicles that, in their ongoingness and rhythmic momentum, emphasize the limitless expansiveness of space

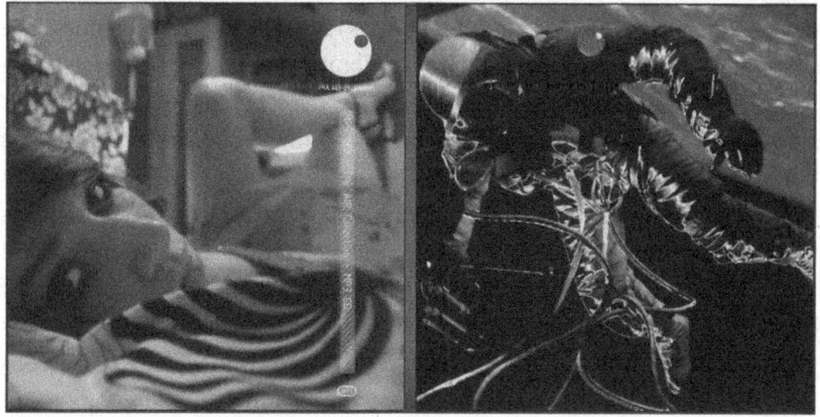

Figure 4.5. Album cover and back cover for AIR, *The AIR Collection* (Fax +49-69/450464, 2007).

traversed. Samples and nonnative sonic signifiers paint natural and outer space as frontiers, often resulting in fantastical cultural mixtures that do not represent their origins as such, but rather the traveler's ingress into psychological depth. The sounds do not harken to the world out there, but rather to the vastness of a psychic terrain "in here" where space folds into time. The delirious schizophonic samplings in these '90s records—largely stemming from the storage capacity of newly commercially available digital samplers like the Akai S900—manifest fever dreams of the hyperlinked information age, digital echoes of the cybernetic whole-earth techno-optimism of '60s psychedelia and '70s New Age. These pluralistic soundscapes, much as musicologist Phil Ford writes of 1950s exotica, conjure utopian premonitions of "imaginary worlds" known to be unreal, yet wished into reality, "incongruously thrust into a present strung with the neural extensions of electronic media."[51] Musically shaded through mixed moods of strangeness, majesty, and wonder, the ambient house albums here more nearly resemble the starry-eyed cosmic rock of Steve Hillage's *Rainbow Dome Musick* (1979) or Klaus Schulze's *Moondawn* (1976) than they do the staider, somberer ambiences of Eno or Budd.

A less enchanted observer might be more dismayed than swayed by these first-world-born white musicians baldly appropriating and recontextualizing styles developed mainly in the Global South and by musicians of color. Ambient house trips often ride the line between celebratory pluralism and a very postmodern, very chill extension of cultural imperialism. In the cases of *Chill Out* and *Air II* especially, the blissful idyll of the ambient house trip hinges on an imperialist symbolic logic that recognizes economically underdeveloped places as wondrous potentialities rather than lived actualities. The sense of expansiveness offered by these albums might even derive strength from cultural and capitalist hegemonies that depict global music culture as an open frontier while disproportionately routing its social and economic benefits to a select few.

At the same time, these albums generally spurn the spurious essentialisms that give rise to the most ethically troublesome cultural appropriations (and to the least generous critiques thereof). They largely avoid the trappings of big-label ambient-adjacent music from the turn of the '90s like Deep Forest's and Enigma's, in which uncredited aboriginal sounds tokenize natives' connection to nature or life force (Deep Forest) or stand as emblems of ancient

[51] Phil Ford, "Taboo: Time and Belief in Exotica," *Representations* 103, no. 1 (Summer 2008): 114.

mysteries (Enigma).[52] More commonly, ambient house's space-making trips do not make a spectacle of cultural difference as primitive or unknowable. Rather, in bypassing the orthodoxies of stay-in-your-lane localism and manifesting the (im)possibility of the far-flung brought near and present, ambient house's unlikely aural connections facilitate psychic escape into the temporally dilated and deconcentrated liminal spacetime of vehicular transportation as such. As the cliché goes, it's about the journey, not the destination, man.

Ambient House's Vehicular Motif

Traveling themes, of course, pervade electronic and nonelectronic dance pop alike: from Cosmic Cars and *der Autobahn* to the Mothership and Soul Train; from house back through hip hop, disco, funk, rock'n'roll; the vehicular thematization of bodily movement runs through popular dance music, typically in connection with a musical pulse, beat, or groove. Yet ambient house records, through vehicular samples and simulations, make a spectacle of departure *from* the groove through dualistic juxtapositions of grounded movement and mental flight. Sonic indexing and high/low contrasts within ambient house's rhythmic grooves synecdochally recall the physicality of EDM while renouncing EDM's imperative to dance.[53] Low percussive sounds and bass attacks are either removed or minimized relative to other sonic elements. High percussive sounds and looped or improvised melodies sew the rhythmic flow of the ambient house track, while unmetered samples and sustained tones both represent and trigger mental drift. Samples and simulations of flight through open space collide with abstract sounds and fragments of speech. Gradual transitions and consistent textures ease the experience into a smooth rather than bumpy ride—although in stops and starts, they can also display ambivalence about these movements from body into head, movement into stillness, and corporeality into immateriality.

[52] On sampling in the music of Deep Forest and Enigma, respectively, see Steven Feld, "A Sweet Lullaby for World Music," *Public Culture* 12, no. 1 (2000): 145–71; Timothy D. Taylor, "A Riddle Wrapped in a Mystery: Transnational Music Sampling and Enigma's 'Return to Innocence,'" in *Music and Technoculture*, ed. René T. A. Lysloff and Leslie C. Gay Jr. (Middletown, CT: Wesleyan University Press, 2003), 64–92.

[53] Music theorist Philip Tagg calls this sort of allusion "genre synecdoche"; see Tagg, *Music's Meanings: A Modern Musicology for Non-Musos* (New York: Mass Media Scholars Press, Inc., 2012), 524–28.

For example, Mixmaster Morris's first LP as The Irresistible Force, *Flying High* (1992), uses rhythmic grooves to conjure the physicality of house music, yet undercuts their imperative to dance by minimizing low percussive sounds and bass attacks. Suggestive samples aid the undercutting: the album opens with the sound of a plane flying overhead, followed by a sample of a man narrating a meditational exercise. "The first phase of our exercise is relaxing through concentration," he says softly, his words blurred by heavy echo. "Place a thin mat upon the floor. Or, if your floor is carpeted, this will do as well. Now, stretch out on the floor, lying flat on your back. Close your eyes . . . ." The music swells; a melodic harp loops alongside a drone, transmorphing through a continuous filter sweep, rhythmically gated to produce a gently chugging sixteenth-note pulse, with instrumental entrances rather than percussive snares or kicks defining the metric profile. Only about eleven minutes into the album, in the following track, does the faintest of kick drums skitter across the rhythmic groove—a light, syncopated tapping that disappears one minute later. It's not until about forty minutes in that a thumping four-on-the-floor beat arrives, a rarity in an album that largely rides by on cymbals high. For the supine listener, the effect is hardly a call to the dance floor, but instead presents a climactic plane of intensity in the album's full unfolding. In the sleeve notes, the phrase "*I THINK THEREFORE I AMBIENT*" appears on the backdrop of a serene, sunny sky (Fig. 4.6).

The KLF's *Chill Out* even more vividly metaphorizes "traveling without moving" with samples and simulations of moving vehicles shooting through the sonic field. The record opens with the rumble of a train and a clattering railroad; and yet, *Chill Out* does not straightforwardly depict or simulate a journey by train from one place to another, but rather replicates the roving head space of a train traveler. A plane *shooms* overhead; a song comes on; a synth arpeggio rises—assorted samples, musical grooves, and melodic riffs overlap and intersect to affectively and metaphorically recreate the rail traveler's "inner" perceptual world. Railroad samples establish an aural "first-person" perspective analogous to an extended point-of-view camera shot. These sounds fade in and out as Lee's pedal steel, Cauty's Oberheim OB-8, and other samples take over, simulating the train's disappearance and reappearance within the traveler's perceptual schema as attention drifts toward external sounds and internal feelings. Quick panning and slow crossfades indicate a traveler lost in reverie, while heavy echo and reverb conflate spatial distance with psychological departure. Body-shaking bass rumbles, car zooms, and patterned rhythms momentarily appear and disappear, briefly

Figure 4.6. "I THINK THEREFORE I AMBIENT." Booklet image from The Irresistible Force, *Flying High* (Rising High, 1992).

drawing attention back to the physical plane. Angelic choirs signal flight through open space, and the howling of wolves and bleating of sheep in the distance identify a rural setting.

The listener's immobilized body, both in anticipation and at ease, is part and parcel of this journey. A sample of an Evangelical Baptist preacher saying "get ready" repeats throughout the album as mantra, suggesting that the listener, although traveling, has yet to get a move on.[54] "Get-get-get-get-get

[54] The exact identity of the man hasn't been confirmed, but various sources speculate that the pastor is Newark-based Reverend Doctor James C. Wade, a nationally known television and AM radio evangelist during the 1960s and '70s.

ready. Get ready." The pastor's demand is consistent with the KLF's warning in a press release advertising *Chill Out*: "Don't bother trying to listen to this LP if you have neither first switched off the lights and then laid your body to rest on the floor," it reads. "Hopefully then the trip will be complete."[55]

The variegated design of the vehicular journey, with its crossfading flights of fancy, assists listener-travelers' mental drift from the music to mental images or thoughts and back. Thin textures and ample silences (particularly during the middle third of the album, such as toward the end of "Elvis on the Radio . . .") make time for even the most fully absorbed listeners to detach momentarily from the musical trip. The sounds of planes appear as aspects of the scenery, but also represent the traveler's attention taking flight from their own physical grounding and musico-vehicular extension, while train and car sounds metaphorize the vessels (the music, one's body) that enable the listener's transport.

Chill Out's sonic contrasts between road vehicles and planes also suggest a metaphorical contrast between house music's earthbound dance versus ambient's high-flying chill. Vehicular sounds and EDM tropes alternately set listeners aloft and bring them down to earth through stark contrasts of register and momentum. In "Madrugada Eterna," a nonpercussive track serenely floating along for nearly eight minutes on a B♭-F choral-pad drone, car sounds have a grounding effect. The track opens with the sound of a car zooming across the stereo field followed by furious honking. Fifty seconds later, following a dreamy pedal steel and electronic organ interlude, another Doppler-effected car careens across the stereo field from left to right (0:57). Unlike the opening sample, however, this *zoom* is chopped up into a whirring rhythmic pulsation, appearing synthetically generated rather than sampled. The *zoom* repeats at 1:03, then passes by one more time—now chugging at half speed (1:09). Was that a house track going by? The slowing effect makes a connection between the grounded vehicle, the grounded body, and physical movement as the "car" reveals itself to be a hi-hat and low-pitched synth lead, timbres reminiscent of the dancefloor DJ set. The momentary appearance of the bass-heavy pulse in the KLF's trip sharply contrasts with the lightness of the drift that surrounds it; the listener is briefly grounded by motorized sound, only to be released again to floating. In an inversion of this move, distant motorcycle and plane sounds act as

[55] KLF Communications, "K.L.F. communications Info. Sheet No. 7," December 1989, http://klf.wikia.com/wiki/KLF_INFO_SHEET_7.

distant, self-standing sonic figures untethered from the propulsive, melodic techno groove that repeatedly cuts out during "Wichita Lineman Was a Song I Once Heard" (for instance at 1:16 and 3:43), signaling the listener's release from bodily groove into mental drift.

What to make of the KLF's vehicular capriciousness? The jumbled presence of planes, trains, and automobiles throughout *Chill Out* seems to signal ambivalence about its own stilling function, heightening the oxymoronic contradiction of ambient house. The KLF sold their album as an opportunity for motionless listeners to enjoy their chill, soften their concentration, and lose themselves to reverie, absorption, or introspection; and yet, *Chill Out*'s mixed vehicular metaphors and stop-and-start grooves belie listeners' presumed inert physicality and full awareness. From start to end, the journey constantly shuttles between physical activation and deactivation, bodily motivation and passive drift, entrainment and enplanement. The album's sonic juxtapositions of the blissful and banal alternately inspire and spurn enthusiasm. With regard to its own utility as a vehicle for chilling out, *Chill Out* seems scattered, perhaps even misleading. As critic Ian McCann wrote for *Vox* in 1992, the album "was regarded as either a joke or a classic, depending on whom you spoke to."[56] "With radar bleeps, eerie sheep bleating and ominous rumbling," another *Mixmag* critic reflected, "it's more likely to induce the screaming horrors than a state of chillage."[57] Equal parts goofy and listless, starting and slack, and entirely aimless, *Chill Out* can leave listeners wondering whether the music was genuinely meant to provide a psychogeographic odyssey, or whether it had just made game of their inertia, satirizing the fact that they evidently had nowhere better to go.

The sonic figure of the train offers a key to interpreting this ambivalence, for trains have long symbolized in Western literature, music, and film the technologization of the human subject.[58] As art scholars Kodwo Eshun and Michael Jarrett observe, twentieth-century popular music (re)presents in both content and form humans' technological conditioning by vehicular transport, a phenomenon that Jarrett calls "the railroading of music."[59]

[56] Ian McCann, "Cali for an Ambience," *Vox*, November 1992, 39.

[57] Dee Johnston, "Chill Downhill," *Mixmag*, December 1999, 190.

[58] Norm Cohen, *Long Steel Rail: The Railroad in American Folksong*, 2nd ed. (Urbana and Chicago: University of Illinois Press, 2000); Lynne Kirby, *Parallel Tracks: The Railroad and Silent Cinema* (Durham, NC: Duke University Press, 1997); Wolfgang Schivelbusch, *The Railway Journey: The Industrialization of Time and Space in the Nineteenth Century* (1977; repr. Oakland: University of California Press, 2014).

[59] Kodwo Eshun, *More Brilliant Than the Sun: Adventures in Sonic Fiction* (London: Quartet, 1998); Michael Jarrett, "Train Tracks: How the Railroad Rerouted Our Ears," *Strategies* 14, no. 1 (2001): 38.

Crossfading samples and sequenced grooves, as Jarrett observes of hip-hop and ambient alike, summon a deconcentrated condition not unlike that of the train traveler who, unable to focus on nearby entities, is forced to adopt a "panoramic" gaze observing distant scenes framed by the wash of colors and textures passing nearby. The noise of the railroad, Jarrett argues, imposes a similarly deconcentrated quality of perception on the train traveler's ear: "Encased in a womb of steel, a sonorous envelope, the chronically distracted rail passenger bathes in patterned noise."[60] Nineteenth-century train travelers once found unsettling this "mechanization" of perception that occurs on trains; but for the twentieth-century traveler, this blurring of sensory experience became a regular, and even enjoyable facet of travel, a pleasure exploited by the patterned-noise-making of electronic musicians like the KLF. The mechanical grooves and arrhythmic skeins of EDM commonly produce transportive sensations like entrainment, momentum, and drift, or what Eshun calls "automotion effects."[61] No wonder vehicular representations so often accompany music that calls listeners to hop on board with the groove that en*trains* the body and mind, pulling them in lockstep with its regularity.[62]

Chill Out's trains, as semaphores for the entraining groove of EDM, extend and trope on the vehicular motif in classic house, techno, funk, and disco, circuits of signification in which motorized vehicles serve as figures of bodily participation and mimesis. This signifying chain, although not exclusive to this lineage, extends directly through the dance music of Black Americans who, since the late nineteenth century, responded to industrialized labor and electrified urban life by making the train's rhythms pleasurable to physically inhabit. Between the World Wars, the train became a regular figure in blues lyrics, while jazz grooves took on the clickety-clack of the railroad track—a sound later approximated timbrally and rhythmically in the shuffle of the tap dancer. These appropriations symbolized both national unity and freedom from hardship, their grooves inviting audiences to take up feelings of power and freedom through social

[60] Jarrett, "Train Tracks," 35. Jarrett's argument pulls from Schivelbusch, *The Railway Journey*, 58–60.

[61] Eshun, *More Brilliant Than the Sun*, 82.

[62] Significant musicological discussions of musical entrainment include Martin Clayton, Rebecca Sager, and Udo Will, "In Time with the Music: The Concept of Entrainment and Its Significance for Ethnomusicology," *ESEM CounterPoint* 1 (2004): 1–82; Tia DeNora, *Music in Everyday Life* (New York: Cambridge University Press, 2000), 78–96; Justin London, *Hearing in Time* (New York: Oxford University Press, 2012).

dance.[63] And at least since the Swing Era, identifying these pulsed rhythms as "grooves" also identified the music's capacity to move listeners spiritually and physically.

Grooves, in music theorist Anne Danielsen's words, provoke participation in "marking time with movement."[64] But the ambient house listener is not invited to "do time" with the music, at least not through physical motion; instead, ambient house presents itself as a vehicle for passive occupancy. Although house nominally receives a nod in the style label, marking the pulsed rhythms that occasionally glide through the music's textures, ambient house's drums often receive less emphasis than in much other electronic dance music. Where present, grooves tend toward stiffness: regular rhythmic patterns are often strongly quantized to the beat, eliminating the "participatory discrepancies" with the underlying pulse that can fuel groove feeling; and rhythms often distribute stress evenly across the divisions and subdivisions of the meter, minimizing or eliminating the cross-rhythms that can propel the groove.[65] The flight motif of ambient house's trips thus seems to signal a departure from house's imperative to move—groove music off the rails.

Yet for these reasons, the "ambient" of ambient house, like the flying vehicles therein, may not only signal a departure from the body, but also from the Afrodiasporic aesthetics that historically fueled EDM's motoricity. As I probe in the latter half of this chapter, there is nothing essentially "white" about ambient house's departures from the groove; yet ambient became racialized as a white style by way of a mind-body binary that locates the moving body at the center of black authenticity, and that maps disembodied mind onto racial whiteness. The racial whiteness of self-described ambient artists like Mixmaster Morris and the KLF may hence have played a role in their troping on the EDM groove as a musical topic whose field of reference is the moving body, with the figure of the airplane signaling their symbolic distance from this field. As one 1992 *Vox* feature teased (out) the connection between ambient music's evident whiteness and bodily stillness, "Many modern psychedelic drugs have rendered the white raver unable to dance, returning him to his usual un-funky state. Hence the rise of

[63] Joel Dinerstein, *Swinging the Machine: Modernity, Technology, and African American Culture between the World Wars* (Amherst: University of Massachusetts Press, 2003).

[64] Anne Danielsen, *Presence and Pleasure: The Funk Grooves of James Brown and Parliament* (Middletown, CT: Wesleyan University Press, 2006), 203.

[65] Charles Keil, "Participatory Discrepancies and the Power of Music," *Cultural Anthropology* 2, no. 3 (August 1987): 275–83; see also Weidenbaum, *Selected Ambient Works Volume II*, 23.

Ambient, ideal for the terpsichorially-challenged."[66] Ambient house's vehicular reconfigurations of the dance groove, it seems, not only represented the chill-out concept guiding the productions, but also something of the social identities of its makers.

Ambient EDM's Second Wave and the Making of a "Beatless" Popular Genre

"The Sound of the Beatless and the Stoned"

"This is post-rock, post-rave music, the sound of the Beatless and the Stoned." So summarized critic Neil McCormick in an April 1994 feature on ambient in British *GQ*, well capturing the genre's position following its growth from the "ambient house" of 1990–91 into an agglomeration of styles hyped in hip music media.[67] In that interim, a trickle of rock fans, particularly indie rockers drawn to stylistic experimentation, had come to embrace electronic music through well-publicized ambient acts like The Orb, Aphex Twin, and Brian Eno, with some even unironically regarding electronica as the rock of the future. Meanwhile as the rave, injected with amphetamines and furious breakbeats, went from an under- to overground phenomenon, clubbers resistant to EDM's mainstreaming sought in ambient psychedelia an alternative to raving, if not altogether a replacement for it. Ambient's enveloping timbral explorations, of course, also continued to magnetize stoners both within and outside these post-rock, post-rave crowds, matching and replicating the cloudy, ruminative detachment of the cannabis mellow.

But "Beatless"? As music writer Marc Weidenbaum notes, "beatless" became the operative word in 1990s music journalism to describe this new crop of ambient music, despite the fact much of it still bore a pulse, looped rhythms, and percussive beats derived from EDM.[68] Moving toward the mid-'90s, however, post-rockers and post-ravers adopted the standalone "ambient" to categorize the least percussive of these derivations, giving Eno's concept new life as genre. Producers and DJs increasingly regarded "ambient" as the abstraction of an EDM recording—the "ambience" of the track, without the skeletal "beat." "The presence of a beat defines dance music," as

[66] McCann, "Cali for an Ambience," 42.
[67] Neil McCormick, "The Big Chill," *British GQ*, April 1994, 119–23.
[68] Weidenbaum, *Selected Ambient Works Volume II*, 11–32.

DJ/producers Ewan Pearson and Jeremy Gilbert summed in their 1999 EDM study *Discographies*. "The absence of one defines 'ambient' proper."[69]

McCormick's "Beatless," however, refers to ambient's genre culture in addition to the music, at once punning on the Beat Generation (and The Beatles) while also metaphorizing ambient listeners' presumed disinclination to dance. All such referents, more to the point, find common association with the white bohemian, a cultural figure—usually male—too aloof or in-his-head to connect with the pulse of life around him. Which is just where McCormick proceeds with his description of ambient: "It is made," he continues, "almost exclusively, by white men who were tiring of the rave scene and never had much rhythm anyway." Interviewee Phil Hartnoll of Orbital supports the estimation. "At the moment this is the most horribly male-dominated kind of music there is," Hartnoll avers. "It's very white too. Men and their buttons."[70] The two were not alone with such observations; a small handful of critics and musicians around 1993–94 contested the terms by which the "ambient" genre label coalesced almost exclusively around white and light-skinned artists. "The media gives us one idea of what ambience is about," summarily notes DJ/producer Tony Thorpe in a 1994 *DJ Mag* article. "But they don't seem to want to acknowledge the part that black music has always played."[71]

Between the early- and mid-1990s, media discourses around ambient's "beatlessness" largely located the genre's cerebral hipness in the music of white men, and through distinction from genres gendered feminine (like new age) and racialized as nonwhite (like house, or popular music as a whole). In regularly canonizing the contributions of light-skinned men, these discourses tacitly configured ambient music as an expression of hip highbrow white masculinity. Concomitant representations of ambient music as the emanation of disembodied minds (rather than of individuals), in combination with blanket claims to ambient having "no rules," derived from and reinforced gendered and racial stereotypes rendering white masculinity transcendent and universal, and accordingly sanctioned the regular omission of women and nonwhite artists from the ambient genre. The latter half of this chapter exhumes these discourses, as well as the underground ambient scenes of the UK that informed this genre construction.

[69] Jeremy Gilbert and Ewan Pearson, *Discographies: Dance Music, Culture and the Politics of Sound* (New York: Routledge, 1999), 94.

[70] McCormick, "The Big Chill," 120–21.

[71] Andy Chrysell, "Shhhhhhhhhhh," *DJ Mag*, May 12–25, 1994, 27.

Brain Candy? Ambient Techno and IDM

The rise of ambient techno in the United Kingdom portended chill out's second wave. Detroit techno's postsoul electrofunk, although already present in the United Kingdom's late-1980s rave wave, became increasingly pronounced in European club nights and chill-out areas in the early '90s. Local DJs and producers took cues from originators like Derrick May, as well as from newer contemporaries like Carl Craig (Psyche/BFC) and Octave One, who occasionally convoked misty pads, warm synth strings, and cloudy atmospherics moving slowly over a warped groove. Mixmaster Morris championed Craig's work as a model. "Carl Craig was making ambient techno as far back as '87 or '88," Morris remarked of Craig's "Neurotic Behavior" demo, a dusky synth-strings-and-sequencer odyssey that Craig later, with May, reworked into a dance track. "His first track was totally ambient, and when he took it to the record label, they said 'Put some drums on it and speed it up.' That's what record labels used to say."[72] Now, however, a handful of independent European record labels were signing artists like The Black Dog, B12, Plaid, and Stasis, who sought to "do the UK equivalent" of Detroit techno.[73] "Ambient techno" became shorthand for this style.

During this time, "ambient techno" was in print and industry media also becoming synonymous with any and all EDM-for-home-listening, increasingly a selling concept in the LP-oriented record industry. By the end of 1992, artists like Aphex Twin, Future Sound of London, Ultramarine, System 7, and Biosphere had contributed techno albums waving the ambient banner, and record labels like FAX, Apollo, Beyond, and Rising High boasted specialization in ambient. But perhaps most responsible for popularizing home-listening EDM—especially among listeners outside the European rave scene—was Sheffield label Warp Records. Coming hot off several dance-floor hits, and encouraged by The Orb's success, Warp's owners were eager to showcase music "that had a reference to dance music but wasn't aimed at the dancefloor."[74] They gathered several tracks for the 1992 compilation (and later series) *Artificial Intelligence*, a title that label cofounder Rob Mitchell proposed to lampoon stereotypes of EDM production as

[72] Rob Green, "Licensed to Chill: Mixmaster Morris," *The Mix*, December 1994, 100–102.

[73] Oli Warwick, "Welcome to the New Age Disco: The Untold Story of London Techno, 1989–1997," *Red Bull Music Academy*, July 16, 2015, https://daily.redbullmusicacademy.com/2015/07/london-techno-untold-story.

[74] Benji B, interview with Steve Beckett, *Red Bull Music Academy*, 2007, https://www.redbullmusicacademy.com/lectures/steve-beckett-the-warp-factor.

computer-automated rather than human-driven.[75] Yet when the collection, marketed by the label as "electronic listening music" or "armchair techno," sold beyond expectations, the irony evaded some fans, several of whom in '93 started referring to the music therein as "intelligent dance music" (IDM) or "intelligent techno."[76] The tag caught on with new listeners, many of whom had listened mostly to rock, never participated in a rave, and evidently dismissed club-oriented music as unintelligent.[77] Accordingly, while the busy, spiky percussion and intricate rhythmic knots associated with the *AI* series bore little stylistic continuity with earlier ambient audio, the music's orientation toward the home listener led journalists, fans, and artists to apply the "ambient" label to the records' "headphone techno."[78]

The rise of IDM dovetailed with ambient music's discursive orientation around intelligence, which reversed the valence of hardcore techno culture's mind-oriented lingo. Whereas 'ardcore fans spoke positively of their favored music as "mental," "nutty," and brain-damaging, Britain's chillmongers understood their music as heady and brain-awakening.[79] "Over the last five years techno got faster, harder and more macho," reflected Mixmaster Morris in 1993. "I hate that. I want people to make music that is more emotionally engaging, strange, and more effective at stimulating minds."[80]

As more and more artists—almost entirely white European men, despite the music's Black American influences—around 1992 became associated with ambient techno, critics increasingly insisted that the somatic and perceptual ease of the ambient experience did not preclude artistic daring or cognitive insight: as Ian McCann wrote for *Vox* in '92, ambient music, unlike new age, is "adventurous" and "a challenging musical genre"; while a '93 *Newsweek* feature by Joshua Cooper Ramo proposed ambient may offer, if

[75] Erik Morse, "Warp Records and the Birth of Popular Electronic Music," *The Believer* 73, July 1, 2010, https://believermag.com/warp-records-and-the-birth-of-popular-electronic-music/.

[76] The term "intelligent dance music" was coined in August 1993 by the eponymous electronic mailing list related to *Artificial Intelligence* and Aphex Twin. The list was hosted on Hyperreal, an online forum originally dedicated to the San Francisco rave scene.

[77] Warp cofounder Steve Beckett recalls the 1993 "See the Light" US tour as a particular turning point in the popularization of electronic listening music among rock fans: "It was during that time when we first started switching kids who were into indie rock and had always dismissed electronic music as mindless music for idiots. And they started to realize it had a lot more depth to it than that." Morse, "Warp Records."

[78] Sherman, "Twin Bleeps: The Aphex Twin, *Selected Ambient Works '85–'92*," *New Musical Express*, November 21, 1992, 36.

[79] Reynolds, *Energy Flash*, 50, 112.

[80] Alix Sharkey, "Saturday Night: The Techno Ice-Cream Van Is on Its Way," *The Independent*, June 26, 1993, 35.

not "a route to enlightenment," at least "brain candy."[81] As with their psychedelic and new-age predecessors, ambient records were commonly described as psychoactive, producing altered states of consciousness; as Joe Brown wrote for the *Washington Post* in '93, ambient is "techno-trance music for meditating, daydreaming, hallucinating. (Warning: Don't use when driving or operating heavy machinery.)"[82] Yet these intoxicating records, and the listening culture surrounding them, were also commonly deemed "progressive," "experimental," and "cerebral"; ambient was "more subversive" than new age, and "more reflective than heart-pumping techno."[83] In short, ambient recoded new-age ease and EDM ecstasy in terms of stoner chill, underground weird, and detached intellectualism—which, not coincidentally, aligned ambient's musical ideals with idealizations of hip highbrow white masculinity.

Not Just a Comedown: The '90s UK Ambient Scene

As a transatlantic market for "electronic listening music" and "ambient techno" coalesced between 1992 and '94, the updated sounds of ambient also suffused and consolidated a heady translocal music scene radiating out from London. Finding footholds in digital-age cyber-optimism and technophilia, in a resurgence of interest in psychedelic drugs like LSD and ketamine, and in the explosion of novel ambient/EDM fusions from UK producers, practitioners in the ambient scene circulated opportunities for achieving altered states of mind and embodiment through immersive electronic ambiences. For this loose coalition of countercultural types, "ambient" emblematized mental liberation from the limits of physical embodiment, signaling less a singular musical style than a collective astral dream-space.

Prior to ambient EDM's second wave, Balearic clubs and a handful of raves had toyed with new-age concepts and sounds, including Whirl-y-gig—the long-standing acid-soaked "world" electronica night ending with an ambient-soundtracked "parachute dance"—and Steve Strange's short-lived Dream Age at the Hippodrome. Most spectacularly making way for

[81] McCann, "Cali for an Ambience," 42; Joshua Cooper Ramo, "Cruising to Enlightenment," *Newsweek*, November 15, 1993, 84A.

[82] Joe Brown, New Wrinkles in Ambient Time, *Washington Post*, January 1, 1993, n16.

[83] Greg Kot, "Subversive Sound Sculpture—with a Beat"; Neil Spencer, "Samplers Full of English Embroidery," *The Observer*, August 29, 1993, 50.

ambient's second coming, however, was Spacetime, the first major party wherein ambient DJ sets played more than a secondary role. Beginning in late 1989, the East London studio party drew special attention for the whimsical artistry set forth by the hosts, fashion designers Richard Sharpe and Mia Manners, who decked the space in suspended holographic foils. Although invite-only at first, the party generated buzz when it turned out technoheads equally enjoyed socializing in less dance-centric musical environments. Sets and live performances by resident DJ Mixmaster Morris (donning Sharpe's holographic clothing), as well as Jonah Sharp, Paul Hartnoll of Orbital, and Mr. C of The Shamen, took partygoers on rides from freeform space music to pumping techno and back.[84] "The eccentric decor created an environment where musical exploration was really at home," recalls Jonah Sharp, who also promoted the event. "We would play records across genres and also attempt live sets—there were no limits to what we could do; we were experimental above all else."[85] Although Spacetime shut down in 1992 due to overcrowding, the party's rapid ascent in popularity forecasted ambient's quiet boom.

Later in 1992, Telepathic Fish, a South East London "ambient tea party," became a beacon for the newly forming ambient microscene. The initial December event was one of many squat parties in London that, at the time, were regularly attracting hundreds of attendees with top-shelf DJs and the promise of a truly underground experience. Telepathic Fish's organizers—a miniature collective of art students, DJs, and computer programmers who called themselves Openmind (Fig. 4.7)—first modeled their underground event on the postrave chill out.[86] "After raves we used to chill out in each others' bedrooms," explained Kevin Foakes, one of Openmind's four. "Now we've turned the bedroom into a party."[87] On this first night, roughly three hundred attendees flocked to the collective's East Dulwich apartment where the living room appeared upside-down (the ceiling had been painted like a floor, and included an inverted bucket and mop) and a side room contained mattresses and a pile of stacked TVs airing music videos. After paying the £1 entrance fee, partygoers could lounge, drink Indian tea, spliff up, and daze out to the all-night set by Mixmaster Morris (coming in live from the kitchen!). The event's success led the group to secure a larger warehouse space in

[84] Anniss, "Ambient House."
[85] Sharp, interview with author.
[86] Openmind's members included Kevin Foakes, Chantal Passamonte, David Vallade, and Mario Tracey-Aguera.
[87] Reynolds, *Energy Flash*, 174.

Figure 4.7. Openmind collective & Telepathic Fish DJs; from top to bottom: Kevin Foakes (aka Strictly Kev/DJ Food), Mario Aguera, Chantal Passamonte (aka Mira Calix), David Vallade. Photographer unknown. ©1994 Openmind. Used by permission.

Brixton for the following iterations in May, July, and October 1993, for which digital-chic flyers announced "ambient frequencies and trance transmissions all night" along with "deep sea decor" and "21st century visuals" (Fig. 4.8). On the decks appeared Openmind DJs, as well as Morris and Aphex Twin, with Matt Black (Coldcut) doing computer-generated projections, and a giant amoeba (or jellyfish, depending on whom you asked) continuously inflated and deflated by a vacuum cleaner motor. By this time, Openmind had

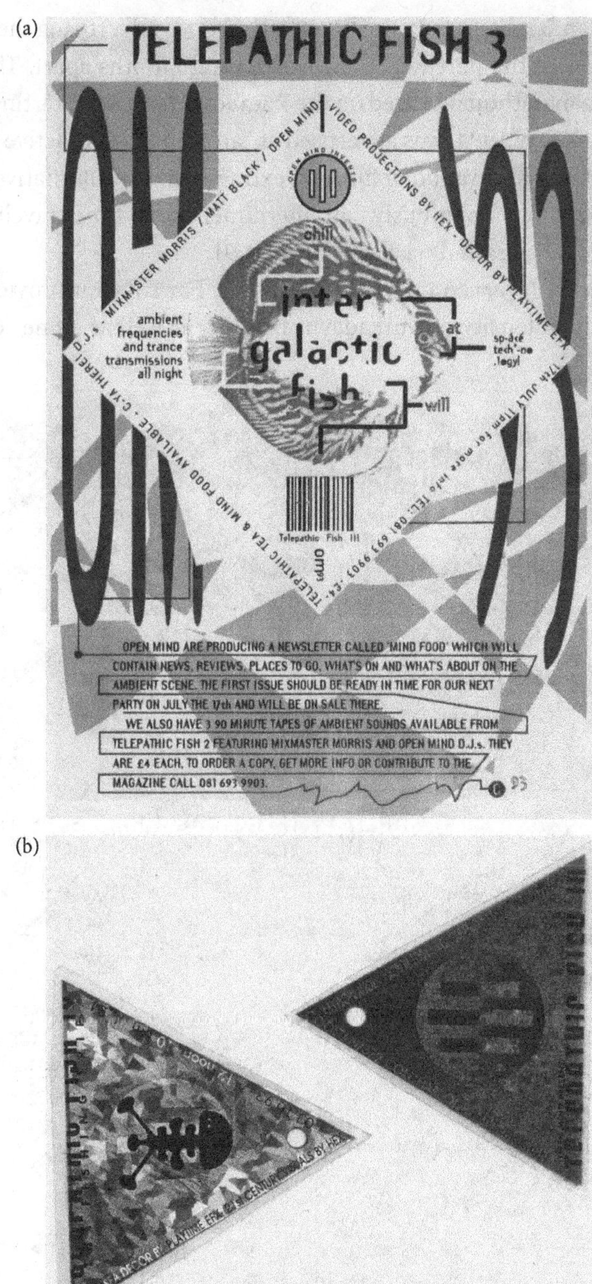

Figure 4.8. Telegraphic Fish 3 & 4 flyers and holographic foils. Design by Openmind. ©1993 Openmind. Used by permission.

also started an "ambient fanzine" titled "Mindfood" advertising the next several iterations of the party, each thrown several months apart. The group's final event, a marathon modeled on the Rainbow Gathering starting at 6 a.m. on New Year's Day 1994, was advertised as "an ambient eco-active gathering of the tribes and celebration of life," "an extravaganza of alternative and DIY culture," and, most ambitiously, "an interdimensional time traveling day of higher consciousness and relaxation" (Fig. 4.9).

Telepathic Fish served numerous purposes. For some, it provided an escape from the intensity of workaday urban life, as well as a fine comedown

Figure 4.9. Flyer for Openmind's Roundhouse New Years Day 1994 event. Designer unknown. ©1993 Openmind. Used by permission.

from a weekend of hard raving. "Our parties are as close to getting it together in the country as you can get in London," Openmind member Chantal Passamonte (aka Mira Calix) said in 1993.[88] As Foakes recalls, the events doubled as art installations and performance venues for the budding DJs and VJs in Openmind.[89] But perhaps most significantly, the party's DJs brought together styles like hip hop, dub, dream pop, progressive trance, and ambient techno in the name of a singular fantastical, absorbing musical experience. As one *Mindfood* writer reflected of the second Telepathic Fish, "It was chilling out for the sake of it, not just a comedown from something more frantic; being enveloped by the ambience instead of just ignoring it."[90]

Telepathic Fish served as a catalyst for a handful of ambient-centric events in London and elsewhere over the next several years, many of which likewise offered immersive audio, eye-popping visuals, and New Age "paratechnologies" social and cerebral.[91] The Ambient Club at Jackson's Lane Community Theatre in Highgate, for instance, promised to "digress your stress" with "spatial sounds," kinetic projection, multiscreen video, CD mobiles, smart drinks, massage, and a brain machine.[92] The Big Chill, an all-Sunday event at Islington's Union Chapel, boasted "Global Ambient Soundscapes" as well as an art gallery, board games, café, tea stall, a jamming room, a children's area, and free internet access.[93] North of the border, in Edinburgh's The Cooler, The Blue Room soothed listeners well into Monday morning; while in Glasgow, DJ/producer JD Twitch and friends hosted a "Sunday evening soiree" called Sonora to bring in transportive live acts like Zoviet France and "beatless" DJ sets from Richie Hawtin and Andrew Weatherall.[94] And in Amsterdam, three Ambient Weekend festivals at the Melkweg drew hundreds of listeners to spacey repose.

More regular and long-lasting than these chapels of chill, however, were EDM club nights in which ambient styles, if not always the main feature, were

[88] Ibid., 175.

[89] Foakes, interview with author.

[90] JC, "Chilled," *Mindfood*, Spring 1993, n.p.

[91] I borrow the term "paratechnology" from religion scholar Olav Hammer, who uses it to describe "alternative" technologies that sport scientific rhetoric but are not accepted as scientific by academics; see Hammer, *Claiming Knowledge: Strategies of Epistemology from Theosophy to the New Age* (Boston: Brill, 2004), 239–43.

[92] Brain machines, also known as mind machines, use rhythmic patterns of light and sound, purportedly to produce changes in brain wave activity.

[93] The weekly Big Chill event gave birth to the eponymous annual music festival in 1995 that, over the years, grew to attract tens of thousands of visitors.

[94] "FACT mix 214: Optimo," January 17, 2011, https://www.factmag.com/2011/01/17/fact-mix-214-optimo/.

crucial ingredients within an assortment of electronic styles and sounds. Oscillate, a series of Birmingham club nights initiated in '92 by Scylla Magda and Bobby Bird, was one of the first. Flyers advertised a "total ambient groove" for "maximum mental hygiene," with ambient dub and techno sets keeping crowds moving amid junk-art lighting installations.[95] The fortnightly Friday night party expanded in popularity over the years as it nurtured ambient-techno up-and-comers like Autechre and Higher Intelligence Agency (HIA), along with well-known acts like Orbital and The Orb's Alex Paterson, creating a much-needed venue for performers exploring musical possibilities between spaced-out chill and grinding hardcore.

Over in London, starting in '93, the quickly famed Megatripolis night gave ambient atmospherics a foregrounded presence. Fraser Clark, writer and editor for the magazine *Encyclopaedia Psychedelica* (later *Evolution*), had long predicted a digital upgrade of the New Age hippie into the tech-savvy '90s "zippie," and so he, with his partner Sionaidh Craigen, formulated the party with the goal of fusing New Age and rave cultures.[96] Attendees of their weekly "voyages" at Heaven could rave to techno and trance on the main floors, enjoy ambient and chill-out music in "The Well," and in the "Techno Silence Suite" partake in "edutainment" like lectures, film screenings, and shiatsu classes.[97] The night, as with Telepathic Fish, found favor not just with ravers drawn to weed over speed, but all sorts of "techno-hippies" as described in a 1993 feature: "crusts, squatters, doles, spliff-heads, white dreads, New Agers, post-punks, travelers, ravers." For these "diverse tribes of 1990s counterculture," ambient music had become a favored source of disembodied mental stimulation.[98]

Although Clark's "zippie" label remained more of a media buzzword than a common point of identification for the scene—Foakes recalls that so-called zippies were just one contingent within ambient's diverse coalition—the tag handily captured the cyberdelic tendencies of gatherings like Megatripolis, Telepathic Fish, and the Big Chill.[99] Clark's "zippie" figure brought the digital optimism of the 1980s and '90s to bear on the hip mysticism of the '60s and '70s, rebooting old-school psychedelia and New Age techno-therapy with

[95] Oli Warwick, "Nightclubbing: Oscillate," *Red Bull Music Academy*, June 28, 2017, https://daily.redbullmusicacademy.com/2017/06/nightclubbing-oscillate.

[96] Jules Marshall, "Zippies!," *Wired*, May 1994, https://www.wired.com/1994/05/zippies/.

[97] Megatripolis's original venue was The Marquee before moving to Heaven.

[98] Matthew Collin, "Turn On, Tune In, Sort It Out," *The Observer Life*, December 5, 1993, 4.

[99] Foakes, interview with author.

the sounds and technologies of the age of personal computing. The coinage coincided with the Californian invention of "New Edge" by the editors of cyberculture magazine *Mondo 2000* to describe the rising neopsychedelic counterculture that, at the turn of the 1990s, reconfigured "cyberspace" as a hallucinogenic "electronic frontier" beyond physical place and embodiment.[100] British fashion press spoke of zippies as seeking the thrill of the "liberating mental trip" via small-scale technologies and tools of "sexy science" like digital graphics, virtual reality, smart drugs, holograms, brain machines—and, of course, ambient music.[101] Apocryphal as such descriptions might have been, the specter of the zippie within the ambient scene was substantial enough for media commentators like *Vox* critic Ian McCann to jokingly list "zippie" technologies as "Ambient Paraphernalia" while writing that the "New Edge" school "aims to make Ambient a challenging musical genre."[102] A *Wired* magazine feature on the zippie similarly identified ambient house acts The Orb and the KLF, along with the "very chilled-out ambient-techno" found at Telepathic Fish and Megatripolis, as "zippie favorites."[103]

The new-edgy figure of the zippie occupied the midpoint between two stylistic tendences bookending the ambient microscene, with some nights leaning largely into psychedelic trance (like Megatripolis) and others pushing arty leftfield abstraction (like Oscillate). In the former camp, psychedelic and progressive styles dominated Megadog, the massively popular touring update to hippie gathering Club Dog. Megadog regularly billed top live acts from the jammier crevasses of ambient techno, trance, dub, and psych rock starting in '93, including ambient "supergroup" System 7, "New Edge folk" band Psychick Warriors ov Gaia, "ethno-ambient" act Banco de Gaia, and ambient techno bigshots like Orbital, Ultramarine, Aphex Twin, and HIA. On the other end of the spectrum, Quirky at Brixton's Vox Club leaned away from hippie and progressive trance vibes, becoming a magnet for artsier heads in the scene between 1993 and '95 by billing rising ambient stars like Seefeel, Global Communication, and Biosphere. As the UK EDM scene diversified, the slow divergence of an art-oriented highbrow electronic

[100] Turner, *From Counterculture to Cyberculture*, 162–64; Dorien Zandbergen, "Silicon Valley New Age: The Co-Constitution of the Digital and the Sacred," in *Religions of Modernity: Relocating the Sacred to the Self and the Digital*, ed. Stef Aupers and Dick Houtman, International Studies in Religion and Society (Boston: Brill, 2010), 161–86.

[101] "1990: Review of the Year," *The Face*, January 1991, 16.

[102] McCann, "Cali for an Ambience," 41–42.

[103] Marshall, "Zippies!"

underground from psychedelic and progressive scenes foretold the fragmentation of ambient's delicate coalition in the mid-'90s.

Abroad, ambient began to gain a discreet public presence in the early '90s, albeit on a smaller scale, in places like San Francisco, Frankfurt, and Tokyo. San Francisco, with perhaps the most robust rave scene in the States during the early '90s, circulated ambient music in the chill rooms of parties like A Rave Called Sharon or the Woopy Ball festival, as well as underground pop-up parties hosted by the S.P.A.Z. crew or by Jonah Sharp's Reflective Records.[104] In Frankfurt, Club XS drew large crowds for its ambient nights; while major acts like The Orb and Mixmaster Morris attracted audiences in Tokyo.

Scattered as they were, participants in the translocal ambient scene of the early- to mid-'90s were commonly bound by an appetite for unconventional musical styles and sounds, often homegrown, independently produced, and covertly distributed. "I could be playing crappy remixes of Lisa Stansfield at the Ministry for big money," as Mixmaster Morris told *The Independent* in '93, "but I'd rather nurture this scene. It's mushrooming. There are tens of thousands of people making their own electronic music at home now, and it's growing all the time."[105] To Morris's point, club nights could not have sustained the scene without the participation of small independent record labels and specialist record stores. Rockitt's Ambient Soho, established at the end of Berwick Street in late 1993, provided an especially important central hub for players in London's ambient scene by distributing homemade cassettes and small-batch releases, as well as by promoting ambient events, bringing like-minded DJs together while giving greater visibility to the genre within the city.

The public visibility of chill out's second wave, however, largely dissipated in 1995, even as events like the Big Chill Festival persisted. Ambient rooms in clubs and at parties, as Jonah Sharp and Mixmaster Morris both recall, were either replaced with "jungle rooms"—named after the more popular style of dubwise, body-rumbling drum-and-bass head music—or yet more dance floors.[106] Meanwhile, DJs still seeking experimental outlets began performing in more rarefied institutional spaces. Perhaps the counterintuitive notion of the social gathering for introspective head trips was destined to be short-lived. "I always kind of envisaged ambient as more home listening,"

104 Sharp, interview with author.
105 Sharkey, "Saturday Night," 35.
106 Sharp, interview with author; Anniss, "Ambient House."

as Foakes now reflects. "We did it in the clubs because that was the biggest outlet for it."[107] Yet as the home-listening genre drew the attention of the music media mainstream, becoming a major inlet into the EDM world for both rock and art-music converts, ambient's underground chill iced over into something much more forbidding.

The Establishment Goes Ambient

"Ambient music. Top of the charts. What can I say? I told you so." It is August 1992, a month following the debut of The Orb's *U.F.Orb* at #1 on the UK Albums chart, and Brian Eno is feeling vindicated. *New Musical Express*, the prominent off-mainstream UK rock rag that trashed his ambient records a decade prior, declares Eno "the most important man in pop," and regards *Music for Airports*, in hindsight, "one of the most influential records of the last 20 years, if not ever."[108] Two months later, The Orb grace the cover of *NME*, and the feature ponders, now that "it's hip to be weightless," whether the duo heralds "the future of rock'n'roll."[109] One month after this, in a fawning review of Aphex Twin's *Selected Ambient Works '85–'92, NME* reviewer Sherman proclaims that "the ambient theme has taken huge evolutionary step" with ambient techno, and anticipates the day when "this exciting brand of musician and music" finds widespread recognition.[110]

But ambient's rise to recognition, if *NME*'s fervor was any indication, had arrived. Up to this point, record promoters struggled to capitalize on the rave boom, having found it difficult to establish artist visibility and longevity based on EDM's singles market and lack of lead vocalists. Few critics, moreover, had an apparatus for gauging EDM's adrenaline-pumping and ass-shaking capacity, given the music press's long-standing inability to appreciate styles that put a premium on intensities of bodily sensation and pleasure.[111] Ambient's album-based head music, however, made EDM legible to pop critics and rock fans who considered contemplative headphone

[107] Foakes, interview with author.

[108] Stuart Maconie, "A Huge Ever Growing Pulsating Brian That Rules from the Centre of the Ultraworld," *New Musical Express*, August 22, 1992, 24–25.

[109] Stephen Dalton, "A Giant Bleep for Mankind," *New Musical Express*, October 10, 1992, 19.

[110] Sherman, "Twin Bleeps," 36.

[111] On the popular music press's historical aversion to styles that prize physical intensity, see Leslie M. Meier, "In Excess? Body Genres, 'Bad' Music, and the Judgment of Audiences," *Journal of Popular Music Studies* 20, no. 3 (2008): 240–60

or personal listening the best way to assess recorded music's aesthetic value. Homing in on a handful of artists with distinctive individual styles, pop mags like *NME* helped ambient achieve market parity with vaunted indie rockers in the United Kingdom between 1992 and '94, with its biggest artists regularly selling albums internationally in the tens of thousands, and with hype spreading to North America, Europe, and Japan.[112] Come March 1994, a *New York Times* feature would declare ambient to be a "booming album-based genre, appealing both to burned-out ravers and to people who never really cared for dance music in the first place."[113]

In that period, EDM tracks in ambient styles steadily gained distribution within underground markets via ever-sprouting independent labels. In addition to the labels aforementioned, the UK's Planet Dog, em:t, Sentrax, and Chill Out, as well as German label Recycle or Die, spread ambient throughout Europe; while in the United States, imprints like Kranky, Instinct, Silent, and Reflective Records began to establish ambient rosters and sublabels. Most releases on these labels had limited production and distribution through local EDM retailers during this period, but committed fans and DJs took pride in the music's subterranean delivery and publicity, whether on white-label vinyls or through dedicated World Wide Web communities like Hyperreal.[114]

More influentially for the mainstreaming of ambient, several large independent labels scooped up acts like The Orb (Island) and Future Sound of London (Virgin, who signed the duo for a whopping £400K), with some also establishing ambient-focused sublabels (like the Virgin-run Astralwerks). The hipper-than-ever Warp propelled Aphex Twin's *On* EP to #24 and *Selected Ambient Works, Vol. II* to #11 on the UK charts, while Warner Bros.-owned Sire provided international distribution. Album-length ambient compilations also proved important avenues to mainstream markets, providing broad exposure for artists otherwise unsigned or relegated to specialty retailers. The compilation format, as former Astralwerks A&R Peter Wohelski explains, allowed independents "to test the market relatively risk-free—either signed for really cheap, or [licensed] through one of their major label subsidiaries. It didn't cost them anything."[115] Among the dozens of

[112] Sharkey, "Saturday Night," 35.

[113] Simon Reynolds, "Techno Wars: A House Divided over Beats," *New York Times*, March 13, 1994, 32.

[114] On Hyperreal's ambient community, see Weidenbaum, *Selected Ambient Works Vol. II*, 63–66.

[115] Michaelangelo Matos, "How the Major Labels Sold 'Electronica' to America," *NPR*, August 18, 2011, https://www.npr.org/sections/therecord/2011/08/18/139747383/how-the-major-labels-sold-electronica-to-america.

compilations released during this period, *Ambient Dub Vols. 1–3* (Beyond), *Excursions in Ambience* (Caroline), *A Brief History of Ambient vols. 1–4* (Virgin), *Feed Your Head* (Planet Dog), and *Chill Out or Die!* (Rising High) introduced many a listener to the assorted EDM-inspired permutations of ambient audio.

And permutations, there were many. For myriad reasons—the musical omnivory of ambient DJs, the mixed subcultural coalition undergirding the UK ambient scene, the flexibility and stylistic diversity of ambient audio, the freedom permitted by the digital sampler—the second wave of ambient EDM saw a proliferation of ambient subgenres and substyles.[116] "Ambient music" came to represent an openness, even limitlessness of sonic possibilities, described by some as "genre-defying" and "music with no rules," or what critic Ian McCann, riffing on a Warp press release, called "make-up-your-own-bullshit music."[117] Ambient artists' "bullshit" still cleaved to the perennial themes of the natural, technological, and cosmic, albeit often with little regard for the sonic discretion Eno originally sought. "In keeping with its chameleon nature," as Biba Kopf wrote in a July 1993 record review, "Ambient . . . now describes anything remotely atmospheric (i.e., you can hear crickets chirruping), electronic or cosmically orientated, regardless of the Wagnerian playback settings," applications that "make a nonsense of Eno's definition."[118] Commentators often conjectured, as did Mixmaster Morris, that ambient's definition had swung wide open "as soon as it started to mean House without any drums in it."[119] But more accurately, artists were now rediscovering and reinterpreting the fluid applications of ambient audio that already preceded and exceeded Eno's original vision, but in new contexts and idioms.

For instance, indie rock and pop acts producing droning, reverberant atmospheres through guitar-band instrumentation served both as gateway drugs for electronic-music newbies and as an exciting new realm of musical possibility among scenesters. "Indie ambient" encompassed a variety of overlapping sounds, including the gauzy, sumptuous textures of '80s dream-pop

[116] Kembrew McLeod discusses the proliferation of EDM subgenres as a function of record merchandising strategies and accelerated consumerism, among other things; see McLeod, "Genres, Subgenres, Sub-Subgenres and More: Musical and Social Differentiation within Electronic/Dance Music Communities," *Journal of Popular Music Studies* 13, no. 1 (2001): 59–75.

[117] Dominic Pride, "Euro Subculture Offers Ambience with Attitude," *Billboard*, July 23, 1994, 1; Ian McCann, "Twin Speaks," *NME*, February 13, 1993, 39.

[118] Biba Kopf, "Review: *Neroli* by Brian Eno," *The Wire*, July 1993, 54.

[119] McCormick, "The Big Chill," 120.

favorites The Cocteau Twins, Lush, and Spacemen 3; the distorted washes of gentler shoegaze acts Spiritualized and Slowdive; and the grandiose soundscapes of pre-post-rockers Seefeel, Main, and Labradford. Some critics interpreted indie's ambient turn as a rejection of punk discontent and postpunk cynicism, with Simon Reynolds calling rock's new atmospherism a "a nouveau hippy riposte to grunge's punk revivalism," and with Cliff Jones regarding ambient "the hippy's revenge for the years of post-punk ridicule."[120] More directly for the "nouveau hippies" and cynical cyberpunks alike, indie ambient enabled stoned explorations of the possibilities generated by guitar pedals and reverb processors to privilege texture over meaning. Whether merely gorgeous or punker-than-punk, indie ambient bands, many of whom were signed to large imprints with international distribution, further bridged the indie rock and EDM undergrounds.

Yet as 1993 pressed into '94, some promoters and critics pushing against perceived "hippie" leanings in the genre curated alternative genealogies of ambient's sinister side. A host of style tags emerged to describe strands of electronic experimentation, especially in and around the industrial genre, that had been largely neglected in media discourses around ambient. Such labels included "ambient industrial," "dark ambient," and "isolationism," a term coined by critic and DJ/producer Kevin Martin in a September 1993 *Wire* article and popularized by his 1994 *Ambient 4: Isolationism* Virgin compilation. The "unresolvable tensions [lying] at the heart of Isolationism," Martin wrote, betray the clichéd, nature-sound-riddled "shallow utopias" dominating ambient compilations. Isolationism's distorted, dissonant, and "asocial" music, traceable through industrial, noise, dub, techno, metal, and Krautrock, "sounds as paranoid as it does panoramic," and "thankfully questions more than it answers," providing an antidote to ambient's "sedating veneer."[121] Simon Reynolds, in a follow-up piece, described isolationism as a reaction against the "cozy, dozy pleasance" of ambient artists like Pete Namlook, The Irresistible Force, and The Orb—whom he calls "closer in spirit to New Age" than ambient—turning their "nonspecific bliss" inside-out into dread.[122] Lauded isolationists like Zoviet France, PGR, Coil, Lustmord, Paul Schütze, and Asmus Tietchens, along with the music of associated labels like

[120] Simon Reynolds, "Easy Lizzzzning," *Melody Maker*, October 2, 1993, 50; Cliff Jones, "Quiet Storm," *The Face*, October 1993, 153.
[121] Kevin Martin, "Fantastic Voyage—A Personal Take," liner notes for *Ambient 4: Isolationism*, Virgin, AMBT 4, 1994, CD; Kevin Martin, "The Lonely Crowd," *Wire*, September 1993, 32–34.
[122] Simon Reynolds, "Muzak of the Fears," *ArtForum* 33, no. 5 (January 1995): 61–62.

Silent, Barooni, and Extreme, had been perfecting the art of disquiet since the 1980s; but isolationism's critics and curators also folded newer artists like Thomas Köner, Aphex Twin, and Lull into what Silent Records boss Kim Cascone called a necessary "new packaging" of long-ignored ideas in the industrial and electronic avant-gardes.[123]

Isolationism's exploration of ambient's more dour and "difficult" possibilities, marked via simplistic distinctions from ambient's psychedelic lineage, signaled and precipitated the taste-based fragmentation of the ambient scene from late 1993 into mid-decade. The seeds of this fragmentation had been planted since ambient's original highbrow distinctions from new-age ease in the 1980s, which then sprouted in ambient house's technophilic eclipsing of "new age house" in the early '90s. But by the middle of 1994, with features in the *New York Times*, *Newsweek*, *Billboard*, and the *Sunday Times*, and with compilations flooding the electronic music market, the ambient genre label had become so ubiquitous that many in the EDM underground began equating "ambient," much like "new age" before it, with marketing ploy—"the music press's most abused and misused buzz word," as one *Wire* critic wrote in June of '94.[124] The popularization of ambient, in turn, led many within the scene to renegotiate ambient's generic allegiances against an industry-polluted, overstuffed middlebrow mainstream.

As the refrain had gone for nearly a decade, "hippie," and "new age" became shorthand for this middlebrow, and for along with it the crass hip marketing, formulaic "chill-out" functionalism, and middle-of-the-road pandering that represented threats to the genre culture's core value of aesthetic risk. Bemoaning the overt pharmacological functionalism of breezy chill-out compilations, a *Wire* reviewer summarily complained that "a great deal of the Ambient music that's been released over the last year appears to have no raison d'être beyond the chill out room or as an accompaniment to altered states of consciousness."[125] Insiders instead prized music with technical and affective nuance, music irreducible to conventional psychedelic techniques and space topics. As Cliff Jones wrote in *The Face* in '93, "There's a new breed of techno chancer out there whose lazy ambient-by-numbers approach involves little more than a sound effects CD and a synth drone. The unique imagination of the sound obsessives is being lost to a cliché-ridden

[123] Kim Cascone to Hyperreal Ambient Music Mailing List, April 4, 1995, archived by Hyperreal, http://music.hyperreal.org/epsilon/info/isolationism.html.

[124] Jakubowski, "Outline: Electronica," *Wire*, June 1994, 70.

[125] Peter McIntyre, "Review: *Beauty Reports* by Media Form," *Wire*, February 1995, 55.

New Age bastard hybrid."[126] Moby, one of EDM's best-known figures at the time, echoed the sentiment in a '94 piece. "Ambient has become a caricature of itself. Wooshy digital synths, a few pastoral sounds, a waterfall or two. Electronic music has to become more sophisticated."[127] A split between prog-trance tribalism and icy techno abstraction had meanwhile become evident within the ambient scene, with some scenesters repudiating acts that more closely resembled jam bands than techno-auteurs. Ambient, as David Toop applauded in January '94, was transforming from "in-flight muzak for assorted hippies and space cadets" and "New Age de-stress technique" into "a scene which values sociability and mobility."[128] Such critiques of the state of ambient, well-reasoned and well-meaning as they were, smuggled in reductive equations of boring functionalism with "hippie" and "new age" leanings, set against a nebulous artistic purity and social authenticity.

Ironically, in the EDM record market, the terms of ambient's not-new-age sophistication turned out old hat when in 1994 the Chill Out label and a handful of DJs, in a PR blitz and familiar hip marketing move, rebranded classical instrumentals as ambient. "Our idea," reported Chill Out label director Peter Leigh, "is to open up the genre, to mutate ambient into a higher form using classical, jazz, in fact any kind of music."[129] Suggesting the term "post-ambient" to describe this so-called mutation—while yet ignoring most "any kind of music" other than classical, not to mention ambient and space music DJs' former dalliances with the genre—the label released the *Chill Out Classics* compilation featuring "ambient classical" by such composers as Górecki, Satie, Debussy, Messiaen, and Pärt. For maximum hip factor, Chill Out put out the vinyl version as a white label along with a press release name-checking spins at Megatripolis, Sonora, and Oscillate.[130] As with Columbia Masterworks's Music of our Time series and Eno's Obscure label, the gray area between Western art music and ambient audio appeared an untapped resource for solidifying a niche hip high-middlebrow market; the "post-ambient" concept, as Leigh admitted in a *Billboard* feature, was foremost an opportunity for market expansion. "Existing classical labels have contacted us with some fantastic repertoire," as he explained. "It's one way to reach beyond their traditional middle-class consumers."[131]

126 C. Jones, "Quiet Storm," 153.
127 Cliff Jones, "Classic Chills," *The Face*, July 1994, 133.
128 David Toop, "Mellow Fever," *The Face*, January 1994, 92, 97.
129 C. Jones, "Classic Chills."
130 Chill Out Label, press release for *Chill Out Classics Vol. 1*, CHILL001, 1994, LP.
131 Pride, "Euro Subculture Offers Ambience," 135.

Meanwhile, arts and new-music institutions long reluctant to engage with pop finally began to open their doors to select electronic expressions. Ambient was one. The London Design Museum, for instance, hosted a launch party for Eno's Virgin box sets in November 1993, with Eno himself delivering a keynote.[132] In April 1994, sound artist Robin Rimbaud (Scanner) established the Electronic Lounge at London's Institute of Contemporary Arts, a monthly gathering where DJs might be free to "experiment" more than in "regular dance/ambient clubs."[133] And that November, experimental improvisor Ben Neill curated "before and after ambient," a program at Manhattan new music mecca The Kitchen, presenting a collection of "non-linear" work that "evolves organically" to create a "total environmental effect."[134]

Chalk up the pop/avant-garde crossover to the "intoxicating . . . feeling that anything is possible in the contemporary electronic environment," as David Toop wrote in August 1995, just ahead of publishing his dizzying account of "ambient sound" in the twentieth century, *Ocean of Sound*. Toop's book demonstrated how "ambient" might not designate any one style or genre so much as various sorts of musical openness: openness to environments of audition and performance, to techniques of sonic production, to styles of improvisation, to travails across genre boundaries (especially those dividing art and pop). "Music is moving out of the niche market trap into a many-headed beast," as Toop continued, and so, he confessed, it becomes much easier as an electronic composer to say "I do Ambient" than "be cute about 'breaking down boundaries.'"[135]

But "doing ambient music," as this book has demonstrated, largely attained discursive coherence as participants in niche popular and electronic music markets—like Irv Teibel, like Stephen Hill and Anna Turner, like Brian Eno, and like the KLF—negotiated and articulated the virtues of their ambient audio relative to other popular and electronic musics. Only after several decades of these negotiations would a significant mass of musicians entertain the possibility, as Pete Namlook liked to report, that a genre called ambient might be the "classical music of the future."[136] And only in the mid-'90s,

[132] Toop, "Mellow Fever," 94.

[133] Erkki Rautio, "Scanner Interview," *pHinnWeb*, April 1996, http://www.phinnweb.org/5HT/interviews/scanner/.

[134] Ben Neill, program for "before and after ambient" at The Kitchen, November 4–5, 1994, archived at *The Kitchen*, http://archive.thekitchen.org/wp-content/uploads/2015/01/Program_beforeandafterambient_1994.pdf.

[135] David Toop, "On Fax Wars, Ambient Confusion, Bald Jazzers and Bo Diddley," *Wire*, August 1995, 74.

[136] Mark Prendergast, "Ambience Chaser," *The Independent* (London), December 16, 1994, 26.

following various repudiations of ambient's psychedelic, new age, and dance-oriented EDM inheritances in popular discourses, would highbrow experimental, electronic, and classical avant-garde scenesters begin to seriously acknowledge the artistic merits of ambient audio. Whatever freedoms "ambient" communicated to the art world had been prepared by, and partly predicated on, this boundary work.

Ambient Music's White Racialization

"Melody is not the point. The beat has gone missing. And there is little hint of a pulse." The byline to Robert Sandall's 1994 feature on ambient in London's *Sunday Times*, like many such articles of the time, begins by describing what ambient music lacks. Melody, the beat, a pulse—these are elements to be expected of "pop's technobrat auteurs"; and yet, Sandall says, to understand the Future Sound of London or Aphex Twin, you cannot look to Kraftwerk, nor Yello, nor really any of the electronic pop or rave music of the last fifteen years. No, you must look to the Euro-American avant-garde—Brian Eno, Steve Reich, Karlheinz Stockhausen, John Cage—to understand the ambiences drawing in today's "pop kids." "In retrospect," Sandall gathers, "the astonishing thing is not so much the manner in which Eno drew the attention of a rock audience to musical ideas that had been around for well over a decade, it is the fact that that audience was prepared to listen."[137]

Ambient's frames of comparison had shifted significantly by the mid-1990s. What had been formerly described as an experimental take on easy listening or new age was now understood as a "beatless" abstraction of EDM or synth-pop; as described in a '93 article, "dance music minus the drums, pop stripped to its elemental form, where only the atmosphere remains."[138] Ambient's definition-by-negation of the EDM/pop "beat" implicitly nullified the music's presumed physical stimulation; no wonder, then, that ambient drew the attention of high-middlebrow rock audiences better than did techno or dance-pop, for "chilling out" far better resembled former highbrow norms of "serious" artistic contemplation than did dancing. Explicit distinctions from other EDM helped the press's ambient champions position

[137] Robert Sandall, "But Where's the Tune?," *Sunday Times (London)*, March 13, 1994.
[138] Sharkey, "Saturday Night," 35.

the genre as high art over mere dance fodder, as in *NME*'s celebration of the "carefully measured dimensions" and "near-classical" beauty of Aphex Twin's *Selected Ambient Works '85–'92* LP (1992), which exemplified "headphone techno as an art" mercifully "void of any rave rhythms or E-fuelled mantras."[139] Such claims, as sociologist Sarah Thornton argued in her book *Club Cultures*, extended lines from earlier rock criticism that located legitimacy in intellectualized "head" music in contrast to dance music genres "debased" by association to a feminized mainstream.[140]

But in retrospect, perhaps the strangest aspect of ambient features like Sandall's was the attention heaped onto avant-garde experimentalism relative to the decades of head music in rock, jazz, dub, new age, and most of all, EDM, that informed ambient musicians' methods, and that prepared audiences reared on rock and pop to listen. Music writers in the 1990s commonly substantiated ambient's highbrow aspirations through specific references to established white male avant-garde composers and experimental art-rockers while glossing over the EDM innovators and styles more directly informing ambient's "technobrat auteurs." Ambient, according to one *Newsweek* writer, had made the "spiritual cleanliness" yielded by the works of John Cage into "a presence in modern club music"—although, as he went on to acknowledge, "disco tunes" and "techno music" too created spaces for introspection.[141] The Orb's *Adventures* LP, cracked another writer for *The Washington Post*, although largely inspired by dub, due to its length "might as well be sending its royalties directly to Philip Glass."[142] Ambient's psychedelic lineage, when mentioned, often served either as a point of contrast, or as a qualifying stylistic marker. Critical coverage drifted toward highbrow credentializing as ambient's expansions from the electronic to the indie-rock underground, and from these niches into the media mainstream, accelerated. Much as when distinctions between ambient and an industry-diluted new age had elevated ambient's status in the mid–late 1980s, specifications of ambient's avant-garde cultural authority in the '90s helped shore up the reputation of a hyped genre under threat of becoming, as The Orb's Paterson put it, "just another sales pitch for anything featuring a bird or an ocean wave;" or, as *The Observer* observed, "a catch-all term for virtually any electronic record

139 Sherman, "Twin Bleeps," 36

140 Sarah Thornton, *Club Cultures: Music, Media and Subcultural Capital* (Hanover, NH: Wesleyan University Press, 1996), 3, 11.

141 Joshua Cooper Ramo, "Cruising to Enlightenment," *Newsweek*, November 15, 1993, 84A.

142 Mark Jenkins, "Orb's House Mix: Glazed-over Ears," *Washington Post*, November 15, 1991, n14.

milder than the most frenetic, heart-pumping examples of House."[143] And importantly, such accrediting discourses did not simply name-check and trace boundaries from the outside; they also conventionalized the sounds and stated aesthetic ideals of self-appointed "ambient" record producers, DJs, and listeners active in the EDM scene and experimental undergrounds, organizing them as expressive norms of a legible market formation.

Rarely acknowledged, however, was how these expressive ideals were tacitly predicated on the presumption of a white male genre culture. This presumption, as detailed throughout this book, has roots in popular discourses idealizing stylistic fluidity, affective detachment, cerebral introspection, and disposition to physical ease as qualities of white high-middlebrow and hip white male fashion and comportment. Discursive gestures to Eno, a white European who himself foregrounded ambient's white avant-garde lineage, naturalized the association of these qualities with racial whiteness. Later artists and commentators posited the irrelevance of "black" genres like jazz/fusion, soul, R&B, dub, hip hop, and deep house to these musical ideals, primarily configuring ambient's boundaries through alignments with, and distinctions from, genres racialized as white, including avant-garde experimentalism, light-classical easy-listening, new age, and prog rock. The genre's masculinity, meanwhile, could be taken for granted due to the narrow social construction and gatekeeping of electronic music production and DJing as a boys' club (never mind the long-standing innovations by femme, trans, and queer musicians in the realm).[144]

Few inquiries into ambient's genre culture lingered on the identities and cultural communities of its makers and listeners (unlike, say, hip-hop, techno, or house); and yet, discourses since 1990 overwhelmingly constructed the genre almost entirely around alignments with, and distinctions from, the contributions of white and light-skinned men. Sandall's article provides one example of this; Cliff Jones's October '93 feature in *The Face* another: here, Jones makes reference to the influence of Brian Eno, John Cage, La Monte

[143] Neil Spencer, "Pilots of Inner Space for Ecstasy Kids," *Observer*, June 5, 1994, 5; Spencer, "Samplers Full of English Embroidery," 50.

[144] On women's participation in electronic music culture(s), and barriers encountered therein, see Rebekah Farrugia, *Beyond the Dance Floor: Female DJs, Technology, and Electronic Music Culture* (Chicago: Intellect, 2012); Tara Rodgers, *Pink Noises: Women on Electronic Music and Sound* (Durham: Duke University Press, 2010). On the role of queers and trans people in the development of rave culture(s), see Luis-Manuel Garcia, "Whose Refuge, This House?: The Estrangement of Queers of Color in Electronic Dance Music," in *The Oxford Handbook of Music and Queerness*, ed. Fred Everett Maus and Sheila Whiteley (New York: Oxford University Press, 2018), doi:10.1093/oxfordhb/9780199793525.013.49.

Young, David Tudor, Cornelius Cardew, Joe Meek, the BBC Radiophonic Workshop, White Noise, Pink Floyd, the "Cologne school" of Krautrock (Neu, Can, Faust, Kraftwerk, Tangerine Dream), The Orb, Andrew Weatherall, Paul Oakenfold, the KLF, Harold Budd, Ennio Morricone, Ryuichi Sakamoto, Aphex Twin, The Black Dog, B12, Sven Vath, and William Orbit—but not one black or brown composer—on ambient music.[145] Ian McCann's 1992 *Vox* article on the rise of ambient identified only Aqua Regia among the style's nonwhite predecessors and leaders.[146] Such overwhelmingly light-skinned genealogies indeed reflected common points of reference by ambient musicians and listeners; and yet they also regularly excluded the equally relevant work of artists such as Miles Davis, Pharaoh Sanders, Ravi Shankar, Minnie Riperton, Lee "Scratch" Perry, Alice Coltrane, Laraaji, Larry Heard, Derrick May, or Carl Craig. Genre representations had a colorist bent, with most ambient artists of color being light-skinned and of Asian descent. *The Wire* magazine's 1993 "An A–Z of Ambient" guide only identifies a single artist of color, "Marion [sic] Zazeela" (whose blurb is one unfortunate line: "LaMonte [sic] Young's wife");[147] while Virgin Records's *A Brief History of Ambient* compilation series, one of the most ethnically and racially diverse representations of the genre at the time, featured five non-Asian artists of color (Laraaji, Baaba Maal, Prince Far I, Tony Thorpe [as Voyager], and Sufi) out of eighty-four. (Another ten were Asian, making the "history of ambient" represented still predominantly white.)

Ambient EDM's white racialization took form, in part, amid what several writers have called a "whitewashing" of EDM's history that occurred in the wake of the United Kingdom's rave boom.[148] Originally, house and techno's Black American innovators sought to unsettle common assumptions of "black music" by creating styles that, in techno founder Juan Atkins's words, "repudiated an ethnic designation."[149] Their "racelessness" was strategic, a scrambling of the racialized mind/body binary that, as sociologist Sarah Thornton describes, roots blackness in "emotive and embodied sound" while assuming whiteness of the "disembodied, invisible and high-tech."[150]

[145] Jones, "Quiet Storm," 153.

[146] McCann, "Cali for an Ambience," 38–42.

[147] "An A–Z of Ambient," 11.

[148] Caspar Melville, *It's a London Thing: How Rare Groove, Acid House and Jungle Remapped the City* (Manchester: Manchester University Press, 2019), 225; Matthew Collin, *Rave On: Global Adventures in Electronic Dance Music* (Chicago: University of Chicago Press, 2018), 108.

[149] Sean Albiez, "Post-Soul Futurama: African American Cultural Politics and Early Detroit Techno," *European Journal of American Culture* 24, no. 2 (2005): 142.

[150] Thornton, *Club Cultures*, 72–73.

House and techno's "postsoul" aesthetic deconstructed this binary by incorporating the muted affect and roboticism associated with white artists like Kraftwerk and Gary Numan (who themselves humorously exaggerated these qualities in their own appropriations of Black American funk styles).[151] These racialized dynamics, however, became lost on many listeners whose initial exposure to EDM occurred through UK rave—which was, by most accounts, a largely white affair.[152] As the 1990s progressed, new audiences high on rave's revolutionary rhetoric and the deluge of EDM made by white Europeans wrongly heard EDM's robotic "racelessness" as white European invention—and as "rootless" in spirit—unaware of how house and techno's "raceless" sound was born of racial politics.[153] Atkins, in response, came to decry the growing association of techno with whiteness as "brainwashing," while his colleague Derrick May, detecting "no spirit, no soul" in the new "raw, purist" strains of UK acid and hardcore, lamented the Brits' "prostitution" of techno.[154]

Ambient's reinvention as a subgenre of EDM, having arisen in Europe, participated in this broader whitewashing. Few people, it seems, noticed. In the sustained absence of discussion on race, the whiteness of ambient's genre culture may well have appeared to participants as merely atmospheric—"normative, benign, and frequent," as literary scholar André Carrington characterizes white authorship within the science fiction genre.[155] And the appearance of "ambient" as a label descriptive of environments, rather than of the subject(s) or persona(e) therein, rhetorically clouds the salience of race to the genre's anglophone formation, tacitly sanctioning the processes by which genre discourses repeatedly omitted the contributions of dark-skinned musicians.[156] Where pervasive whiteness is assumed to be transparent, normal, and universal, rather than remarkable or even relevant, race becomes exnominated from discourse; as cultural studies scholar John Fiske explains, "A key strategy of whiteness is to avoid definition and explicit presence."[157]

[151] Albiez, "Post-Soul Futurama"; Eshun, *More Brilliant Than the Sun*, -006.

[152] Reynolds, *Energy Flash*, 56. Black British DJs and racially mixed parties, however, facilitated the UK acid explosion, as documented in Melville, *It's a London Thing*, 211–73.

[153] Thornton, *Club Cultures*, 76.

[154] Albiez, "Post-Soul Futurama," 149; Phil Cheeseman, "DJ Profile: Derrick May," *DJ Mag*, June 1992, 16.

[155] André M. Carrington, *Speculative Blackness: The Future of Race in Science Fiction* (Minneapolis: University of Minnesota Press, 2016), 17.

[156] On the "salience of race" to genre, see Mark C. Jerng, *Racial Worldmaking: The Power of Popular Fiction* (New York: Fordham University Press, 2018), 2.

[157] John Fiske, *Media Matters: Race and Gender in U.S. Politics*, rev. ed. (Minneapolis: University of Minnesota Press, 1996), 41.

Race's absence from ambient's media coverage, with this in mind, may be understood as a distinctive feature of its colorist racial frame. In the same vein, the empty soundscapes of white ambient artists might well be heard, in their seeming selflessness, as a tacit and (perhaps) unintended representation of "atmospheric" white subjectivity.

The correlation of "not moving" with mental "traveling" underscores the relevance of a disembodied middle-class whiteness to the ambient formation. "Part of what makes white people socially white," as cultural theorist Richard Dyer notes, lies in the Christian construct of, and self-identification with, an invisible, extracorporeal "mind" that the white middle-class subject accesses through effacement of the body.[158] This Cartesian mind-over-matter ideology, as Dyer explains, goes hand-in-hand with the spirit of white colonialist "enterprise," as both imply a continuity of the white self with a mind that lacks geographical boundaries, traverses "blank" landscapes, and holds command over (one's own and others') fleshly bodies.[159] "True whiteness," as Dyer deadpans, "resides in the non-corporeal."[160]

In this vein, it was ambient's conventionalization as "beatless" EDM—and the symbolic alignment of beatless EDM with the liberation of mind from physical embodiment—that most definitively, and enduringly, reified the ambient genre's white racialization. The redefinition of the ambient label, already associated with white masculinity, took shape around the classed, gendered, and racialized mind-body dualism organizing EDM authenticity. Most white male participants in the ambient genre, rather than challenging this dualism, passively drew ironic cool from the correlation between bodily stillness (or stiffness), mental stimulation, and "rational" white masculinity, while yet also retaining the looseness of EDM's funky grooves and space music's cloudy drifts. Commentators' perception of ambient as "beatless," as with the assumption of ambient as "dance music that isn't dance music!," accordingly said more about the white male ambient musician's or

[158] Richard Dyer, *White: Essays on Race and Culture* (New York: Routledge, 1997), 45. See also Sara Ahmed, "A Phenomenology of Whiteness," *Feminist Theory* 8, no. 2 (2007): 149–68; Robin James, "In but Not of, of but Not In: On Taste, Hipness, and White Embodiment," *Contemporary Aesthetics* Special Volume 2 (2009), http://www.contempaesthetics.org/newvolume/pages/article.php?articleID=549.

Anna Bull and James Johnson similarly describe classical music listening and performance as techniques of self-control and bodily transcendence; see Anna Bull, *Class, Control, and Classical Music* (New York: Oxford University Press, 2019), 24, 104; James H. Johnson, *Listening in Paris: A Cultural History* (Berkeley: University of California Press, 1995), 195.

[159] Dyer, *White*, 31–34.

[160] Ibid., 45.

listener's presumed disconnection from his physical body than it did about the music. Accordingly, and likely unintentionally in most cases, ambient's "beatlessness" also pronounced distance from music associated with individuals hegemonically marked as inescapably embodied: "black-music-that-isn't-Black" and "femme-music-that-isn't-female."

Despite such implications, as writer Chester Anderson presciently argued of head music decades prior, ambient music is not disembodied.[161] As Gilbert and Pearson explain, "Although ambient has often been thought of as 'head music' in comparison to 'body music' (which is for dancing to) this is a naïve formulation. Ambient music is not an object of contemplation: it is a source of affect. It may not make us dance, but its effects are just as directly physical as those of other dance musics."[162] "Chilling out," by extension, is no less embodied than other modes of listening that involve movement; in fact, as some studies of embodied cognition in music listening suggest, ambient's motionless travelers may be responding mimetically to the seemingly effortless music.[163] Yet while ambient "beatlessness" promotes physical disengagement more than arousal, it does not follow that the music is any more mind-expanding than dance-oriented house or techno, much of which, as Kodwo Eshun has thoroughly demonstrated, can be just as (if not more) heady, a "hyperembodiment" of intelligence that "overrides that pre-modern binary that insists the dancefloor is all mindless bodies and the bedroom nothing but bodiless minds."[164]

During ambient EDM's second wave, Eshun was one of just a small handful of critics and journalists who remarked on, and sometimes contested, the terms by which the ambient genre coalesced around mostly white European artists. In 1993 he observed ambient as one of several strains of white pastoralism in British techno wherein the "bland" nature-sound folksiness of

[161] Chester Anderson, "Notes for the New Geology," *San Francisco Oracle*, February 1967, 2, 23.

[162] Gilbert and Pearson, *Discographies*, 94.

[163] Music theorists Arnie Cox and Naomi Cumming have developed "mimetic" hypotheses of musical listening that suggest listeners subconsciously hear music as if a human were creating it and interpret the music by subconsciously or consciously imitating the gestures or comportment necessary to create its sounds. At times, these imitations manifest overtly, as in the case of dancing and singing along. Long attacks and drones, perceived as gentle and automatic, may hence well suggest the overt embodied performance of staying in place. Arnie Cox, *Music and Embodied Cognition: Listening, Moving, Feeling, and Thinking* (Bloomington: Indiana University Press, 2016); Naomi Cumming, "The Subjectivities of 'Erbarme Dich,'" *Music Analysis* 16, no. 1 (1997): 5–44. See also Ian Cross, "Listening as Covert Performance," *Journal of the Royal Musical Association* 135, Special Issue no. 1 (2010): 67–77; Istvan Molnar-Szakacs and Katie Overy, "Music and Mirror Neurons: From Motion to 'E'motion," *Scan* 1 (2006): 235–41.

[164] Eshun, *More Brilliant than the Sun*, -002, 22.

acts like The Irresistible Force and Ultramarine—a sound that surely would have been called "new age house" several years prior—"wants to assert white English roots."[165] A '94 *DJ Mag* feature on ambient also took issue with the style's presumptive whiteness by pointing out that artists like Sun Ra, Miles Davis, and Derrick May "developed hypnotic music that gives Tangerine Dream a run for their money any day."[166] Meanwhile David Toop, taking note in a '94 *Wire* feature on The Orb of the erasure of deep house artists Larry Heard and Marshall Jefferson from ambient histories, made a point to shift some of the blame from "ignorant journalists" to "record company crooks (some in the UK) who succeeded in murdering the motivation of these [Black EDM] artists."[167] (Toop was also among the first to note that hip hop's sample-collage aesthetic, exemplified by the Bomb Squad or Ice Cube, presents an alternative, unrestful vision of ambient music in which the audio atmosphere of a track is constantly shifting, a furious music of ambiences.)[168]

Perhaps the most sustained interrogation of ambient's white racialization came from *Wire* critic (and now publisher) Tony Herrington in a 1994 editorial on "Black Ambient." Based on the prevailing definition of ambient as a "largely pulseless electronic hush," Herrington wrote, "Ambient is a uniquely white, male, European concern."[169] But this essentialization of ambient, he goes on to say, fails to consider the world of atmospheric possibilities opened up by Chicago's AACM experimentalists, by dub producers King Tubby and Lee Perry, by the afro-pop of Salif Keita or Geoffrey Oryema, by the twisted underground rock of A.R. Kane, the hazy trip-hop of Tricky, the haunted house of Moody Boyz, even by the scuzz and warp of long-aged Delta blues recordings, all of which, Harrington proposes, opens a wormhole out of race-based musical essentialisms. "Black Ambient releases black music from both the strictures of its own history and our trammeled expectations of it," as Herrington explained. "It allows Black musicians to become *something else*, other than the stagolee figure, gangsta lean, jazz messenger, love man, trouble girl or soul diva."[170]

[165] Kodwo Eshun, "Outline: Techno," *The Wire*, August 1993, 70.
[166] Chrysell, "Shhhhhhhhhhh," 27.
[167] David Toop, "Passage to the Underworld," *The Wire*, July 1994, 40.
[168] David Toop, "High Tech Mindscapes, Real Life Dramas," *The Wire*, December 1991/January 1992, 34.
[169] Tony Herrington, "Outline: Ambient," *The Wire*, April 1994, 74.
[170] Herrington, "Outline: Ambient," 74.

Black ambient, had the notion been more deeply considered in popular media discourses and industry constructions, might well have also allowed ambient music to become *something else*, even while largely remaining pulseless, electronic, hushed. And some deconstructions of "ambient music" in the years leading up to the millennium headed in this direction—not just Toop's aforementioned *Ocean of Sound*, which located "ambient music" as just one of a multitude of ambient musics from around the globe, but also in the early work of Paul D. Miller, aka DJ Spooky that Subliminal Kid, who was one of several artists seeking to bridge ambient aesthetics with hip-hop, jazz, and dub in the short-lived "illbient" style.[171] These interventions, however, did little to affect the white racialization of the ambient genre, which even these authors rarely outright discussed as such. Moreover, ambient already had a reputation for being radically open-ended, despite itself, and so these interventions may not have appeared as a social strategy so much as an aesthetic inevitability. "The common denominator of all ambient musics is a sense of openness," as Miller wrote in 1994. "There are no barriers in this music, which can contain almost any tone, from the harshest guitar feedback to the smoothest rustle of water."[172] And yet ambient's widely held aspiration to total openness, literalized by the seeming boundlessness and frictionlessness of musical recordings conventionalized by the "ambient" category, held fast to its narrowly racialized and gendered construction as it entered the increasingly genre-flexible internet media age of the twenty-first century. Now as then—and even here, in this book, as elsewhere—women and artists of color elude historicization and canonization in this most "open" of genres known as ambient, which has for decades rhetorically channeled and elevated the experiences and expressions of boundless, frictionless, "beatless" hip high-middlebrow white masculinity.

[171] On illbient, see Jesse Stewart, "DJ Spooky and the Politics of Afro-Postmodernism," *Black Music Research Journal* 30, no. 2 (2010): 337–62; Laurent Fintoni, "Detuning the City: An Oral History of Illbient," *Red Bull Music Academy*, August 18, 2014, https://daily.redbullmusicacademy.com/2014/08/illbient-oral-history.

[172] Paul D. Miller, "Surround Sound," *ArtForum* 33, no. 5 (January 1995): 101.

Coda: Ambient Music in the 21st Century

"Have you heard of *The Disintegration Loops*?"

While writing my PhD dissertation on ambient music in the early–mid 2010s, this inquiry, almost invariably directed at me by another white male grad student, became a predictable refrain. It typically resulted in sharing admiration for the now-canonic ambient elegy released in 2002 by Brooklyn-based recording artist William Basinski, *The Disintegration Loops*, which unlike many ambient records made for a fine discussion piece thanks to the compelling story and context of its making.

To retell it: In August 2001 Basinski was digitally recording loops from some twenty-year-old tapes of orchestral music. Entranced by the majestic dirge emerging from one loop, the artist created a looping countermelody on his Voyetra synthesizer and let the loops run. Unintentionally, particles of iron oxide began flaking off under the tape head as the tape looped; ironically, the transducer intended to preserve the sounds was eroding the magnetic pigment encoding them. This process of disintegration became digitally recorded as the looping continued, resulting in the first of several works in which, as Basinski recalls, "the life and death of the melody was redeemed in another medium."[1]

Despite the automaticity of the process, Basinski's results are emotionally poignant, with the warped tape's waver introducing a weeping quality to the sounds, dampened high frequencies mellowing their sorrowful ache, and string-horn-and-snare textures lending dignity to their disappearance into reverberation and silence. The loss of sound itself, like increasingly faltering sobs, seem to register the sadness of material destruction in human terms. And so, the mournful pieces took on unforeseen metaphorical resonances

[1] Kiran Sande, "'To Be There, and to See It . . . Was Hell.' Unspooling the past with William Basinski," May 28, 2009, *FACT Magazine*, http://www.factmag.com/2012/11/10/interview-william-basinski/.

Turn On, Tune In, Drift Off. Victor Szabo, Oxford University Press. © Oxford University Press 2023.
DOI: 10.1093/oso/9780190699307.003.0006

following the destruction Basinski saw unfold from his apartment several weeks later that September:

> We had been up on the roof all day. That night, my neighbor had a penthouse on the other side of the building and had a video camera up there; I got a tape and I asked her if she'd help me set it up, and so I framed this static shot of downtown where the smoke was, where the towers used to be, and I just let the tape run out. So I managed to capture the last hour of daylight for that day, and then the next day I got the tape and put it with the first *Disintegration Loops 1.1* and made this accompanying film.

Through his own record label, Basinski went on to release the first installment on CD and mp3 in 2002 accompanied by stills from his film of the Twin Towers going up in dust. Five installments followed. Over the next several years, critical praise for the cycle spread rapidly; on the tenth anniversary of the 9/11 attacks, The Wordless Music Orchestra performed an arrangement of *Loops 1.1* at the Metropolitan Museum of Art in New York; and one year following, the cycle was reissued as a box set of LPs. Basinski's memorial had become monumental.

It would also later become, despite my affection for the piece, a bit of an annoyance, for rarely did my grad school discussions about *The Disintegration Loops* generate deeper insights than "what a cool piece," save the occasional debate over whether it qualified as disaster opportunism. No one, it seemed, wished to mull over the deep sadness of the music, or interpret the disintegrative process as metaphor, or dissect the means by which it provides (or does not provide) catharsis, or debate whether the live performance did justice to the original. Rather, instead, I could not help but cynically feel at the receiving end of some dude's demonstration of his cultural capital and erudition, of his profound interior depth, and of his knowledge of high art—leading me, eventually, to sympathize a great deal with the young woman in a popular 2018 meme (Fig. C.1).[2]

Then again, my own snobbishness (*Disintegration Loops*, again?) was probably also a factor in the disintegration of conversation around Basinski's piece. Perhaps with more generosity, I could have fostered discussions like the one that ignited my own love of ambient music as a student at the University

[2] Andrew Ellis, Twitter post, September 23, 2018, 9:26 am, https://twitter.com/Ellis_Samizdat/status/1043854224587714560.

Figure C.1. William Basinski's *The Disintegration Loops* appears in an Internet meme.

of Michigan in the mid-2000s. I remember it well, having taken place at a chilled-out fall party steeped in red wine and weed, my curiosity piqued in conversation with the cute skinny white hipster hosting the soirée. (I myself was a wannabe-hipster, never "chill" or stoic enough to fit in, but always eager to find common ground in cool music and weird art.) I had been enjoying the music creeping in at the edges of my perception—synth moodscapes that were weighty but not heavy, melancholic but not depressing, grandiose but not overwhelming—and asked what it was. The host told me, to my surprise, that it was M83's *Dead Cities, Red Seas & Lost Ghosts*, a 2003 album I had formerly dismissed as boring. "Have you heard of Satie?" he asked, before proceeding to explain the concept of furniture music, of which I was unaware. Suddenly, the music clicked; while I formerly thought of M83 as derivative, I realized, through Satie's avant-garde conceptual abstraction, how it might, as ignorable music, have interesting effects. Since that time, closer listens to the album revealed a rich world of texture and tone color, as well as a slow-to-unfold tunefulness that had previously eluded me. The hip high-brow framing, affirming my own sense of belonging in a highly individualistic and well-read crowd, disposed me to the music's affective pleasures. I sought out more music like it. I found ambient music.

And yet, ten years later—with considerably "higher" education in musicology and cultural studies under my belt—I would come to attribute my aesthetic epiphany to the social mechanisms that had prepared it, including my own aspirations to cultural capital and intellectualism; my own investment in racial whiteness; and the status-elevating validation accorded by concepts like "furniture music" and "ambient music." I could not help but read similar aspirations into those *Disintegration Loops* inquiries, and I had the urge to dismiss them as a result. And yet, that M83 epiphany, that tug toward immersion in melancholic sound, that continuous drift toward ambient music over other varieties of ambient audio, rarely felt—or feels—socially aspirational; rather, these connections and attunements, from my perspective, provided retreats into introspection, opportunities to connect with my underlying sadness; as well as a way of letting go of preconceptions, of overthinking music, of snobbery; an opening up of possibilities formerly unexplored. Was this, as sociological accounts of taste had me defensively wondering, such a bad thing?

I suppose this book is my answer. The shorter answer, I think, is no; and yet, I must add that so long as media and fan discourses around ambient disregard the music's affective resonances and socioaesthetic meanings, so long as ambient records are imagined as high-art abstractions rather than popular highs, the genre may become, I fear, a cultural rut. Over the last ten years, media discourses on ambient music have weathered the same grooves as they loop, again and again, around the same non-insights: ambient, you might learn, has been making a "comeback" or receiving "renewed interest" nearly every year, as though the evolution and invention of new ambient styles was reviving a dormant artform rather than a consistent feature of a vibrant pop genre.[3] Relatedly, the ambient genre, you might read, is an "amorphous" genre with "nearly limitless applications," a genre that "can be almost anything," a genre that is "so dynamic that we can't even define what it is," a

[3] Sharon Oliver, "'Chill Music' Makes a Comeback in the Time of COVID-19," Culture Sonar, May 6, 2020, https://www.culturesonar.com/chill-music-makes-a-comeback-in-the-time-of-covid-19/; Lanre Bakare, "Lost in Muzak: How Ambient Became Cool," *The Guardian*, January 3, 2020, https://www.theguardian.com/music/2020/jan/03/how-ambient-music-became-cool-brian-eno-peach.

style that "can be pretty much anything you want."[4] Eluding definition, of course, has long been a marked feature of ambient's ever-white-male-centric genre culture, an elusion that conveniently also steers clear of considering the complications and baggage of sonic and social convention, of musico-cultural politics, of stylistic appropriation and reinterpretation. (Claims that we have entered a "post-genre" era or that one's music is "genre-less," it bears noting, are commonly predicated upon similar identities and elusions.)[5]

Genres of music, thankfully, change; indeed, they can become "almost anything" through collective contention with their cultures and histories. People often think of music genres as stable categories, but they are more accurately social musicodiscursive *processes* that only appear stable due to the reifying nature of institutions and corporations that typically profit from making these processes predictable. And so perhaps it is not just possible, but indeed necessary to acknowledge that masculinism, elitism, and racism have historically informed the illusion that ambient is a timeless, limitless form of abstract art; and to affirm that there, indeed, is nothing essentially masculinist, or elitist, or racist about ambient music, nor about the aspiration to timelessness and limitlessness. Only by way of a collective effort to both honestly recognize and de-essentialize ambient music's socioaesthetic formation might the parameters of the genre culture expand, permitting true evolution rather than orbiting around the same tired clichés. In this spirit, I would like to affirm this possibility by glimpsing at some records emerging out of ambient music's psychedelic present that suggest promising trajectories along which the genre might grow.

Ana Roxanne's records, ~~~ (2019) and *Because of a Flower* (2020), illustrate not just the multifarious antecedents of ambient music in ambient audio, but also the remarkable potential for sensitive self-expression in their synthesis. Influences of classical minimalism in the vein of Philip Glass or Meredith Monk ("I'm Every Sparkly Woman," "A Study in Vastness"), nature sounds ("It's a Rainy Day on the Cosmic Shore," "Venus,"), Hindustani singing

[4] Patric Fallon, "Nothing Is True, Everything Is Permitted: Wolfgang Voigt, Lawrence English, and Others Ponder the State of Ambient Music," *XLR8R*, August 13, 2014, http:// www.xlr8r.com/features/2014/08/nothing-is-true-everything-is-permitted-wolfgang-voigt-lawrence-english-and-others-ponder-the-state-of-ambient-music/; Joe Muggs, "Return to the Chill-Out Room: When Did Ambient Music Last Have It So Good?" *FACT Magazine*, October 9, 2014, http://www.factmag.com/2014/10/09/ambient-2014-round-up-joe-muggs/.

[5] Robin James, "Is the Post- in Post-Identity the Post- in Post-Genre?," *Popular Music* 36, no. 1 (2017): 21–32.

("Nocturne"), Windham Hill style new age ("- - -") are all evident; so is the dream-pop of Cocteau Twins or Julee Cruise ("Camille"), the indie ambient and postrock of Grouper and Low ("Suite Pour L'Invisible"), and throughout, Eno's pop/ambient hybrids, particularly as heard on *Another Green World*. What feels especially vital about Roxanne's music is not only the way in which she so seamlessly brings these elements together, but also the intensely personal manner in which she does so. Each ambience, it seems, vulnerably exposes an intense stillness and vastness within Roxanne, especially by way of her silky, ghostly voice, which assumes a full presence on most of her tracks. (This vulnerability, this heart, links her music to a great deal of *Hearts of Space*'s space music). Roxanne's personal narrative around her music, divulged in a series of interviews, further connects her music to a project of self-exposure, particularly with regard to her coming-out as intersex and revealing, through sound, a subjectivity exploring gender expressions. Hence tracks like "Camille" and "Suite Pour L'Invisible," both dedicated to the legacy of early intersex writer Herculine Barbin, and the latter also to "anyone who's ever had to feel invisible in some way."[6] The ambient drones and patterns of her music educe spaces to embrace the fullness of one's own many-gendered existence; or as she asserts over deliriously sequenced looping Moog arpeggios in her Chaka Khan and Whitney Houston cover, "I'm Every Sparkly Woman," that "it's all in me."

Psychedelic experiments in ambient mellow have long wafted through the history of hip-hop production. At least in the last thirty years, one could point to the hallucinogenic turntablism of producers like RZA, J Dilla, and Madlib that mixes cinematic spoken-word samples with ambient audio across fusion jazz, prog rock, psychedelic soul, and soft R&B. The vein of production has resurfaced with the downcast vinyl crackle of UK trip-hop in lo-fi hip hop ("lo-fi," for short), a subgenre popularized via the "Beats to Relax/ Study to" YouTube channel, and arguably the most popular style of ambient audio among young adults in the United States today. One might also note the codeine-drowsed leanback of chopped-and-screwed hip hop, largely creditable to DJ Screw and his Houston collaborators' mixtapes of time-stretched samples and benumbed MCing, as another intoxicating (and intoxicated) fusion of rap and ambient audio.

[6] Cat Zhang, "The Radiant Slowness of Ana Roxanne," *Pitchfork*, April 14, 2021, https://pitchfork.com/features/rising/the-radiant-slowness-of-ana-roxanne/.

In the last several years, one might hear these developments coming together in the entrancements of ambient rap MCs such as Ka, Boldy James, Navy Blue, Mach-Hommy, Roc Marciano, and Earl Sweatshirt, all of whom regularly enact verbal dada hypnosis over cloudy, reverb-soaked plumes of jazz and soul. "MTOMB" by Earl Sweatshirt (Thebe Kgositsile), featuring Liv.e, offers just one taste of this new crop of hip hop that flickers between absorbing, heady rap presentation and low-key lush-yet-loopy vibe. Producer The Alchemist—a common collaborator with several of the aforementioned artists—lays a cushy, laidback beat out of smooth-R&B act Mtume's "Theme for the People," with singer Liv.e's chopped and filtered mezzo, and assorted atmospheric sound effects, feathering Mtume's pitched-down "pray for the people" loop. Kgositsile's introspective lyrics dizzyingly contract memories into a single verse through dream-logic lateral shifts across time, setting, and addressee. His high-baritone straight-tone deadpan delivery is loose, behind the beat, and subtly unpredictable: the enjambed continuation of steady syllabic flow across bars takes precedence over metric-lyrical correspondence, yet with small drops in intonation at line breaks offering easy impacts all over the metric grid; while his rhythmic diction ever-shifts from a rocking polyrhythmic lilt to even-rhythm arrivals and back, anchored by emphatic accents when the rhymes match the beat structure. All of which is a very technical way of describing what makes the track at once a wonder and a wash; an invitation to follow Kgositsile's taking stock of "bones to pick out," but also atmospheric occasion to "salt the rims and pour a drink out / and sip . . . mmm."

There is far more to write about vaporwave—an internet-born genre of music largely composed of time-stretched, echo-soaked samples of late-twentieth-century MOR pop and muzak—than I can write here; thankfully, much has been written already.[7] Suffice it to say that vaporwave fans are almost certainly familiar with the 2015 release 新しい日の誕生 (*Birth of a New Day*)

[7] For a fine scholarly introduction to vaporwave, see Ken McLeod, "Vaporwave: Politics, Protest, and Identity," *Journal of Popular Music Studies* 30, no. 4 (2018): 123–42. See also Georgina Born and Christopher Haworth, "From Microsound to Vaporwave: Internet-Mediated Musics, Online Methods, and Genre," *Music & Letters* 98, no. 4 (2018): 601–47; Laura Glitsos, "Vaporwave, or Music Optimised for Abandoned Malls," *Popular Music* 37, no. 1 (2017): 100–118; Adam Harper, "The New Hi-Tech Underground," in *Seismographic Sounds: Visions of a New World*, ed. Theresa Beyer, Thomas Burkhalter, and Hannes Liechti (Bern: Norient, 2015), 484–87; Grafton Tanner, *Babbling Corpse: Vaporwave and the Commodification of Ghosts* (Winchester, UK: Zero Books, 2016); Andrew Whelan and Raphaël Nowak, "'Vaporwave Is (Not) a Critique of Capitalism': Genre Work in an Online Music Scene," *Open Cultural Studies*, no. 2 (2018): 451–62.

by 2814, a collaboration between UK artists telepath (Luke Laurila) and HKE (David Russo) that was, upon its release, instantly hailed in online communities as a watershed in the genre's evolution. Whereas most prior vaporwave artists blatantly plundered consumer-culture kitsch through rough edits, tape hiss, and recognizable samples to summon a retrofuturist aesthetic, 2814 avoided these nostalgia-triggering elements while retaining vaporwave's surrealistic production techniques (time-stretching and pitch-shifting, multiband filtering, wah and phaser effects, bitcrushing and other forms of distortion). The creators ended up calling their style "dreampunk," described by HKE as providing "introspective respite that takes in the modern technological world as a lucid dream."[8] The evocative neon luminescence of the cityscape on the album cover offers a visual analog for the radiant multitimbral textures of the recorded tracks, with extensively filtered sounds producing liquid layers of shadow and light, and with tunnelly convolution reverb and distant sirens suggesting the enclosed, hard-walled spaces of the city. Slow phaser effects are nearly omnipresent on the record, leading layered sounds to whirl around and melt into one another in unpredictable fashion, giving the tracks a dreamy, hallucinatory halo. In "悲哀" ("Sorrow"), for instance, woozy drones, a gently rolling 52-bpm drum shuffle, a mist of maracas, and splashes of dissonant noise wash and churn together, phaser-swept. Gooey, warm synths soften the texture, rocking back and forth in a C♭maj9–B♭m11 pendulum, flickering almost imperceptibly between expectancy and ennui. On occasion, a chiming electric piano wistfully adorns the texture with sparse melodic arpeggiations. 恢复 ("Recovery"), the album opener, offers a less clouded pensiveness. The track both begins and ends with shimmering, chorused pianos, echoing and cascading over one another on an Fm11. In between, droning synth hums, cymbal splashes, and chirruping pads pile up and recede in surging fashion over an intermittent undulating F-E♭ bass murmur. The track, like the best ambient EDM of yore, is a masterclass in manufactured flow; the album, unlike the carbon-copy dreamy drones sleepily filling most ambient playlists, incarnates a singular, splendid sonic hallucination.

In an inversion of 2814's sparkling techno-urban dreamworld, James Ferraro's nightmarish 2013 *NYC, Hell 3:00am* compresses what Ferraro

[8] Andrew Daly, "An Interview with David Russo AKA HKE," *Vinyl Writer Music*, April 11, 2021, https://vinylwritermusic.com/an-interview-with-david-russo-aka-hke/.

calls the "dark and decayed" conditions of twenty-first-century New York into an ambient-blues odyssey of the mind.[9] Forged from the artist's "ritual" recording sessions after midnight, the mural-like album freezes late-nighttime NYC into a claustrophobic, drugged, and hotbox standstill. The album's dragging, detuned loops, plodding languidly alongside drones, samples, and Ferraro's ad-libbed R&B vocals, conjure the dingy dimness of a David Lynchian basement club or cramped studio bedroom. Ferraro's voice, typically courting some girl with sweet supplications like those of Usher or The Weeknd, easily melts into the recorded mix and eludes concentration; but unlike most smooth soulsters, he doesn't seem to want or care to be understood, with delivery typically off-pitch and hanging behind the beat, sometimes delivered through extreme autotune ("Fake Pain"), reduced to lulling la-da-da-das ("Eternal Condition"), scarcely comprehensible in the mix ("City Smells," "Irreplaceable"), or uncomfortably intimate ("Close Ups"), yet always rendering disassociation from his own desirous entreaties like a half-asleep lounge singer. On "Cheek Bones," the hint of a skittering trap beat over synth arpeggios and looped vocal samples queasily gestures toward radio-friendly pop; but more often haunted organ ("Close Ups"), dour keyboard loops ("Upper East Side Pussy"), and trudging synth strings ("Irreplaceable") bog the music down in unfriendly, unholy murk. Throughout the album, irruptions of robotic voices blaring brand names ("TOYOTA" "XEROX" "MTV") and the detritus of desire ("MONEY" "SEX TAPE PIXELLATION" "TOM CRUISE") pock the song cycle with reminders of corporate-induced fetishism. Media coverage of the 9/11 attacks ("Close Ups") and repeat intrusions of police sirens and walkie talkie bookending a slowed-down loop of a man muttering "n***a" ("Stuck 2," "N***as," "Stuck 3 (RATS)"), replicate the ever-present sonic intimations and perpetuations of racist media and state power, i.e., "American violence" (as looped at the end of the album). Ferraro's post-9/11 NYC hell, in toto, fully immerses the listener in the American violence of a failed empire paranoiacally clinging to supremacy, and in the severely stoned, sexed-up subjective space that inadequately distracts the mind from these surroundings.

[9] Miles Bowe, "Q&A: James Ferraro on NYC's Hidden Darkness, Musical Sincerity, and Being Called 'The God of Vaporwave,'" Stereogum, October 11, 2013, https://www.stereogum.com/1504091/qa-james-ferraro-on-nycs-hidden-darkness-musical-sincerity-and-being-called-the-god-of-vaporwave/interviews/.

If recorded music can alter consciousness by replicating one's tripped-out headspace, can it do the same by replicating other forms of mental disarrangement, even illness? Such is the wager of The Caretaker (Leyland Kirby)'s *Everywhere at the End of Time* (2016–19), a series of six albums that uses loops and manipulations of ballroom dances to simulate the long decline of a terminally ill dementia patient. The first three albums or "stages" largely feature extended loops of wax- and shellac-encoded big-band and light orchestral dance music, with surface pops, crackles, scratches, skips, and hiss preserved (or even amplified), suggesting the faulty materiality of memory. As the series progresses through stage 3 into stages 4 and 5, hisses, skips, and other disruptions begin to take over, with musical features becoming entirely defamiliarized through filtering and distortion. Confusion reigns in stage 4, which especially registers a palpable anxiety, sometimes bordering on terror, as sounds become scrambled and garbled, vocals are rendered unintelligible, unplaceable horns blare, static and fuzz pervade, and the sound unpredictably cuts in and out. Stages 5 and 6 document the slow forgetting of forgetting, with pitched sounds increasingly absent as stretches of crackle, fuzz, and remnants of reverberation and echo fill an agnosic emptiness. What might have, in less capable hands, become a shallow exploitative spectacle of illness (akin to what some today describe as "trauma porn") instead, through thoughtful pacing and emotional sensitivity, invites empathy with the infirm who so often undergo social death long before their physical one. Unexpectedly, the piece became a social-media phenomenon in late 2020 as teenagers on TikTok posed and accepted the "Caretaker Challenge" to listen to the 6½-hour piece in full. Through TikTok memes and YouTube comments (posted under the album that now boasts over 24 million views), thousands of listeners attest to the piece's heavy emotional impact, many of whom also share personal stories about dementia and loss. In doing so, they rebuke the contention that the isolative trips of ambient music, by nature, equate to individualized therapy or entail social atomization, as though they could not also condition meaningful communication and mutual care.

Ambient techniques and styles have suffused film scores for decades; often, it seems, supplying subjective texture to narratives and vignettes of humans' encounters with, and entanglements within, measurelessly complex human-made institutions and catastrophes. Briefly, three recent examples:

Fatima Al Qadiri supplies the bewitching score to Mati Diop's dreamy *Atlantique* (*Atlantics*, 2019), a film that tells the tale of Ada, lover of exploited construction worker Souleiman but pledged in marriage to another, who begins to experience supernatural phenomena after Souleiman disappears to migrate to Europe via a deadly ocean route. Early in the film, the terrible enticement of the ocean, and of a better life, is communicated, unspoken, by the hypnotically looping four-note thumb-piano motif of "Souleiman's Theme," rendering Souleiman's dilemma atmospheric over cycling synth strings, the rattle of the car engine, Souleiman's companions singing an antiphonal tune, and most consequentially, the beckoning, ultimately engulfing drone of the ocean waves.

Adam Curtis's experimental documentary *Can't Get You Out of My Head* (2021), an "emotional history of the modern world," presents, over the course of six hour-long episodes, thematically overlapping narratives historicizing, from the personal perspective of those who lived and orchestrated them, the psychological and technological apparatuses of mass-scale social control. Clips of ambient music by artists like Stars of the Lid and William Basinski underscore documentary footage with wonder and woe, with the pieces' tranquility sometimes belying the extremity of violence, political upheaval, and human manipulation depicted—for instance, toward the end of the second episode in which the gentle, sympathetic mournfulness of Brian McBride's "Overture (For Other Halfs)" offsets, with ugly irony, Curtis's narration of the devising of data-driven logistics to surveil and preempt grassroots opposition to the concentrated power of multinational corporations and global finance.

In my experience, no film so powerfully conjoins the promise and peril of ambient isolationism with the themes of the filmic narrative as Paul Schrader's *First Reformed* (2018). The film follows the crisis of faith and descent into despair of Ernst Toller, pastor of the fictional First Reformed Church in Albany County, New York, following his failure to address the fears of a fatally suicidal climate activist (slash-alarmist/slash-realist, depending on your perspective). Gripped by guilt, Toller undertakes the process of researching impending climate disaster, which, compounded by the existential crisis of his own stomach cancer, leads him to contemplate a violent act of eco-terrorism. We, the viewers, are invited to partake in Toller's withdrawal into a bleak, antisocial worldview through the disconsolate sonic smog of dark-ambient pioneer Lustmord (Brian Williams). The suffocating darkness of Toller's perspective only finds light through the character of the widowed Mary, who, seeking solace in the radicalized reverend before the film's final act, invites him to find grounding through a physically intimate meditation. Gazing into each other's eyes, Toller finds himself lifted, floating weightlessly through the starry void of outer space, then gliding calmly over snowcapped mountains, dense forests, cool blue rushes of water, all as Lustmord cloaks the "magical mystery tour" in a heavenly synth-organ-accompanied vocalise, gentle layers of an A♭-B♭-D♭-E♭ collection hanging placidly over a E♭–D♭ pendulum in the bass. But then Toller's face creeps out from behind Mary's, and, as rows of trees melt into rows of car traffic, the serene choral bliss is punctured with a discordant whirring bass swell and sinister laugh; voices droop as Toller and Mary drift off-screen, and a sea of discarded tires, industrial factory smoke, a razed forest, rotten rivers of plastic waste, and scorched earth take over the screen, all accompanied with distressing low-string swells and dissonant bass drones (Fig. C.2). The dreadful, unredemptive ambivalence of Lustmord's ambient seems only too well suited to accompany Toller's drift into desperation, the all-too-relatable result of proudly interiorizing ecological awareness while forgetting one's imbrication within, and responsibility to, the social ecology in which one also exists.[10]

Many of these musical projects do not fall squarely into the ambient category as it is commonly conventionalized today; some conventionalists might even argue, in one breath, that while "ambient can be anything," not all of these projects are ambient. And yet each of these projects involves sonic and affective design elements that find precedent in ambient music's psychedelic past, including: the use of steady-state sounds to expand time and entrance minds; the discovery of calm through vulnerable, intimate, gentle sounds; the vivid swirls of tone color, reverb, and pitch that conjure associations with technologized spaces; the surrealistic production effects that replicate and trigger modes of intoxication, enchantment, and disorientation; and perhaps most often, ambivalent mixtures of feeling—of stoicism and intensity, of dreamy detachment and melancholic dwelling, of ataraxia and ataxia, hyperpresence and numbness, mixtures that all too well replicate the affective textures involved in desiring solace

[10] *First Reformed*, directed by Paul Schrader (2018; New York: A24), https://www.amazon.com/dp/B07D6T8JZP, 1:24:18.

Figure C.2. Reverend Toller (Ethan Hawke) has dark ecological visions.

and stability and comfort and coherence and quiescence within a reality that can often feel like a profoundly unmoored slow-motion catastrophe. If ambient music is to be anything—and if the participants in its genre culture were to seek in ambient music social worth to match its aesthetic aspirations—then I believe its psychedelic past provides a good place to start.

So does the music of other genres. This does not mean, contrary to some idealist accounts, that we can wish away genre labels, as though these musical divisions are not already deeply connected to our thoroughly commodified public and political lives. Perhaps instead of imagining the end of genre, we can creatively reimagine genres as socioaesthetic frameworks for affiliation across assumed social and cultural divisions. The ambient genre, in this sense, might not serve as shorthand expression of some idealized identity or conventional style, but rather index a process of relation (perhaps a process involving isolation, reflection, cogitation, introspection) that is mediated through head music of all different sorts. To rethink the genre in such a fashion may never amount to revolutionary social praxis or resist music's commodification—to a certain extent, it necessarily takes for granted the divisive conditions that it mediates—but it does drop the veneer of social autonomy that can make ambient music seem "outside" its always-already shared, and always-already commodified, social conditions.

As with ambient's highbrow validators in the past, I have been tempted to find redemption in what I find aesthetically most captivating about well-made ambient music: in how it registers, through layered sounds, the feeling of being ensconced within our designed environments; and in how its sonic mimeses of atmosphere provide frames or bubbles from inside which to attain a second-order perspective on the ways in which environments shape subjective experience. And yet, as the history of the psychedelic counterculture also well illustrates, altered consciousness does not alter society. Personal epiphanies are not contagious. Awareness is not enough. As literary critic Timothy Morton argues, the reflexive individualistic consumption of ambient unease, as though reality were a bad dream, risks fueling the intoxicating delusion that one can live permanently taking it all in "from the outside" in a cynical mode.[11]

At the same time, there appears plenty to redeem the ongoing practice of making and sharing ambient music. Should we not value the music's ability to scale down the pervasive, ambient anxiety of inhabiting a globe that often seems to be, thanks to human hubris, careening out of control? To this point, as critic Jon Pareles in an April 2020 *New York Times* article remarks of Brian Eno's ambient back catalog, the genre seems uncannily "prepared for" the "open-ended, unstructured time, with undercurrents of foreboding" accompanying such crises as the Covid-19 pandemic, and as such appears "particularly suited to orchestrate this uneasy historical moment."[12] Is it not a worthwhile venture to channel the anxieties of contemporary crisis into muted expressions of grief, uncertainty, and powerlessness from which loss, unease, and uncontrol can be more manageably inhabited at a slower, controlled pace?

Well—perhaps not, if that is the only thing we are doing with ambient music. The notion that ambient music exists, as the *NYT* article byline puts it, to provide "atmospheric soundtracks for uneasy times" comes awfully close to resigning the music, like an eerie underscore, as mere backdrop to and mirror of humanity's demise. For similar reasons, various writers have

[11] Timothy Morton, *Ecology without Nature: Rethinking Environmental Aesthetics* (Cambridge, MA: Harvard University Press, 2007), 109–23.

[12] Jon Pareles, "Brian Eno's 15 Essential Ambient Works," *New York Times*, April 29, 2020, https://www.nytimes.com/2020/04/29/arts/music/brian-eno-ambient-songs.html.

interpreted Basinski's *Disintegration Loops* as apocalyptic art; for instance, David Keenan, in the record's first major review in *Wire* magazine, mused, "It was as if [Basinski] had been unwittingly commissioned to soundtrack the end of the world."[13] Brandon Kreitler hears Basinski's music as a specter, "music as the memory of music," haunted by the supposition that "we are *after* history, but drowning in its artifacts: slabs of etched vinyl, wax, cassette tapes, film reels."[14] Musicologist Joanna Demers has likewise read the piece as "apocalyptic art" that, worrisomely, aestheticizes human annihilation and "doesn't allow for contingency."[15]

Yet as sociopolitical and ecological catastrophes continue to shatter dreams of global stability, then the perseverance of Basinski's piece in our cultural memory, as of the many examples of ambient music's living psychedelic past, also give reason for hope rather than paralysis; for their mere continued existence as interesting objects—objects that foster interpretation, circulate socially, and mediate and resonate unpredictably with historical currents—retains the promise of relational contingency, should we provide it that supplement. Ambient music alone will never stanch the disintegration of Earth's social and biological ecosystems; but *we* might find in ambient music, presuming its relational power as popular art, models for inhabiting the planet in sympathy, peace, and solidarity with global life. This music, understood as part of an ongoing historical social process, would not merely "soundtrack" or spectrally echo an unlivable world by creating isolative bubbles in regimented time, but could rather condition living memories, ecological affinities, and interpersonal communion via the nonlinear sociomusical space of our media-saturated lives. The point would not be arrival at some completed "healed" or wholly "aware" state; it would be part of a continual process of healing and reconciliation through the cloud of unknowing that is our profoundly fractured geopolitical and technological ecology. The aim would not be drifting off; but rather digging in, descending deeper.

As documented throughout this book, the impulse among ambient musicians and listeners to rescue ambient audio from its psychedelic past, status jockeying notwithstanding, has often been based on the recognition

[13] David Keenan, "The Disintegration Loops," *The Wire*, August 2002, 61.

[14] Brandon Kreitler, "The Music Was Dying," *Brooklyn Rail*, June 2009, https://brooklynrail.org/2009/06/music/the-music-was-dying.

[15] Joanna Demers, "The Ethics of Apocalypse" (paper presented at the meeting of the American Musicological Society, New Orleans, November 1–4, 2012); see also Joanna Demers, *Drone and Apocalypse: An Exhibit Catalog for the End of the World* (Winchester, UK: Zero Books, 2015), esp. 82–83.

that deracinated, interiorized trips could never deliver on countercultural dreams of personal healing and global kinship. It is not, however, clear that ambient music's withdrawals into vague, unsettling reminiscence of our ecological reality, as though we were living, undead, after history, are worth salvaging *without* these dreams. The collectivized hunts for universality, quests for wholeness, and hunger for unitive and transpersonal experiences that transcend entrenched hypercommodified divisions if nothing else confirm our immanence in a social world through which we might attain unity with others, despite ourselves. Could we bring these aspirations, if not to ambient music itself, to the culture that values it? Ambient music need not cater to these quests by projecting shallow utopias or universalisms into the world; more ideally, its unsettled harmonies might permit us, slowly, peaceably, maybe even on our own time and in our own spaces, to wrestle with the affective complications of seeking wholeness in disintegrating conditions. Ambient's genre culture might also, in this spirit, be imagined as a social space that takes interdependence across presumed difference, via the spread of inhabitable environments, as a core value—a value that might reorient the production and consumption of head music away from psychologized escapes into "far out" interiors of the self, and toward the making and partaking of dreamworlds for a shared here, out there.

Bibliography

Abbate, Carolyn. "Music: Drastic or Gnostic?" *Critical Inquiry* 30, no. 3 (Spring 2004): 505–36.

Achtermann, Mark Edward. "Yes, But Is It Music? Brian Eno and the Definition of Ambient Music." In *Brian Eno: Oblique Music*, edited by Sean Albiez and David Pattie, 85–104. New York: Bloomsbury Academic, 2016.

Adelt, Ulrich. *Krautrock: German Music in the Seventies*. Ann Arbor: University of Michigan Press, 2016.

Adorno, Theodor. *Introduction to the Sociology of Music*. Translated by E. B. Ashton. 1962; repr. New York: Continuum, 1976.

Ahmed, Sara. "A Phenomenology of Whiteness." *Feminist Theory* 8, no. 2 (2007): 149–68.

Aitken, Hugh G. J. *Syntony and Spark: The Origins of Radio*. New York: John Wiley & Sons, 1976.

Ake, David. "The Emergence of the Rural American Ideal in Jazz: Keith Jarrett and Pat Metheny on ECM Records." *Jazz Perspectives* 1, no. 1 (May 2007): 29–59.

Albiez, Sean. "Post-Soul Futurama: African American Cultural Politics and Early Detroit Techno." *European Journal of American Culture* 24, no. 2 (2005): 131–52.

Albright, Thomas. *Art in the San Francisco Bay Area: 1945–1980*. Berkeley: University of California Press, 1985.

Allen, John. "Ambient Power: Berlin's Potsdamer Platz and the Seductive Logic of Public Spaces." *Urban Studies* 43, no. 2 (February 2006): 441–55.

Altman, Rick. *Film/Genre*. London: BFI, 1999.

Anderson, Chester. "Notes for the New Geology." *San Francisco Oracle*, February 1967.

Anderson, Tim J. *Making Easy Listening: Material Culture and Postwar American Recording*. Minneapolis: University of Minnesota Press, 2006.

Anderson, Virginia. "British Experimental Music: Cornelius Cardew and His Contemporaries." Master's thesis, University of Redlands, 1983.

Anderson, Virginia. "Systems and Other Minimalism in Britain." In *The Ashgate Research Companion to Minimalist and Postminimalist Music*, edited by Keith Potter, Kyle Gann, and Pwyll Ap Siôn, 87–106. Burlington, VT: Ashgate, 2013.

Anniss, Matt. "Ambient House: The Story of Chill Out Music, 1988–95." *Red Bull Music Academy*, February 17, 2016. https://web.archive.org/web/20190327060903/https://daily.redbullmusicacademy.com/specials/2016-ambient-house-feature.

Armstrong, David. *A Trumpet to Arms: Alternative Media in America*. Boston: South End Press, 1981.

Ascott, Roy. "Behaviourist Art and the Cybernetic Vision." *Cybernetica: Revue de l'Association Internationale de Cybernétique* 10, no. 1 (1967): 25–56.

Ashby, W. Ross. *An Introduction to Cybernetics*. 2nd ed. London: Chapman & Hall, 1957.

Augé, Marc. *Non-Places: An Introduction to Supermodernity*. Translated by John Howe. 2nd ed. New York: Verso, 2008.

Aurobindo, Sri. *The Integral Yoga: Sri Aurobindo's Teaching and Method of Practice*. Twin Lakes, WI: Lotus Press, 1993.

Baer, Hans A., John Hays, Nicole McClendon, Neil McGoldrick, and Raffella Vespucci. "The Holistic Health Movement in the San Francisco Bay Area: Some Preliminary Observations." *Social Science & Medicine* 47, no. 10 (November 1998): 1495–501.

Baldwin, J., and Stewart Brand, eds. *Soft-Tech*. New York: Penguin Books, 1978.

Bangs, Lester. "Eno." *Musician, Player & Listener* 21 (November 1979): 38–44.

Bangs, Lester. "Eno Sings with the Fishes." In *Mainlines, Blood Feasts, and Bad Taste*, edited by John Morthland, 243–49. New York: Anchor, 2002.

Barber, Simon. "Smooth Jazz: A Case Study in the Relationships between Commercial Radio Formats, Audience Research and Music Production." *The Radio Journal—International Studies in Broadcast and Audio Media* 8, no. 1 (2010): 51–70.

Barbiero, Daniel. "After the Aging of the New Music." *Telos* 82 (Winter 1989–90): 144–50.

Barnes, Stephen H. *Muzak: The Hidden Messages in Music*. Studies on the History and Interpretation of Music, Vol. 9. Lewiston, NY: The Edwin Mellen Press, 1988.

Becker, Judith. *Deep Listeners: Music, Emotion, and Trancing*. Bloomington: Indiana University Press, 2004.

Belgrad, Daniel. *The Culture of Feedback: Ecological Thinking in Seventies America*. Chicago: University of Chicago Press, 2019.

Benjamin, Walter. "Surrealism." In *Walter Benjamin, Selected Writings*, edited by Marcus Bullock and Michael W. Jennings, 2:207–18. 1929, repr. Cambridge, MA: Belknap, 2004.

Bentley, Christa Anne. "Los Angeles Troubadours: The Politics of the Singer-Songwriter Movement." PhD diss., University of North Carolina, 2016.

Berland, Jody. "Locating Listening." In *The Place of Music*, edited by Andrew Leyshon, David Matless, and George Revill, 129–50. New York: Guilford, 1998.

Berman, Leslie. "New Age Music?" In *Not Necessarily the New Age: Critical Essays*, edited by Robert Basil, 250–68. Buffalo, NY: Prometheus, 1988.

Bernstein, David W., ed. *The San Francisco Tape Music Center: 1960s Counterculture and the Avant-Garde*. Berkeley: University of California Press, 2008.

Bhogal, Gurminder Kaur. *Details of Consequence: Ornament, Music, and Art in Paris*. New York: Oxford University Press, 2013.

Bijsterveld, Karin, Eefje Cleophas, Stefan Krebs, and Gijs Mom. *Sound and Safe: A History of Listening behind the Wheel*. New York: Oxford University Press, 2014.

Binkley, Sam. *Getting Loose: Lifestyle Consumption in the 1970s*. Durham, NC: Duke University Press, 2007.

Birosik, Patti Jean. *The New Age Music Guide*. New York: Collier Books, 1989.

Björnberg, Alf. "On Aeolian Harmony in Contemporary Popular Music." Department of Musicology, University of Göteborg, 1984. http://www.tagg.org/others/othxpdfs/bjbgeol.pdf.

Born, Georgina, and Christopher Haworth. "From Microsound to Vaporwave: Internet-Mediated Musics, Online Methods, and Genre." *Music & Letters* 98, no. 4 (2018): 601–47.

Bourdieu, Pierre. *Distinction: A Social Critique of the Judgement of Taste*. Translated by Richard Nice. 1979; repr. Cambridge, MA: Harvard University Press, 1984.

Boutin, Aimée. "'Ring Out the Old, Ring In the New': The Symbolism of Bells in Nineteenth-Century French Poetry." *Nineteenth-Century French Studies* 30, nos. 3–4 (Spring–Summer 2002): 266–80.

Bracewell, Michael. *Re-Make/Re-Model: Becoming Roxy Music*. Cambridge, MA: Da Capo, 2007.

Brackett, David. "'Where's It At?': Postmodern Theory and the Contemporary Musical Field." In *Postmodern Music/Postmodern Thought*, edited by Judy Lochhead and Joseph Auner, 207–31. New York and London: Routledge, 2002.

Brand, Stewart. *The Whole Earth Catalog: Access to Tools*. Menlo Park, CA: The Portola Institute, 1968.

Brecht, Berthold. "A Short Organum for the Theatre." In *Brecht on Theatre: The Development of an Aesthetic*, edited and translated by John Willett, 179–208. 1947–48; repr. New York: Hill and Wang, 2001.

Brown, Steven, and Töres Theorell. "The Social Uses of Background Music for Personal Enhancement." In *Music and Manipulation: On the Social Uses and Social Control of Music*, edited by Steven Brown and Ulrik Volgsten, 126–60. New York: Berghahn Books, 2006.

Bryson, Bethany. "Anything but Heavy Metal: Symbolic Exclusion and Musical Dislikes." *American Sociological Review* 61, no. 5 (October 1996): 884–99.

Bull, Anna. *Class, Control, and Classical Music*. New York: Oxford University Press, 2019.

Bull, Michael. *Sound Moves: IPod Culture and Urban Experience*. New York: Routledge, 2007.

Bull, Michael. *Sounding Out the City: Personal Stereos and the Management of Everyday Life*. New York: Berg, 2000.

Cage, John. "Experimental Music." In *Silence: Lectures and Writings*, 7–12. Cambridge, MA: MIT Press, 1961.

Cage, John. *I–VI*. Cambridge, MA: Harvard University Press, 1990.

Campion, Nicholas. *The New Age in the Modern West: Counterculture, Utopia and Prophecy from the Late Eighteenth Century to the Present Day*. London & New York: Bloomsbury Academic, 2016.

Carby, Hazel V. "The Multicultural Wars." *Radical History Review* 54 (1992): 7–18.

Carl, Robert. *Terry Riley's* In C. Studies in Musical Genesis, Structure, and Interpretation. New York: Oxford University Press, 2009.

Carpenter, Edmund, and Marshall McLuhan. "Acoustic Space." In *Explorations in Communication*, edited by Edmund Carpenter and Marshall McLuhan, 65–70. Toronto: Beacon Press, 1960.

Carrette, Jeremy, and Richard King. *Selling Spirituality: The Silent Takeover of Religion*. New York: Routledge, 2005.

Carrington, André M. *Speculative Blackness: The Future of Race in Science Fiction*. Minneapolis: University of Minnesota Press, 2016.

Carroll, Noël. "Art and Mood: Preliminary Notes and Conjectures." *The Monist* 86, no. 4 (2003): 521–55.

Carson, Charles D. "'Bridging the Gap': Creed Taylor, Grover Washington Jr., and the Crossover Roots of Smooth Jazz." *Black Music Research Journal* 28, no. 1 (Spring 2008): 1–15.

Casey, Edward S. *Remembering: A Phenomenological Study*. 2nd ed. Bloomington: Indiana University Press, 2000.

Chave, Anna C. "Minimalism and the Rhetoric of Power." *Arts Magazine* 64, no. 5 (January 1990): 44–63.

Chayka, Kyle. *The Longing for Less: Living with Minimalism*. New York: Bloomsbury, 2020.

Christenson, Peter G., and Jon Brian Peterson. "Genre and Gender in the Structure of Music Preferences." *Communication Research* 15, no. 3 (June 1988): 282–301.

Clarke, Eric F. *Ways of Listening: An Ecological Approach to the Perception of Musical Meaning*. New York: Oxford University Press, 2005.

Clayton, Martin R. L. "Free Rhythm: Ethnomusicology and the Study of Music without Metre." *Bulletin of the School of Oriental and African Studies* 59, no. 2 (June 1996): 323–32.

Clayton, Martin, Rebecca Sager, and Udo Will. "In Time with the Music: The Concept of Entrainment and Its Significance for Ethnomusicology." *ESEM CounterPoint* 1 (2004): 1–82.

Cohen, Norm. *Long Steel Rail: The Railroad in American Folksong*. 2nd ed. Urbana and Chicago: University of Illinois Press, 2000.

Cole, Ross. "'Fun, Yes, but Music?' Steve Reich and the San Francisco Bay Area's Cultural Nexus, 1962–65." *Journal of the Society for American Music* 6, no. 3 (August 2012): 315–48.

Cole, Ross. "'Sound Effects (O.K., Music)': Steve Reich and the Visual Arts in New York City, 1966–1968." *Twentieth-Century Music* 11, no. 2 (2014): 217–44.

Coleman, James William. *The New Buddhism: The Western Transformation of an Ancient Tradition*. New York: Oxford University Press, 2002.

Collin, Matthew. *Altered State: The Story of Ecstasy Culture and Acid House*. Rev. ed. London: Serpent's Tail, 2009.

Collin, Matthew. *Rave On: Global Adventures in Electronic Dance Music*. Chicago: University of Chicago Press, 2018.

Conrad, Emilie. *Life on Land: The Story of Continuum*. Berkeley: North Atlantic, 2007.

Cope, David H. *New Directions in Music*. 5th ed. Dubuque, IA: WM. C. Brown Publishers, 1989.

Copland, Aaron. *What to Listen for in Music*. 1939; repr. New York: McGraw-Hill, 1957.

Corbin, Alain. *Village Bells: Sound and Meaning in the 19th-Century French Countryside*. Translated by Martin Thom. New York: Columbia University Press, 1998.

Courtwright, David T. "The Routine Stuff: How Flying Became a Form of Mass Transportation." In *Reconsidering a Century of Flight*, edited by Roger D. Launius and Janet R. Daly Bednarek, 209–22. Chapel Hill: University of North Carolina Press, 2003.

Cox, Arnie. *Music and Embodied Cognition: Listening, Moving, Feeling, and Thinking*. Bloomington: Indiana University Press, 2016.

Crary, Jonathan. *Suspensions of Perception: Attention, Spectacle, and Modern Culture*. Cambridge, MA: MIT Press, 1999.

Cross, Ian. "Listening as Covert Performance." *Journal of the Royal Musical Association* 135, Special Issue no. 1 (2010): 67–77.

Cumming, Naomi. "The Subjectivities of 'Erbarme Dich.'" *Music Analysis* 16, no. 1 (1997): 5–44.

Curtis, Adam, director. *Can't Get You Out of My Head*. BBC Film, 2021.

Daniélou, Alain. "The Influence of Sound Phenomena on Human Consciousness." Translated by Paul Huebner and Ralph Metzner. *Psychedelic Review* 7 (1966): 20–26.

Danielsen, Anne. *Presence and Pleasure: The Funk Grooves of James Brown and Parliament*. Middletown, CT: Wesleyan University Press, 2006.

Dayal, Geeta. *Another Green World*. 33⅓ Series. New York: Bloomsbury Academic, 2009.

De Visscher, Eric. "'There's No Such a Thing as Silence . . .': John Cage's Poetics of Silence." In *Writings about John Cage*, edited by Richard Kostelanetz, 117–33. Ann Arbor: University of Michigan Press, 1993.

Debord, Guy. "A User's Guide to Détournement." In *Situationist International Anthology*, edited and translated by Ken Knabb, rev. ed., 14–20. 1956; repr. Berkeley, CA: Bureau of Public Secrets, 2006.

Dell'Antonio, Andrew. *Listening as Spiritual Practice in Early Modern Italy*. Berkeley: University of California Press, 2011.

Demers, Joanna. *Drone and Apocalypse: An Exhibit Catalog for the End of the World*. Winchester, UK: Zero Books, 2015.

Demers, Joanna. *Listening through the Noise: The Aesthetics of Experimental Electronic Music*. New York: Oxford University Press, 2010.

deMoll, Lane, ed. *Rainbook: Resources for Appropriate Technology*. New York: Schocken Books, 1977.

Dennis, Brian. "Repetitive and Systemic Music." *The Musical Times* 113, no. 1582 (December 1972): 1036–38.

DeNora, Tia. *After Adorno: Rethinking Music Sociology*. New York: Cambridge University Press, 2003.

DeNora, Tia. *Music in Everyday Life*. New York: Cambridge University Press, 2000.

DeRogatis, Jim. *Turn on Your Mind: Four Decades of Great Psychedelic Rock*. Milwaukee: Hal Leonard, 2003.

Dinerstein, Joel. *Swinging the Machine: Modernity, Technology, and African American Culture between the World Wars*. Amherst: University of Massachusetts Press, 2003.

Diop, Mati, director. *Atlantics*. Netflix, 2019.

Douglas, Susan J. *Listening In: Radio and the American Imagination*. New York: Random House, 1999.

Doyle, Peter. *Echo and Reverb: Fabricating Space in Popular Music Recording, 1900–1960*. Middletown, CT: Wesleyan University Press, 2005.

Doyle, Peter. "From 'My Blue Heaven' to 'Race with the Devil': Echo, Reverb and (Dis)Ordered Space in Early Popular Music Recording." *Popular Music* 23, no. 1 (2004): 31–49.

Drury, Nevill. *The Elements of Human Potential*. Longmead: Element Books, 1989.

Duckworth, William. *Talking Music*. New York: Schirmer Books, 1995.

Dulken, Stephen van. *Inventing the 20th Century: 100 Inventions That Shaped the World*. London: The British Library, 2000.

Durr, R. A. *Poetic Vision and the Psychedelic Experience*. Syracuse, NY: Syracuse University Press, 1970.

Dyer, Richard. "In Defense of Disco." In *On Record: Rock, Pop, and the Written Word*, edited by Simon Frith and Andrew Goodwin, 351–58. New York: Pantheon Books, 1990.

Dyer, Richard. *White: Essays on Race and Culture*. New York: Routledge, 1997.

Echard, William. *Psychedelic Popular Music: A History through Musical Topic Theory*. Bloomington: Indiana University Press, 2017.

Eglash, Ron. "Cybernetics and American Youth Subculture." *Cultural Studies* 12, no. 3 (July 1998): 382–409.

Eisenstein, Sergei. "A Dialectic Approach to Film Form." In *Film Form: Essays in Film Theory*, edited and translated by Jay Leyda, 45–63. 1931; repr. Orlando, FL: Harcourt Brace & Co., 1977.

Eno, Brian. "Aurora Musicalis." *Artforum* 24, no. 10 (Summer 1986): 76–79.

Eno, Brian. *A Year with Swollen Appendices*. London: Faber & Faber, 1996.

Eno, Brian. "Foreword to *Experimental Music: Cage and Beyond*, 2nd ed., by Michael Nyman," xi–xiii. New York: Cambridge University Press, 1999.

Eno, Brian. "Generating and Organizing Variety in the Arts." *Studio International*, 192, no. 984 (November–December 1976): 279–83.

Eno, Brian, Russell Mills, and Rick Poynor. *More Dark Than Shark*. London: Faber & Faber, 1986.

Eshun, Kodwo. *More Brilliant Than the Sun: Adventures in Sonic Fiction*. London: Quartet, 1998.

Farrugia, Rebekah. *Beyond the Dance Floor: Female DJs, Technology, and Electronic Music Culture*. Chicago: Intellect, 2012.

Feld, Steven. "A Sweet Lullaby for World Music." *Public Culture* 12, no. 1 (2000): 145–71.

Felski, Rita. *Hooked: Art and Attachment*. Chicago: University of Chicago Press, 2020.

Felski, Rita. "The Invention of Everyday Life." *New Formations*, no. 59 (1999): 15–31.

Felski, Rita. *The Limits of Critique*. Chicago: University of Chicago Press, 2015.

Ferguson, Marilyn. *The Aquarian Conspiracy: Personal and Social Transformation in the 1980s*. Los Angeles: J.P. Tarcher, 1980.

Fink, Robert. *Repeating Ourselves: American Minimal Music as Cultural Practice*. Berkeley: University of California Press, 2005.

Fisher, Mark. *Something in the Air: Radio, Rock, and the Revolution That Shaped a Generation*. New York: Random House, 2007.

Fiske, John. *Media Matters: Race and Gender in U.S. Politics*. Rev. ed. Minneapolis: University of Minnesota Press, 1996.

Fiske, John. *Reading the Popular*. Boston: Unwin Hyman, 1989.

Ford, Phil. *Dig: Sound and Music in Hip Culture*. New York: Oxford University Press, 2013.

Ford, Phil. "Somewhere/Nowhere: Hipness as an Aesthetic." *The Musical Quarterly* 86, no. 1 (Spring 2002): 49–81.

Ford, Phil. "Taboo: Time and Belief in Exotica." *Representations* 103, no. 1 (Summer 2008): 107–35.

Foucault, Michel. *Technologies of the Self: A Seminar with Michel Foucault*. Edited by Luther H. Martin, Huck Gutman, and Patrick H. Hutton. Amherst: University of Massachusetts Press, 1988.

Frank, Thomas. *The Conquest of Cool: Business Culture, Counterculture, and the Rise of Hip Consumerism*. Chicago: University of Chicago Press, 1997.

Frith, Simon. "Art versus Technology: The Strange Case of Popular Music:" *Media, Culture & Society* 8, no. 3 (1986): 163–79.

Frith, Simon. "Towards an Aesthetic of Popular Music." In *Music and Society: The Politics of Composition, Performance, and Reception*, edited by Richard Leppert and Susan McClary, 133–49. New York: Cambridge University Press, 1987.

Frith, Simon, and Howard Horne. *Art into Pop*. New York: Methuen, 1987.

Frow, John. *Genre*. New York: Routledge, 2005.

Fuller, R. Buckminster. *Ideas and Integrities: A Spontaneous Autobiographical Disclosure*. 1963; repr. New York: Collier Books, 1970.

Gale, Emily Margot. "Sounding Sentimental: American Popular Song from Nineteenth-Century Ballads to 1970s Soft Rock." PhD diss., University of Virginia, 2014.

Gann, Kyle. *American Music in the Twentieth Century*. New York: Schirmer, 1997.

Garcia, Luis-Manuel. "Crowd Solidarity on the Dance Floor in Paris and Berlin." In *Musical Performance and the Changing City*, edited by Fabian Holt and Carsten Wergin, 227–50. New York: Routledge, 2013.

Garcia, Luis-Manuel. "Whose Refuge, This House? The Estrangement of Queers of Color in Electronic Dance Music." In *The Oxford Handbook of Music and Queerness*, edited by Fred Everett Maus and Sheila Whiteley, 35–62. New York: Oxford University Press, 2018.

Gaston, E. Thayer. "Psychological Foundations for Functional Music." *American Journal of Occupational Therapy* 2, no. 1 (February 1948): 1–8.

Gebser, Jean. *The Ever-Present Origin*. Edited by Noel Barstad and Algis Mickunas. Revised. Athens: Ohio University Press, 1991.

Gendron, Bernard. *Between Montmartre and the Mudd Club: Popular Music and the Avant-Garde*. Chicago: University of Chicago Press, 2002.

Gibson, James J. *The Ecological Approach to Visual Perception*. Classic Edition. Psychology Press Classic Editions. 1986; repr. New York and London: Psychology Press, 2015.

Giddens, Anthony. *Modernity and Self-Identity: Self and Society in the Late Modern Age*. Cambridge, UK: Polity Press, 1991.

Gilbert, Jeremy, and Ewan Pearson. *Discographies: Dance Music, Culture and the Politics of Sound*. New York: Routledge, 1999.

Glitsos, Laura. "Vaporwave, or Music Optimised for Abandoned Malls." *Popular Music* 37, no. 1 (2017): 100–118.

Goodman, David. "Distracted Listening: On Not Making Sound Choices in the 1930s." In *Sound in the Age of Mechanical Reproduction*, edited by David Suisman and Susan Strasser, 15–46. Philadelphia: University of Pennsylvania Press, 2010.

Gopinath, Sumanth. "Reich in Blackface: Oh Dem Watermelons and Radical Minstrelsy in the 1960s." *Journal of the Society for American Music* 5, no. 2 (May 2011): 139–93.

Gopinath, Sumanth. "The Problem of the Political in Steve Reich's 'Come Out.'" In *Sound Commitments: Avant-Garde Music and the Sixties*, edited by Robert Adlington, 121–44. New York & Oxford: Oxford University Press, 2009.

Gopinath, Sumanth S. "Contraband Children: The Politics of Race and Liberation in the Music of Steve Reich, 1965–66." PhD diss., Yale University, 2005.

Gordon, Alastair. *Spaced Out: Radical Environments of the Psychedelic Sixties*. New York: Rizzoli, 2008.

Gosse, Van. *Rethinking the New Left: An Interpretative History*. Gordonsville, VA: Palgrave Macmillan, 2005.

Graham, James. "Musique en Fer Forgé: Erik Satie, Le Corbusier and the Problem of Aural Architecture." *AA Files*, no. 68 (2014): 3–15.

Grimshaw, Jeremy. *Draw a Straight Line and Follow It: The Music and Mysticism of La Monte Young*. New York: Oxford University Press, 2011.

Gruen, John. *The New Bohemia*. New York: Grosset & Dunlap, 1966.

Hagood, Mack. *Hush: Media and Sonic Self-Control*. Durham: Duke University Press, 2019.

Halliwell, Martin. *Therapeutic Revolutions: Medicine, Psychiatry, and American Culture, 1945–1970*. New Brunswick, NJ: Rutgers University Press, 2013.

Halpern, Steven. *Tuning the Human Instrument: An Owner's Manual*. Belmont, CA: Spectrum Research Institute, 1978.

Hamel, Peter Michael. *Through Music to the Self*. Translated by Peter Lemesurier. Boulder: Shambhala, 1979.

Hamilton, Jack. *Just around Midnight: Rock and Roll and the Racial Imagination*. Cambridge, MA: Harvard University Press, 2016.

Hammer, Olav. *Claiming Knowledge: Strategies of Epistemology from Theosophy to the New Age*. Boston: Brill, 2004.

Hanegraaff, Wouter J. *New Age Religion and Western Culture: Esotericism in the Mirror of Secular Thought*. Leiden, The Netherlands: E.J. Brill, 1996.

Harper, Adam. "The New Hi-Tech Underground." In *Seismographic Sounds: Visions of a New World*, edited by Theresa Beyer, Thomas Burkhalter, and Hannes Liechti, 484–87. Bern: Norient, 2015.

Hartogsohn, Ido. *American Trip: Set, Setting, and the Psychedelic Experience in the Twentieth Century*. Cambridge, MA: MIT Press, 2020.

Hayles, N. Katherine. *How We Became Posthuman: Virtual Bodies in Cybernetics, Literature, and Informatics*. Chicago: University of Chicago Press, 1999.

Hayles, N. Katherine. "Simulated Nature and Natural Simulations: Rethinking the Relation between the Beholder and World." In *Uncommon Ground: Toward Reinventing Nature*, edited by William Cronon, 409–25. New York & London: W. W. Norton & Company, 1995.

Healy, David. *The Creation of Psychopharmacology*. Cambridge, MA: Harvard University Press, 2009.

Heath, Joseph, and Andrew Potter. *Nation of Rebels: Why Counterculture Became Consumer Culture*. New York: HarperCollins, 2004.

Heelas, Paul. *The New Age Movement: The Celebration of the Self and the Sacralization of Modernity*. Cambridge, MA: Blackwell, 1996.

Henckes, Nicolas. "Magic Bullet in the Head? Psychiatric Revolutions and Their Aftermath." In *Therapeutic Revolutions: Pharmaceuticals and Social Change in the Twentieth Century*, edited by Jeremy A. Greene, Flurin Condrau, and Elizabeth Siegel Watkins, 65–96. Chicago: University of Chicago Press, 2016.

Hennion, Antoine. "Loving Music: From a Sociology of Mediation to a Pragmatics of Taste." *Scientific Journal of Media Education* 34, no. 17 (2010): 25–33.

Hibbett, Ryan. "The New Age Taboo." *Journal of Popular Music Studies* 22, no. 3 (2010): 283–308.

Hicks, Michael. "Mass Marketing the American Avant-Garde, 1967–1971." *American Music* 35, no. 3 (2017): 281–302.

Hicks, Michael. *Sixties Rock: Garage, Psychedelic, and Other Satisfactions*. Urbana: University of Illinois Press, 1999.

Higgins, Hannah. *Fluxus Experience*. Berkeley: University of California Press, 2002.

Hinton, Stephen. *The Idea of Gebrauchsmusik: Musical Aesthetics in the Weimar Republic with Reference to the Works of Paul Hindemith*. New York: Garland, 1989.

Hittleman, Richard. *Guide to Yoga Meditation*. New York: Bantam, 1969.

Holmes, Thom. *Electronic and Experimental Music: Technology, Music, and Culture*. 3rd ed. New York: Routledge, 2008.

Hosokawa, Shuhei. "The Walkman Effect." *Popular Music* 4 (1984): 165–80.

Howland, John. *Hearing Luxe Pop: Glorification, Glamour, and the Middlebrow in American Popular Music*. Oakland: University of California Press, 2021.

Hubbard, Barbara Marx. "The Future of Futurism." *The Futurist* 17, no. 2 (April 1983): 52–58.

Hullot-Kentor, Robert. "From Uplift to Gadgetry: Barbiero, Eno, and New Age Music." *Telos* 82 (Winter 1989–90): 151–56.

Husch, Jerri Ann. "Music of the Workplace: A Study of Muzak Culture." PhD diss., University of Massachusetts, 1984.

Huxley, Aldous. *The Doors of Perception*. London: Thinking Ink Ltd., 2011.

James, Robin. "In but Not of, of but Not In: On Taste, Hipness, and White Embodiment." *Contemporary Aesthetics* Special Volume 2 (2009). http://www.contempaesthetics.org/newvolume/pages/article.php?articleID=549.

James, Robin. "Is the Post- in Post-Identity the Post- in Post-Genre?" *Popular Music* 36, no. 1 (2017): 21–32.

Jarrett, Michael. "Train Tracks: How the Railroad Rerouted Our Ears." *Strategies* 14, no. 1 (2001): 27–45.

Jenkins, Philip. *Mystics and Messiahs: Cults and New Religions in American History*. New York: Oxford University Press, 2000.

Jerng, Mark C. *Racial Worldmaking: The Power of Popular Fiction*. New York: Fordham University Press, 2018.

Johnson, Ann, and Mike Stax. "From Psychotic to Psychedelic: The Garage Contribution to Psychedelia." *Popular Music and Society* 29, no. 4 (October 2006): 411–25.

Johnson, James H. *Listening in Paris: A Cultural History*. Berkeley: University of California Press, 1995.

Johnson, Timothy. "Minimalism: Aesthetic, Style, or Technique?" *The Musical Quarterly* 78, no. 4 (1994): 742–73.

Johnson, Tom. *The Voice of New Music: New York City, 1972–1982*. Eindhoven, The Netherlands: Het Apollohuis, 1989.

Johnston, Jay. "Subtle Anatomy: The Bio-Metaphysics of Alternative Therapies." In *Medicine, Religion, and the Body*, edited by Elizabeth Burns Coleman and Kevin White, 11:69–78. International Studies in Religion and Society. Leiden and Boston: Brill, 2009.

Johnston, Josée, and Shyon Baumann. "Democracy versus Distinction: A Study of Omnivorousness in Gourmet Food Writing." *American Journal of Sociology* 113, no. 1 (July 2007): 165–204.

Jones, Simon C., and Thomas G. Schumacher. "Muzak: On Functional Music and Power." *Critical Studies in Mass Communication* 9, no. 2 (June 1992): 156–69.

Joseph, Branden W. "'My Mind Split Open': Andy Warhol's Plastic Inevitable." In *Summer of Love: Psychedelic Art, Social Crisis and Counterculture in the 1960s*, edited by Christoph Grunenberg and Jonathan Harris, 8:239–59. Tate Liverpool Critical Forum. Liverpool: Liverpool University Press, 2005.

Kassabian, Anahid. *Ubiquitous Listening: Affect, Attention, and Distributed Subjectivity*. Berkeley: University of California Press, 2013.

Kaufman, David. *Ridiculous! The Theatrical Life and Times of Charles Ludlam*. New York: Applause Theatre & Cinema Books, 2002.

Keefer, Cindy. "'Raumlichtmusik': Early 20th Century Abstract Cinema Immersive Environments." *Leonardo Electronic Almanac* 16, nos. 6–7 (2009).

Keightley, Keir. "Long Play: Adult-Oriented Popular Music and the Temporal Logics of the Post-War Sound Recording Industry in the USA." *Media, Culture & Society* 26, no. 3 (2004): 375–91.

Keightley, Keir. "Music for Middlebrows: Defining the Easy Listening Era, 1946–1966." *American Music* 26, no. 3 (Fall 2008): 309–35.

Keightley, Keir. "Reconsidering Rock." In *The Cambridge Companion to Pop and Rock*, edited by John Street, Simon Frith, and Will Straw, 109–42. Cambridge Companions to Music. Cambridge: Cambridge University Press, 2001.

Keil, Charles. "Participatory Discrepancies and the Power of Music." *Cultural Anthropology* 2, no. 3 (August 1987): 275–83.

Keister, Jay. "The Shakuhachi as Spiritual Tool: A Japanese Buddhist Instrument in the West." *Asian Music* 35, no. 2 (2004): 99–131.

Keith, Michael C. *Voices in the Purple Haze: Underground Radio and the Sixties*. Westport, CT: Praeger, 1997.

Khalsa, Nirinjan Kaur. "When Gurbani Sings a Healthy Happy Holy Song." *Sikh Formations* 8, no. 3 (December 2012): 437–76.

Kim-Cohen, Seth. *Against Ambience and Other Essays*. New York: Bloomsbury Academic, 2016.

King, Jason. "The Sound of Velvet Melting: The Power of 'Vibe' in the Music of Roberta Flack." In *Listen Again: A Momentary History of Pop Music*, edited by Eric Weisbard, 172–99. Durham, NC: Duke University Press, 2007.

Kirby, Lynne. *Parallel Tracks: The Railroad and Silent Cinema*. Durham, NC: Duke University Press, 1997.

Kirk, Andrew. "'Machines of Loving Grace': Alternative Technology, Environment, and the Counterculture." In *Imagine Nation: The American Counterculture of the 1960s & '70s*, by Peter Braunstein and Michael William Doyle, 353–78. New York: Routledge, 2002.

Kirk, Andrew G. *Counterculture Green: The Whole Earth Catalog and American Environmentalism*. Lawrence: University of Kansas Press, 2007.

Kostelanetz, Richard. *The Theatre of Mixed Means*. New York: RK Editions, 1980.

Kramer, Jonathan D. *The Time of Music: New Meanings, New Temporalities, New Listening Strategies*. New York: Schirmer, 1988.

Kramer, Michael J. *The Republic of Rock: Music and Citizenship in the Sixties Counterculture*. New York: Oxford University Press, 2013.

Krims, Adam. "The Changing Functions of Music Recordings and Listening Practices." In *Recorded Music: Performance, Culture and Technology*, edited by Amanda Bayley, 68–85. Cambridge, UK: Cambridge University Press, 2010.

Lacasse, Serge. "'Listen to My Voice': The Evocative Power of Vocal Staging in Recorded Rock Music and Other Forms of Vocal Expression." PhD diss., University of Liverpool, 2000.

Land, Jeff. *Active Radio: Pacifica's Brash Experiment*. Commerce and Mass Culture Series. Minneapolis: University of Minnesota Press, 1999.

Lanza, Joseph. "'Beautiful Music': The Rise of Easy-Listening FM." In *The Popular Music Studies Reader*, edited by Andy Bennett, Barry Shank, and Jason Toynbee, 156–63. New York: Routledge, 2006.

Lanza, Joseph. *Easy Listening Acid Trip: An Elevator Ride through Sixties Psychedelic Pop*. Port Townsend, WA: Feral House, 2020.

Lanza, Joseph. *Elevator Music: A Surreal History of Muzak, Easy-Listening, and Other Moodsong*. New York: Picador, 1995.

Lasar, Matthew. *Pacifica Radio: The Rise of an Alternative Network*. Philadelphia: Temple University Press, 2000.

Lasar, Matthew. *Uneasy Listening: Pacifica Radio's Civil War*. Cambridge, England: Black Apollo Press, 2006.

Lasch, Christopher. *Culture of Narcissism: American Life in an Age of Diminishing Expectations*. New York: W.W. Norton, 1978.

Lau, Kimberly J. *New Age Capitalism: Making Money East of Eden*. Philadelphia: University of Pennsylvania Press, 2000.

Le Guin, Elisabeth. "Uneasy Listening." *Repercussions* 3, no. 1 (Spring 1994): 5–19.

Leary, Timothy. *The Politics of Ecstasy*. Berkeley: Ronin, 1998.

Leary, Timothy, George Litwin, Michael Hollingshead, Gunther Weil, and Richard Alpert. "The Politics of the Nervous System." *Bulletin of the Atomic Scientists* 18, no. 5 (May 1, 1962): 26–27.

Lee, Martin A., and Bruce Shlain. *Acid Dreams: The Complete Social History of LSD: The CIA, the Sixties, and Beyond*. Revised. New York: Grove Press, 1992.

Léger, Fernand. "Satie Inconnu." *La Revue Musicale*, no. 214 (June 1952): 137–38.

Lena, Jennifer C. *Banding Together: How Communities Create Genres in Popular Music*. Princeton, NJ: Princeton University Press, 2012.

Leonard, George. *The Silent Pulse: A Search for the Perfect Rhythm That Exists in Each of Us*. New York: E.P. Dutton & Co., 1978.

Levaux, Christophe. *We Have Always Been Minimalist: The Construction and Triumph of a Musical Style*. Translated by Rose Vekony. Oakland: University of California Press, 2020.

Levine, Lawrence W. *Highbrow/Lowbrow: The Emergence of Cultural Hierarchy in America*. Cambridge, MA: Harvard University Press, 1988.

Lewis, George E. "Improvised Music after 1950: Afrological and Eurological Perspectives." *Black Music Research Journal* 16, no. 1 (Spring 1996): 91–122.

Leydon, Rebecca. "The Soft-Focus Sound: Reverb as a Gendered Attribute in Mid-Century Mood Music." *Perspectives of New Music* 39, no. 2 (Summer 2001): 96–107.

Leydon, Rebecca. "Towards a Typology of Minimalist Tropes." *Music Theory Online* 8, no. 4 (2002).

Licht, Alan. *Sound Art: Beyond Music, between Categories*. New York: Rizzoli, 2007.

Lindau, Elizabeth Ann. "Art Is Dead. Long Live Rock! Avant-Gardism and Rock Music, 1967–99." PhD diss., University of Virginia, 2012.

Lingerman, Hal A. *The Healing Energies of Music*. 2nd ed. Wheaton, IL: Quest Books, 1995.

Lysaker, John T. *Brian Eno's Ambient 1: Music for Airports*. Oxford Keynotes. New York: Oxford University Press, 2018.

Macan, Edward L. *Rocking the Classics: English Progressive Rock and the Counterculture*. New York: Oxford University Press, 1997.

Mahon, Maureen. *Black Diamond Queens: African American Women and Rock and Roll*. Durham: Duke University Press, 2020.

Marcus, George H. *Functionalist Design: An Ongoing History*. Munich and New York: Prestel-Verlag, 1995.

Marx, Leo. "The Idea of 'Technology' and Postmodern Pessimism." In *Technology, Pessimism, and Postmodernism*, edited by Yaron Ezrahi, Everett Mendelsohn, and Howard P. Segal. Amherst: University of Massachusetts Press, 1995.

Marx, Leo. *The Machine in the Garden: Technology and the Pastoral Ideal in America*. New York: Oxford University Press, 1967.

Maus, Fred Everett. "Masculine Discourse in Music Theory." *Perspectives of New Music* 31, no. 2 (Summer 1993): 264–93.

McLeod, Kembrew. "Genres, Subgenres, Sub-Subgenres and More: Musical and Social Differentiation within Electronic/Dance Music Communities." *Journal of Popular Music Studies* 13, no. 1 (2001): 59–75.

McLeod, Ken. "Vaporwave: Politics, Protest, and Identity." *Journal of Popular Music Studies* 30, no. 4 (2018): 123–42.

McLuhan, Marshall. *Understanding Media: The Extensions of Man*. 2nd ed. New York: Mentor, 1964.

McNeil, Legs, and Gillian McCain. *Please Kill Me: The Uncensored Oral History of Punk.* New York: Penguin, 1997.

Meier, Leslie M. "In Excess? Body Genres, 'Bad' Music, and the Judgment of Audiences." *Journal of Popular Music Studies* 20, no. 3 (2008): 240–60.

Melton, J. Gordon, Jerome Clark, and Aidan A. Kelly. *New Age Encyclopedia*. Detroit: Gale Research Inc., 1990.

Melville, Caspar. *It's a London Thing: How Rare Groove, Acid House and Jungle Remapped the City*. Manchester: Manchester University Press, 2019.

Messelink, Jennifer. "Mood Albums." *Journal of Popular Music Studies* 33, no. 3 (2021): 45–49.

Michelsen, Anders, and Frederik Tygstrup, eds. *Socioaesthetics: Ambience—Imaginary.* Leiden, The Netherlands: Brill, 2015.

Miller, Farley. "Popular Music and Instrument Technology in an Electronic Age, 1960–1969." PhD diss., McGill University, 2018.

Miller, Paul D. "Surround Sound." *ArtForum* 33, no. 5 (January 1995): 61–62, 101.

Molnar-Szakacs, Istvan, and Katie Overy. "Music and Mirror Neurons: From Motion to 'E'motion." *Scan* 1 (2006): 235–41.

Moorefield, Virgil. *The Producer as Composer: Shaping the Sounds of Popular Music.* Cambridge, MA: MIT Press, 2005.

Morat, Daniel. "Music in the Air—Listening in the Streets: Popular Music and Urban Listening Habits in Berlin ca. 1900." In *The Oxford Handbook of Music Listening in the 19th and 20th Centuries*, edited by Christian Thorau and Hansjakob Ziemer, 335–53. New York and London: Oxford University Press, 2018.

Morrison, Gouverneur, ed. *The Power of Sounds*. Santa Barbara: J.F. Rowny Press, 1932.

Morton, Timothy. *Ecology without Nature: Rethinking Environmental Aesthetics.* Cambridge, MA: Harvard University Press, 2007.

Moylan, William. *Recording Analysis: How the Record Shapes the Song.* New York: Routledge, 2020.

Müller, Lars. *Helvetica: Homage to a Typeface*. Baden, Switzerland: Lars Müller, 2002.

Murphy, Scott. "Scoring Loss in Some Recent Popular Film and Television." *Music Theory Spectrum* 36, no. 2 (2014): 295–314.

Neer, Richard. *The Rise and Fall of Rock Radio*. New York: Villard, 2001.

Nicholls, David. "Getting Rid of the Glue: The Music of the New York School." In *The New York Schools of Music and Visual Arts*, edited by Steven Johnson, 17–56. Studies in Contemporary Music and Culture. New York: Routledge, 2002.

Nyman, Michael. "As the Titanic Went Down." *Music and Musicians* 21 (December 1972): 10–14.

Nyman, Michael. "Believe It or Not Melody Rides Again." *Music and Musicians* 20, no. 2 (October 1971): 26–28.

Nyman, Michael. *Experimental Music: Cage and Beyond*. 2nd ed. New York: Cambridge University Press, 1999.

Nyman, Michael. "Music [Obscure Records]." In *Michael Nyman: Collected Writings*, edited by Pwyll Ap Siôn, 258–61. Burlington, VT: Ashgate, 2013.

Oja, Carol J. "Dane Rudhyar's Vision of American Dissonance." *American Music* 17, no. 2 (Summer 1999): 129–45.

Oliveros, Pauline. *Software for People*. Baltimore: Smith, 1984.

Orledge, Robert. *Satie Remembered.* Translated by Roger Nichols. London: Faber & Faber, 1995.

Orledge, Robert. *Satie the Composer*. Music in the 20th Century. New York: Cambridge University Press, 1990.

Perry, Charles. *The Haight-Ashbury: A History*. New York: Wenner, 2005.

Peterson, Richard A., and Roger M. Kern. "Changing Highbrow Taste: From Snob to Omnivore." *American Sociological Review* 61, no. 5 (October 1996): 900–907.

Pike, Sarah M. *New Age and Neopagan Religions in America*. New York: Columbia University Press, 2004.

Pinch, Trevor, and Frank Trocco. *Analog Days: The Invention and Impact of the Moog Synthesizer*. Cambridge, MA: Harvard University Press, 2002.

Potter, Caroline. *Erik Satie: A Parisian Composer and His World*. Woodbridge, UK: Boydell & Brewer, 2016.

Potter, Keith. *Four Musical Minimalists: La Monte Young, Terry Riley, Steve Reich, Philip Glass*. Music in the Twentieth Century. New York: Cambridge University Press, 2000.

Prendergast, Mark. *The Ambient Century: From Mahler to Trance – The Evolution of Sound in the Electronic Age*. New York: Bloomsbury, 2000.

Potter, Keith, Kyle Gann, and Pwyll Ap Siôn, eds. *The Ashgate Research Companion to Minimalist and Postminimalist Music*. Burlington, VT: Ashgate, 2013.

Priest, Eldritch. "Felt as Thought (or, Music Abstraction and the Semblance of Affect)." In *Sound, Music, Affect: Theorizing Sonic Experience*, edited by Marie Thompson and Ian Biddle, 45–63. New York: Bloomsbury Academic, 2013.

Radano, Ronald M. "Interpreting Muzak: Speculations on Musical Experience in Everyday Life." *American Music* 7, no. 4 (Winter 1989): 448–60.

Reich, Steve. "Music as a Gradual Process." In *Writings on Music, 1965–2000*, edited by Paul Hillier, 34–36. New York: Oxford University Press, 2002.

Reising, Russell. "Melting Clocks and the Hallways of Always: Time in Psychedelic Music." *Popular Music and Society* 32, no. 4 (October 2009): 523–47.

Reynolds, Simon. *Energy Flash: A Journey through Rave Music and Dance Culture*. Berkeley: Soft Skull, 2012.

Reynolds, Simon. "Muzak of the Fears." *ArtForum* 33, no. 5 (January 1995): 61–62, 98, 101.

Reynolds, Simon, and Joy Press. *The Sex Revolts: Gender, Rebellion, and Rock "N" Roll*. Cambridge, MA: Harvard University Press, 1995.

Roberts, Jennifer L. "Lucubrations on a Lava Lamp: Technocracy, Counterculture, and Containment in the American Sixties." In *American Artifacts: Essays in Material Culture*, edited by Jules David Prown and Kenneth Haltman, 167–89. East Lansing: Michigan State University Press, 2000.

Robin, William. *Industry: Bang on a Can and New Music in the Marketplace*. New York: Oxford University Press, 2021.

Rodgers, Tara. *Pink Noises: Women on Electronic Music and Sound*. Durham: Duke University Press, 2010.

Roof, Wade Clark. *Spiritual Marketplace: Baby Boomers and the Remaking of American Religion*. Princeton: Princeton University Press, 1999.

Roquet, Paul. *Ambient Media: Japanese Atmospheres of Self*. Minneapolis: University of Minnesota Press, 2016.

Rose, Barbara. "ABC Art." In *Minimalism: A Critical Anthology*, edited by Gregory Battcock, 274–97. New York: Dutton, 1968.

Rose, Tricia. *Black Noise: Rap Music and Black Culture in Contemporary America*. Music Culture. Hanover, NH: Wesleyan University Press, 1994.

Rosenfeld, Edward. *The Book of Highs: 250 Methods for Altering Your Consciousness without Drugs*. New York: Quadrangle/The New York Times Book Co., 1973.

Rossman, Michael. *New Age Blues: On the Politics of Consciousness*. New York: E.P. Dutton & Co., 1979.

Roszak, Theodore. *The Making of a Counter Culture: Reflections on the Technocratic Society and Its Youthful Opposition*. Berkeley: University of California Press, 1995.

Roszak, Theodore. *Unfinished Animal: The Aquarian Frontier and the Evolution of Consciousness*. New York: Harper & Row, 1975.

Rouget, Gilbert. *Music and Trance: A Theory of the Relations between Music and Possession*. Translated by Brunhilde Biebuyck. Chicago: University of Chicago Press, 1985.

Rudhyar, Dane. *The Magic of Tone and the Art of Music*. Boulder: Shambala, 1982. https://www.khaldea.com/rudhyar/mt/.

Rudhyar, Dane. *The Planetarization of Consciousness: From the Individual to the Whole*. New York: Harper & Row, 1970.

Rudhyar, Dane. *The Rebirth of Hindu Music*. orig. 1928; repr. New York: Noble Offset Printers, 1979.

Russell, Peter. *The Global Brain: Speculations on the Evolutionary Leap to Planetary Consciousness*. Los Angeles: J.P. Tarcher, 1983.

Saldanha, Arun. *Psychedelic White: Goa Trance and the Viscosity of Race*. Minneapolis: University of Minnesota Press, 2007.

Satie, Erik. *A Mammal's Notebook*. Edited by Ornella Volta. Translated by Anthony Melville. Atlas Arkhive Five: Documents of the Avant-Garde. London: Atlas, 1996.

Satie, Erik. *Écrits*. Edited by Ornella Volta. Paris: Editions Champ Libre, 1977.

Satprem. *Sri Aurobindo, or The Adventure of Consciousness*. Translated by Tehmi. New York: Harper & Row, 1968.

Schaberg, Christopher. *The Textual Life of Airports: Reading the Culture of Flight*. New York: Continuum, 2012.

Schaefer, John. *New Sounds: A Listener's Guide to New Music*. New York: Harper & Row, 1987.

Schafer, R. Murray. *The Soundscape: Our Sonic Environment and the Tuning of the World*. 1977; repr. Rochester, VT: Destiny Books, 1994.

Scherzinger, Martin. "Curious Intersections, Uncommon Magic: Steve Reich's 'It's Gonna Rain.'" *Current Musicology* 79 (2005): 207–44.

Schrader, Paul, director. *First Reformed*. A24, 2018.

Schur, Edwin. *The Awareness Trap: Self-Absorption Instead of Social Change*. New York: Quadrangle/The New York Times Book Co., 1976.

Scott, Derek B. "Other Mainstreams: Light Music and Easy Listening, 1920–70." In *The Cambridge History of Twentieth-Century Music*, edited by Anthony Pople and Nicholas Cook, 307–35. The Cambridge History of Music. Cambridge: Cambridge University Press, 2004.

Scott, Derek B. *Sounds of the Metropolis: The 19th-Century Popular Music Revolution in London, New York, Paris, and Vienna*. New York: Oxford University Press, 2008.

Sedgwick, Eve Kosofsky. "Paranoid Reading and Reparative Reading; or, You're So Paranoid, You Probably Think This Introduction Is about You." In *Touching Feeling: Affect, Pedagogy, Performativity*, 123–51. Durham: Duke University Press, 2003.

Seigel, Jerrold. *Bohemian Paris: Culture, Politics, and the Boundaries of Bourgeois Life, 1830–1930*. New York: Viking, 1986.

Serra, Ilaria. *The Imagined Immigrant: Images of Italian Emigration to the United States between 1890 and 1924*. Teaneck, NJ: Fairleigh Dickinson University Press, 2009.

Sheppard, David. *On Some Faraway Beach: The Life and Times of Brian Eno*. Chicago: Chicago Review Press, 2009.

Shirley, Ian. *Turn up the Strobe: The KLF, The JAMS, The Timelords: A History*. London: Cherry Red Books, 2017.

Shklovsky, Viktor. "Art as Technique." In *The Critical Tradition: Classic Texts and Contemporary Trends*, edited by David H. Richter, 3rd ed., 775–84. Boston & New York: Bedford/St. Martin's, 2007.

Simpson, Kim. *Early '70s Radio: The American Format Revolution*. New York: Continuum, 2011.

Smith, C. Ray. *Supermannerism: New Attitudes in Post-Modern Architecture*. New York: Dutton, 1977.

Smith, Mark Michael. *Listening to Nineteenth-Century America*. Chapel Hill: University of North Carolina Press, 2001.

Spitzer, Leo. "Milieu and Ambiance: An Essay in Historical Semantics." *Philosophy and Phenomenological Research* 3, no. 1 (September 1942): 1–42.

Sterling, Christopher H., and Michael C. Keith. *Sounds of Change: A History of FM Broadcasting in America*. Chapel Hill: University of North Carolina Press, 2008.

Sterne, Jonathan. "Sonic Imaginations." In *The Sound Studies Reader*, edited by Jonathan Sterne, 1–17. New York: Routledge, 2012.

Sterne, Jonathan. "Sounds like the Mall of America: Programmed Music and the Architectonics of Commercial Space." *Ethnomusicology* 41, no. 1 (Winter 1997): 22–50.

Stewart, Jesse. "DJ Spooky and the Politics of Afro-Postmodernism." *Black Music Research Journal* 30, no. 2 (2010): 337–62.

Stoeber, Michael. "3HO Kundalini Yoga and Sikh Dharma." *Sikh Formations* 8, no. 3 (December 2012): 351–68.

Strickland, Edward. *Minimalism: Origins*. Bloomington: Indiana University Press, 1993.

Stubbs, David. *Future Days: Krautrock and the Birth of a Revolutionary New Music*. Brooklyn: Melville House, 2015.

Stubbs, David. *Mars by 1980: The Story of Electronic Music*. London: Faber & Faber, 2018.

Summer, Lisa. *Music: The New Age Elixir*. Amherst, NY: Prometheus, 1996.

Sun, Cecilia. "Brian Eno, Non-Musicianship and the Experimental Tradition." In *Oblique Music*, edited by Sean Albiez and David Pattie, 29–48. New York: Bloomsbury Academic, 2016.

Sun, Cecilia. "Experiments in Musical Performance: Historiography, Politics, and the Post Cagian Avant-Garde." PhD diss., University of California, Los Angeles, 2004.

Sun, Cecilia. "Resisting the Airport: Bang on a Can Performs Brian Eno." *Musicology Australia* 29, no. 1 (2007): 135–59.

Sutcliffe, Steven J. *Children of the New Age: A History of Spiritual Practices*. New York: Routledge, 2003.

Sutich, Anthony J. "The Founding of Humanistic and Transpersonal Psychology: A Personal Account." PhD diss., The Humanistic Psychology Institute, 1976.

Sutich, Anthony J. "Transpersonal Psychology: An Emerging Force." *Journal of Humanistic Psychology* 8, no. 1 (1968): 77–78.

Tagg, Philip. *Music's Meanings: A Modern Musicology for Non-Musos*. New York: Mass Media Scholars Press, 2012.

Tagg, Philip. "'Universal' Music and the Case of Death." *Critical Quarterly* 35, no. 2 (1993): 54–98.

Tamm, Eric. *Brian Eno: His Music and the Vertical Color of Sound*. London: Faber & Faber, 1988.

Tanner, Grafton. *Babbling Corpse: Vaporwave and the Commodification of Ghosts*. Winchester, UK: Zero Books, 2016.

Taruskin, Richard. "A Harmonious Avant-Garde?" In *The Oxford History of Western Music*, Vol. 6: *Music in the Late Twentieth-Century*, 351–410. New York: Oxford University Press, 2005.

Taylor, Timothy D. "A Riddle Wrapped in a Mystery: Transnational Music Sampling and Enigma's 'Return to Innocence.'" In *Music and Technoculture*, edited by René T. A. Lysloff and Leslie C. Gay Jr., 64–92. Middletown, CT: Wesleyan University Press, 2003.

Teibel, Irv. "Mother Nature Goes Digital." In *Digital Deli*, edited by Steve Ditlea, 224–25. New York: Workman, 1984.

Théberge, Paul. *Any Sound You Can Imagine: Making Music/Consuming Technology*. Middletown, CT: Wesleyan University Press, 1997.

Thornton, Sarah. *Club Cultures: Music, Media and Subcultural Capital*. US Edition. Hanover, NH: University Press of New England, 1996.

Tipp, Cheryl. "An Overview of Early Commercial Wildlife Recordings at the British Library." *IASA Journal*, no. 37 (2011): 47–54.

Tone, Andrea. "Tranquilizers on Trial: Psychopharmacology in the Age of Anxiety." In *Medicating Modern America: Prescription Drugs in History*, edited by Andrea Tone and Elizabeth S. Watkins, 156–79. New York: New York University Press, 2007.

Toop, David. "How Much World Do You Want? Ambient Listening and Its Questions." In *Music beyond Airports: Appraising Ambient Music*, edited by Monty Adkins and Simon Cummings, 1–20. Huddersfield: University of Huddersfield Press, 2019.

Toop, David. *Ocean of Sound: Aether Talk, Ambient Sound and Imaginary Worlds*. London: Serpent's Tail, 1995.

Trower, Shelley. "Nerves, Vibration and the Aeolian Harp." *Romanticism and Victorianism on the Net*, no. 54 (2009). doi:10.7202/038761ar.

Trower, Shelley. "'Nerve-Vibration': Therapeutic Technologies in the 1880s and 1890s." In *Neurology and Modernity: A Cultural History of Nervous Systems, 1800–1950*, edited by Laura Salisbury and Andrew Shail, 148–62. New York: Palgrave Macmillan, 2010.

Tuhus-Bugrow, Rebecca. *Personal Stereo*. Object Lessons. New York: Bloomsbury Academic, 2017.

Turner, Ann. "The National Center for Experiments in Television." *Radical Software* 2, no. 3 (1972): 46–51.

Turner, Anna, and Stephen Hill. *Music from the Hearts of Space: Guide to Cosmic, Transcendent and Innerspace Music*. San Francisco: Music from the Hearts of Space, 1981.

Turner, Fred. *The Democratic Surround: Multimedia & American Liberalism from World War II to the Psychedelic Sixties*. Chicago: University of Chicago Press, 2013.

Turner, Fred. *From Counterculture to Cyberculture: Stewart Brand, The Whole Earth Network, and the Rise of Digital Utopianism*. Chicago: University of Chicago Press, 2006.

Valle, Ronald S. "The Emergence of Transpersonal Psychology." In *Existential-Phenomenological Perspectives in Psychology: Exploring the Breadth of Human Experience*, edited by Ronald S. Valle and Steen Halling, 257–68. New York: Plenum Press, 1989.

Vanel, Hervé. *Triple Entendre: Furniture Music, Muzak, Muzak-Plus*. Urbana: University of Illinois Press, 2013.

Volta, Ornella. *Satie / Cocteau: Les Malentendus d'une Entente*. Bègles, France: Le Castor Astral, 1993.

Wainwright, Jean. "Mediated Pain: Andy Warhol's Exploding Plastic Inevitable." In *Across the Great Divide: Modernism's Intermedialities, from Futurism to Fluxus*, edited by Christopher Townsend, Alex Trott, and Rhys Davies, 158–86. Newcastle upon Tyne, UK: Cambridge Scholars Publishing, 2014.

Walker, Jesse. *Rebels on the Air: An Alternative History of Radio in America*. New York: New York University Press, 2001.

Watkins, Holly. "Musical Ecologies of Place and Placelessness." *Journal of the American Musicological Society* 64, no. 2 (Summer 2011): 404–8.

Weidenbaum, Marc. *Selected Ambient Works Volume II*. 33⅓ Series. New York: Bloomsbury Academic, 2014.

Weisbard, Eric. *Top 40 Democracy: The Rival Mainstreams of American Music*. Chicago: University of Chicago Press, 2014.

Welch, Allison. "Meetings along the Edge: Svara and Tāla in American Minimal Music." *American Music* 17, no. 2 (1999): 179–99.

Whelan, Andrew, and Raphaël Nowak. "'Vaporwave Is (Not) a Critique of Capitalism': Genre Work in an Online Music Scene." *Open Cultural Studies*, no. 2 (2018): 451–62.

Whiteley, Sheila. *The Space between the Notes: Rock and the Counter-Culture*. London: Routledge, 1992.

Whitesell, Lloyd. "White Noise: Race and Erasure in the Cultural Avant-Garde." *American Music* 19, no. 2 (2001): 168–89.

Whiting, Steven Moore. *Satie the Bohemian: From Cabaret to Concert Hall*. New York: Oxford University Press, 1999.

Wiener, Norbert. *Cybernetics: Or Control and Communication in the Animal and the Machine*. 2nd ed. New York: MIT Press and John Wiley & Sons, 1961.

Wild, Lorraine, and David Karwan. "Agency and Urgency: The Medium and Its Message." In *Hippie Modernism: The Struggle for Utopia*, edited by Andrew Blauvelt, 44–57. New York: Distributed Art Publishers, 2015.

Williams, Andrew. *Portable Music and Its Functions*, Vol. 6: *Music [Meanings]*. New York: Peter Lang, 2007.

Williams, Paul, and Brian Edgar. "The Primal Is the Political: Psychotherapy, Engagement, and Narcissism in the 1970s." *American Quarterly* 70, no. 1 (March 2018): 79–100.

Williams, Richard. *The Blue Moment: Miles Davis's "Kind of Blue" and the Remaking of Modern Music*. London: Faber & Faber, 2009.

Williams, Rosalind H. *Dream Worlds: Mass Consumption in Late Nineteenth-Century France*. Berkeley: University of California Press, 1982.

Willis, A. J. "The Ecosystem: An Evolving Concept Viewed Historically." *Functional Ecology* 11, no. 2 (April 1997): 268–71.

Wolfe, Tom. *The Electric Kool-Aid Test*. New York: Picador, 1968.

Young, La Monte. "Lecture 1960." *Tulane Drama Review* 10, no. 2 (1965): 73–83.

Zagorski-Thomas, Simon. *The Musicology of Record Production*. Cambridge, UK: Cambridge University Press, 2014.

Zak, Albin. *The Poetics of Rock: Cutting Tracks, Making Records*. Berkeley: University of California Press, 2001.

Zandbergen, Dorien. "Silicon Valley New Age: The Co-Constitution of the Digital and the Sacred." In *Religions of Modernity: Relocating the Sacred to the Self and the Digital*, edited by Stef Aupers and Dick Houtman, 161–86. International Studies in Religion and Society. Boston: Brill, 2010.

Zimmerman, Nadya. *Counterculture Kaleidoscope: Musical and Cultural Perspectives on Late Sixties San Francisco*. Ann Arbor: University of Michigan Press, 2008.

Selected Discography

2814. 新しい日の誕生 *(Birth of a New Day)*. Dream Catalogue, DREAM_86, 2015, mp3.
808 State. "Pacific State." *Quadrastate*. Rephlex, CAT 808, 2008, CD. Originally released in 1989.
Air. *Air II*. Fax +49-69/450464, PK 08/85, 1994, CD.
Ashra. *New Age of Earth*. MG.ART, MG.ART 402, 2008, CD. Originally released in 1976.
Basinski, William. *The Disintegration Loops*. 2062, 2062 0201, 2002, CD.
Beaver & Krause. *In a Wild Sanctuary*. Warner Bros., WS 1850, 1970, 33 rpm.
Bhagavan Das. *Ah*. Pacific Arts, PACR7-111, 1978, 33 rpm. Originally released in 1972.
Brouk, Joanna. "The Creative." *Hearing Music*. Numero Group, NUM069, 2016, CD.
Bryars, Gavin. *The Sinking of the Titanic*. Virgin, 7243 8 45970 2 3, 1998, CD. Originally released in 1975.
Budd, Harold. *The Pavilion of Dreams*. Editions EG, EEGCD 30, 1992, CD. Originally released in 1978.
Budd, Harold, and Brian Eno. *Ambient 2: The Plateaux of Mirror*. Editions EG, EEGCD 18, 1987, CD. Originally released in 1980.
Caretaker, The. *Everywhere at the End of Time*. History Always Favours the Winners, 2019, FLAC.
Carlos, W. *Sonic Seasonings*. Columbia, KG 31234, 1972, 33 rpm.
Chandler, Geoffrey. *Starscapes*. Unity, UR 706, 1980, 33 rpm.
Davis, Miles. "He Loved Him Madly." *Get Up with It*. Columbia, C2K 63970, 2000, CD. Originally released in 1974.
De La Sierra, Jordan. *Gymnosphere: Song of the Rose—Music for the Well-Tuned Piano*. Numero Group, NUM059, 2014, CD. Originally released in 1978.
Deuter. "Haleakala Mystery." *Haleakala*. Kuckuck, 2375 042, 1978, 33 rpm.
Eno, Brian. *Ambient 1: Music for Airports*. Editions EG, AMB001, 1978, 33 rpm.
Eno, Brian. *Ambient 4: On Land*. Editions EG EEGCD 20, 1987, CD. Originally released in 1982.
Eno, Brian. *Another Green World*. EG, EGCD 21, 1987, CD. Originally released in 1975.
Eno, Brian. *Apollo: Atmospheres & Soundtracks*, Brian Eno, Roger Eno, and Daniel Lanois, EG, EGCD 53, 1990, CD. Originally released in 1983.
Eno, Brian. *Discreet Music*. Editions EG, EEGCD 23, 1987, CD. Originally released in 1975.
Eno, Brian, and Robert Fripp. *Evening Star*. Editions EG, EEGCD 3, 1988, CD. Originally released in 1975.
Eno, Brian, and Robert Fripp *(No Pussyfooting)*. Island, HELP 16, 1973, 33 rpm.
Ferraro, James. *NYC, Hell 3:00am*. Hippos in Tanks, HIT 026, 2013, mp3.
Göttsching, Manuel. "Quasarsphere." *Inventions for Electric Guitar*. Spalax, 14245, 1998, CD. Originally released in 1975.
Halpern, Steven. *Spectrum Suite*. SRI Records, SRI 770, 1976, 33 rpm.
Hamel, Peter Michael. *Nada*. Ginkgo, SM 1807-2, 1994, CD. Originally released in 1977.

Hassell, Jon, and Brian Eno. *Fourth World, Vol. 1—Possible Musics*. Editions EG, EEGCD 7, 1987, CD. Originally released in 1980.

Hillage, Steve. *Rainbow Dome Musick*. Virgin, VR1, 1979, 33 rpm.

Horn, Paul. *Inside*. Epic, BXN 26466, 1968, 33 rpm.

Iasos. *Inter-Dimensional Music*. Inter-Dimensional Music, 2013, CD. Originally released in 1975.

Irresistible Force, The. *Flying High*. Rising High, RSN CD5, 1992, CD.

Jefferson, Marshall, presents Truth. "Open Our Eyes (Celestial Mix)." *Open Our Eyes*. Big Beat, BB-0003, 1988, 33 rpm.

The KLF. "3 A.M. Eternal (Blue Danube Orbital)." Uncredited remix by The Orb. *3 A.M. Eternal: The UK Mixes*. KLF Communications, KLF 005R, 1989, 45 rpm.

The KLF. *Chill Out*. Wax Trax!, WAXCD 7155, 1991, CD. Originally released in 1990.

The KLF. *Space*. KLF Communications, SPACE CD 1, 1990, CD.

The KLF vs. Pet Shop Boys. "It Must Be Obvious (UFO Mix)." *So Hard (The KLF vs. Pet Shop Boys)*. Parlophone, 560-20 4062 2, 1990, CD.

Laraaji. *Ambient 3: Day of Radiance*. Editions EG, EEGCD 19, 1987, CD. Originally released in 1980.

Laraaji (credited to Edward Larry Gordon). *Celestial Vibration*. Universal Sound, US LP30, 2010, 33 rpm. Originally released in 1978.

Malachi. *Holy Music*. Verve, V6-5024, 1967, 33 rpm.

Mr. Fingers. *Ammnesia*. Jack Trax, CD FING 2, 1989, CD.

Orb, The. "A Huge Ever Growing Pulsating Brain That Rules from the Centre of the Ultraworld—Loving You (Orbital Mix)." *A Huge Ever Growing Pulsating Brain That Rules from the Centre of the Ultraworld*. Big Life, BLR 27CD, 1990, CD. Originally released in 1989.

Orb, The. *The Orb's Adventures beyond the Ultraworld*. Big Life, BLRDCD 5, 1991, 2xCD.

Palestine, Charlemagne. *Bells Studies*. Alga Marghen, alga049, 2015, 33 rpm.

Papathanassiou, Vangelis. *Entends-Tu Les Chiens Aboyer?* Barclay, 80234, 1975, 33 rpm.

Reich, Steve, Richard Maxfield, and Pauline Oliveros. *New Sounds in Electronic Music*. Odyssey, 32 16 0160, 1967. LP.

Reich, Steve. *Live/Electric Music*. Columbia Masterworks, MS 7265, 1968, 33 rpm.

Riley, Terry. *In C*. Columbia Masterworks, MS 7178, 1968, 33 rpm.

Riley, Terry. *Persian Surgery Dervishes*. Mantra, MANTRA 077, 1992, CD. Originally released in 1972.

Riley, Terry. "Poppy Nogood and the Phantom Band." *A Rainbow in Curved Air*. Columbia Masterworks, MS 7315, 1969, 33 rpm.

Roxanne, Ana. ~~~. Self-released, 2019, mp3.

Roxanne, Ana. *Because of a Flower*. Kranky, krank230, 2020, mp3.

Sanders, Pharaoh. "Let Us Go into the House of the Lord." *Summun Bukmun Umyun—Deaf Dumb Blind*. Impulse!, M 59199, 1970, 33 rpm.

Schulze, Klaus. "Floating." *Moondawn*. Magnum America, MACD 067, 1996, CD. Originally released in 1976.

Scott, Tony, Shinichi Yuize, and Hōzan Yamamoto. *Music for Zen Meditation (and Other Joys)*. Verve, V6-8634, 1965, 33 rpm.

Stearns, Michael. *Ancient Leaves*. Continuum Montage, CM1001, 1980, LP. Originally released in 1977.

Sweatshirt, Earl, feat. Liv.e. "MTOMB." *Feet of Clay*. Warner, 2019, mp3.

Syntonic Research, Inc. *Environments: Disc 1*. Atlantic, SD 66001, 1970, LP. Originally released in 1969.

Syntonic Research, Inc. *Environments: Disc 2*. Atlantic, SD 66002, 1970, LP.

Syntonic Research, Inc. "Intonation." *Environments: Disc 7*. Syntonic Research Inc., SD 66007, 1976, 33 rpm.

Tangerine Dream. *Zeit*. Ohr, OMM 2/56021, 1972, 33 rpm.

Tangerine Dream. *Phaedra*. Virgin, VR 13-108, 1974, 33 rpm.

Various Artists. *Ambient House: The Compilation by DFC*. BCM Records, BCM 50422, 1990, CD.

Various Artists. *Ambient 4: Isolationism*. Virgin, AMBT 4, 1994, CD.

Various Artists. *Artificial Intelligence*. Warp, WARP CD 6, 1992, CD.

Wolff, Henry and Nancy Hennings, with Drew Gladstone. *Tibetan Bells*. Island, SMAS-9319, 1972, 33 rpm.

Index

For the benefit of digital users, indexed terms that span two pages (e.g., 52–53) may, on occasion, appear on only one of those pages.

Tables, figures, and boxes are indicated by *t*, *f*, and *b* following the page number